MOVE.

CHOREOGRAPHING YOU

Published on the occasion of the exhibition
Move: Choreographing You
Hayward Gallery, London
13 October 2010 – 9 January 2011

Haus der Kunst, Munich
10 February – 15 May 2011

Kunstsammlung Nordrhein-Westfalen, Düsseldorf
16 July – 25 September 2011

Exhibition curated by Stephanie Rosenthal
Exhibition organised by Anna Gritz and Siobhan McCracken Nixon
Assisted by Chelsea Fitzgerald
Exhibition Archive co-curated by André Lepecki and Stephanie Rosenthal
Exhibition Archive organised by Chelsea Fitzgerald

Exhibition supported by the German Federal Cultural Foundation and Louis Vuitton

KULTURSTIFTUNG DES BUNDES

LOUIS VUITTON

Published by Hayward Publishing
Southbank Centre
Belvedere Road
London, SE1 8XX, UK
www.southbankcentre.co.uk

Art Publisher: Mary Richards
Publishing Co-ordinator: Faye Robson
Project Manager: Rosalind Horne
Sales Manager: Deborah Power
Texts by Isabelle Graw and Stephanie Rosenthal translated by Gerrit Jackson
Catalogue designed by Melanie Mues, Mues Design
Printed in the UK by Butler Tanner & Dennis

A catalogue record for this book is available from the British Library

ISBN: 978 1 85332 282 2

Distributed in the UK by
Cornerhouse Publications
70 Oxford Street, Manchester M1 5NH
tel: +44 (0)161 200 1503
fax: +44 (0)161 200 1504
www.cornerhouse.org/books

Distributed in Europe by
Buchhandlung Walther König,
Ehrenstr. 4, 50672 Köln, Germany
www.buchhandlung-walther-koenig.de

Distributed in all territories excluding the UK and Europe by The MIT Press of the Massachusetts Institute of Technology, 55 Hayward St, Cambridge, Massachusetts, 02142-1315, USA, www.mitpress.mit.edu

Cover: Mike Kelley, *Adaptation: Test Room Containing Multiple Stimuli Known to Elicit Curiosity And Manipulatory Responses (Graham Action)* (1999/2010, detail). Photograph by Fredrik Nilsen. Images courtesy Kelley Studio.

MOVE.

EDITED BY STEPHANIE ROSENTHAL

CHOREOGRAPHING YOU

With essays by
SUSAN LEIGH FOSTER
ANDRÉ LEPECKI
PEGGY PHELAN

SOUTHBANK CENTRE
HAYWARD PUBLISHING

ARTS COUNCIL ENGLAND

CON

Texts by: Eleonora Fabião, Isabelle Graw, Anna Gritz, Martin Hargreaves, Paul Kaiser, André Lepecki, Julienne Lorz, Helen Luckett, Siobhan McCracken Nixon, Eva Martinez, Nicky Molloy, Noémie Solomon and Åsmund Thorkildsen.

T EN T S

FOREWORD

Move: Choreographing You is the first major exhibition to explore the fertile cross-currents flowing between contemporary art and dance over the past fifty years. Bringing together seminal artists and choreographers, the exhibition charts their shared interest in everyday movements, balance, and the passage of our bodies through space. Beginning in the 1960s with Allan Kaprow's Happenings and the collaborative performances created by dancers and artists at New York's Judson Memorial Church, *Move* chronicles a crucial turn in the development of contemporary art that has become increasingly important in recent years as a growing number of artists have used dance and performance to explore the choreography, and scripting, of routine behaviours. Much of this art also aims to give us an expanded awareness of how we can physically interact with our environment, using our entire bodies (and not just our heads) as a tool for gaining experience and knowledge.

Organised by Hayward Chief Curator Stephanie Rosenthal, *Move* elaborates a new approach to presenting the mutually influential relationship between art and dance. In addition to major sculptural works and installations – some of which visitors actively engage with – the exhibition features constant performances in the gallery. It also includes a touch-screen digital archive that brings together photographs and films of over 100 of the most important performance works from the last half-century, allowing visitors to explore the larger historical trajectory of this ongoing dialogue between contemporary art and dance. Audiences can further engage with this subject through an expanded programme of talks and performances across Southbank Centre.

A ground-breaking exhibition in many ways, *Move* adds a substantial new chapter to the Hayward Gallery's continuing engagement with types of art that address aspects of everyday life, and that draw on other disciplines and cultural spheres. Ambitious in its presentation as well as its ideas, this show could not have realised without the extraordinary generosity of many individuals and institutions. First and foremost, I would like to thank the German Federal Cultural Foundation for their leading support. We are also very grateful for the crucial support of Louis Vuitton, The Henry Moore Foundation and the Institut für Auslandsbeziehungen.

Stephanie Rosenthal deserves high praise for her extraordinary work in curating this adventurous show, which is both a call to action for every visitor and a pioneering survey of a critical strand in recent art history. Our gratitude also goes to the many people with whom Stephanie collaborated, including André Lepecki, Professor of Performance Studies at New York University, who co-curated the contextual archive section. Amanda Levete Architects devised the unique and elegantly playful exhibition design. Unit9 provided the innovative digital design for the archive. We are all very grateful to the Trinity Laban Conservatoire of Music and Dance for helping to bring new life into the galleries through their collaboration. We also thank Nicky Molloy and Eva Martinez for co-curating the live performances in the Queen Elizabeth Hall and Purcell Room.

In addition I wish to thank the many distinguished contributors to this catalogue: Peggy Phelan, Susan Leigh Foster and André Lepecki for their insightful essays, with incisive shorter texts on artists provided by Eleonora Fabião, Isabelle Graw, Anna Gritz, Martin Hargreaves, Paul Kaiser, Julienne Lorz, Helen Luckett, Siobhan McCracken Nixon, Eva Martinez, Nicky Molloy, Noémie Solomon and Åsmund Thorkildsen. Thanks also go to designer Melanie Mues for her excellent work in bringing a sense of movement and flair to this book, and to Mary Richards, Hayward Art Publisher, and Rosalind Horne, Freelance Editor, for skillfully supervising and managing all aspects of this publication.

My deep thanks and appreciation also go to Assistant Curators Siobhan McCracken Nixon, Anna Gritz and Exhibition Assistant Chelsea Fitzgerald, who did a brilliant job overseeing the countless tasks involved in putting this complex exhibition together. Hayward Operations Manager Matt Nightingale, Senior Technician David Wood and Registrar Vicky Skelding ably rose to the challenges of planning and installing the exhibition. Helen Luckett did her usual superb job of writing and editing texts for the exhibition guide and wall labels, while Hayward General Manager Sarah O'Reilly adroitly managed the many taxing organisational issues poised by such an ambitious show.

For their keen support of this project, I would personally like to thank Southbank Centre CEO Alan Bishop and Artistic Director Jude Kelly as well as Southbank Centre's Board of Trustees. Finally, and most importantly of all, our gratitude goes to the many artists in this exhibition whose work has inspired and moved us in many ways.

Ralph Rugoff
Director, Hayward Gallery

CHOREOGRAPHING YOU

CHOREOGRAPHIES IN THE VISUAL ARTS

Stephanie Rosenthal

Venice Biennale, *12th June, 2009. I am at the Arsenale in front of the installation* The Fact of Matter *by the choreographer and dancer William Forsythe. Rings suspended at various heights invite me to float through the room, using hands and feet to swing from one to the next. I am reasonably fit, which makes the first part fairly easy. I move quickly from ring to ring without the need to think twice about taking the path that requires the least effort, because I possess the strength. As my strength begins to wane, I try to use my reserves effectively, switching hands and feet with strategic smarts in order to traverse the room as quickly as possible. When my strength fades in earnest, I lack the energy to think strategically and switch to mere perseverance, and finally I reach the goal. With my feet back on the ground, I feel as though I were flying – my arms and legs appear to be lifting off – I had escaped gravity for a moment. The tension in my muscles abates, and I perceive changes in my own body with great clarity.*

Since the late 1990s, Forsythe has created installations that engage with the fundamental questions of choreography. These 'choreographic objects' have been shown in exhibitions, biennials and festivals worldwide over the past decade. Forsythe is not the only choreographer who has suddenly been embraced by the world of visual arts – La Ribot, Boris Charmatz and many others are regularly showing in art exhibitions internationally. Increasing numbers of artists, notably Tacita Dean, Pablo Bronstein and Kelley Nipper to name a few, are discovering an interest in dance and choreography and are integrating it into their work, either in the form of performance, or in their video or film works. Forsythe asks whether choreography can elaborate an expression of its principles that is independent of the body:

> Denigrated by centuries of ideological assault, the body in motion [...] is still subtly relegated to the domain of raw sense: precognitive, illiterate. Fortunately, choreographic thinking, being what it is, proves useful in mobilizing language to dismantle the constraints of this degraded station by imagining other physical models of thought that circumvent this misconception. What else, besides the body, could physical thinking look like?[1]

The answer to this question can be found in the 'choreographic object' – sculptures and installations that Forsythe sees as materialisations of choreographic thinking. In an extension of Forsythe's ideas, I will argue that certain installations represent a form of choreography, works where the visual arts and dance interpenetrate and the categories dissolve.

What may seem new to us today has roots that go as far back as the mid-twentieth century. Two authors, Peggy Phelan and André Lepecki, approach this fascinating history from different perspectives in this publication. In 1958, the American artist and creator of the Happening, Allan Kaprow, concluded his essay on 'The Legacy of Jackson Pollock' with the words:

> Young artists of today need no longer say, 'I am a painter' or 'a poet' or 'a dancer'. They are simply 'artists'. All of life will be open to them. They will discover out of ordinary things the meaning of ordinariness. They will not try to make them extraordinary but will only state their real meaning. But out of nothing they will devise the extraordinary and then maybe nothingness as well. People will be delighted or horrified, critics will be confused or amused, but these, I am certain, will be the alchemies of the 1960s.

These words represent an attitude shared by an entire generation of artists after the end of the Second World War, when different forms of art entered into an often seamless fusion. In keeping with Kaprow's euphoric assertion, this essay attempts to outline those borderline areas where the visual arts and dance become indistinguishable in the context of the art exhibition: the intersections between installation or sculpture and choreography.

Our traditional Western conception of what unites art and dance is primarily based on the ways in which dance has been treated as a motif in sculptures, paintings and films, as well as on the scenarios that artists have produced for choreographies. Accordingly, exhibitions and discussions in books consider the relationship between art and dance largely on the level of representation.[2] Instead, I would like to come back to Kaprow's 'Legacy of Pollock'. To Kaprow, Pollock's Action Paintings take a step towards the Environment:

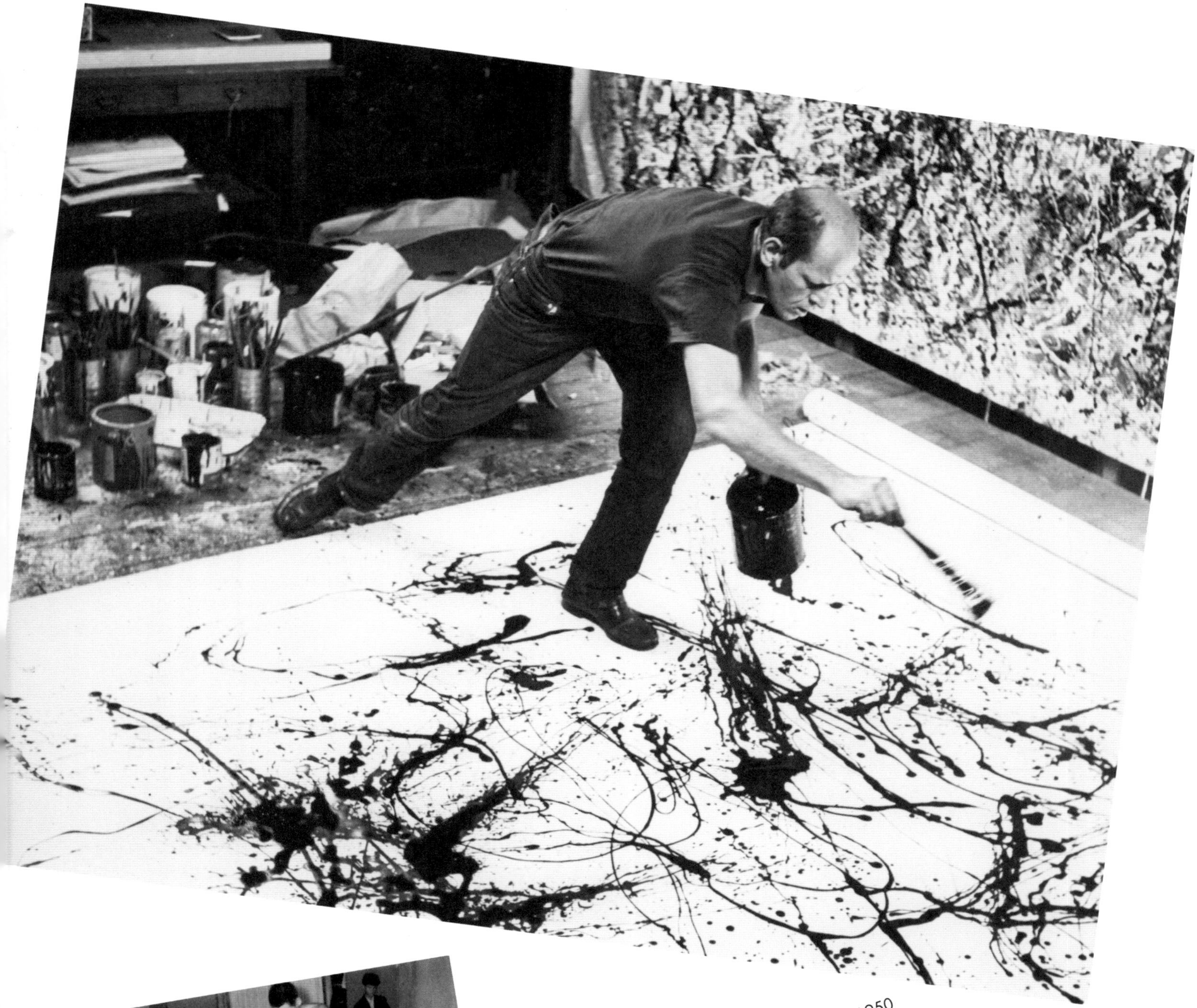

Hans Namuth, *Jackson Pollock*, 1950

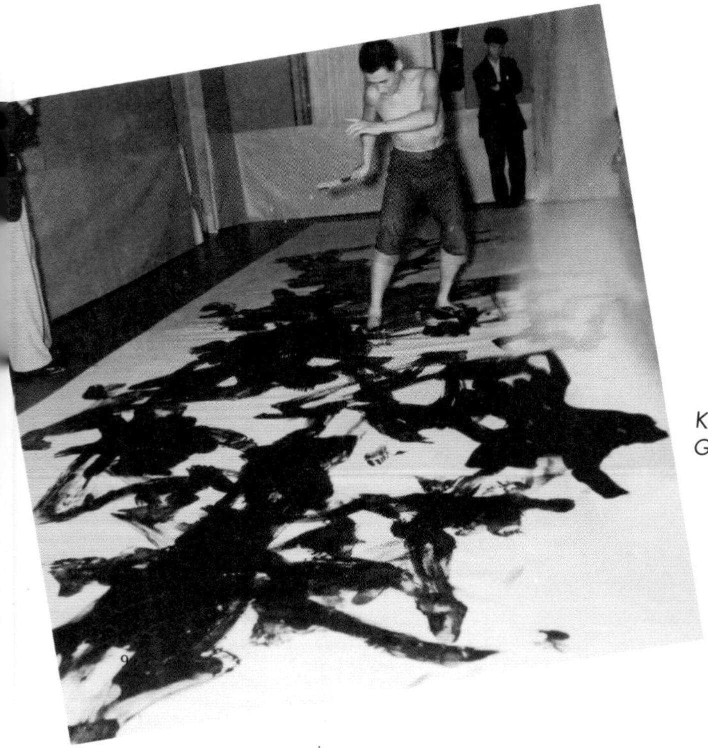

Kazuo Shiraga, *Shiraga painting with his feet at the Gutai Art Exhibition, Tokyo*, 1956

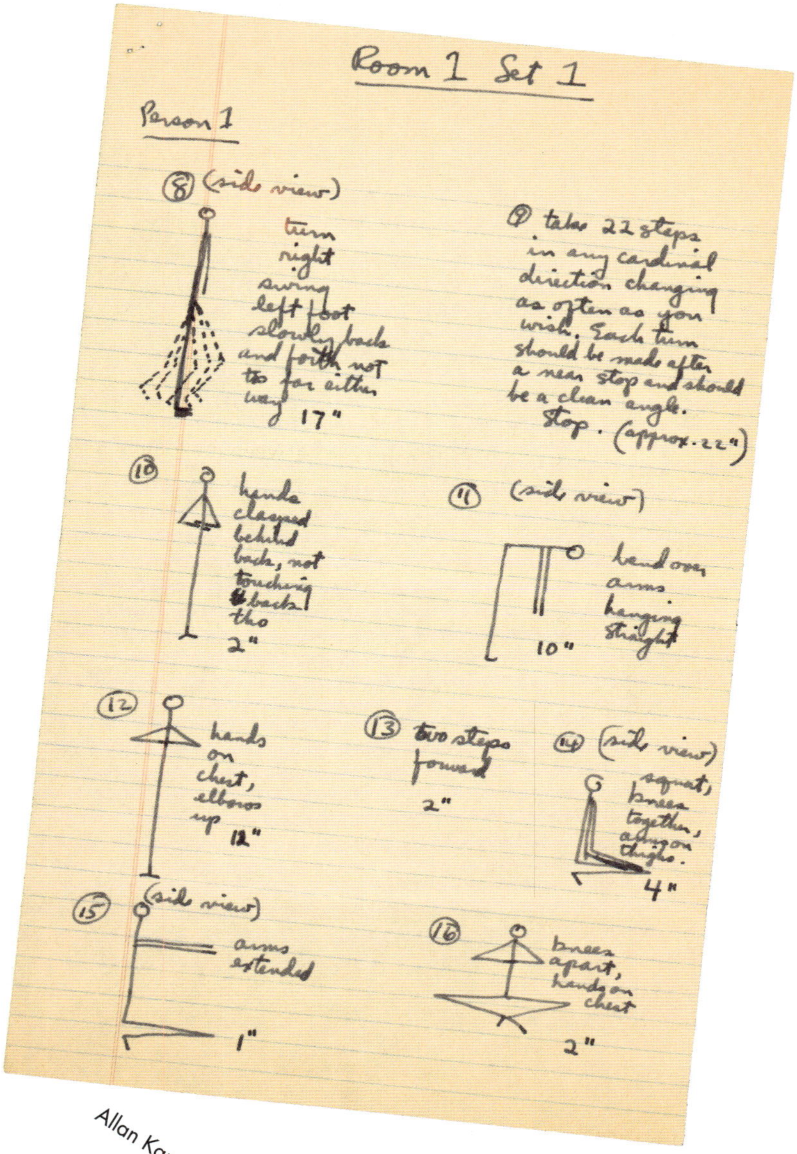

Allan Kaprow, *18 Happenings in 6 Parts: Movement Score*, p. 2, 1959

> The space of these creations is not clearly palpable as such. We can become entangled in the web to some extent and by moving in and out of the skein of lines and splashings can experience a kind of spatial extension [...] But what I believe is clearly discernible is that the entire painting comes out at us (we are participants rather than observers), right into the room.[3]

By virtue of their large dimensions, the paintings turn the viewer into a participant. Pollock's creative process is defined by a rhythmical movement across the canvas, an action evidenced by the lines of paint; the emphasis is not on the result but on the process. The traces of paint render movement palpable to the viewer. Hans Namuth's film of Pollock working supports this reading: the artist's canvas appears as a stage, the act of painting as a dance (p. 9). At almost the same time, Kazuo Shiraga, a co-founder of the Japanese Gutai group, also brought movement into his work. Suspended from a rope, he slid his naked feet across the canvas after dipping them in paint, leaving the traces of his circular movements (p. 9). In another work, he wiggled his way through mud, imprinting his movements into the ground and turning the world into his canvas (p. 132). Finally, in Yves Klein's 'Anthropometries', female bodies became brushes, the artist their choreographer (p. 141). In each instance, the process is just as important as the result. Traces of paint record movement and thus convey it to the viewer. This renders them a form of choreography.

I understand choreography to be any descriptive notation or, in the wider sense, prescription of movement. With this definition I follow Susan Leigh Foster's essay in this publication, as well as William Forsythe's notion that choreography is 'a class of ideas', with the idea being 'a thought or suggestion as to a possible course of action'.[4]

Simone Forti: Dance Constructions

One could argue that since the late 1950s the term 'choreography' has also been applicable to painting, sculpture and installation art. Works of art invite visitors to an exhibition to perform certain movements, effectively creating a choreography for them. Movement becomes an element of the artwork by virtue either of the traces it leaves on the canvas or of the interaction between viewer and work. My interest, then, is in the ways in which artists strategically employ choreography in their installations and sculptures.

The choreographer, performance artist and writer Simone Forti created works that would prove seminal to this development. In 1959, she and her husband, the artist Robert Morris, moved from California to New York. In California they had attended the workshops of Anna Halprin – one the leading dance figures at this time. The works Forti created in New York became seminal for the development of dance.[5] *See-saw*, for example, was first performed in 1960, at the Reuben Gallery, New York, a hot spot of the artistic avant-garde co-founded by Kaprow. It was here, a year earlier, that Kaprow had realised his *18 Happenings in 6 parts*, establishing the Happening as a concept.

See-Saw consisted of a simple instruction:

This piece, performed by a man and a woman, is about twenty minutes long. It requires a plank about eight feet long, and a saw-horse, used together as a see-saw. At each end of the plank, three hooks correspond to hooks placed in the two opposite walls. Elastics are attached from the hooks in the walls to the hooks in the boards, forming a long line from the wall to wall which zigs and zags as the see-saw shifts balance back and forth. Attached to the bottom of one side of the see-saw is a noise-making toy that goes 'moo' every time it is tipped.[6]

There must have been a lot of laughter when Morris and Yvonne Rainer first rehearsed the piece with Forti. And it was a historic moment, too. They were suddenly able to say: 'This is dance! Forget everything you've seen on the stage until now.' There were no predefined structures; instead, the dancers followed a 'task line'. During every performance, they had to tackle anew the task that they had set themselves; the see-saw became the choreographic basis and the point of departure for their improvisation. Everyday movements became dance, and dance became everyday; life and art united.

Similarly, *Slant Board*, which Forti first presented in 1961 as part of *Five Dance Constructions and Some Other Thing*, used a wooden structure to test new forms of movement in subtle ways:

> The piece begins when three or possibly four people, wearing tennis shoes for traction, get on the ramp [...] The movement should not be hurried, but calm, and as continuous as possible. The activity of moving around on such a steep surface can be strenuous even when done casually. If a performer needs to rest, she may do so by using the ropes in any way she can to assume a restful position. But the performers must stay on the board for the duration of the piece.[7]

This performance, too, took place not on a stage but in a gallery-like room.

Forti's dance constructions enabled the dancers to test the gravitational heft and physical capabilities of their bodies: their movements are only slightly stylised and dance is reduced to its basic vocabulary. Forti, in parallel with choreographers from the Judson Dance Theater,[8] among them many of Merce Cunningham's students, explored these alternative forms of movement, calling the traditional parameters of dance into question.

Only a short time earlier, expressive dance had dominated the scene. Choreographers such as Martha Graham (1894–1991), had championed the primacy of emotion over movement. The young generation now sought to sever the cohesion between movement and music, to make more room for randomness and improvisation, and to explore new compositional procedures. Rather than the 'emotional-expressive force of movement', at issue was a 'plastic-fluctuating creative force'.[9] The repetition of simple sequences of movements became a popular device – one of numerous parallels between dance and Minimalism in the visual arts.[10] Choreographers now examined the physical features of the body, its relation to the space and time of movement. They left the stage, realising their performances instead in places such as the Reuben Gallery, the Judson Memorial Church or in the urban space – sites that dissolved the classical theatrical situation and allowed the audience to form a circle around the performance rather than sitting in rows of seats frontally facing a stage. Other examples of this phenomenon include pieces by Steve Paxton, Robert Rauschenberg and Deborah Hay,[11] as well as Rainer, who, in works such as *Room Service* (1963), *Parts of Some Sextets* (1965) or *The Mind is A Muscle* (1968), used 'found objects' such as mattresses, car tyres, chairs, ladders, etc.[12] Some of these choreographies recall

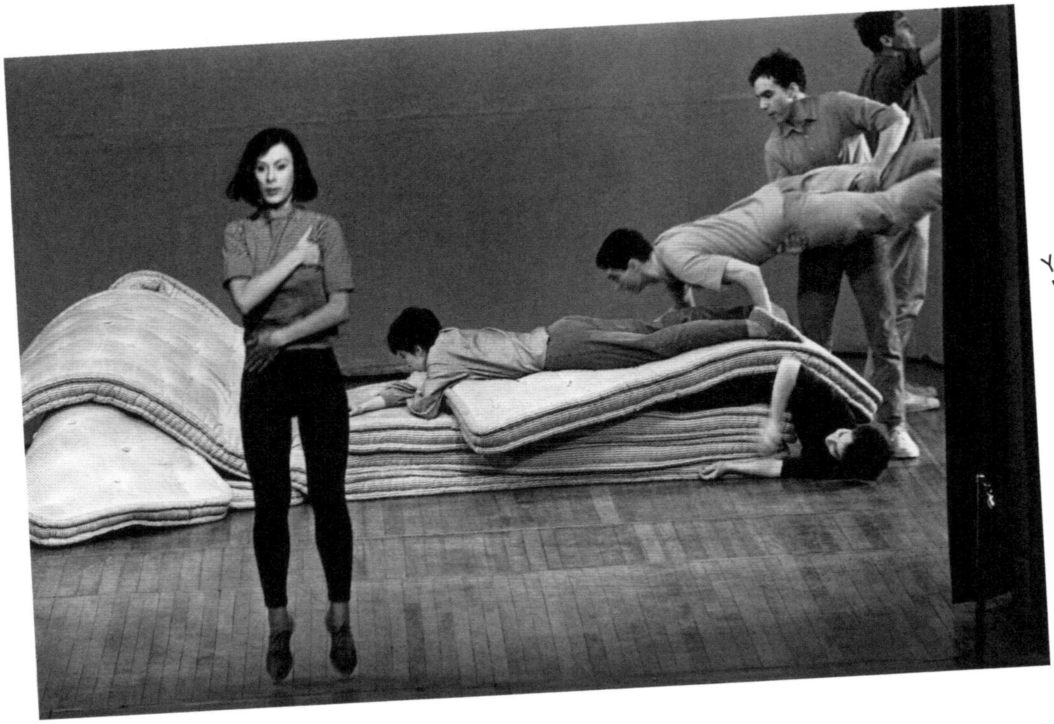

Yvonne Rainer, *Parts of Some Sextets*, 1965
Photo by Peter Moore © Estate of Peter Moore/
VAGA, NYC

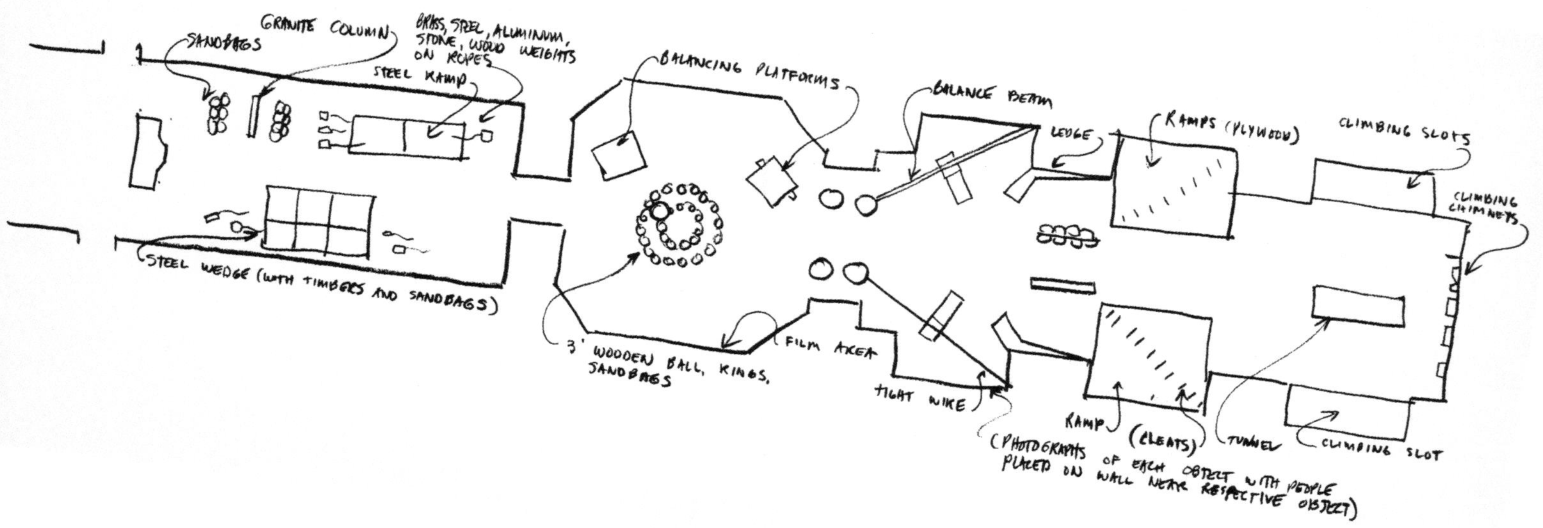

Robert Morris, Sketch of Robert Morris exhibition.
Taken from Tate Gallery publicity leaflet, 1971

gymnastic exercises: the dancers drop from a high bar or vault over piles of mattresses. Rainer emphasised the role played by the objects in this context: they enabled the dancers to 'move or be moved by some *thing* rather than by oneself.'[13]

Forti, who from the early 1960s worked with large, simple wooden structures, would exercise a vital influence over artists such as Morris. She saw these structures, which she had asked Morris to build for her, not as sculptures but as purely pragmatic 'movement apparatuses'. They often suggest gymnastics or playground equipment; everyday sequences of movement came front and centre, fusing life and art. This credo – and a love of improvisation – also informed work being done in other fields, such as music (John Cage) or the visual arts (Kaprow), causing a revolution in the New York arts scene of the 1960s.

Kaprow wanted participants, not spectators, for his art. Pollock's Action Paintings created the first spark: 'Pollock [...] left us at the point where we must become preoccupied with and even dazzled by the space and objects of our everyday life, either our bodies, clothes, rooms, or, if needed, the vastness of Forty-second Street.'[14] Kaprow saw himself as an 'Un-Artist/Non-Artist'.[15] With his Happenings, he stepped outside the arts scene and into public space. Through artists such as Forti, Rainer and Robert Whitman, he was in touch with the Judson Dance Theater. Unlike his later Happenings, the *18 Happenings in 6 Parts* were based on a detailed script running to around 50 pages. In this context is interesting to note that these sequences of movements, though highly stylised, evinced a simplicity and a proximity to everyday life that reveal significant parallels with the later works of the Judson Dance Theater.

The interest – shared by an entire generation of visual artists – in the unique event, in playfulness and an exploration of one's own body, was reflected in the developments in postmodern dance. The critique of the reification, and hence commodification, of the work of art reached a climax. No wonder, then, that artists welcomed dance as a way to elude the art market, and capitalism with it. Both Conceptual art and Minimalism lent expression to this desire by changing the status of the work of art: while some bade farewell to objecthood, turning the idea into the work, others emphasised it. The works discussed here build a bridge between these two approaches.

The Visitor Starts to Dance

I'd rather break my arm falling off a platform than spend an hour in detached contemplation of a Matisse.
Robert Morris, 1971[16]

In all the pieces discussed so far, the performers were either trained dancers or fellow artists. A clear distinction was still made between performers and audience, although the way in which the latter was positioned already assigned it a completely new role. One exception was the choreographer Trisha Brown's *The Stream* (1970) (pp. 66–7): she placed her work in public space – right in the middle of New York's Union Square – making it available to a general audience. Arranged inside a U-shaped wooden structure were pots and pans filled with water. Passers-by could either step into the water or swerve to avoid it.[17] Artists such as Rainer also considered the role of the spectator; not for nothing does Carrie Lambert-Beatty call Rainer a 'sculptor of spectatorship'.[18]

It was Morris who took the decisive step in 1971, creating, in an installation for the Tate Gallery in London (pp. 70–3), what was explicitly a choreography for the exhibition space. The visitor was to experience the show through his own body: 'The show is more environmental than object-like, offers more possibility – or even necessity – of physically moving over, in, around, rather than detached viewing.'[19] He staged a course of sculptures made from a variety of simple materials such as wood or metal in the Tate's Duveen Galleries, thus realising a choreography that required neither instructions nor rehearsals but allowed visitors to experience the work through their own bodies. 'The works were based on progressive physical difficulty as one proceeded toward the end of the space', he commented.[20] There were slanted wooden surfaces to be ascended with the help of ropes, tunnels to be crawled through, see-saws and parallel bars to be balanced on, and a wheel that let visitors roll upside down. In contrast to Forti's works, his installation turned the audience into dancers. His sketches demonstrate the precision with which he balanced the arrangement of the objects, which made use of the entire length of the hall. The fact that the show had to be closed after only four days for safety reasons is evidence that Morris had succeeded in realising sculptures as 'instructions to act'.

We can draw a direct line from Morris's Tate exhibition to Forti's earlier choreographies. In the late 1950s, Morris had occasionally accompanied his wife to Anna Halprin's workshops in San Francisco.[21] Forti recalls:

> I remember vividly the movement Bob did on this particular day. He had observed a rock. Then he lay down on the ground. Over a period of about three minutes he became more and more compact until the edges of him were off the ground, and just the point under his center of gravity remained on the ground.[22]

It is as though Morris had become his own sculpture. At the Judson Memorial Church, he realised choreographies such as *Arizona* (1963) and *Site* (1964), whose central motif was the act of moving heavy sheets of plywood.[23] In these dance pieces he tested what would later become the foundations of his installations; at the same time, he created his early Minimalist works such as *Untitled (Slab)* (1962).

What Morris and other artists learned from dance was the presence of the body, on a visual and physical level:

> My involvement in theatre has been with the body in motion [...] In retrospect this seems a constant value which was preserved. From the beginning I wanted to avoid the pulled-up, turned-out, anti-gravitational qualities that not only give a body definition and role as 'dancer' but qualify and delimit the movement available to it. The challenge was to find alternative movement.[24]

Other choreographers with the Judson Dance Theater left a lasting impression on Morris's work, as did Yvonne Rainer, with whom he was romantically involved off and on between 1964 and 1971. As Richard Serra said, Rainer's performances led to a new conception of the body in art: 'the body's movement not being predicated totally on image or sight or optical awareness, but on physical awareness in relation to space, place, time, movement'.[25]

Bruce Nauman and Dan Graham: 'A Sort of Dance'

The works of Bruce Nauman and Dan Graham can likewise be considered in this context. In the 1960s, Nauman approached sculpture via dance and performance art, testing the limits of his own body and inviting the viewer to do the same in works such as *Corridor Installation (Nick Wilder Installation)* (1970) or *Green Light Corridor* (1970) (pp. 68–9). He undertook experiments on himself resembling those of the Californian choreographers, focusing on spontaneous, unpretentious, everyday movements. In his early performance pieces from the 1960s, objects not unlike Forti's constructions invited specific movements: 'An awareness of yourself comes from a certain amount of activity and you can't get it from just thinking about yourself. You do exercises, you have certain kinds of awareness that you don't have if you read books.'[26] By the late 1960s, his performances had come to consist of actions pure and simple, no

Bruce Nauman, *Dance or Exercise on the Perimeter of a Square (Square Dance)*, 1967–8

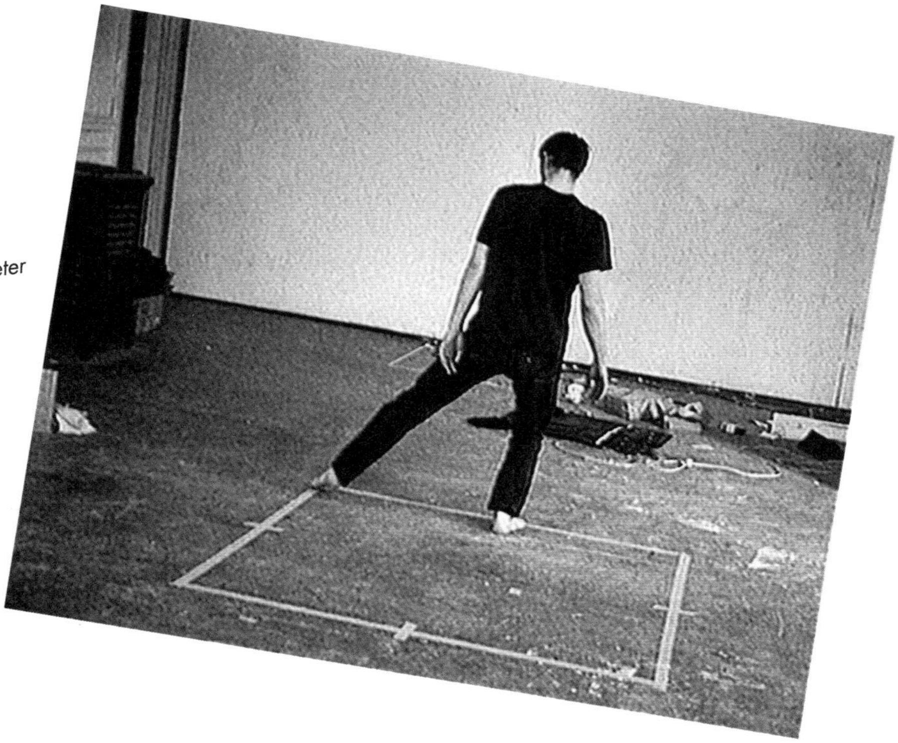

longer involving objects. He also recorded movement studies on film or video. In works such as *Dance or Exercise on the Perimeter of a Square* (1967–8) (p. 13), *Slow Angle Walk (Beckett Walk)* (1968) and *Bouncing in the Corner* (1968), he repeated certain movements to the point of exhaustion. At the time, Nauman talked to the choreographer Meredith Monk. 'Meredith Monk [...] had thought about or seen some of my work and recognized it. [...] I thought of them as dance problems without being a dancer, being interested in the kinds of tension that arise when you try to balance and can't. Or do something for a long time and get tired.'[27] He also recalls that it 'was really good to talk to someone about it. Because I guess I thought of what I was doing as a sort of dance because I was familiar with some of the things that Cunningham and others had done, where you can take any simple movement and make it into a dance just by presenting it as a dance.'[28]

Soon after his performances and works on film and video, Nauman began to make simple corridors constructed from plywood panels. These works, which fused performance and sculpture, ranged from single corridors to multiple corridors connected to produce the appearance of labyrinths, some of them with integrated video recording systems. With its narrow interior spaces, which could, in some parts only be traversed by walking sideways and its green lighting and sound-absorbing walls, *Green Light Corridor* (1970) created a very specific – to some visitors, claustrophobic – situation that generated a heightened perception of the body.

Although his corridors solicited the audience's participation, the visitor-participant could not alter the fundamental structure of the work in any way.[29] Nauman deliberately controlled his audience:

> All you could really do was just walk in and walk out and it really limited the kinds of things that you could do. [...] Because I don't like the idea of free manipulation [...] I really had some more specific kinds of experiences in mind and [...] I wanted to make kind of play experiences unavailable, just by the preciseness of the area.[30]

The extent to which the artists permitted participation varied from work to work, and was not always subject to their control. Nauman remembers, for example, how dissatisfied Morris was that the audience completely changed one of his works when he had not intended this to happen.[31] The artists recognised the important point that participation might also take place purely in the imagination.[32]

Dan Graham, too, closely studied the perception of the body in the early 1970s. Forti's influence on him was decisive.[33] In works such as *Helix/Spiral* (1973), realised in collaboration with Forti, he called into question conventional notions of space, image and visual perception. His filmic performances often aimed at observing and discovering himself and the other in space. He uses the camera and/or the monitor to achieve a defamiliarising effect. The user sees a time-delayed and distanced representation of his own movements. Once again, simple movements play a central role; lifted out of their context, they can be perceived in their essence.[34]

Morris, Nauman and Graham, unlike Forti, turn exhibition visitors into dancers. 'I wanted a situation where people could use their bodies as well as their eyes',[35] Morris wrote. The formats and sizes of his works enabled an experience of the body in its concrete existence in space; with this aim, Morris also described a central desideratum of Minimalism;[36] the primacy of the co-presence of work and viewer over the internal structure of the artwork is considered a constitutive feature of Minimal art.

This situation-specificity of the experience of art prompted the critic Michael Fried to charge the artists with 'theatricality', calling instead for the creation of a lasting and timeless presence.[37] But Morris saw his works as bridges leading to a more intense perception of the viewer's own body.

> From the body relating to the spaces of the Tate via my alterations of the architectural elements of passages and surfaces to the body relating to its own conditions [...] the progression is from the manipulation of objects, to constructions which adjust to the body's presence, to situations where people can become more aware of themselves and their own experience.'[38]

Dan Graham, Detail from Roll, Binocular Zoom, Helix/Spiral, Helix/Spiral (Simone Forti), Sunset to Sunrise, 1969–73

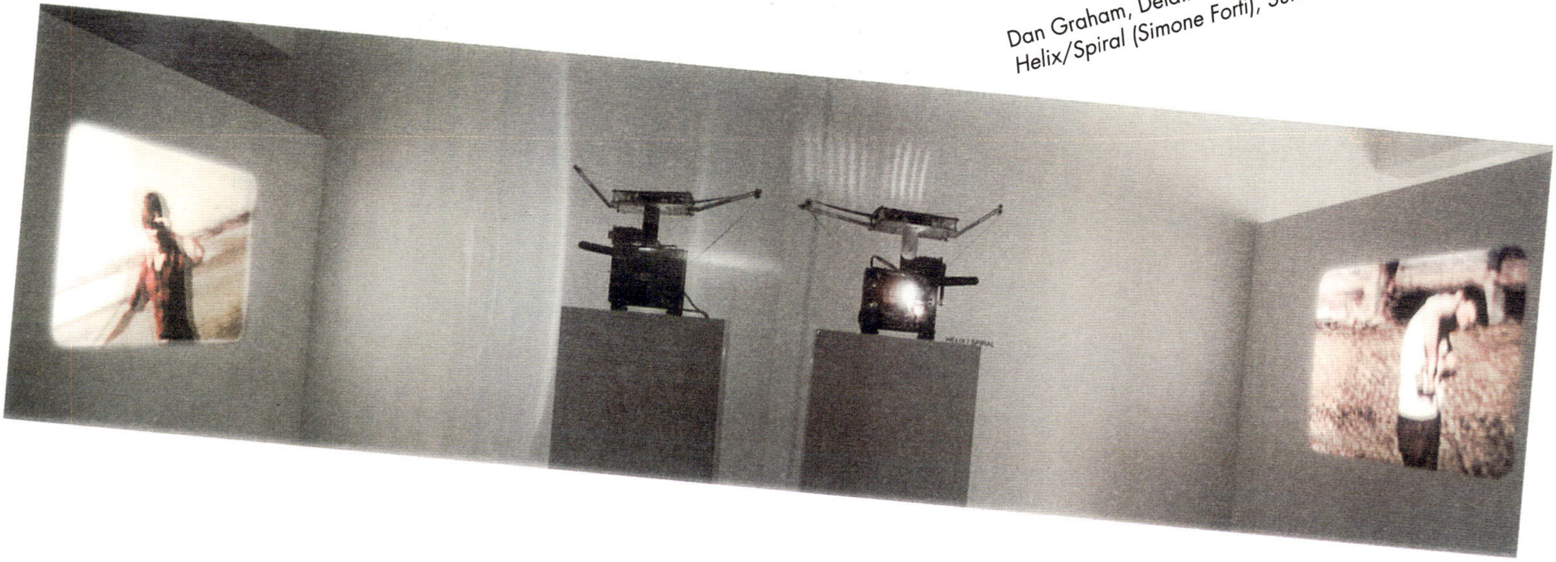

Lygia Clark: Connecting Interior and Exterior Worlds

At around the same time, the Brazilian artist Lygia Clark developed an interest in the interrelation between human being and object, which led to her belief that her sculptures truly existed only in interaction with the viewer:

> Deep down, the object is not the most important thing. The thought – the meaning which it lends to the object, to the act, is what matters: That which goes from us to the object [...] In my work, if the spectator does not propose himself towards the experience, the work does not exist.[39]

The results were works such as the *Máscaras sensoriais* (Sensory Masks, 1967), *Pedra e ar* (Rock and Air, 1966), or *Camisa-de-força* (Straight Jacket, 1969) (p. 60), most of which were simple constructions made of plain materials that offered sensual surfaces. Clark describes her *Straight Jacket* as follows:

> Stones and six nylon sacking bags. One of the bags covers the head. On the bottom end of the bag, connected to it by an elastic band, a smaller bag with a stone inside it. At each side of the large bag, another bag covers each arm, and a little bag containing stones hangs from each of them by an elastic band.[40]

This description must be read as an instruction to the viewer, who is to slip into the objects as if into a piece of apparel. This contact with the body, Clark believed, was of central importance; her works were designed to stimulate a re-evaluation of everyday routine movements. The sensuality of her works speaks to an erotic life and experience of the body very different from the experience of the Americans. In the late 1970s, her interests led her to the 'Relational Objects' that she employed in her therapeutic practice, using them to unleash emotions that would enable patients to experience a new sense of union with the world. Rather than turning the human body into a sculpture, she sought to create an opportunity for the members of her audience to experience their own bodies and the effects that objects have on them.

In 1969, Clark realised *The House is the Body* (pp. 60–3): a series of narrow rooms defined by various materials – fabric, rubber, plastic, hairs – into which visitors were able to enter in fixed succession, as if passing through the human body. The rooms were entitled 'Penetration', 'Ovulation', 'Germination' and 'Expulsion'. In this and other works, it was important to Clark that the viewer should be able to perceive the work with their various senses. As Guy Brett wrote:

> Clark's innovation had far-reaching implications. According to a perceptive recent analysis of the nature of 'visuality' in modern western culture, our current ways of seeing have been decisively influenced by a historical process whose effect has been 'to sunder the act of seeing from the physical body of the observer, to decorporealize vision.' [...] It becomes fascinating to interpret Lygia Clark's experiments in the 1960s as a pioneering attempt to re-integrate visual perception with the body as a whole, to reconnect the interior and the exterior world, and the knower and the known.[41]

Like Clark's works, the 'Paßstücke' (Adaptives) that the Austrian artist Franz West began to realise in the 1970s turn viewers into participants, inviting us to adapt the sculptures to our own bodies or to connect with them by means of movement. As Åsmund Thorkildsen remarks in this publication, West, like Clark, changed the relationship between object and viewer, opening up new levels of perception (pp. 78–81). In some cases, he exhibited photographs or films that offered instructions; paraphernalia that we can thus read as choreographies of sorts. The artist himself, his friends and dancers, served as interpreters. An even subtler realisation of the same intention can be found in his pieces of furniture, which explicitly instructed the user to perform certain actions.

Between 1963 and 1969, Franz Erhard Walther created his *1. Werksatz* (First Work Set): an ensemble of fabric objects to be engaged by the beholder. His *2. Werksatz* (Second Work Set) consisted of metal walk-in objects such as the *Standing Piece in Two Sections* (1974) (pp. 56–9). In what he called 'work-actions' and 'work-presentations', Walther invited the members of his audience to experience sensual perceptions through their own bodies. In Isabelle Graw's text on Walther for this publication, she explores that his main interest with these works, distinct from Clark, was in the question of the extent to which the viewer's body is itself the sculpture.

Choreographic Objects

By creating works that demand physical exertion, these artists championed the idea of experiencing the world with the entire body. In a variety of ways, this generated a new awareness that we do not perceive with our eyes alone. They realised 'choreographic objects', as Forsythe calls them, as 'an alternative site for the understanding of potential instigation and organization of action to reside'.[42] These works draw our attention to the fact that objects are not self-sufficient entities, or as dancer and choreographer Rudolf Laban put it in his book *The Language of Movement* (1966): 'Movement is, so to speak, living architecture – living in the sense of changing emplacements as well as changing cohesion.'[43] By prompting viewers to experience the works with their own bodies, these 'continuous exchanges and movement' are rendered evident and palpable, changing our understanding of art in profound and lasting ways that become applicable to other situations as well. As Morris writes:

> We've become blind from so much seeing. Time to press up against things, squeeze around, crawl over – not so much out of a childish naïveté to return to the playground, but more to acknowledge that the world begins to exist at the limits of our skin and what goes on at that interface between the physical self and external conditions doesn't detach us like the detached glance.[44]

Perception as Action

In the mid-twentieth century, the question of the role played by the body in our perception of our environment was raised in many

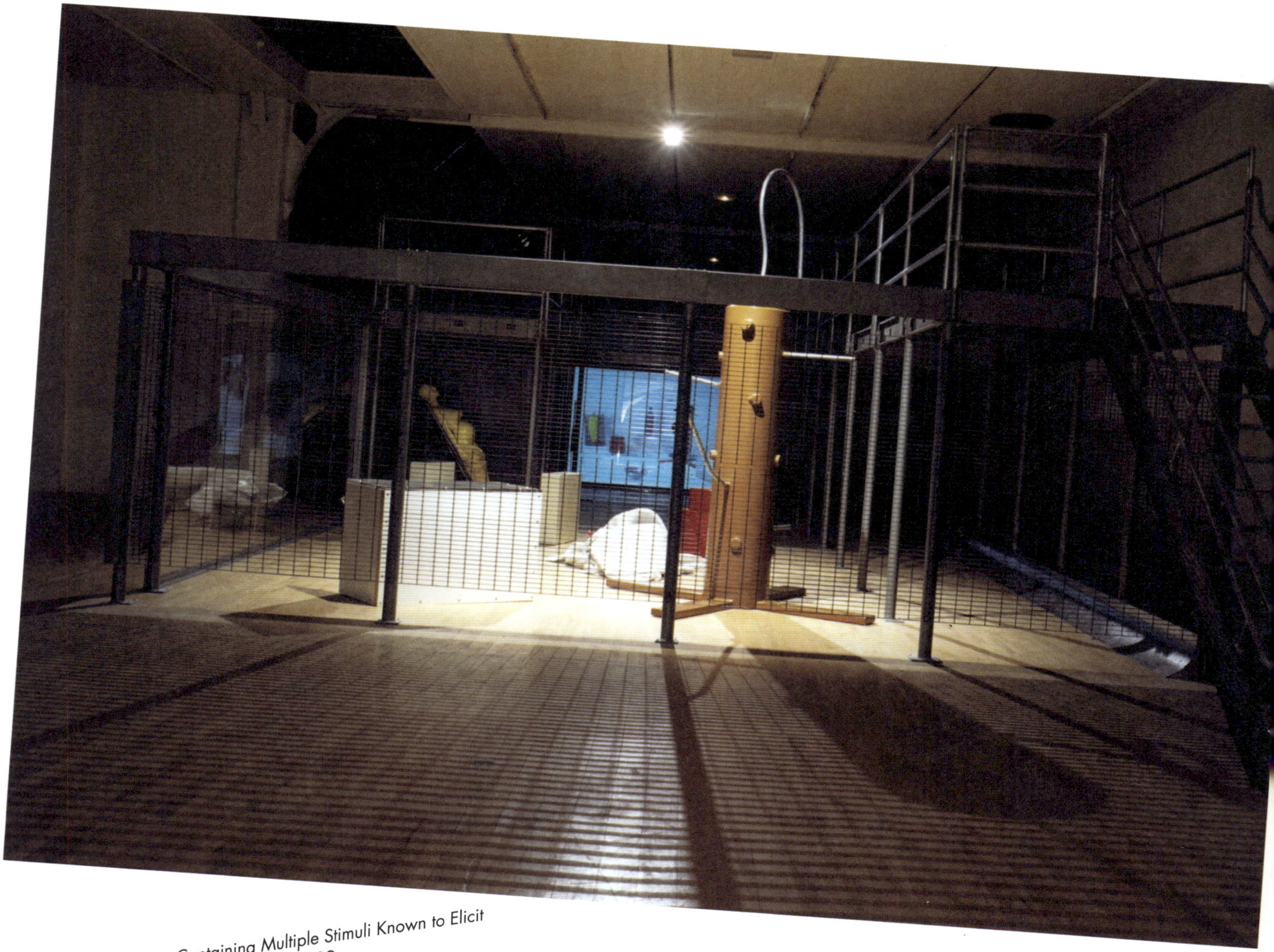

Mike Kelley, *Test Room Containing Multiple Stimuli Known to Elicit Curiosity and Manipulatory Responses*, 1999

areas. After the Second World War, artists seem to have returned to existential questions such as the relationship to one's own body. The interest in Zen Buddhism, primitive cultures and phenomenology, as well as the Hippie movement, were to a certain degree all rooted in the same origin: the desire for a more primordial experience of the world.

In his *Phenomenology of Perception* (1945; the first English translation was available in 1962), Maurice Merleau-Ponty argues that 'the world surrounds and engenders us' and that we ought to stop 'seeing the world as a counterpart'.[45] Unlike, say, Kant or Descartes, Merleau-Ponty considered the human body our decisive connection to the world. It is, he writes, not only 'our anchor in the world'[46] but also, more importantly, 'that by which it is possible for us to have a world at all.'[47] In his *Gestalt Therapy*, which became very fashionable, Frederick Perls likewise examined the phenomenon of body-consciousness. This lent his book great interest in the eyes of Morris and Nauman.[48] John Dewey's *Art as Experience* and John Huizinga's *Homo Ludens*, both written in 1934, were also frequently mentioned by artists who accorded great importance to the playful approach to the world and the experiential gain offered by art. The desire arose to question the status of art and to redefine its mission in society. In the 1960s, Happenings, Conceptual art and Minimalism made this desire a central issue. This development culminated in the wish to re-evaluate the action of the exhibition visitor. In dance, this was nothing new: the object of perception was already immaterial, being constituted 'on site and in the act in the materiality of the body'.[49]

In his book *Action in Perception*, Alva Noë describes perception as already being an action: 'Perceiving is a way of acting. Perception is not something that happens to us, or in us. It is something we do [...] The world makes itself available to the perceiver through physical movement and interaction.'[50] He also argues that:

> [...] seeing is much more like touching than it is like depicting. Consider the bottle again, which you touch with eyes closed. The bottle is there in your hands. By moving your hands, by palpation, you encounter its shape. Vision acquires content in exactly this way. You aren't given the visual world all at once. You are in the world, and through skillful visual probing – what Merleau-Ponty called 'palpation with the eyes' – you bring yourself into contact with it. You discern its structure and so, in that sense, represent it. Vision is touch-like. Like touch, vision is active.[51]

The viewer is given responsibility for decisions regarding his own perception, which is an active process.

Social Choreography

The 'choreographic' art of Morris, Nauman, Clark, West and Walther was defined by sequences of movement guided by sculptures or installations. These works intensified viewers' experiences of their bodies, changing their understanding of what perception means. Viewers – whom we should now call users – became components of the work. These shifts simultaneously emphasised and cancelled the objecthood of the work. On the one hand, sculpture was reconceived as a solicitation to action – in contradistinction to the auratic and untouchable work of art. On the other, the focus on action and movement entirely dissolved the objecthood of art. This second aspect, in particular, owed much to the engagement with dance.

Two generations later, artists such as Mike Kelley, Pablo Bronstein and Tania Bruguera were able to presuppose this engagement as a given. Their interest in choreography focused on degenerated, artificial, or manipulated patterns of behaviour. Choreography became the image of our own world, with its external powers controlling the physical, psychological and spatial aspects of our actions. It thus became a mirror of socio-political structures and mechanisms of manipulation. In his book on *Social Choreography*, Andrew Hewitt has shown 'how choreography has served not only as a secondary metaphor for modernity but also as a structuring blueprint for thinking and effecting modern social organization.'[52]

Mike Kelley's work *Adaptation: Test Room Containing Multiple Stimuli Known to Elicit Curiosity and Manipulatory Responses* (1999/2010) (pp. 86–9), examines forms of human behaviour such as aggression and the exaggerated need for physical affection, as well as strategies of manipulation. Among his references are the psychologist and behavioural researcher Harry Harlow, the choreographer Martha Graham, the artist Isamu Noguchi, and the scholar of aggression Albert Bandura. All of them share an interest in primitive human actions that resemble the behaviour of children or animals. Harlow studied the mother-child relationship in baby monkeys, using simulacra that were reminiscent of children's or a dog's toys. Kelley borrows the shapes of Harlow's objects for his own sculptures, bringing them to the size and dressing them in the colours of Noguchi's sceneries for Graham from the 1940s, which, in turn, drew on the primitive sculptures created, for instance, by Max Ernst or Oskar Schlemmer. We can read Kelley's objects as paying homage to modernity: their colours recall both Piet Mondrian's paintings and the figures in Schlemmer's *Triadic Ballet* (1922). The objects are placeholders: in Harlow's experiments, for the mother who offers either warmth or food; in Kelley, for human emotions that require a sympathetic body. They are simulacra representing the human need for love and its flipside, aggression. In Kelley, they quench the human longing for affect.

An integral part of the work is a film that shows a choreography for two dancers by Anita Pace, as well as four performers (two women and two men) who interrupt this choreography. The two women carry out actions towards the objects that alternate between aggression and affection; two men, sometimes in monkey costumes, sometimes in street clothes, imitate the behaviour of monkeys. Both sequences of actions gesture toward primitive forms of behaviour in humans. Whereas Graham was the inspiration for Pace's choreography, the actions of the performers were inspired by Bandura's scientific films. Bandura studied the interrelation between aggression in childhood and the consumption of violent television programmes. Kelley is interested in Graham's use of simple and direct movements that are often the expression of an internal emotional structure. Like Bandura and Harlow, Kelley also examines human behaviour. In the original version of *Test Room...* (1999), a cage enclosed the sculptures, over which a ramp was provided for observers. In the later adaptation, Kelley released the objects from the cage. The choreography was now performed live and not only played on film; the visitors were given the opportunity to interact with the objects themselves. The choreography became a more central part of the ensemble and lent expression to the manipulation to which human behaviour is subject.

Kelley turns the user into the test subject. He is able to train his muscles as though at a gym, or, like a dancer, use the objects as action instructions or movement aids. At the same time, however, he also becomes a behavioural researcher observing himself. Central to the work is not the invitation to use the objects, but the challenge to reflect on what this invitation could mean, and lays bare our degenerated society. Kelley also adds another layer – one in which we become aware of how we are manipulated. The participant becomes the viewer of his own participation; to question this process critically is part of his role. In Kelley's work, we can experience not only our own bodies, but also what manipulation and heteronomy feel like.

Rather than delivering a moralistic lecture, Kelley offers no explanation and no way out. The people in the film learn nothing from their interaction with the objects and remain isolated and incapable of communication. As in his earlier work *Educational Complex* (1995), Kelley exhibits 'our true, chaotic social conditions, rather than some idealized dream of wholeness'.[53] Unlike the artists of the 1960s and 1970s, Kelley's interest is not in liberating, or raising awareness of the body, but rather in elaborating its state of being controlled.

Choreography as Expression of Manipulation

Other artists, similarly, employ choreography as a means to, as well as an expression of, manipulation. The British artist Pablo Bronstein has realised drawings, paintings, installations and performances in which he combines mechanisms of dance with architecture and Queer politics, with a primary focus on social codes and stereotypes.

Bronstein specifically refers to the early baroque era and the concept of *sprezzatura* coined by Baldassare Castiglione. *Sprezzatura* describes an elegant courtly attitude that, despite conforming to a canon of precise rules, aims to seem natural and uncontrived. As Bronstein explains, however, 'I am not interested in its courtly manifestation, more the legacy and how it developed through baroque into classical ballet.'[54] He confronts sequences of movements that match the criteria of *sprezzatura* with the canonical movements of contemporary dance, where natural and seemingly prosaic movements that are not too distant from those of everyday life and deliberately subjected to gravity have been predominant since the Judson Dance Theater's work. The sweating and heavily breathing body is accepted as an inevitable consequence of physical exertion; there is no need to hide it. Bronstein, by contrast, calls the concept of a 'natural movement' in question: 'I've been interested in pedestrian movement for a while, which is based in postmodern dance history. My work balances two ideas of "natural" or artificial behaviour.'[55]

In *Magnificent Triumphal Arch in Pompeian Colours* (2010) (pp. 110–13), Bronstein places an architectonic arch in the centre of the room. The ornamented structure gestures towards the architecture of public squares. Architecture, like movement, embodies different social and political values:

> There are buildings that exist entirely within the paradigm of power and structure, and are perceived as truthful, honest, or better still, are not perceived at all. They are so within the convention that they are comparable to learnt codes of behavior that are perceived as natural – 'normal' gender-specific behavior of mannerisms.[56]

The arch through which the performers can step during the exhibition creates a disruption or knot in their everyday movements: the straight line (which matches the style derived from the Judson Dance Theater) becomes the flourish (movements inspired by *sprezzatura*). Bronstein's choreography represents everyday movement without being everyday movement; the performers act in accordance with the precepts of *sprezzatura*, which, to present-day eyes, looks contrived, mannered and affected. 'The body politics of *sprezzatura* would be codified as queer politics now [...] I love order and power and how you actually subvert power by sexualising it.'[57]

Bronstein's works refer to the intersection between architecture and dance as a way to address the issue of politicised space. The arch in the room defines not a transition from indoors to outdoors but, more simply, from one form of behaviour to another; it is an indicator of change or being different. The disruption takes place in the action, triggered by an architectonic form. We are thus under the direction of an architectonic element that points to the architecture of public urban spaces – and, more abstractly, under that of the social system for which the arch stands. Choreography lends form to such manipulative strategies.

Lack of control over one's own body is the subject of João Penalva's work *Widow Simone (Entr'acte, 20 Years)* (1996) (pp. 82–5). In what seems like a documentary in a variety of media, he tells the story of a dancer who has performed the role of Widow Simone in the ballet *La Fille mal gardée* for more than 20 years and yet does not have the right to transmit the choreographies to others or, in this case, to teach the artist himself. The dancer, that is to say, is a mere puppet: an object.[58]

As André Lepecki points out, control is also a central aspect in Tania Bruguera's work *Untitled (Kassel)* (2002) (pp. 90–3). On the one hand, she choreographs the movement within and outside of her installation; on the other, she reveals the extent to which our environment choreographs us. Blindingly bright lights suggest the floodlit atmosphere of a camp or prison. The loading of guns and the sound of heavy boots marching along an elevated catwalk heighten the sense of oppression and imprisonment.

In Isaac Julien's nine-screen installation *TEN THOUSAND WAVES* (2010) (pp. 114–17), people slosh like water from continent to continent – not always of their own volition, but forced by political or economic circumstances. This work examines a more abstract form of choreography; at the same time, the editing and the way in which the installation directs the viewer conforms to a subtle choreography of its own.[59]

In her work *Walk the Chair* (2010) (pp. 118–21), the choreographer La Ribot gives the visitor a free choice between spectatorship and participation. Scattered across the gallery space are folding chairs with a variety of seat cushions. If visitors accept the invitation to sit down, they become both spectators and performers. The chairs themselves bear instructions for movement: reading the sentences inscribed on them requires turning and lifting them, folding them up and unfolding them again. Visitors determine their own role, taking responsibility for their actions; La Ribot merely creates the initial situation.[60]

Spaces of Action

The works of Tino Sehgal and Xavier Le Roy confront the visitor not with an object but with an interpersonal situation. In works such as *Instead of Allowing Some Thing to Rise Up to Your Face Dancing Bruce*

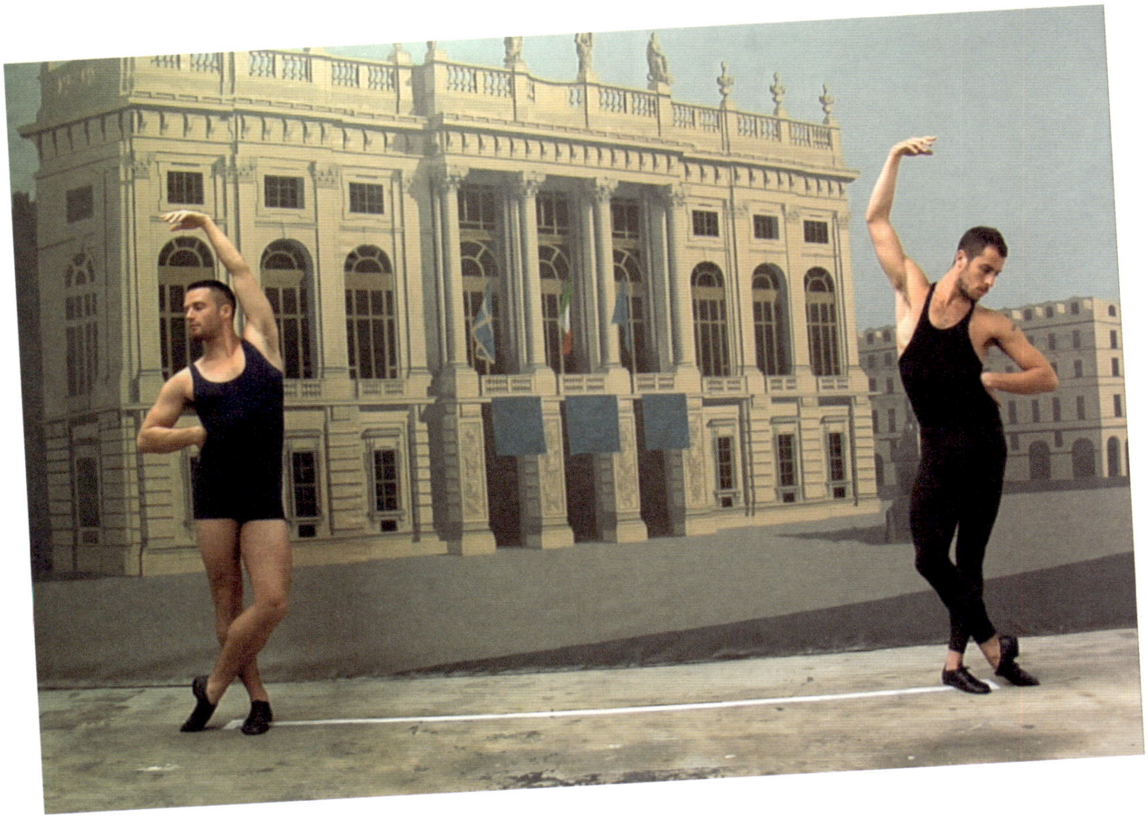

Pablo Bronstein, *Passeggiata*, 2008

and Dan and Other Things (2000), Sehgal attaches central importance to the interaction between 'interpreter' and viewer. He employs choreography in very precise ways as a sculptural means. Despite their performative character, his works are considered sculptural pieces that exist for a certain period of time and then disappear when the performing artist is gone. Sehgal choreographs the movements of his interpreters in such a way that they acquire a semblance of objecthood. He achieves this effect by enjoining his dancers to move gradually, almost as though in slow motion; rather than moving through the room, moreover, the interpreters lie on the floor. The work thus requires a different form of observation from that employed when watching a performance. In the case of *Instead of Allowing...*, the sequence of movements borrows from works by Nauman and Graham.[61]

The interpreter is the work of art; the visitor, the beholder. The relationship between the two is a decisive element of the work. Sehgal's works are in constant flux due to (however minimal) modifications of the interpretation, but more importantly, by virtue of the particular response of each individual viewer. Nonetheless, he succeeds in lending these ephemeral events a 'work- and object-like status'.[62] Accordingly, he requires that his pieces, like paintings or sculptures, should be on view for the entire duration of an exhibition. In 1970, Nauman framed the idea of leaving an entire exhibition room to a dancer for a certain period of time every day; he penned a clear set of instructions:

> The dancer, dressed either in street clothes or in training wear, enters the large room of a gallery. The attendants clear this room; they merely permit the spectators to watch through the door. The dancer walks through the room, slightly ducked, as though the ceiling were about 30 centimetres below his own height; he looks straight ahead, without establishing direct eye contact with the audience [...] After completing the performance, the dancer leaves the room; the attendants permit the audience to enter again.[63]

In Sehgal's work, however, the viewer is not excluded from the room; to the contrary, his presence is of decisive importance. The focus is on what takes place in the interaction between work and viewer. The interpreter in *Instead of Allowing...* involves the visitor by looking directly at him, with his hands forming a rectangle as though holding an imaginary camera.[64] The involvement of the viewer is even more immediate in works such as *This is Good* (2001) (pp. 128–9), where he becomes a protagonist, for it is him alone to whom the interpreter's performance is addressed. In *This is Good*, Sehgal defines a specific choreography for the museum attendants, who in turn become a choreographic means in the hands of the visitor. The actions of the attendant, unfamiliar in the museum context, solicit new actions on the part of the visitor. Dorothea von Hantelmann points out the fundamental shift that takes place in Sehgal's oeuvre:

> Sehgal's works do not employ material objects at all. Instead, they insist on the specific features of the moving (acting and speaking) body and the possibilities it offers to engender meaning. It is this principle that marks their essential innovative position [...] It is not only – and perhaps not even primarily – what these choreographies represent on, say, a metaphorical, allegorical, or expressive level that matters; what is decisive, rather, is the fact that this body-medium can take place in the context of the visual arts, with its focus on objects, that it can exist and circulate as a work of visual art.[65]

Unlike Conceptual art, then, Sehgal's work is directed not against art as a commodity, but against the form of the commodity itself. His is a critique of 'a social model of production in which matter is transformed into (capital or consumer) goods, a model the visual arts reproduce'.[66]

What Hantelmann writes about Sehgal also applies to Xavier Le Roy and his work *production* (2010) (pp. 122–3), developed in collaboration with Mårten Spångberg: 'The fact that the works are produced in different fashion ultimately also engenders a different beholder; a visitor who is not a receptive entity but instead an agent who exercises creative and responsible influence over the work.'[67] In Le Roy and Spångberg's view, choreography consists of 'artificially staged action(s) and/ or situation(s)',[68] and this is exactly what they realise, with the help of trained dancers, for the entire duration of an exhibition. The action, as such, is the work. They call the dancers with whom they work 'participants', for it is ultimately they who determine their actions, Le Roy and Spångberg having defined the parameters and 'choreographed the space of action'. Such a space is opened up to the visitors as well: the performers invite them to participate in a conversation about work – a choreography of intellectual exchange.

In collaboration with the performers, Le Roy and Spångberg have developed methods that help stimulate the visitor's interest in this communication. The exchange between them can range from a short dialogue to a guided tour of the entire exhibition. It can begin with a conversation that is individual in each instance, addressing the visitor's views and reflecting the performers' very personal opinions. But the exchange can also begin with the execution of a piece of choreography. The result is a dialogue – whether physical or verbal – about questions of choreography, as if sculpting a thought process. The participants in Le Roy and Spångberg's work become 'living sculptures' who exist only at the moment of conversation. Clark spoke of a 'communal body'; what they create is something similar: a body created by communication.[69] Comparable to the bodies that shift on top of one another and become 'entangled' in Forti's *Huddle* (1961) (pp. 44–5), Their work accumulates ideas. At its centre stands the human being, his physical presence, gestures, language – and not the dancer, exhibition visitor or artist. The work is about an exchange of ideas between individuals in a concrete, material and present situation – an important act of reflective assurance in a time of virtual worlds.

As Michael Kliën writes: 'Choreography is everywhere, always, in everything. I no longer see in pictures. I see movement and interrelation, exchange and communication between bodies and ideas.'[70] We are only beginning to discover the extent to which dance and the visual arts inspire one another and shape our view of the environment in which we live. An engagement with choreography seems to offer us the opportunity to free art – and hence the world – from the predominance of the object. Sehgal, Le Roy and Spångberg

what Forsythe describes as the form of choreography that defined the beginning of the twenty-first century. The focus of attention is on human action, and this may also explain the recent surge in popularity that choreography has enjoyed in a great variety of fields. It is connected to the call for self-determination in action and the conviction that art can guide us in this self-determination. The museum is no longer conceived merely as a place where objects are on view, but also as a site where 'values and ideologies are represented in works of art'.[72] The critical engagement with choreography provides the visual arts with strategies that allow it to show people that they are responsible for their own actions – that they can, may and must act according to their own will.

1 William Forsythe, 'Choreographic Objects', in: *Suspense*, exh. cat., Ursula Blickle Stiftung, Kraichtal, Markus Weisbeck for Ursula Blickle Stiftung (ed.), JRP/ Ringier Kunstverlag AG, Zürich, 2008, p. 6.
2 See, for example, *Tanz in der Moderne*, exh. cat., Haus der Kunst, Munich, 1996; *Tanz, Sehen.*, exh. cat., Museum für Gegenwartskusnt, Siegen, 2007, *Dance with Camera*, Institute of Contemporary Art, Philadelphia, 2009;
3 Allan Kaprow, 'Legacy of Jackson Pollock', in Allan Kaprow, *Essays on the Blurring of Art and Life*, Jeff Kelley (ed.), University of California Press, Berkeley and Los Angeles, 1996, p. 6.
4 Forsythe, 'Choreographic Objects'.
5 Both pieces were part of *Five Dance Constructions and Some Other Things*, which Forti staged in a 1961 concert series at the Yoko Ono Studio organised by La Monte Young.
6 Simone Forti, *Handbook in Motion*, p. 39.
7 Ibid., p. 56.
8 For more on the Judson Dance Theater, see Sally Banes, *Democracy's Body. Judson Dance Theater 1962–1964*, Ann Arbor, Michigan, 1980.
9 Sabine Huschka, *Merce Cunningham und der Moderne Tanz. Körperkonzepte, Choreographie und Tanzästhetik*, Königshausen & Neumann, Würzburg. 2000, p. 35.
10 See Yvonne Rainer's tally of the similarities between Minimal sculpture and dance: 'A quasi survey of some "minimalist" tendencies in the quantitatively minimal dance activity midst the plethora, or an analysis of Trio A', in *Minimal Art. A Critical Anthology*, Gregory Battcock (ed.), p. 263.
11 Deborah Hay, *Will They or Won't They?'*, 1963 (performed by Barbara Dilley, Alex Hay, Deborah Hay, Robert Rauschenberg); Robert Rauschenberg, *Map Room II*, 1965 (performed by Alex Hay, Deborah Hay, Steve Paxton, Robert Rauschenberg).
12 For a more detailed discussion of these works, see Carrie Lambert-Beatty, *Being Watched. Yvonne Rainer and the 1960s*, MIT Press, Cambridge, MA, p. 75ff, as well as Noel Carrol, 'Yvonne Rainer and the recuperation of the everyday life', in *Yvonne Rainer: Radical Juxtaposition 1961–2002*, exh. cat. Rosenwald-Wolf Gallery, The University of the Arts, Philadelphia, 2002, pp. 75–125.
13 Rainer, 'A quasi survey', in *Minimal Art. A Critical Anthology*, p. 269.
14 Allan Kaprow, 'Legacy of Jackson Pollock', in *Essays on the Blurring of Art and Life*, p. 7.
15 Cf. Allan Kaprow, 'The Education of the Un-Artist, Part I' (1971), in *Essays on the Blurring of Art and Life*, pp. 97–109.
16 For a continuation of this quote please see p. 16 of this volume.
17 *Trisha Brown: Dance and Art in Dialogue, 1961–2001*, exh. cat., Addison Gallery of American Art, Phillips Academy, Andover, Massachusetts, 2002, p. 307.
18 'On the conviction that Rainer's area of exploration in the 1960s was not exactly "things in themselves" but things-in-themselves to watch. Eyeing this difference, I have come to see Rainer as not only a shaper of dances and mover of bodies but a sculptor of spectatorship. Seen this way, Rainer's work becomes a – perhaps the – bridge between key episodes in postwar art. For this was a period in which issues of spectatorship came to the fore everywhere, in both literal and theoretical ways.' Lambert-Beatty, p. 9.
19 Letter to Michael Compton, 19 January 1971, about his exhibition at the Tate Gallery, London.
20 Morris in an interview with Simon Grant, *Tate Etc*, issue 14, Autumn 2008..
21 Many artists who would later be important choreographers in New York had been Halprin's students. Her work championed improvisation in dance and emphasised the physical self-discovery of her students.
22 Simone Forti, *Handbook in Motion* (1974), Northampton, 1998, p. 31.
23 For a more detailed discussion of these works, see *Robert Morris. The Mind/Body Problem*, exh. cat., Solomon R. Guggenheim Museum, New York, 1994, pp. 158–59, 168–69.
24 Robert Morris, *Notes on Dance*, The Tulane Drama Review, Vol. 10 no. 2, Winter 1965, pp. 179–186, p. 179.
25 Richard Serra, in 'Interview with Lynne Cooke and Michael Govan', in *Richard Serra: Torqued Ellipses*, Dia Center for the Arts, New York, 1997, p. 28. Quoted in Lambert-Beatty, p. 4.
26 Bruce Nauman, 'Interview mit Willoughby Sharp,' in *Bruce Nauman, Interviews 1967–1988*, Verlag der Kunst, Amsterdam, 1996, p. 49.
27 See Nauman, 'Interview mit Willoughby Sharp,' in *Bruce Nauman, Interviews 1967–1988*, p. 49.
28 See Nauman, 'Interview mit Lorraine Sciarra,' in *Bruce Nauman, Interviews 1967–1988*, pp. 79–80.
29 See Nauman, 'Interview mit Willoughby Sharp,' in *Bruce Nauman, Interviews 1967–1988*, p. 15.
30 'Because an interesting thing was happening. A lot of people had taken a lot of trouble educating the public to participate – if I put this stuff out here, you were supposed to participate. And certain kinds of clues were taken that certain sculptures were participatory.' Ibid., p. 82.
31 Nauman, 'Interview with Lorraine Sciarra', p. 82.
32 With its discovery of mirror neurons, neuroscience has demonstrated that the same neurons in the brain are activated whether we perform an activity ourselves or merely observe it without performing it.
33 Graham himself mentioned Forti as one of the most important influences on his work of the late 1960s. See *Tanzen, Sehen*, exh. cat., Museum für Gegenwartskunst Siegen, Frankfurt am Main, 2007, p. 123.
34 For a more detailed discussion, see ibid. p. 122ff.
35 Morris in an interview with Simon Grant, *Tate etc.*, Issue 14, Autumn 2008.
36 See Robert Morris, 'Notes on Sculpture', in *Minimal Art. A Critical Anthology*, Gregory Battcock (ed.), pp. 222–235.
37 Michael Fried, 'Art and Objecthood', in *Minimal Art. A Critical Anthology*, pp. 116–147.
38 Letter to Michael Compton, Tate Archive, March 1971.
39 Lygia Clark, in *Lygia Clark*, exh. cat., Fundació Antoni Tàpies, Barcelona, 1997, p. 227.
40 Ibid., p. 242.
41 Guy Brett, in ibid., p. 22.
42 Forsythe, 'Choreographic Objects', p. 7.
43 Rudolf Laban, *The Language of Movement, A Guidebook to Choreutics*, Plays, Inc., Boston 1978, 3ff., quoted in Sabine Huschka, Merce Cunningham und der Moderne Tanz. Körperkonzepte, Choreographie und Tanzästhetik, Verlag Königshausen&Neumann, Würzburg, 2000, p. 92.
44 Letter to Michael Compton, 19 January 1971, about his exhibition at the Tate, Gallery, London.
45 Maurice Merleau-Ponty, *Phänomenologie der Wahrnehmung*, de Gruyter Studienbuch, Berlin, p. 103.
46 Ibid., p. 174 .
47 Ibid., p. 176.
48 'I read a book called *Gestalt Therapy* that was important because it has to do with awareness of your body and a way of thinking about it.' Bruce Nauman, 'Interview with Lorraine Sciarra', p. 79. Perls, too, was a member of Halprin's circle.
49 Dorothea von Hantelmann, *How to do things with art. Zur Bedeutsamkeit der Performativität von Kunst*, Diaphanes, Zurich, 2007, p. 170.
50 Alva Noe, *Action in Perception*, MIT Press, Cambridge, MA, 2004, p. 1.
51 Ibid., p. 73.
52 Andrew Hewitt, *Social Choreography. Ideology as Performance in Dance and Everyday Movement*, Duke University Press, Durham and London, 2005, p. 14.
53 Mike Kelley in John Welchman (ed.), *Mike Kelley, Minor Histories. Statements, Conversations, Proposals*, MIT Press, Cambridge, MA, 2004, p. 319. Education is only one among many factors that shape our development. 'My education must have been a form of mental abuse, of brainwashing. How else could I have engaged for so long in activities that pointed so overtly toward my own repressed abuse without becoming consciousness of it?' (*Minor Histories*, p. 320) For a more detailed discussion of 'Educational complex, see *Educational Complex Onwards. 1995–2008*, exh. cat., Wiels, Brussels, Zurich, 2009.
54 Pablo Bronstein, in *Interview between Pablo Bronstein and Rebecca May Marston*, 4 November 2007, New York. See http://07.performa-arts.org/
55 Ibid.
56 Pablo Bronstein in: *Displayer*, p. 44.
57 Pablo Bronstein in *Interview between Pablo Bronstein and Rebecca May Marston*, ibid.
58 See Julienne Lorz's text on João Penalva's *Widow Simone* (1996), pp. 82–5 in this volume.
59 Helen Luckett examines the various narrative threads in Isaac Julien's work, pp. 114–17 in this volume.
60 See André Lepecki's more detailed discussion of La Ribot, pp. 60–3 in this volume.
61 For a more detailed discussion of this work see Hantelmann, *How to do things with art*, p.153.
62 Ibid., p. 146.
63 Bruce Nauman, Dance Piece, in: *Bruce Nauman:*, exh. cat., Museum für Neue Kunst MNK, ZKM Karlsruhe, Hatje Cantz, Ostfildern-Ruit, 1999, p. 61.
64 Hantelmann, *How to do things with art*, p. 151.
65 Ibid., p. 152.
66 Tino Sehgal, quoted in Hantelmann, *How to do things with art*, p. 171.
67 Ibid., p. 192.
68 See *Corpus*, http://www.corpusweb.net/answers-4349.html
69 For a more detailed discussion of Lydia Clark's 'communal body,' see: pp. 60–3 in this volume.
70 Michael Kliën, *Book of recommendations*, published by Daghdha Dance Company, 2008 p. 24.
71 Hantelmann, *How to do things with art*, p. 175.
72 Tino Sehgal, quoted in ibid., p. 190.

MOVING CENTRES

Peggy Phelan

In recent years, Euro-American curators and commentators have begun to consider the dense lines of connection and tension between the visual arts and dance.[1] As is often the case, this interest comes several decades after artists had tangled them, unfurled them, woven them into knotted textured nets thick enough to fling, to climb, to fly away on.[2] And it also comes after centuries of profound intermingling of art forms in the performance traditions of Africa, Asia and among indigenous people the world over. But the fact that critical attention has been belated and geo-politically uneven does not make it unnecessary or less vital. Indeed, the rather slow pace of dominant institutions lumbering toward consideration of dance and performance illuminates something quite radical in the core of movement-based thinking. As a philosophical and epistemological injunction 'movement' punctures the ideological assumption that the centre is permanent, stable, secure. Thus the task before us is to shift from a consideration of the aesthetic dimensions of movement to a consideration of movement as ethical principle and practice.

By way of prelude then, let us mark out the critical two-step we dance here. In the manner of Ana Mendieta's *Silueta* series, we bow to the depressing impression left by ignoring moving bodies in the central narrative forms of art history; and then, having marked the outline of these missing bodies with hers, we turn to acknowledge that these traces of absences are not especially privileged signifiers in the history of art but rather quotidian shadows left by an absence so repetitive as to be (almost) routine. The unexamined shadows of women and people of non-white cultures are abundant ghosts in the history of Western art: rather than list and measure all these missing bodies (of work and lack of work) here we may simply note that one of the centre's most consistent habits is making margins. Bodies of work that take movement as their subject and form are perhaps especially neglected since they can tell us so much about centring, and the function of centres, as ethical practice.

Traditional art history places visual objects in a linear narrative that allows for substitutions and new favourites while remaining faithful to a teleological structure in which apprentice becomes genius. This narrative arc can be repeated and preserved regardless of school, historical period, genre or media. Small surprise then that some aspects of movement-based arts – ephemerality, improvisation and somatic grace, for example – cannot be easily inserted into the narrative structure of art history.[3] Moreover, these same qualities, and perhaps especially ephemerality, complicate the security of the visual object as such. Nonetheless, such work belongs in the critical tradition of art history because dance and movement performance are irreducibly visual arts. And artists themselves have continually moved between the genres of painting, sculpture and dance, renewing and expanding the boundaries of each form in the process.

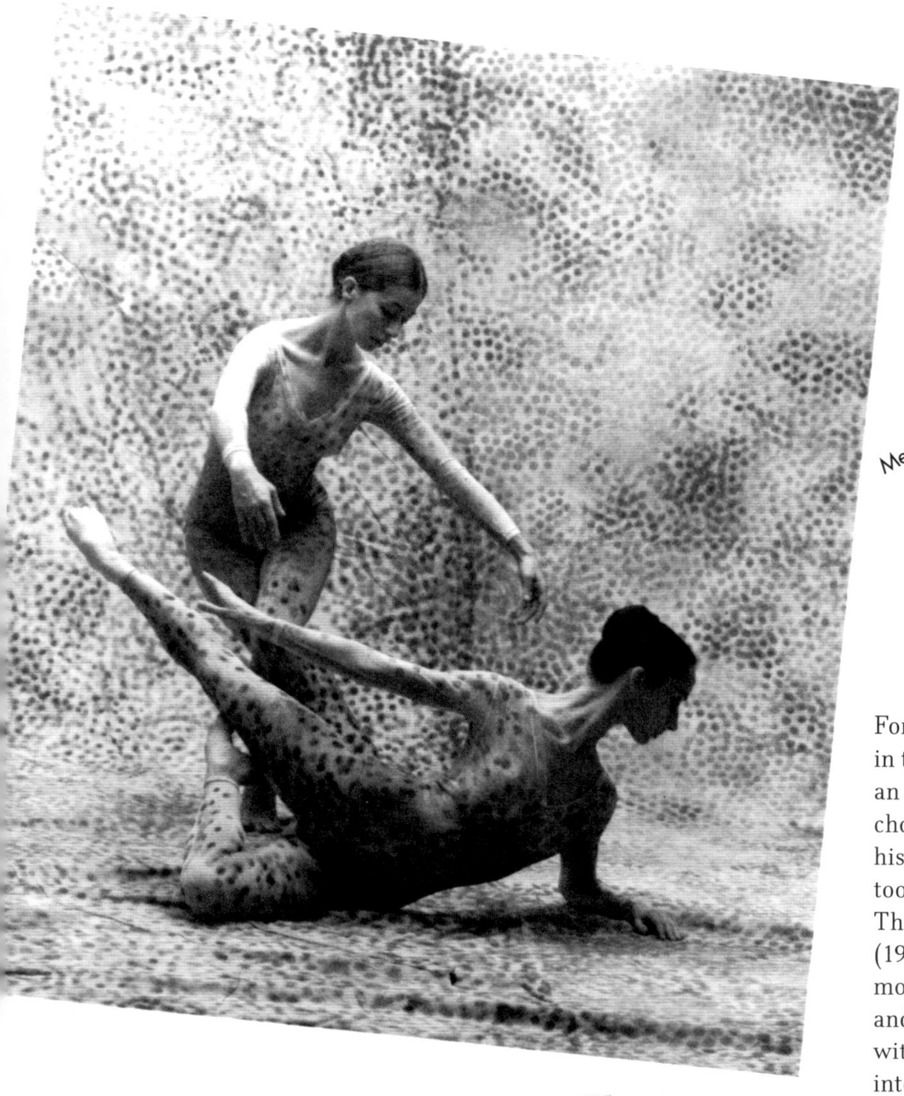

Merce Cunningham, Still from *Summerspace*, 1958

For example, while we now easily locate Rauschenberg's 'combines' in the space between sculpture and painting, 'combine' also connotes an action imperative with roots in Rauschenberg's collaborations with choreographers Merce Cunningham and Trisha Brown. Although his task was mainly defined as creating sets or decor, Rauschenberg took dance principles and applied them to painting and sculpture. Thus the lyrical loop of his slide show for Brown's *Glacial Decoy* (1979) performs a dance of images that both support and ignore the movement of Brown's dancers. Similarly, his pointillist back cloth and matching costumes for Cunningham's *Summerspace* (1958) wittily and seriously meditates on the choreographer's longstanding interest in points in space (*en pointe, d'accord*) and the leap that upends gravity – the *grand jeté* that opens onto flight. (Unlike many of Cunningham's later dances, the piece is largely vertical, with numerous jumps and turns. Indeed, it is probably his most balletic work.) To call these 'collaborations' might risk missing the points of contact and the points of departure already at work among these fecund artists. Brown's grasp of the essential through-line in the grammar of form and content across the arts prompts her own flowing account of her artistic epiphany:

> I had left the West Coast for the East, left the middle class for a classless society of artists, found myself caught on the fulcrum of social change for women. In the classes that I took with Robert Dunn when I got to New York, we were applying John Cage's concepts of chance to dance composition, and it suddenly connected for me. I had a sense of myself as separate from all the other people in the world, and that gave me a concept of how one might make art. And I use the word purposely, as applied to all disciplines. My training was in dance and choreography, but my connection was to form and content, as for any artist. And once I understood that, it was just a matter of time before I could flesh it out.[4]

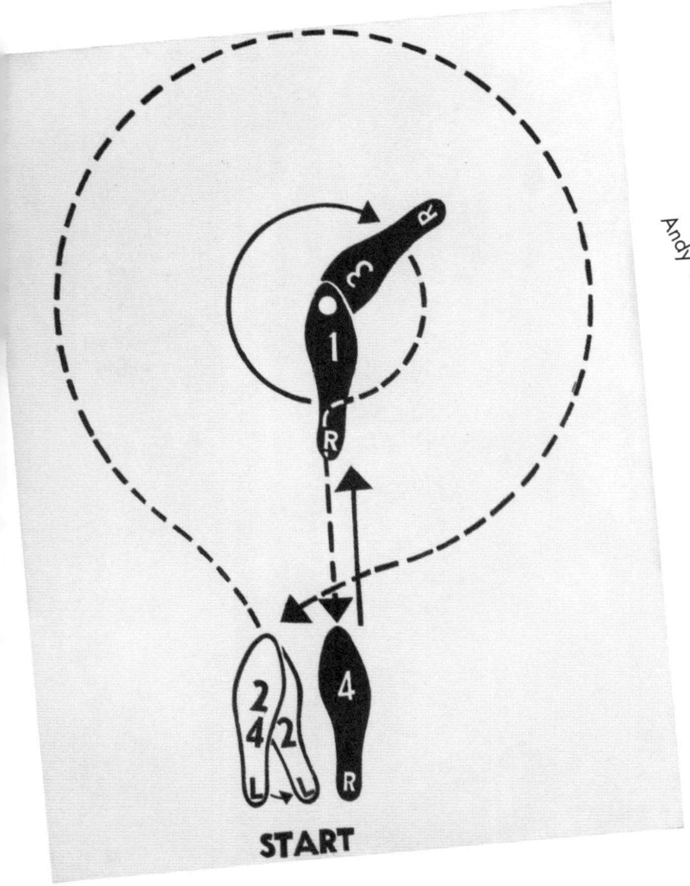

Andy Warhol, *Dance Diagram*, 1962

Fleshing out the relationship between dance and visual arts, however, often requires the intervention of film and photography.[5] For example, when Jackson Pollock was creating his abstract paintings, the sheer physicality of his labours, indeed, the art of his dancing, were documented by Hans Namuth in both still photographs and a short film. While his centrality to the narrative of Euro-American art history in the post-war period cannot be gainsayed, his achievement exposes a crucial relationship between art-making and art object. But it was Namuth's images, rather than Pollock's canvases that spurred Harold Rosenberg to conceptualise 'Action Paintings', a conceptual critical category that drew lines between painting and the larger arena of movement-based art.[6] Art historians such as Paul Schimmel and Amelia Jones have astutely analysed the importance of Pollock for the development of performance and live art in the post-war period.[7] The documentation of Pollock painting, rather more than the paintings themselves, also advanced a clearer understanding of the visual artist as dancer.

Rhythm and Sound

The intricate and repeated rebalancing of Pollock's foot, the lyrical throw of the paint across the horizontal canvas, and the rhythmic torso twists are graceful dances caught by Namuth's camera (p. 9).[8] Once seen, the images of process and making frame the experience of looking at Pollock's paintings. Namuth's photographic documents, in other words, explain the compositional method that produced the often densely enigmatic surface of Pollock's paintings, even while they render the canvases belated remnants of the primary art, the art of action captured in photographs and on film. However, Pollock's actions were neither as silent as Namuth's photographs nor as continuous as the film suggests. The stop and start, choppy back and forth conveyed by the web of lines on Pollock's drip paintings tends to be smoothed over by the work of Namuth's editing and by the soundtrack added after the fact.[9]

The physical difficulty of Pollock's art was taken up with especial acuity by the Japanese Gutai artists. Kazuo Shiraga's *Challenging Mud* (1955) (p. 132), for example, returns us to the scene of the horizontal arena but removes both the canvas and the brush from the action while retaining the camera. Shiraga's gripping performance of wrestling through wet mud is now registered art historically as a photograph. We miss the grunt, the sweat, the mess. We miss as well the sound of the skin sliding and resisting its own materiality. This missing is precisely the ephemeral force of the live performance; recognising this absence, museological practice has been focused on re-enacting and re-doing canonical performances in an effort to release and repeat something of the force of the original live event.[10]

The remarkably still and unswerving single camera loaded with black and white film that recorded Marina Abramović and Ulay's collaborative relational work from the 1970s might be seen as a neutral corrective to some of Namuth's attempts to 'art up' Pollock's gestures. The static frame of the camera emphasises the velocity and force of the artists' bodily encounter, particularly when it edges them out of the tight frame. The 'thud' of their bodies' encounter also reminds us of the dialogical relationship between mover and observer, between actor and witness. In their many explorations of the couple, Ulay and Abramović provide a model for the self/other relationship that rehearses the force and tension of the encounter with their art for

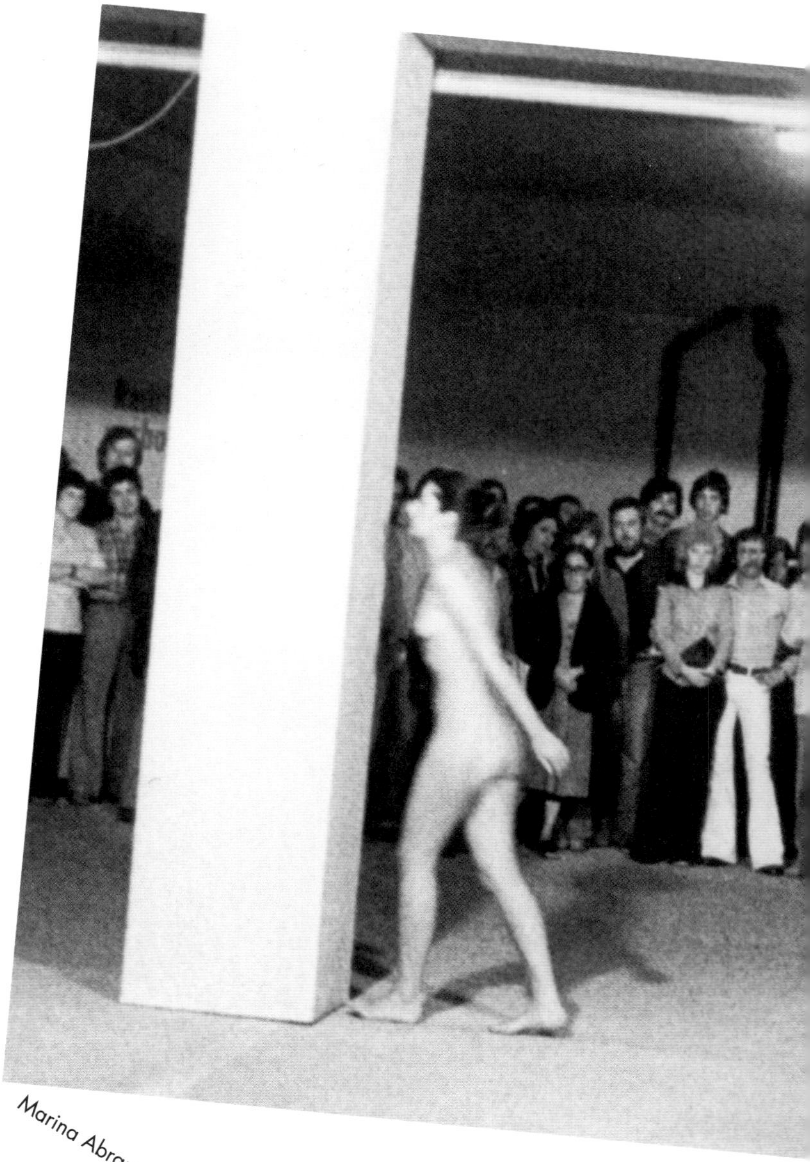

Marina Abramović & Ulay, Still from Expansion in Space, 1977

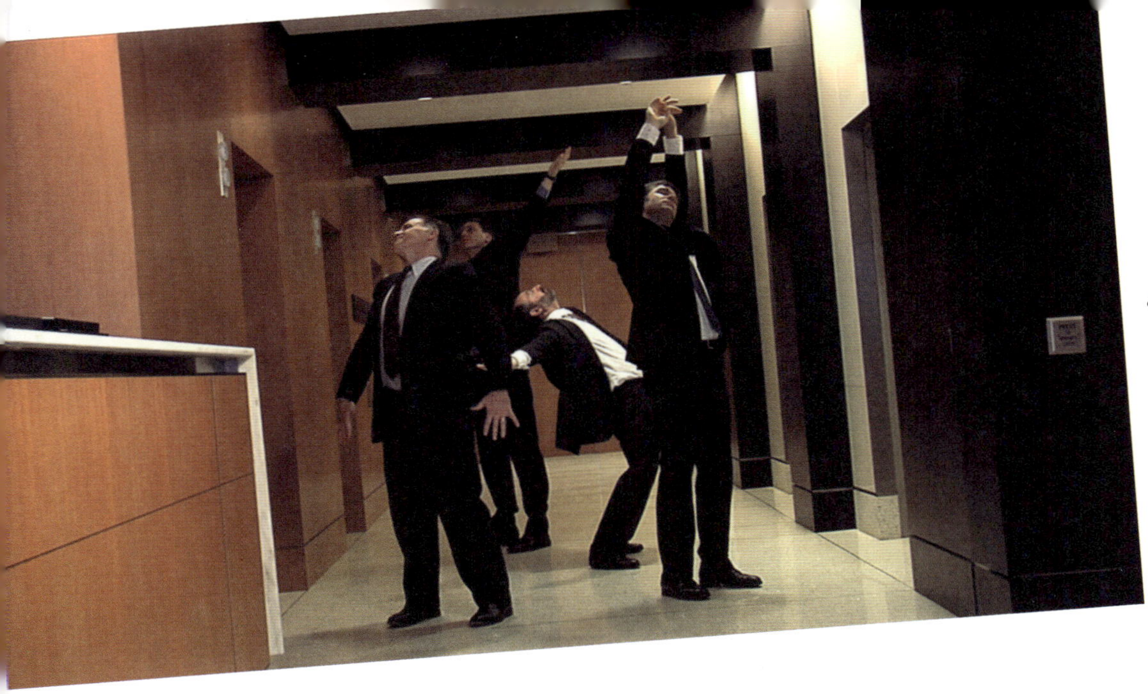

Ann Carlson and Mary Ellen Strom, *Sloss, Kerr, Rosenberg & Moore*, 2007

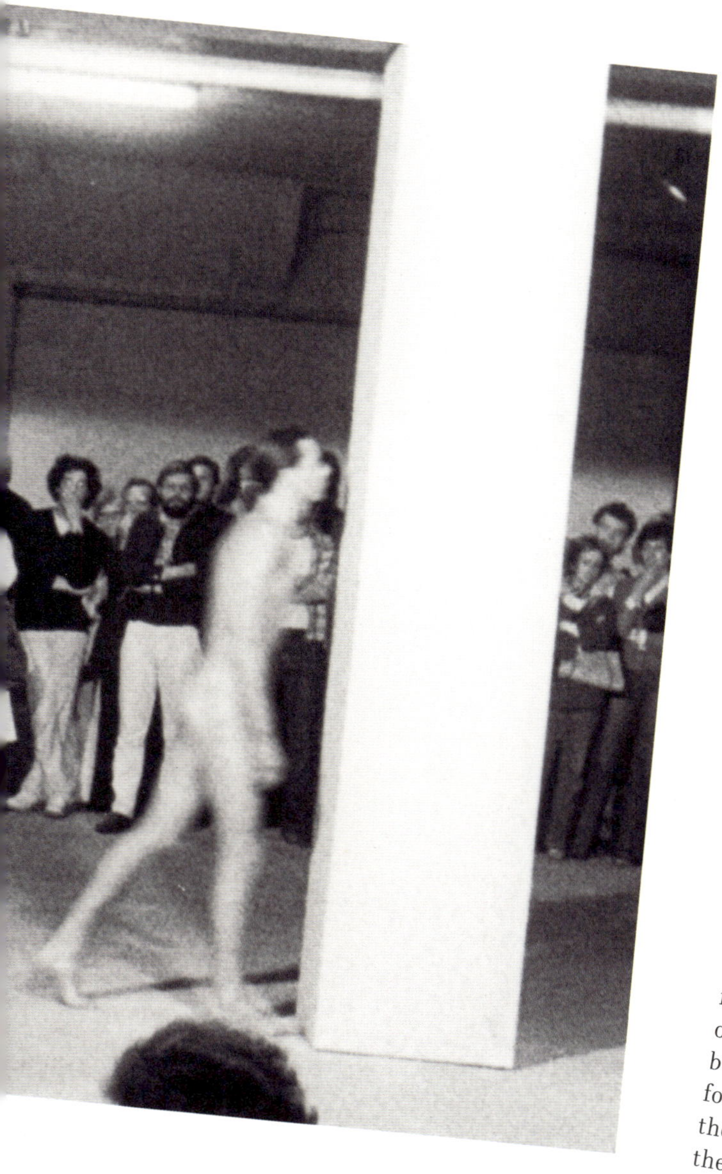

the spectator. To grasp their performance of loving relation, we thud against the limit of our own sense of bodily and amorous limit.

Working the other way around, Ann Carlson's and Mary Ellen Strom's 2007 single-channel video, *Sloss, Kerr, Rosenberg, and Moore*, reminds us that the music of memory is crucial to our sense of movement. The talking, gesticulating lawyers who perform Carlson's choreography underscore how much of our lives are spent matching gesture to word – a drama of balancing *le mot juste* with justice itself. The video documents and updates a dance with the same performers that Carlson choreographed in 1986. Thus the lawyers in their concentrated suits, caught moving in and against the frame of the camera, rehearse and release the baggier concentration of the viewer. Both performer and viewer are united in the effort to match the unfurling choreography to some other gesture – seen, rehearsed, forgotten. What we remember, then, is not *what* we have forgotten but *that* we have forgotten. We remember that we don't. The video, *Sloss, Kerr, Rosenberg, and Moore*, does not restore our memories of the 'original' performance choreographed by Carlson; rather, the video sutures our forgetting to the images moving on the surface of the screen. This kinetic melody, the music of memory, the back and forth rhythm of embodied temporality, is accentuated by the sound score, a series of utterances that are not legal arguments at all, but striking phrases, poses really, that match rhetorical gestures with physical ones. 'I didn't say no I know I know . . . I didn't say no . . . I didn't know.' *Sloss, Kerr, Rosenberg, and Moore* captures the poignant comedy of our attempts to make the match stick. Indeed, the video is usually projected as a loop, a continual circling around the bodies' melodic remembering of its forgetting.

Following Pollock's decision to place the canvas on the floor and his injunction to be 'in the painting', Janine Antoni covered the floor of the Anthony d'Offay Gallery, London with a canvas and filled a bucket of black hair dye. Using her hair as a brush, Antoni, on all fours, painted her way across the floor of the entire gallery, displacing the spectators who had come to see *Loving Care* in 1993. Following the feminist critique of influential predecessors, especially perhaps the brilliant example of Carolee Schneemann, Antoni's process piece reminds us of the gendered nature of art history – *Loving Care* renders Antoni at once the artist and the made thing. Her physical position on all fours, the posture of the maid, also puns on the movement between the maid and hair colourist on one knee, and artist and well-heeled client on the other.

Environments and Silver Clouds

The anti-war movement, the civil-rights movement, the feminist and gay-rights movements all exerted pressure on static and still art. Sculpture began to investigate the bodily acts of throwing and carving, as in Richard Serra's *Hand Catching Lead* (1968) (p. 145) or Eleanor Antin's *Carving: A Traditional Sculpture* (1972), and to exploit, rather than hide, its own process of erosion, decay and disappearance. From Kaprow's tyre-strewn *Yard* (1961) to Robert Smithson's salt-drenched *Spiral Jetty* (1970), art of the 1960s and 1970s became increasingly attuned to the dynamic arc of 'the life of art', a life everywhere informed by changing rhythms of sun, tide, climate, gravity. Materials ranging from Walter De Maria's lighting rods to Eva Hesse's latex seemed alive with temporality, aquiver with finitude. Andy Warhol created *Silver Clouds* (1966), helium sculptures, and exhibited them floating at Leo Castelli's gallery in New York. Cunningham saw them and asked Warhol if he could use them as the environment for his 1968 *Rainforest*. The pillows and the dancers moved independently but on the same stage, appearing to each other as a kind of weather – the dancers were a blur reflected in the silver foil of the clouds, and the clouds responded to the dancers' physical motion by changing the direction of their floating.

Inspired by Pollock's horizontal canvases, Warhol also created *Dance Diagrams* (1962) (p. 23), silk-screened blown-up images from How-to-Dance books, and displayed them on the floor. The images themselves, outlines of men's shoes, condense the movement between imagining making a move and implanting a foot on the canvas. That pause marks the space of imagined movement and calls for a change in spectatorial orientation: to see the *Dance Diagrams* one looks down towards one's feet and encounters Warhol's outline of a shoe making a step just in advance of one's own. This doubling of spectator glance and image seen puns on the pair – the two steps that feet seem to guarantee. As with so much of Warhol's art, the pun disguises a more rigorous send-up or put-down. High art in the 1960s, Warhol contends, tends to look down on how-to practical illustration in favour of rigorous Abstract Expressionism. The foot's appeal as visual object tends to be confined to foot fetishists or shoe salesmen, and selling shoes and drawing naked feet were Warhol's primary calling cards in the early part of his career. Nietzsche's remark in *The Gay Science* is apposite here: 'At times we need a rest from ourselves by looking upon, by looking *down* upon, ourselves and, from an artistic distance, laughing *over* ourselves or weeping *over* ourselves. We must discover the *hero* no less than the *fool* in our passion for knowledge.'[11] For Warhol, high art's movement from Abstract Expression to Pop art has something of this Nietzschean two step about it. Two shoes then: one for the fool, one for the sage, both dancing across the image seen.

Three Separate, Each Central

The remarkable story of the first Happening in 1952 at Black Mountain College, in which John Cage, Merce Cunningham, David Tudor, Robert Rauschenberg and an unnamed dog all performed at once, has mythic status in the history of art. For most critics, Black Mountain's importance stems from its insistence that 'separate but equal' art forms could occur simultaneously, with none taking up the dominant focus and none playing a supporting part. Cunningham put it this way:

> What we have done in our work is to bring together three separate elements in time and space: the music, the dance, and the décor, allowing each one to remain independent. The three arts don't come from a single idea which the dance demonstrates, the music supports and the décor illustrates, but rather that they are three separate elements each central to itself.[12]

Cunningham's matter-of-fact celebration of centrality within multiplicity may be related to a larger attempt to reject hierarchical structures of dominance and submission that underwrite gender, sexuality and power more generally. The epistemological achievement of Cunningham's idea, however, comes from a radical trust in movement as such. More than a matter of aesthetics, movement-based thinking suggests that a static architectural zone called the centre is a fiction. One may be centre-stage but only in passing. Chance procedures, which both Cage and Cunningham employed, further eroded the notion of a fixed form or shape. While these decentering aspects of thinking can be linked to Buddhist beliefs about impermanence and flow, one need not be spiritually minded to notice that there is something counterintuitive, and perhaps also counterproductive, between rigorous rehearsal and chance procedures. The rehearsal serves the idea of getting it right, while chance procedure invites the mistake. Rauschenberg, Warhol, Bruce Nauman and Tacita Dean were all eager to collaborate with Cunningham; for each of these artists, the potential error in transmission was as vital as the transmission itself – since that potential allowed liveness itself to emerge. This is the very liveness that moves artists to new (self) conceptions. Take, for example, the printer's error that turned Rauschenberg into a choreographer in 1963:

> At the Pop Art Festival in Washington, D.C., Rauschenberg mistakenly was listed in the program as 'choreographer' rather than as stage manager of the Judson group. When he read the program, he decided to take on the challenge. Discovering that the performances were to take place in a roller-skating rink called America on Wheels, he designed costumes, learned to roller-skate, and prepared a dance routine for himself and two dancers.[13]

What this account fails to mention, however, is that the 'costumes' are really white wings, parachutes refashioned to mimic birds and to draw and dance a line. The drawn line becomes three dimensional

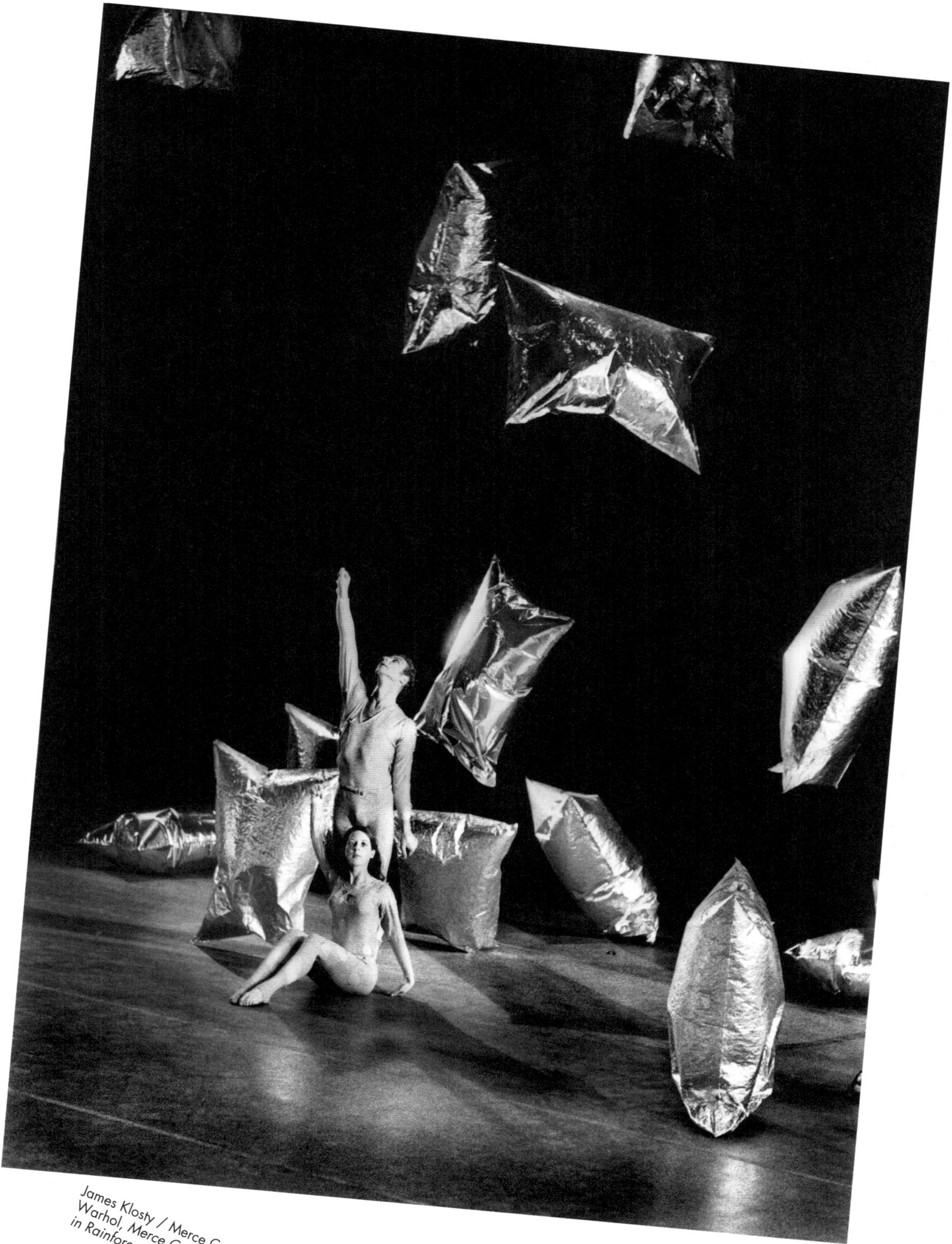

James Klosty / Merce Cunningham / Andy Warhol, Merce Cunningham and Meg Harper in Rainforest, 1969

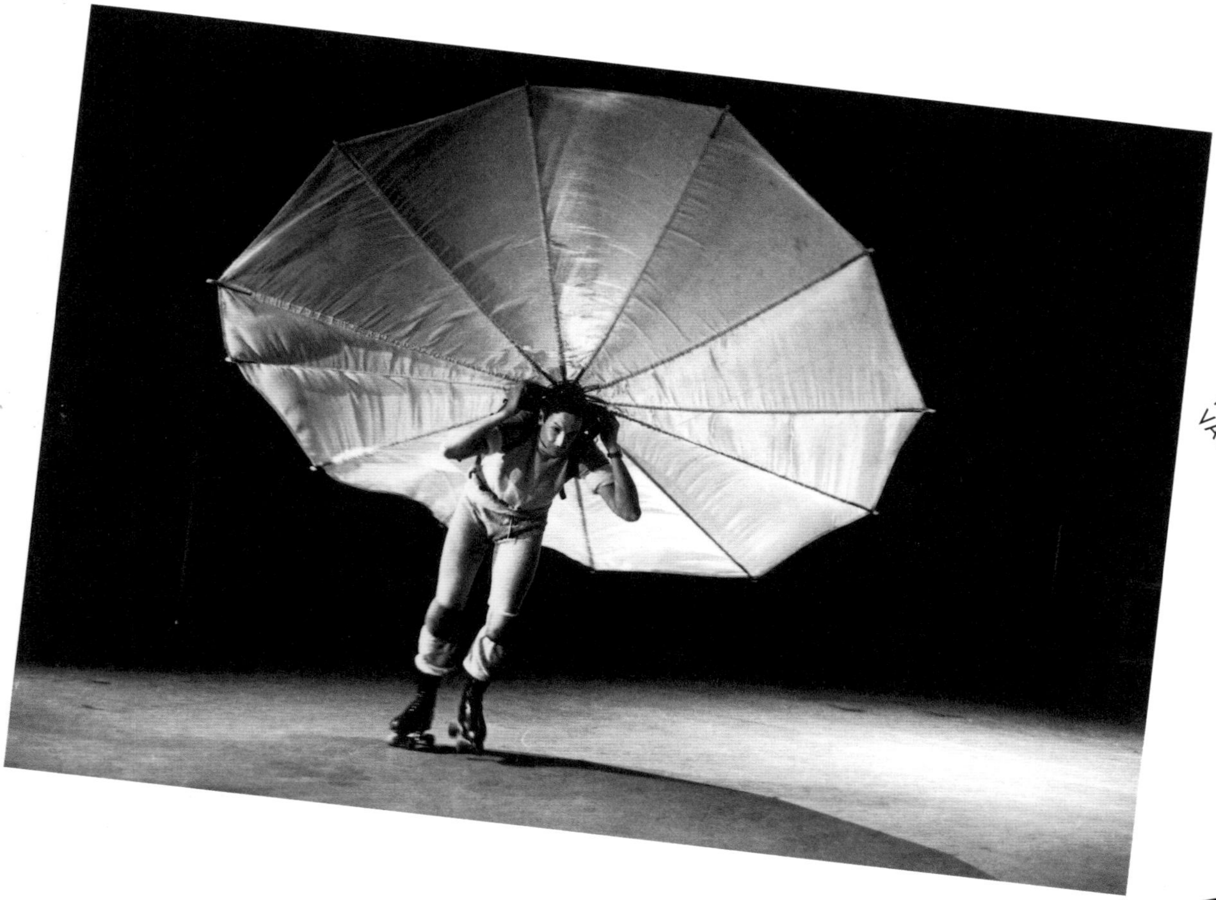

Robert Rauschenberg, Still from Pelican, 1965
Photo by Peter Moore © Estate of Peter Moore/
VAGA, NYC

Samuel Beckett, Still from *Quad I and II*, 1982

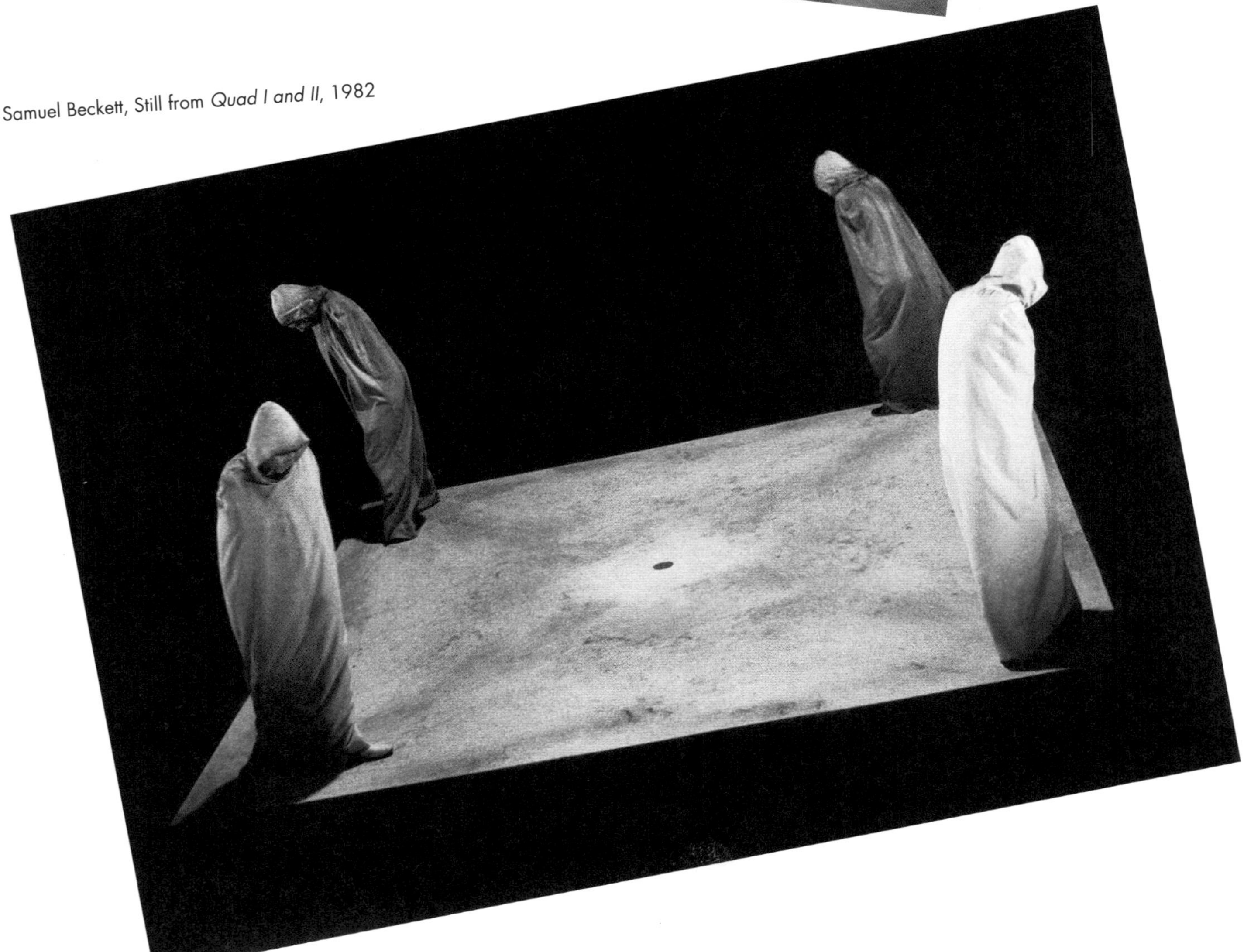

in live performance and the painter's hand animates a living canvas. The apparent ease and fearlessness of moving from 'stage manager' to 'choreographer' is written into the performance as the flight itself, the leap from one task to another – from the leap of thinking of oneself as one, to the task of imagining oneself as many. The hero laces one roller skate and the fool, the other.

This radical trust in movement across tasks may also shed light on why so many remarkable performers with the Judson Dance Theater were ex-Cunningham dancers. For what Cunningham was willing to do, perhaps for reasons that far exceed the aesthetic as such, was to create extraordinarily complicated, difficult choreography and then allow it to take its place, or not, within the larger current of a collaborative work. Sometimes long parts of his dance were performed in the dark.

In this sense, Cunningham's method is the exact opposite of Samuel Beckett's rigid graphs and precise strictures on lighting and counting. Take, for example, the wordless plays he made in the 1980s for German television, *Quad I* and *Quad II*.[14] In the first version, four actors wearing differently coloured hooded costumes pace across a grid. Once inside the square, each dancer takes six steps lengthwise and six steps diagonally across the space. The middle of the square, which functions as a kind of horizontal bull's eye in a target, must be bypassed on the left-hand side only. Beckett's score for the piece specifies that 'some ballet training' on the part of the actors would be helpful.[15] Beckett's *Quad* reminds us of the importance of the grid for painting. Piet Mondrian, Paul Klee, Ellsworth Kelly and Agnes Martin frequently employed the grid as a way of mapping the viewer's eye across the colour field, and as with Rauschenberg's *Pelican* (the performance mentioned above), Beckett dramatises the animation at the core of many great paintings.[16] Beckett's *Quad I* is filmed in colour with percussion. In *Quad II* the four dancers wear all white and the sound score is composed only of the shuffling of the dancers' feet against the tick-tock swing of a metronome. Both pieces have each dancer moving to the left upon arrival in the centre: collisions are avoided because each dancer yields to the anticipated arrival of the next. In other words, *Quad* maps the force of the forever-in-motion centre, a void quivering with the approaching presence of the other, of the next. The focus on the centre allows us to see that it is simultaneously too empty and too crowded; the centre is a whirring blur rather than a static point.

Pedestrian Poses

Beckett crafted his art around a profound inquiry into movement and paralysis whose ethical dimensions are often overlooked. Written in the long shadow of the Second World War, Beckett's masterpiece, *En Attendant Godot* (Waiting for Godot, 1949), ends by suspending the rhythm of call and response that creates the melodic dialogue of the play's two tramps. Didi says to Gogo, 'Let's go', while the stage direction reads: 'They do not move.' The desire to move, to traverse the grid of expectation and disappointment, hope and despair, partners with the desire to avoid change, to remain still, to give up, and to give in. In *Endgame* (1957), the verbal and physical dialogue between Clov and Hamm finds its rhythmic balance in Hamm's command to have his wheelchair placed right in the centre, a location that the play itself continually displaces. If the oscillation between movement and stillness is the central metaphor of Beckett's most famous plays, the oscillation he comes to in the wordless dances of *Quad I* and *II* some thirty years later is one between the deepening furrows around the central void and the accumulating weight of the ever-pressing crowd. *Quad* sets in motion an instantiation of a world in which there are no words left and thus faces and images have become indistinguishable; there is only the shuffling toward and away, the yielding to and the running from, the blank other. We can call this blank death, or sleep, or the beloved, or the stranger. (There are no words.) The form and structure of the encounter produces the same kinetic rapid shuffle. And it is this shuffle, the fact of its motion and repetition, that constitutes the drama of the human – to be alive is to move, to be continually decentred, never quite arriving, never quite leaving, but taut within the pull of each desire.

The task-like focus on the grid in *Quad* resonates with Judson's interest in everyday walking,[17] a story well told by Sally Banes, while the relentless repetition of the choreography brings to mind Pina Bausch's attention to obsessive repetitions in the choreography she created in the 1980s. *Quad* is rarely mentioned in dance history because Beckett's work is assigned to the history of theatre rather than to dance. But I think there is much to be gained by considering Beckett a choreographer. He created characters who were confined to full-body urns, garbage cans, wheelchairs, buried in mounds of sand. He tied Pozzo and Lucky to each other in *Waiting for Godot* and had them run in and out of the light, a notion that both Cunningham and Twyla Tharp expanded for dance. In all of Beckett's plays the difficulty of moving – physically, amorously, philosophically – forms the dramatic kernel of the plot. And it becomes immediately clear that stillness is no real answer. Clov spends the opening ten minutes of *Endgame* walking stiff-legged across the stage, going up and down a ladder and hauling it back and forth, without words. *Not I* (1972), Beckett's monologue written for Billie Whitelaw, choreographs her mouth opening and closing in the dark theatre.

For theatre scholars, thinking of *Not I* as an innovation in choreography risks downplaying its verbal virtuosity. The text spoken in *Not I* is a vivid dramatisation of the difficulty of the dual tasks of utterance and comprehension; in that sense *Not I* can be profitably read in relation to the difficulty of assessing bodily utterance more broadly, a project near and dear to dance. Beckett's concentration on the movement of the mouth opens onto a consideration of its substitutive function, its capacity to stand in for the vagina, the anus and the ear. The mouth is just one source of saying, the one perhaps privileged most within theatre history, but other body parts have their own eloquence.

Among these, the heavy fall of the foot has been a haunting Beckettian rhythm for Bruce Nauman. In his *Slow Angle Walk (Beckett Walk)* (1968), Nauman videotaped himself walking slowly around a track marked out on the studio floor. As he paces, arms behind him, he lifts his leading leg high in the air before letting it fall with a thud; then the second leg repeats the lift and fall of the first. This goes on for sixty minutes. Nauman's awkward walk, one that is difficult both to perform and to observe, is further complicated by his decision to lay the camera on its side, so that he appears to be walking up the wall. Reflecting on the piece in 1972, Nauman recalled:

> My problem was to make tapes that go on and on, with no beginning or end. I wanted the tension of waiting for something to happen, and then you should just get drawn into the rhythm of the thing [...] *Slow Angle Walk* has to do with a description by Beckett of traveling to someone's house. The body movements are like exercises – bending, rotating, and raising one leg, going on and on. It's a tedious, complicated process to gain even one yard.[18]

Nauman's retrospective account neatly condenses the physical performance of walking with a metaphysical meditation on movement more broadly. In these early video pieces there is at once coolness, a calm straightforward documentation of performance in which something as simple as rotating a camera on its side transforms the solidity of the figure/ground relation so central to visual coherence and ordered gravity.[19] Nauman's repeated return to issues of orientation in his video work makes literal the ongoing drama of shifting and unstable ground central to the performance of looking, a task that we invariably begin too late and never fully finish. Nauman's apprenticeship as a reader of Beckett, a job he gave himself in 1966, has sustained his own experiments in movement and confinement for some forty years. His *Performance Corridor* pieces (begun 1969), which involve a disorientation in space and image relation, owe much to Beckett. The installations ask the viewer to walk into a tight corridor and once inside one sees one's image on a monitor at the end of the space. When one walks towards it, the image shrinks. This sense of approaching without arriving is at once Beckettian and psychoanalytical. It reminds us that moving toward is also, deeply, a disorienting moving away. In *Green Light Corridor* (1970) (p. 68), the installation is illuminated by a Jell-o-green neon light, suggesting a kind of expansiveness that is then curtailed and radically foreshortened by the narrowness of the corridor itself. Nauman's sculpture exposes the gap between the look of the thing and the feel of the thing; he shows us the chasm between the swift immateriality of light and the slow go of making it in the blink of his neon flash.

Coda

In a wonderful interview about *Glacial Decoy*, Trisha Brown remarks that she no longer cares if her work is called dance or movement or theatre. She prefers to think of it as trying 'to fall off the air'. It remains to be seen if art history itself will risk such a leap; my suspicion is that it would rather archive Yves Klein's *Leap into the Void* and deconstruct the hidden figure/ground relation in Pollock's abstract webs. And maybe that's fair enough. Sometimes the witness can be motivated to catch the body when it falls. And maybe that move is just as beautiful, just as valuable, as our plummeting embrace of air.

1 See, for example, *Trisha Brown, Art and Dance in Dialogue*, Hendel Teicher (ed.), MIT Press, Cambridge MA, 2002; Carrie Lambert Beatty: *Being Watched: Yvonne Rainer and the Art of the Sixties*, MIT Press, Cambridge MA, 2009. Anna Chave, 'Minimalism and Biography', in *Art Bulletin*: 82, 1 (March 2000), pp. 149–163, which is particularly good on Simone Forti and Robert Morris. See also *Yvonne Rainer: Radical Juxtapositions 1961–2002*, Sid Sachs (ed.), University of the Arts, Philadelphia, PA, 2002. Also notable is Trisha Brown's major role in many recent surveys of Robert Rauschenberg, and the numerous lines of collaboration undertaken by Andy Warhol and well documented within the vast Warhol literature. See also the exhibition *Dance with Camera*, curator Jenelle Porter, Institute for Contemporary Art, University of Pennsylvania, September 2009, and Contemporary Arts Museum, Houston, Texas, August 2010.

2 On flying see Elizabeth Streb, *How to Become an Extreme Action Hero*, Feminist Press, New York, 2010. On the intermingling of line and dance see my essay, 'The Interior of Us', in *Helena Almeida*, Isabel Carlos (ed.), Museum of Contemporary Art, Lisbon, 2003.

3 See Peggy Phelan, 'Shards of a history of performance art: Pollock and Namuth Through a glass, darkly', in *A Companion to Narrative Theory*, James Phelan and Peter J. Rabinowitz (eds.), Blackwell, London and New York, 2006, pp. 499–515.

4 Trisha Brown in Rosyln Sulcas, 'Trisha Brown: choreography that spans continents and oceans', *Dance Magazine*, April 1995.

5 Walter Benjamin was the first to argue that the invention of photography rendered all other visual arts photographic. See Peggy Phelan, 'Haunted Stages: Performance and the Photographic Effect', in *Haunted: Contemporary Photography, Video, Performance*, Guggenheim Museum, New York, 2010, for a fuller discussion.

6 Harold Rosenberg, 'American Action Painting', in *Artnews*, December 1952.

7 Paul Schimmel, *Out of Actions: between performance and the object, 1949–1979*, Museum of Contemporary Art, Los Angeles and Thames and Hudson, London, 1998; Paul Schimmel, 'Only Memory can carry it into the future', in *Allan Kaprow: Art as Life*, Getty Museum, Los Angeles, 2009, pp. 8–19; Amelia Jones, *Body Art: Performing the Subject*, University of Minnesota Press, 1998, where she coins the phrase 'the Pollockian performative'.

8 See Peggy Phelan, 'Shards'.

9 Morton Feldman's score (a cello duet) was added by Paul Falkenberg, a more experienced film editor than Namuth. They also added a tape recording of Pollock responding to an interviewer's questions. (They cut out the questions, thus underlining the auratic aspect of Pollock's statements.)

10 Two of the most prominent exhibitions were *Seven Easy Pieces* at the Guggenheim Museum in New York in 2005, in which Marina Abramović re-enacted seven canonical performance texts and her exhibition at the Museum of Modern Art in New York, *The Artist is Present* in 2010.

11 Friedrich Nietzsche, *The Gay Science*, Bernard Williams (ed.), Cambridge University Press, Cambridge, MA, 2001, p. 107.

12 Merce Cunningham, 'Merce Cunningham in conversation with Jacqueline Lesschaeve', Marion Boyars, New York, 1991, p. 137.

13 Mary Lynn Kotz, *Rauschenberg: Art and Life*, Harry Abrams, New York, 2004, pp. 122–123.

14 The broadcaster was Süddeutscher Rundfunk.

15 Beckett's stage directions for *Quad* include instructions for changing the number of movers. He mapped the piece for six duos and four trios. In the performance for four dancers, he differentiated each part with a letter, A, B, C, D. He also colour-coded each trajectory across the grid. Here Beckett was following in the footsteps of the Bauhaus choreographer and designer Oskar Schlemmer, whose abstract meditations on dance, in pieces such as *Slat Piece* and *Dance in Space* of the late 1920s, extended sculptural ideas to movement.

16 See my 'Lessons in Blindness from Samuel Beckett', *PMLA* 119, No. 5, 2004, pp. 1279–88, for more on Beckett's complicated dialogue with painting.

17 A story well told by Sally Banes in *Democracy's Body: Judson Dance Theatre 1962–64*, Duke University Press, Durham, North Carolina, 1993 and *Greenwich Village 1963: Avant Garde Performance and the Effervescent Body*, Duke University Press, Durham, North Carolina, 1996.

18 Nauman quoted in *Bruce Nauman: Work from 1965 to 1972*, Jane Livingston and Marcia Tucker (eds.), Los Angeles County Museum of Art, Los Angeles and Praeger, New York, 1972, p. 26.

19 In addition to *Slow Angle Walk*, *Stamping in the Studio* and *Revolving Upside Down*, Nauman also inverted the figure/ground relation in *Pacing Upside Down* (1968) and *Bouncing in the Corner, no 2: Upside Down* (1969).

Choreographing Your Move

Susan Leigh Foster

How is your body moving as you read this? Is your shoulder shrugging? Your hand scratching? Your toe curling or uncurling? Do you want to stretch? Shift your weight? Look away? Are these impulses to move in one way or another part of a more elaborate routine? Is this the time in your day when you read? Are you sitting or lying in the place where you typically read? Could these movements and their routines constitute a choreography? And if so, are you choreographing your day? Or is it choreographing you?

The term 'choreography' has gone viral. In the last five years it has suddenly been mobilised as a general referent for any structuring of movement, not necessarily the movement of human beings. Choreography can stipulate both the kinds of actions performed and their sequence or progression. Not exclusively authored by a single individual, choreography varies considerably in terms of how specific and detailed its plan of activity is. Sometimes designating minute aspects of movement, or alternatively, sketching out the broad contours of action within which variation might occur, choreography constitutes a plan or score according to which movement unfolds. Buildings choreograph space and people's movement through them; cameras choreograph cinematic action; birds perform intricate choreographies; and combat is choreographed. Multiprotein complexes choreograph DNA repair; sales representatives in call centres engage in improvisational choreography; families undergoing therapy participate in choreography; web services choreograph interfaces; and even existence is choreographed.

Choreography, then, would seem to apply to the structuring of movement in highly diverse occasions, yet always where some kind of order is desired to regulate that movement. Prior to this current widespread application of the term, choreography had enjoyed two distinct meanings since it was neologised in 1700. It first referred to the art of notating dance on paper using symbols, and subsequently it named the act of self-expression through the creation of a dance. A brief examination of these two earlier usages may provide insight into choreography's contemporary meaning. It might also illumine aspects of *Move: Choreographing You*, the exhibition that this book documents.

Choreography was the name given to the first successful and widely used form of dance notation, invented by Pierre Beauchamps, Louis XIV's dancing master, and put into print by Raoul Auger Feuillet. Choreographies were notated scores of dances, and choreographers were the people who could read and write the notation. In this first meaning, choreography established an innovative and enduring relationship between the body, space and printed symbol.

Although many other dancers and scholars had attempted to document dancing, Feuillet's system asserted the radical proposition that all dancing is composed from a small number of essential motions: 'Positions, Steps,

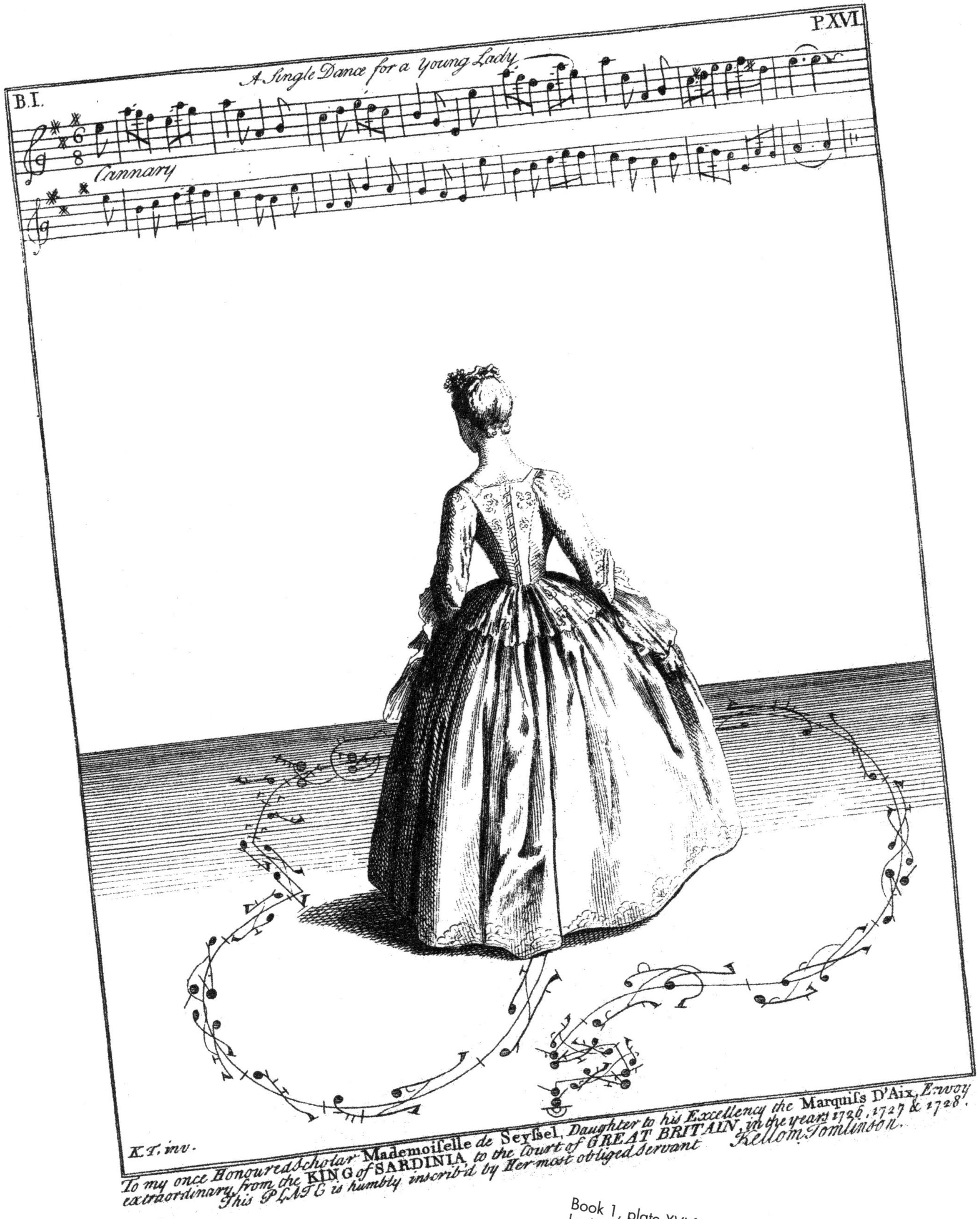

Book 1, plate XVI from *The Art of Dancing Explained* by Kellom Tomlinson (London, 1735)

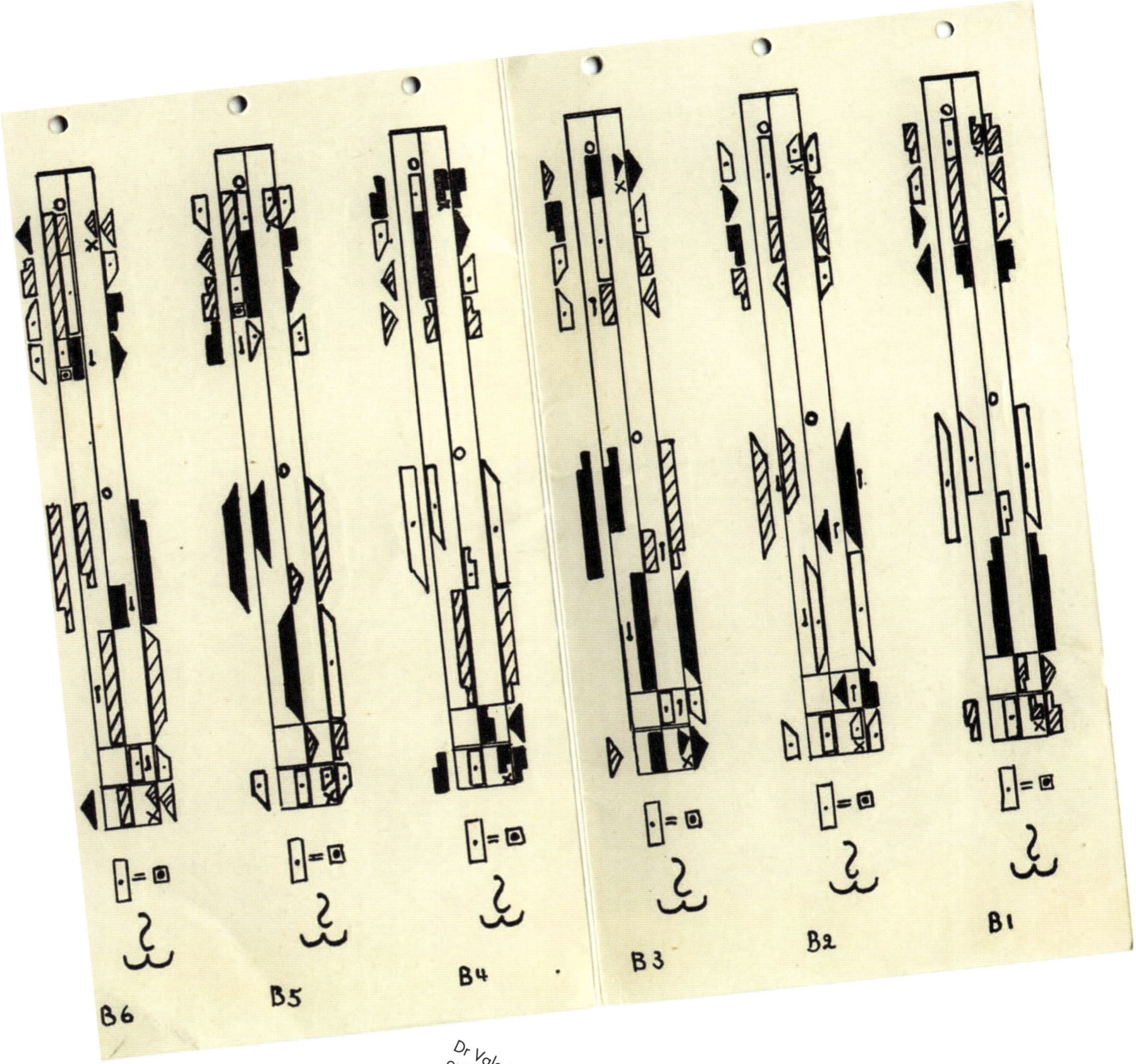

Dr Valerie Preston-Dunlop, Dance notation card sent out on Rudolf Laban's 70th birthday, 1949

Sinkings, Risings, Springings, Capers, Fallings, Slidings, Turnings of the Body, Cadence or Time, Figures, etc.'[1] The system then integrated these elements into a single planimetric representation of the dancing body that highlighted its directionality, the path it took through space, and the motions of the feet and legs. A single line notating the dancer's path was embellished on either side by characters indicating the positions and actions of the feet and legs. There was very little reference made to arm or hand motions or to possible movements of the torso or head. Instead, the notation positioned the body as a vertical and singular entity travelling across a geometrically defined horizontal grid.

By asserting that a small number of seemingly neutral motions or aspects of the body subtended all dance movements, the notation seemed to verify and produce infinite variation in dancing. The symbols appeared to reference neutral motions or aspects of the body, signifying principles of movement that referred only to the movement's direction, timing, and the spatial orientation of the body performing it. These could be varied and recombined in an infinite number of ways to produce any and all dances. Movement, although infinite in its variations, was thereby reduced to a set of possibilities to elevate and lower, to trace a semi-circle or line, etc.

The notation regularised all dancing by assimilating any and all motions into a single system of principles, and it also taught dancers to maintain a single directional orientation as they moved through space by cultivating a bird's eye view of their own path. As part of the instructions for learning to read the notation, Feuillet discussed the relationship of the aspiring choreographer to the surrounding environment, emphasising that it was crucial to keep the top of the page of notation aligned with the front of the room. He even provided detailed instructions for positions of the hands in order to maintain that alignment as one performed a quarter turn. For dancers of Feuillet's time, the body's ability to remain oriented with respect to the fixed horizontal planes of floor and paper was far from given. Feuillet thus found it necessary to provide these meticulous instructions so that dancers could maintain a kind of 'true north' even as their bodies wound along a circuitous path.

Both the principles underlying all movement and the abstract horizontal plane upon which dancing occurred worked to create a specific conceptualisation of the body's relationship to space. Feuillet's system was based on a notion of space in which bodies and their movements could be organised according to abstract and geometric principles. Each individual body consisted of a centrality that extended itself outwards in space towards a periphery, and as it moved into and through space, its movements were characterised as value-free. Any labour entailed in traversing this space went unregistered. Within such a space, neutral bodily features and motions, such as those identified in Feuillet notation, operated to confirm the existence of an absolute set of laws to which all bodies should conform. Thus the notation erased the local origins of dance steps in order to place all dancing on the plane of pure geometry where each dance's specificities could be documented using the same universal principles. The notation bound the dancing to the ground on which it occurred, not to its indigenous location, but rather to an abstract and unmarked ground. It also cultivated an omniscient point of view from which to observe the pathways of all dancers across this abstract plane. Dancers disciplined by the notation could track their own progress through space in relation to others.

By the middle of the eighteenth century, choreography fell out of use as a form of notation largely because concert dance evolved into a new genre of performance – the pantomime ballet. In this genre the facial expressions and postures that conveyed the drama being enacted were equally as important as the virtuoso steps and phrases of movement, and the notation had no capacity to document these expressive elements. Where the notation continued to influence dance was in the pedagogy for dance training in both concert and social dance practices. Aspiring students learned the positions, the basic steps and the combinations of steps that the notation had identified. They assimilated the criteria for evaluating excellence in performance that had been established through the notation's codification of the vocabulary.

Over the course of the nineteenth century the term choreography was rarely invoked, and when it was, it referred indiscriminately to the acts of making, performing and learning dance. It returned with a new urgency and immediacy at the beginning of the twentieth century in response to the radical approaches to dance-making evident in the Ballets Russes productions when they were presented in both London and New York. Because the dances evidenced such new vocabularies and novel scenarios, critics found it necessary to name, for the first time, the art of making dances as a distinct pursuit, separate from learning or arranging dances.

Choreography was then taken up enthusiastically by those involved in the new modern dance, where it began to specify the unique process through which an artist not only arranged and invented movement, but also melded motion and emotion to produce a danced statement of universal significance. In 1933, dance critic and apologist for the new modern dance John Martin asserted this apocalyptic vision of the role of the artist:

> The major purpose of the artist is to make known to you something that is not already known to you, to make you share his revelation of something higher and nearer the truth, to rob the material symbol of some of its appearance of substance and disclose the essence, the reality, of which it is a transient representation.[2]

Unlike entertainment, which offered only a momentary escape, genuine art should lift viewers up, giving them a permanent new vantage point from which to glimpse either the ultimate or the infinite. Dance as an art form used bodily movement, arranged in such a way as to transcend any individual's power to express by rational or intellectual means. Even though people did not speak a common language, Martin explained, they moved 'in generally the same way and for the same reasons', and as a result dance had the capacity to communicate across all cultures, classes and ages.[3]

This use of choreography to name the creative act of formulating new movement to express a personal but also universal concern entailed new kinds of relationships between bodily training, making and performing dance. Where Feuillet notation located all movement along a universal horizontal plane, the new modern techniques foregrounded gravity as a universal within and against which the body articulated its dynamism. In the same way that Feuillet notation occluded the labour of moving from one place to the next, so this conception of gravity rendered equivalent the efforts of all bodies in all places. Students trained in a variety of individually created techniques, each of which explored this relationship between body and gravity as a kind of drama of universal significance. The exercises they practised articulated a very new relationship to space. Rather than progressing along a horizontal plane and tracking that progress in one's awareness, students now learned to flesh out the volumetric body and to explore the tensile and sinuous connections among its parts. They also learned to propel this dynamic corporeality into space, creating momentum and flow as they carved through or launched into their surroundings.

Choreography became the unique process through which this momentum-filled body was tapped as a vehicle for expressing issues of both individual and universal concern. It no longer referenced a standard or shared repertoire of movements, as it had in Feuillet notation. Like the notation, however, it authorised the claim for unique ownership of a given dance. Both meanings of choreography secured the right to proclaim that a given dance was the product of individual invention and the property of that individual.

Since the 1960s, the period documented in this exhibition, the terms choreography and choreographer have undergone yet another set of modifications due to the changing nature of dance composition and performance. The compositional processes of Merce Cunningham challenged the modern conception of dance as the expression of an inner subjectivity by using chance procedures for devising movement and sequencing events. In addition, many artists such as Daniel Nagrin and Anna Halprin began working with improvisation and alluded to the changing outcome of each performance by referring to themselves as the director, rather than the choreographer. The new interest in utilising 'found' movement, such as the pedestrian tasks and activities deployed by Judson choreographers, also provoked a de-centering of the artist-as-genius model of authorship. Artists studying at the newly founded London School of Contemporary Dance likewise explored a variety of new sources for movement vocabulary, arranging movement through work with sculpture, film and slides, and spoken and recorded text. As a result, many artists simply titled the work and then used the word 'by', rather than 'choreographed by'. The subsequent emphasis on borrowing movement from multiple sources and also on integrating dancers' choreography into the piece resulted in yet other nomenclatures, such as 'conceived by', 'directed by', or 'arranged by'.

Throughout this period choreographers collaborated with dancers and also with artists from other media, exploring interdisciplinary modes of performance between dance and theatre, film and video, lighting design, new digital media, and also working with set designers and sculptors. These collaborations took a variety of forms, sometimes juxtaposing performances in the different media, and sometimes constructing new intermedia genres in which neither form would exist without the other. Modern choreographers had integrated different media, based on the premise of an organic functionalism in which each art made a distinctive contribution to the whole. The new collaborations, whether as juxtaposed collages of diverse media or as intermedia integrations of aspects from each art, dismantled and contested any organic differentiation among the arts. Each worked with different materials, but did not, as a result, create unique forms of address. Instead, any and all the arts boasted the capacity to expand perception and illuminate one's apprehension of the world.

These various artistic initiatives reflected a new status for the artist as craftsperson rather than inspired luminary. The terms 'making dances' and 'making new work' came to signify a daily decision to enter the studio and construct movement or to sequence phrases of existing movement, thus signalling a re-definition of the artist as labourer and collaborator who worked with the materiality of movement. Feuillet notation had secured a substantiality for movement, but as an event that could be documented through a lexicon of established principles that were then symbolised on the printed page. Modern dance had imparted a sense of its materiality to movement by articulating a pedagogy of composition and showing its possibilities for repetition, variation and reiteration. For modern choreographers, movement was always placed in the service of the artist, who transformed it into psychological and universal expression. In contrast, the artist as maker of dances assembled movement from diverse sources and arranged it, not as personal expression, but as a statement about movement itself. This imbued the dance with a significance separate from that of its maker's intent, and at the same time, it reinforced the dance as a made event distinct from its execution. The choreography, now allied with the process through which a performance was made rather than the feelings or desires of its maker, became increasingly separated from both the choreographer and the dancer.

It was precisely during this period, when choreography transformed from an act of self-expression into a more impersonal process that could be realised and experienced by individuals in different ways, that the earlier works in *Move: Choreographing You* were created. The possibilities inherent in this new notion of choreography have continued to be explored by artists up to the present. Many of the works in the exhibition construct a collaboration between artist and audience members such that the piece is only realised through the unique actions and reactions of each viewer. Many emphasise a process over a product, inviting viewers to witness an event rather than an object. As a result, a number of the works presented here, even if they are attributed to a given artist, cannot assert authorship in the same way that earlier artworks, based on the object, or dances, based on their choreography, have claimed.

In this new paradigm of choreography, space takes on a new identity as something that is protean, malleable and co-created. Not the geometrically defined system of coordinates in which horizontal and vertical positions can be determined, nor the viscous medium through which the momentum-filled body enunciates itself, space becomes a co-production between body and surroundings. It is not something through which you move, but something that you define in the act of moving. Each body performs a duet with space.

However, the body that performs this duet is not presumed to be a constant and stable entity. Many of the works in *Move* offer propositions or hypotheses about physicality itself: what if the body acts and interacts this way? What if the world and the bodies in it operate according to this logic? What if perceiver and perceived are mutually defining? Following on from these kinds of questions, I would suggest that the way you are currently experiencing your body as you read is quite different from the myriad ways in which you felt embodied as you moved through the exhibition itself.

Implicit in *Move*, then, is the suggestion of choreography as an inclusive naming of diverse patternings of movement – from troop movements to board-room discussions, to dog training and commuter flow – all events to which the term has recently been applied. In many of these recent implementations of choreography, however, there has been an intimation that bodies are being choreographed by a very authoritarian, Manichean even, wielding of power. Some of the usages suggest that the choreography is something that is happening to us, and we are simply part of it regardless of our willingness to participate. *Move* inspires us to realise that we do have agency in these situations, and that choreography is never possible, does not even exist, without the performance of all the bodies summoned into it.

1 John Weaver, *Orchesography, or the Art of Dancing*, H. Meere, London, 1706, p. 2.
2 John Joseph Martin, *The Modern Dance*, A. S. Barnes, New York, 1933, p. 79.
3 Ibid., p. 84.

Merce Cunningham, Dance notation from Rainforest, 1968

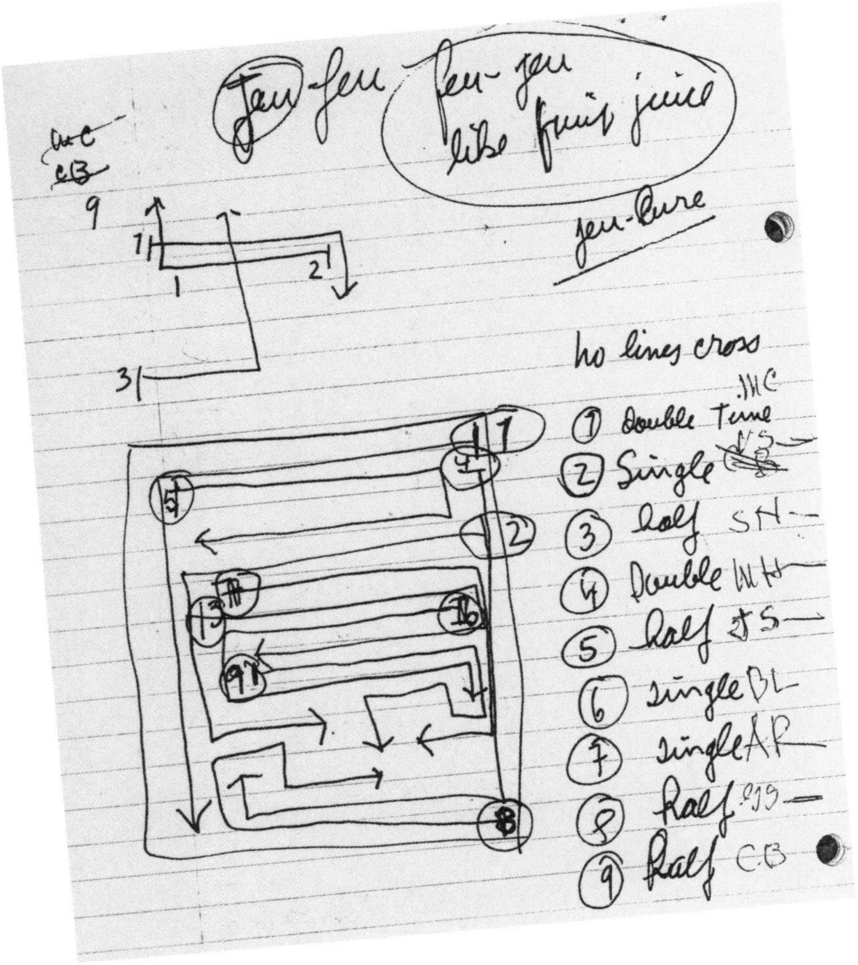

Artists

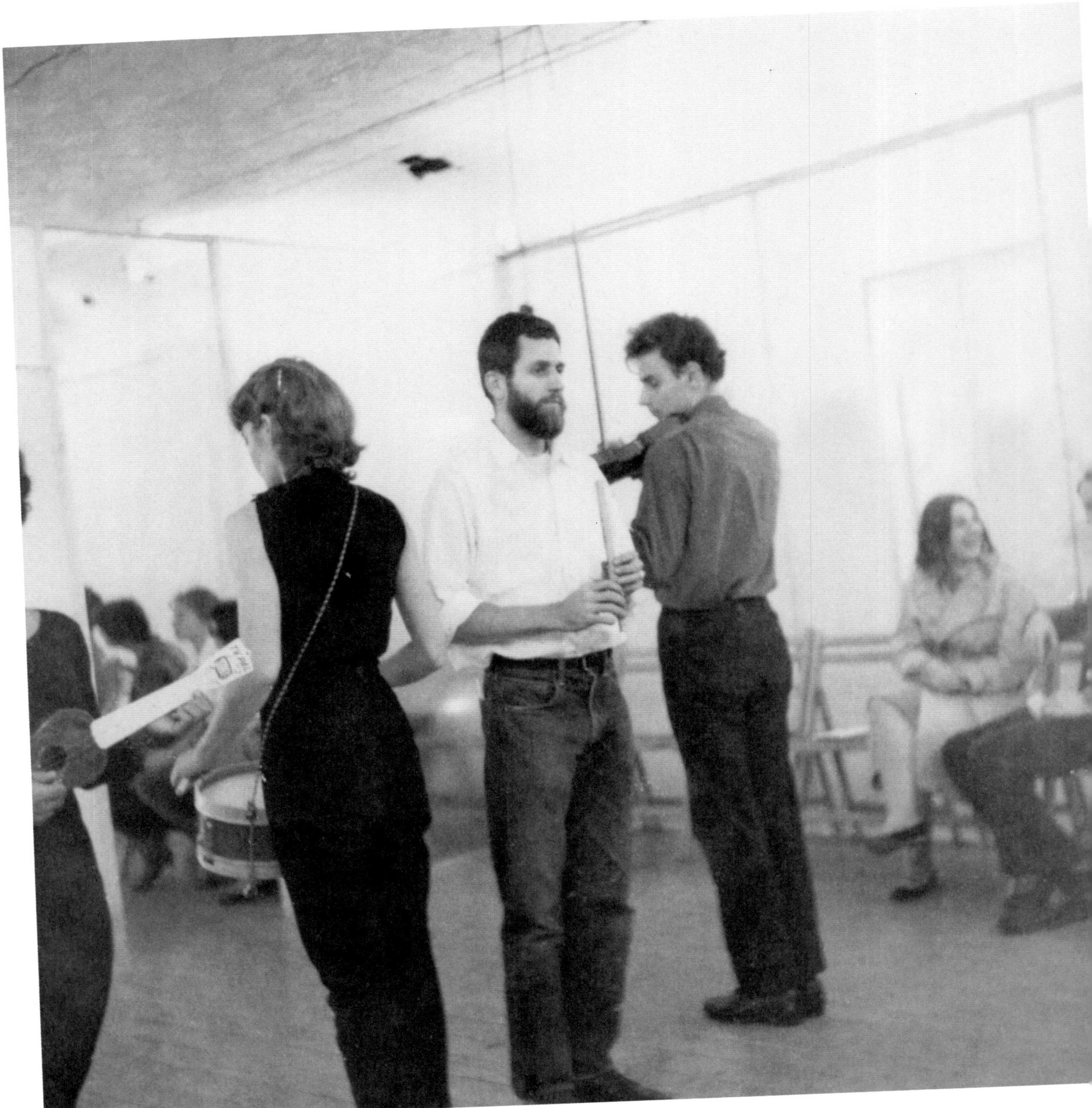

Allan Kaprow, 18 Happenings in 6 Parts: Room 1, Set 4, October 1959

Allan Kaprow
18 Happenings in 6 Parts (1959) reinvented in 2010 by Rosemary Butcher

First performed at the opening of the Reuben Gallery in New York City in October 1959, Allan Kaprow's *18 Happenings in 6 Parts* is widely regarded as an iconic moment in the history of the avant-garde. Meticulously scripted by Kaprow, this complex assemblage of heterogeneous elements – movements, live and recorded sounds, spoken words, smells, electric lights, films, action painting and sculpture – could be said to mark a turning point in the artist's lifelong experiments in equating art with life. Located halfway between his Environments and Happenings, the work surrounded the audience but could only be partially apprehended. It sought to challenge the boundaries between performers and spectators, and yet by tightly controlling their respective actions, it sits apart from his later Happenings – understood as spontaneous, undirected occurrences.[1]

In 2006, in conjunction with a major retrospective of his oeuvre and a few months before his death, Kaprow authorised the recreation of *18 Happenings in 6 Parts*.[2] The first 'redoing', curated by André Lepecki and Stephanie Rosenthal, took place at the Haus der Kunst, Munich and at the Performa biennial, New York, 2007. Lepecki directed a performance proceeding through a close reading of the hundreds of pages of scores, notes, letters and drawings left by Kaprow while making the original work, as a prompt to re-do it, 'not as before, but once again'.[3] In 2008, when the exhibition travelled to MOCA, Los Angeles, the visual and sound artist Steve Roden was invited by LACE to create a 're-invention' of the work that set up an open, creative exchange between interdisciplinary artists. In *Move: Choreographing You*, the British dance artist Rosemary Butcher is proposing a new re-invention, taking its cue from the choreographic premises offered by Kaprow's seminal work.

One might argue that the historical, formal and aesthetic trajectories of *18 Happenings in 6 Parts* are resonant within the field of dance. First, by methodically scoring every aspect of the work, as Lepecki has argued, Kaprow used a compositional method that allies itself with choreography – that is, the writing of movement on paper as direction for its future execution.[4] Moreover, the sculptural, expressionless body put forth by Kaprow might anticipate some of the Minimalist experiments enacted by the Judson Dance Theater a few years later. As Jeff Kelley acutely observed regarding the idiosyncratic drawings used in his movement notations, Kaprow's 'painted stick figures seem like diagrams waiting for the matter-of-fact avant-garde choreography they foreshadow'.[5] Finally, by drawing attention to the function of the spectators – giving them instruction cards and orchestrating when and where they are to move throughout the piece – the work echoes similar aesthetic concerns at the beginning of the 1960s at the intersection of visual art and dance that question spectatorship. Robert Rauschenberg, for instance, thought 'dance [...] directly responsible for [his] new interest in the spectator's active role'. Dance, then, offers a 'critical relationship' between the performer and the viewer as they combine to create 'a living, palpable force of contact'.[6] By including the audience in the work, and fragmenting its experience across three different rooms and six acts, interspersed with longer periods of time waiting for things to happen, *18 Happenings in 6 Parts* experiments with phenomena familiar to dance audiences – heightened corporeity, movement, ephemerality and duration.

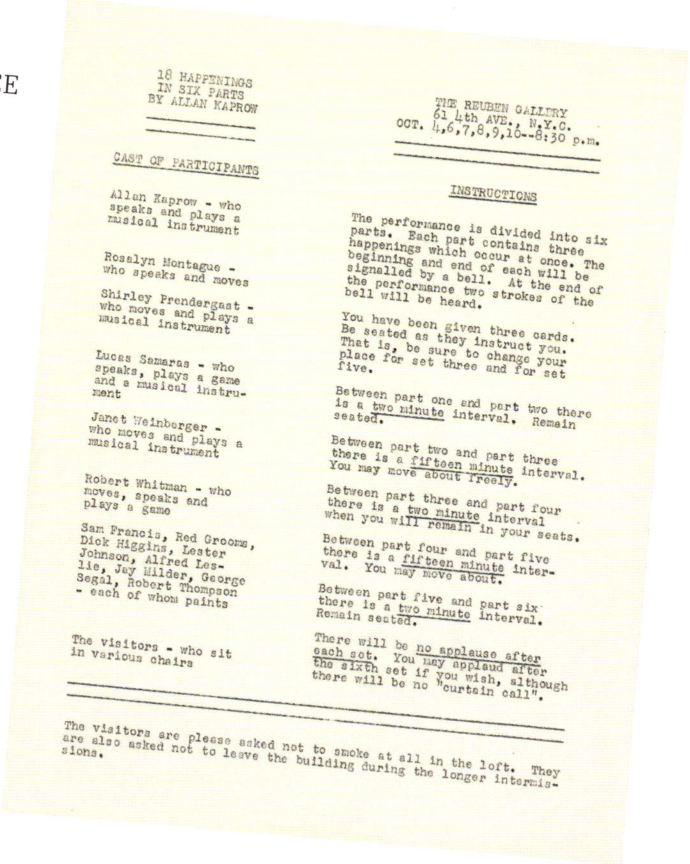

18 HAPPENINGS
IN SIX PARTS
BY ALLAN KAPROW

THE REUBEN GALLERY
61 4th AVE., N.Y.C.
OCT. 4,6,7,8,9,10--8:30 p.m.

CAST OF PARTICIPANTS

Allan Kaprow - who speaks and plays a musical instrument

Rosalyn Montague - who speaks and moves

Shirley Prendergast - who moves and plays a musical instrument

Lucas Samaras - who speaks, plays a game and a musical instrument

Janet Weinberger - who moves and plays a musical instrument

Robert Whitman - who moves, speaks and plays a game

Sam Francis, Red Grooms, Dick Higgins, Lester Johnson, Alfred Leslie, Jay Milder, George Segal, Robert Thompson - each of whom paints

The visitors - who sit in various chairs

INSTRUCTIONS

The performance is divided into six parts. Each part contains three happenings which occur at once. The beginning and end of each will be signalled by a bell. At the end of the performance two strokes of the bell will be heard.

You have been given three cards. Be seated as they instruct you. That is, be sure to change your place for set three and for set five.

Between part one and part two there is a two minute interval. Remain seated.

Between part two and part three there is a fifteen minute interval. You may move about freely.

Between part three and part four there is a two minute interval when you will remain in your seats.

Between part four and part five there is a fifteen minute interval. You may move about.

Between part five and part six there is a two minute interval. Remain seated.

There will be no applause after each set. You may applaud after the sixth set if you wish, although there will be no "curtain call".

The visitors are please asked not to smoke at all in the loft. They are also asked not to leave the building during the longer intermissions.

Allan Kaprow, *18 Happenings in 6 Parts: Cast and Instructions*, 1959

The choreographer Rosemary Butcher has created an innovative body of work over the last three decades. Engaging in collaborative exchanges with a range of experimental practices, most notably visual arts, Butcher created seminal pieces including *Pause and Loss* (1976) and *Touch the Earth* (1987), performed at the Serpentine and the Whitechapel galleries in London respectively. Her dance work was instrumental as she imported some of the crucial aesthetic concerns developed by the Judson Dance Theater in New York to the British dance scene. In her project for *Move: Choreographing You*, Butcher uses the creative and critical weight of *18 Happenings in 6 Parts* as a means to question and push the borders of her own dance practice. She works closely with four performers (Elena Giannotti, Dennis Greenwood, Ben Ash and Lauren Potter) with various artistic backgrounds and sensibilities to foreground the choreographic potential inherent in Kaprow's oeuvre. Questioning the notion of a choreographic activity (what constitutes an activity; how does one make it manifest; how does one translate it from the mind to movement?), the piece experiments with the boundaries between the choreographer, the performer and the spectator; between the act of conceiving, seeing and being seen. Butcher also collaborates with project manager Karsten Tinapp, visual artist and sound co-ordinator Edwin Burdis, researcher Stefanie Sachsenmaier and installation artists Matthew Butcher and Pablo Bronstein, to create an environment that becomes an active element of the dance. Embedding Kaprow's creative spirit into her own practice, Butcher explores the present tense of *18 Happenings in 6 Parts* and what it can do for contemporary bodies. As an inventive and affirmative reassembling of its many forms and contents, the project thus takes to task Kaprow's words written just before the realisation of the original *18 Happenings in 6 Parts*: 'Each of these parts may be re-arranged indefinitely'.[7]

Noémie Solomon

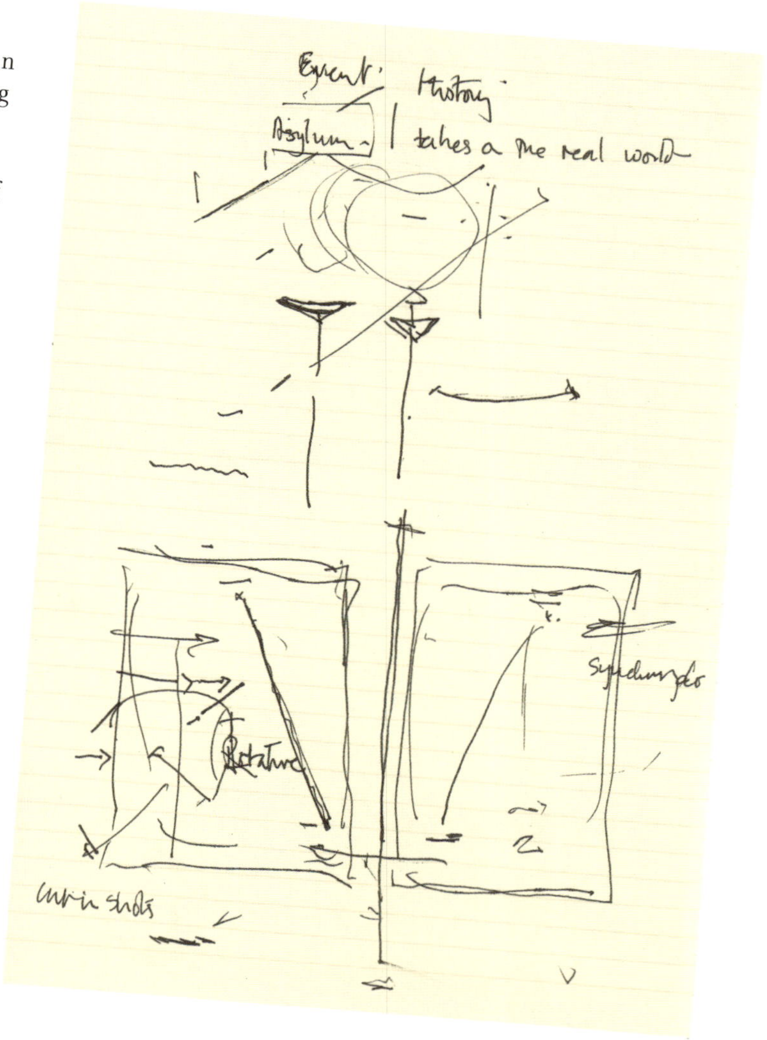

1 This shift in Kaprow's notion of the Happening could explain the artist's lack of interest in re-doing *18 Happenings in 6 Parts*. Kaprow was also profoundly disappointed by the reception of the piece at the time, most notably by John Cage's response, which saw the work as authorial and policing. In 1988, Kaprow created a Happening under the same title, which bore no relation to the original: a number of people met on streets across the city of New York to exchange straw, ending when the straw had completely disappeared. By emphasising the Happening as a transient and non-rehearsed work that takes place without an audience, the 1988 version marks the extent to which Kaprow's work had radically moved on from earlier concerns.

2 *Allan Kaprow – Art as Life* (2006), curated by Stephanie Rosenthal at the Haus der Kunst in Munich, and Eva Meyer-Herman, at the Van Abbemuseum in Eindhoven. The exhibition subsequently travelled to Bern, Genoa and Los Angeles.

3 André Lepecki, 'Not as Before, but Simply: Again' in *Perform, Repeat, Record: Live art in History*, eds. Adrian Heathfield and Amelia Jones, Routledge, London, forthcoming.

4 See Lepecki, 'Zones of Resonances', in this catalogue. My own work in decoding and performing the movement notations in the first re-doing directed by Lepecki engaged closely with the work's sustained choreographic demand. As an example of this hyper-choreography, Kaprow's scores specify that movement should never cross the floor in diagonals, and that the limbs should always be perpendicular or parallel to the architecture.

5 Jeff Kelley, *Childsplay: The Art of Allan Kaprow*, University of California Press, Berkeley, 2004, p. 24.

6 Robert Rauschenberg, quoted in Nancy Spector, 'Rauschenberg and Performance', in *Robert Rauschenberg: A Retrospective*, eds. Walter Hopps and Susan Davidson, Solomon R. Guggenheim Museum, New York, 1997, p. 233.

7 Allan Kaprow, *18 Happenings in 6 Parts*, Papers, The Getty Archive, Los Angeles.

Allan Kaprow was born in Atlantic City, New Jersey in 1927 and died in 2006.
Rosemary Butcher was born in Bristol, England in 1947 and lives and works in England.

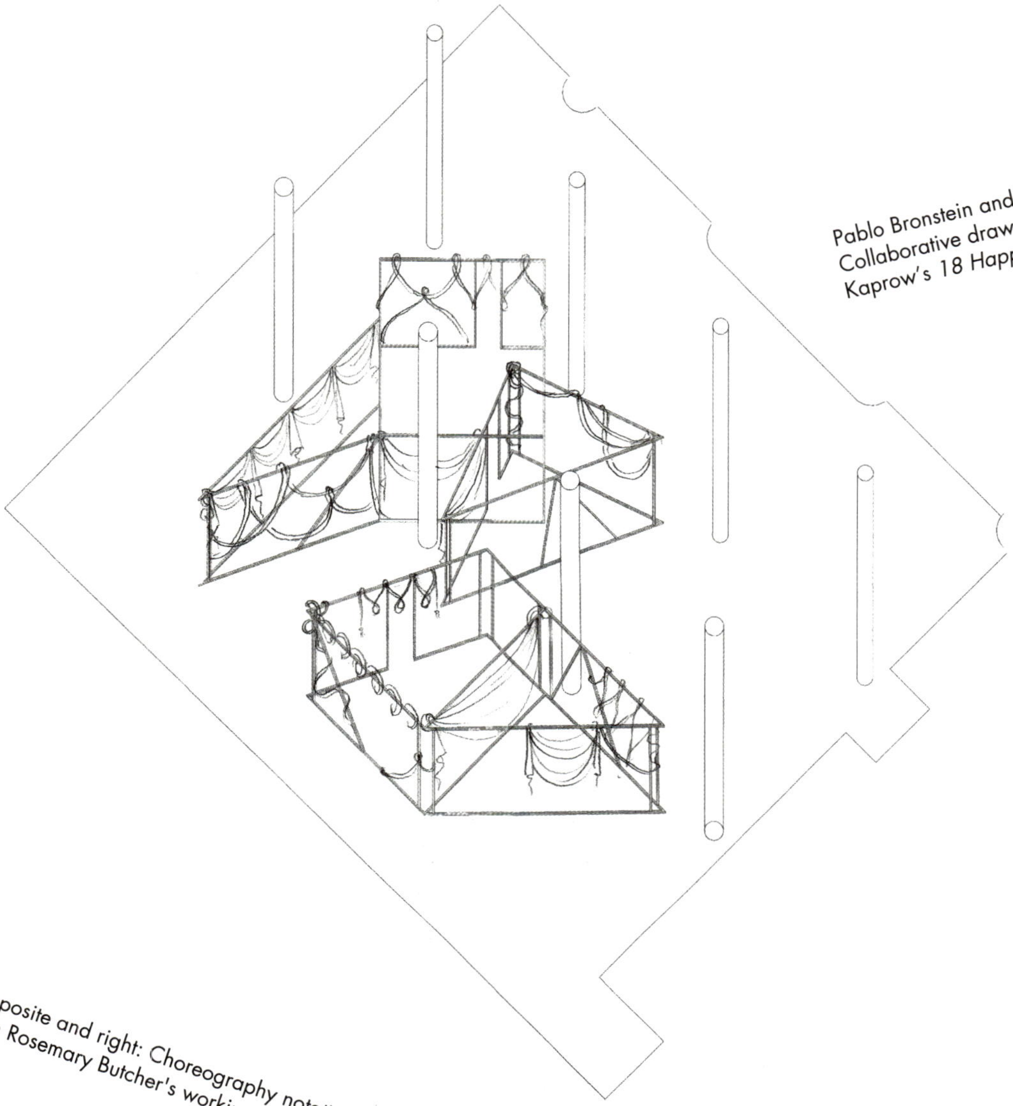

Pablo Bronstein and Matthew Butcher
Collaborative drawing for a new set design of Allan Kaprow's *18 Happenings in 6 Parts*, 2010

Opposite and right: Choreography notation sketches from Rosemary Butcher's working notebook, 2010

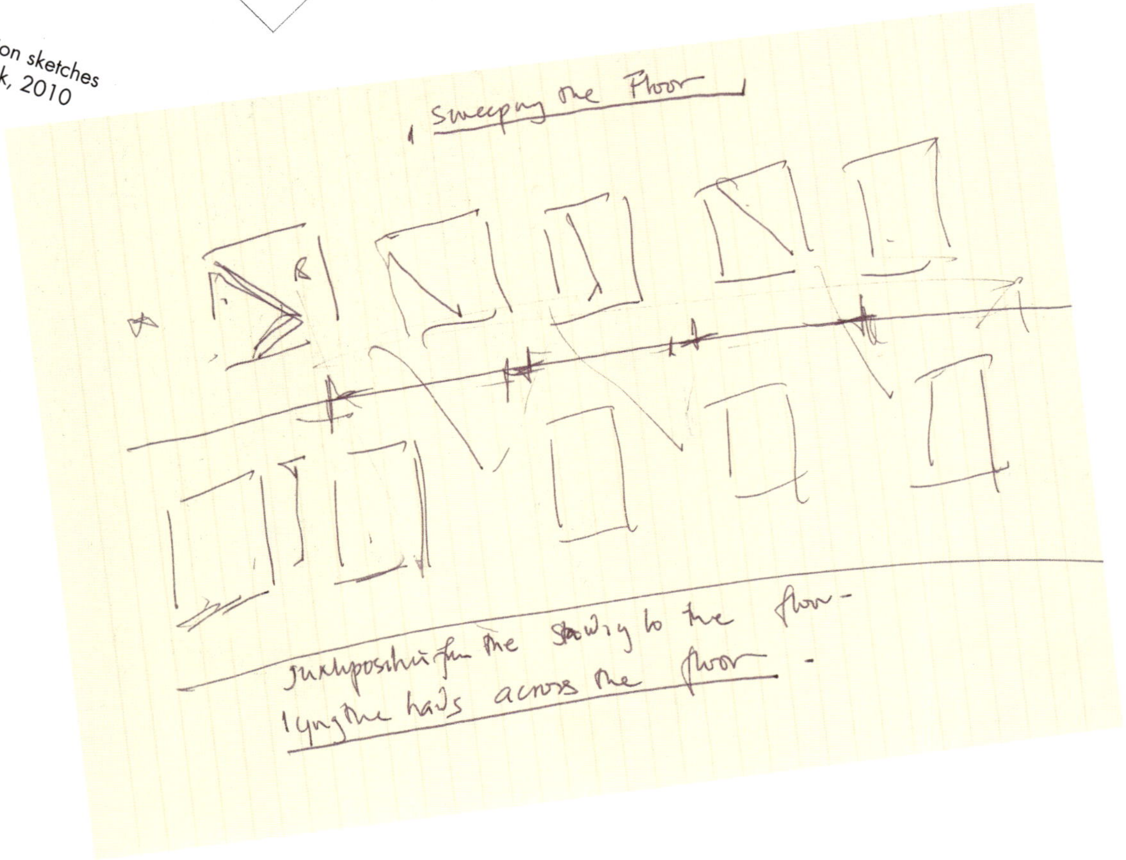

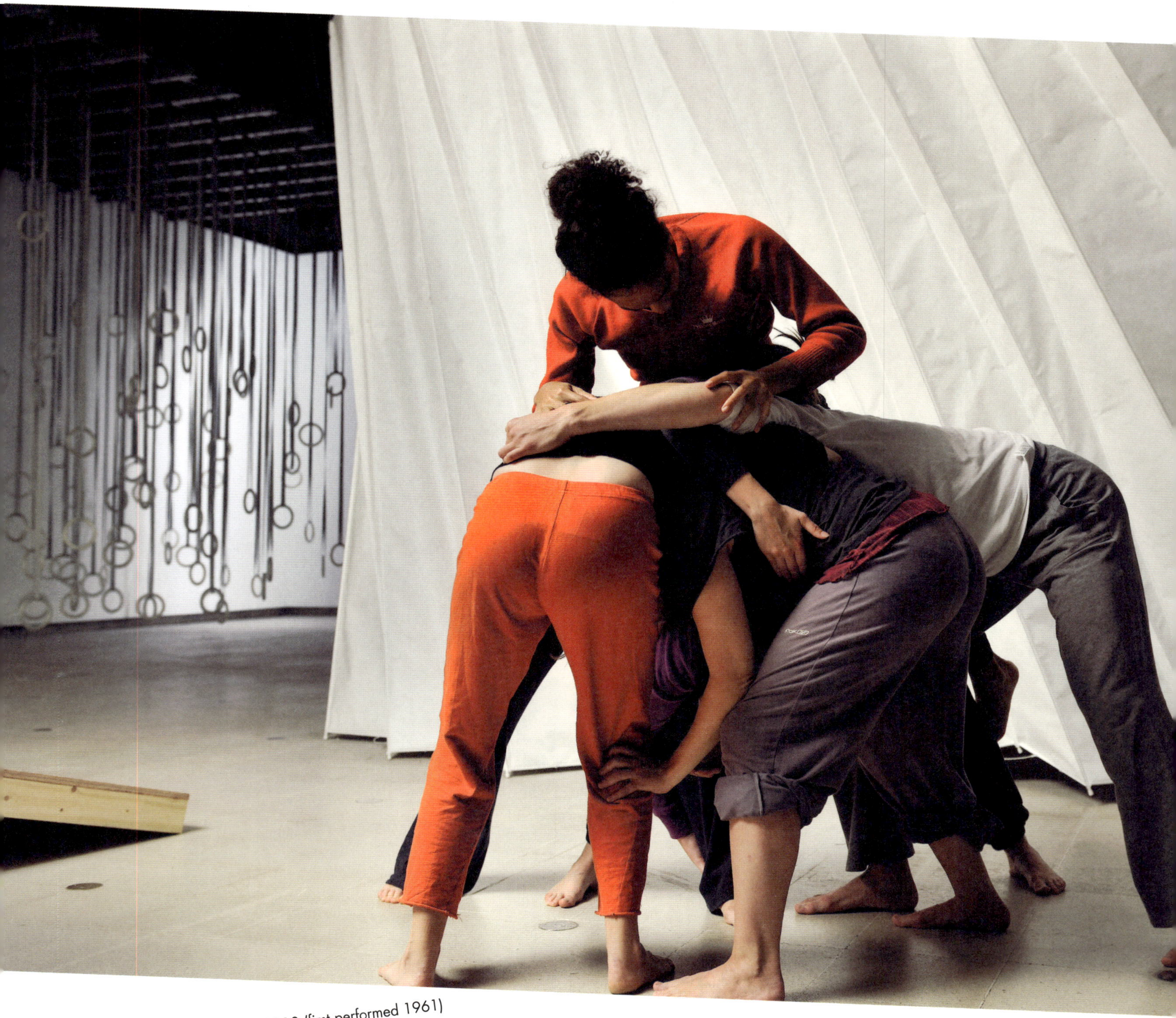

Simone Forti, *Huddle*, 2010 (first performed 1961)

Simone Forti

Huddle (1961); Hangers (1961); Angel (1976); Sleepwalkers (1968/2010); Striding Crawling (1975/2010)

Forti's choreographic work is concerned with kinaesthetic awareness. This is achieved through the effects of defamiliarisation or re-education, and a questioning of the normative behaviours of the human adult, often informed by observing children or animals. She has written that this interest arose out of her four years spent in San Francisco exploring the potential of improvisation with Anna Halprin, who was also an important influence on the work of Trisha Brown and Yvonne Rainer. Halprin's workshops were not about freeing the body but about exploring the restrictions of habit and the possibilities of moving beyond it, through close investigation and studied physical articulation. The result for Forti was an awareness that 'has to do with sensing movement in your own body, sensing your body's changing dynamic configurations'.[1] This internal focus, in contrast to the prevailing modern dance techniques of that period, was derived from the teachings of Martha Graham and Merce Cunningham. Forti moved to New York in 1959 and took classes there, but found them to be too much about a contracted body and a codification of movement, whereas, she says, 'the thing I had to offer was still very close to the holistic and generalised response of infants'.[2]

Together with Rainer, Brown, Steve Paxton and others, Forti attended the composition workshops led by Robert Dunn in 1960–61, based on John Cage's 'chance techniques'. Although never part of the Judson Dance Concert series that emerged from these classes, Forti began to make and present choreographies at events in downtown New York, often alongside experimental performance happenings. Forti's child-like approach became evident as her 'dance constructions' used game scores and playful manipulation of, and by, objects and sculptures. *See-saw* (1960) was a piece made for Yvonne Rainer and Robert Morris (Forti's husband at the time) and it used the eponymous playground structure, with a toy attached that emitted a 'moo' when tilted, as a means to explore balance and equilibrium. It was not entirely formal however; following a section of see-sawing, Rainer had a screaming fit while Morris intoned pages from *Art News* magazine. The following year Forti was invited by composer and Fluxus artist La Monte Young to show work in Yoko Ono's loft. She presented an evening entitled *Five Dance Constructions and Some Other Things* (1961), and she later noted that this event set a template for much of her work that has since followed.

One of these constructions, *Slant Board* (1961), was performed on a wooden ramp at a 45-degree angle with knotted ropes attached to the top. The instruction given to the three dancers was to move up and down and from side to side in a continuous calm manner. They were permitted to rest, but only using the ropes and their body as

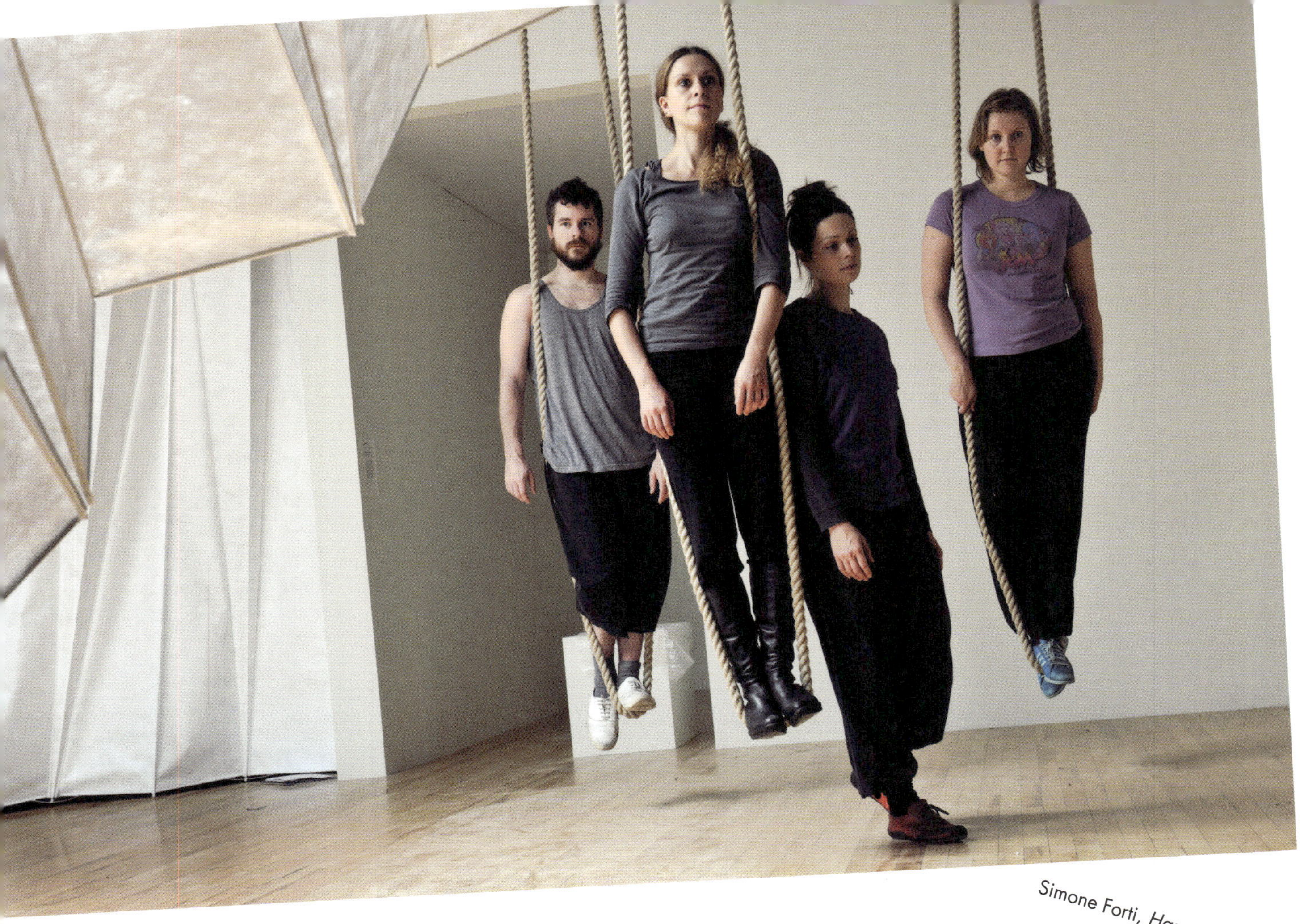

Simone Forti, *Hangers*, 2010 (first performed 1961)

Simone Forti, *Angel*, 1976

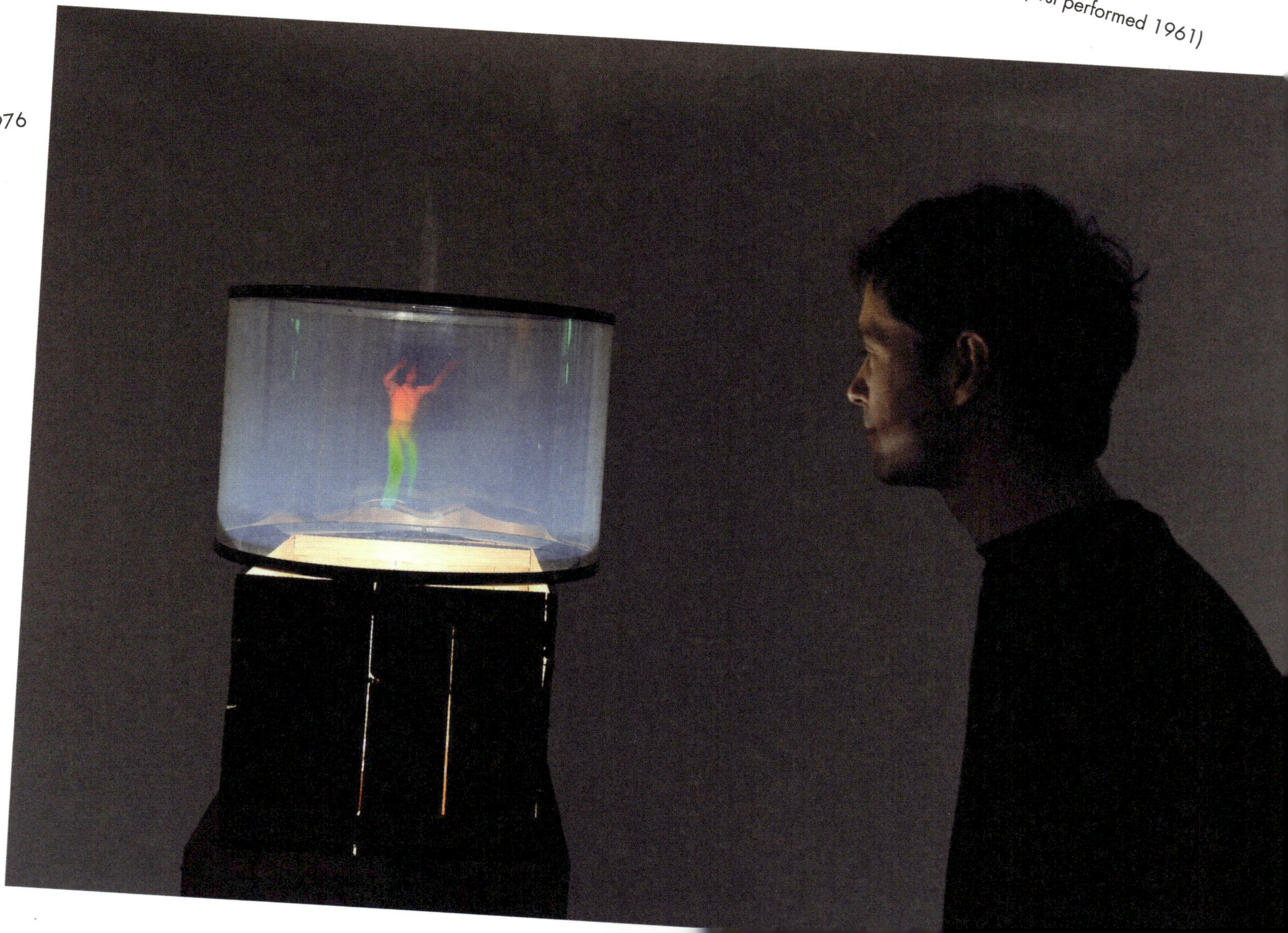

counterweight, and they had to stay on the ramp for approximately ten minutes whilst the audience was free to walk around and observe their negotiations of gravity, geometry and each other. Similar concerns are evident in *Huddle* (1961), presented on the same evening, and in various Fluxus concerts and events since. Six or seven people come together and begin the piece:

> They form a huddle by bending forwards, knees a little bent, arms around each other's shoulders and waists, meshing as a strong structure. One person detaches and begins to climb up the outside of the huddle, perhaps placing a foot on someone's thigh, a hand in the crook of someone's neck, and another hand on someone's arm. He pulls himself up, calmly moves across the top of the huddle, and down the other side. He remains closely identified with the mass, resuming a place in the huddle.[3]

Again spectators are invited to walk around and observe this continuously evolving human structure. Forti even notes that on occasion a dancer would break off and form secondary huddles with audience members who, having watched the piece, intuit the rules and are able to create their own form in response.

Angel (1976) shows a hologram of Forti moving though a series of upper body movements. The spectators activate this solo piece as they move around the sculpture and see the effects of the flickering of the light. The movements are derived from a series of studies Forti conducted on the movements of animals confined to a zoo. Beginning in Rome in 1968, Forti would spend time with animals such as flamingos and polar bears, to understand how they used their repetitive and obsessional movements to try and figure out new relationships to their environment. She felt an affinity with these incarcerated creatures; 'I watched them salvage, in their cages, whatever they could of their consciousness [...] It was the first time in years that I allowed myself to be led by the feedback from my body sensations'.[4] This led to improvisational solo performances, such as *Sleepwalkers* (1968), in which Forti developed a 'dance state' that was for her a releasing of the body, rather than a technique to train the body. 'Some people have a shyness towards entering that state, but everybody does it sometime. Often, at parties, people drop their shyness and enter a dance state. And when I'm in a dance state, the movement that comes out through me enchants me. It can be very simple movement, but it always comes with a sense of wonder, and as one of life's more delicious moments.'[5] *Angel* has echoes of these explorations and perhaps invites the spectator, as the polar bears did, to listen to the rhythm of their pacing and reflect upon the sensations of their own body.

Martin Hargreaves

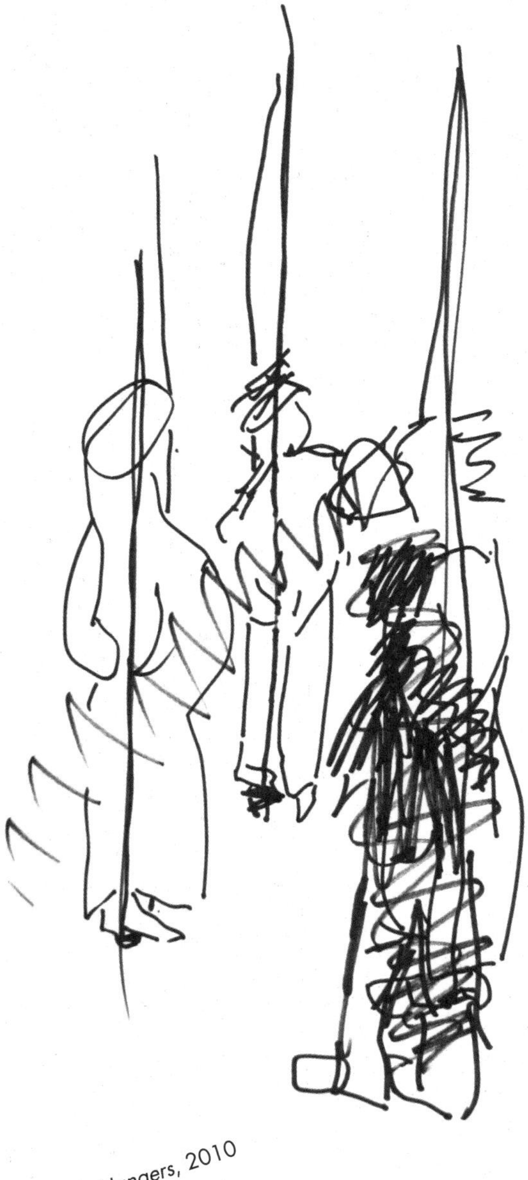

Simone Forti, *Sketch for Hangers*, 2010

1 Simone Forti, *Handbook in Motion*, Nova Scotia College of Art and Design, Halifax and New York University Press, New York, 1974, pp. 29–31.
2 Ibid., p. 34.
3 Ibid., p. 59.
4 Ibid., p. 91.
5 Ibid., pp. 108–9.

Simone Forti was born in Florence, Italy in 1935 and lives and works in Los Angeles.

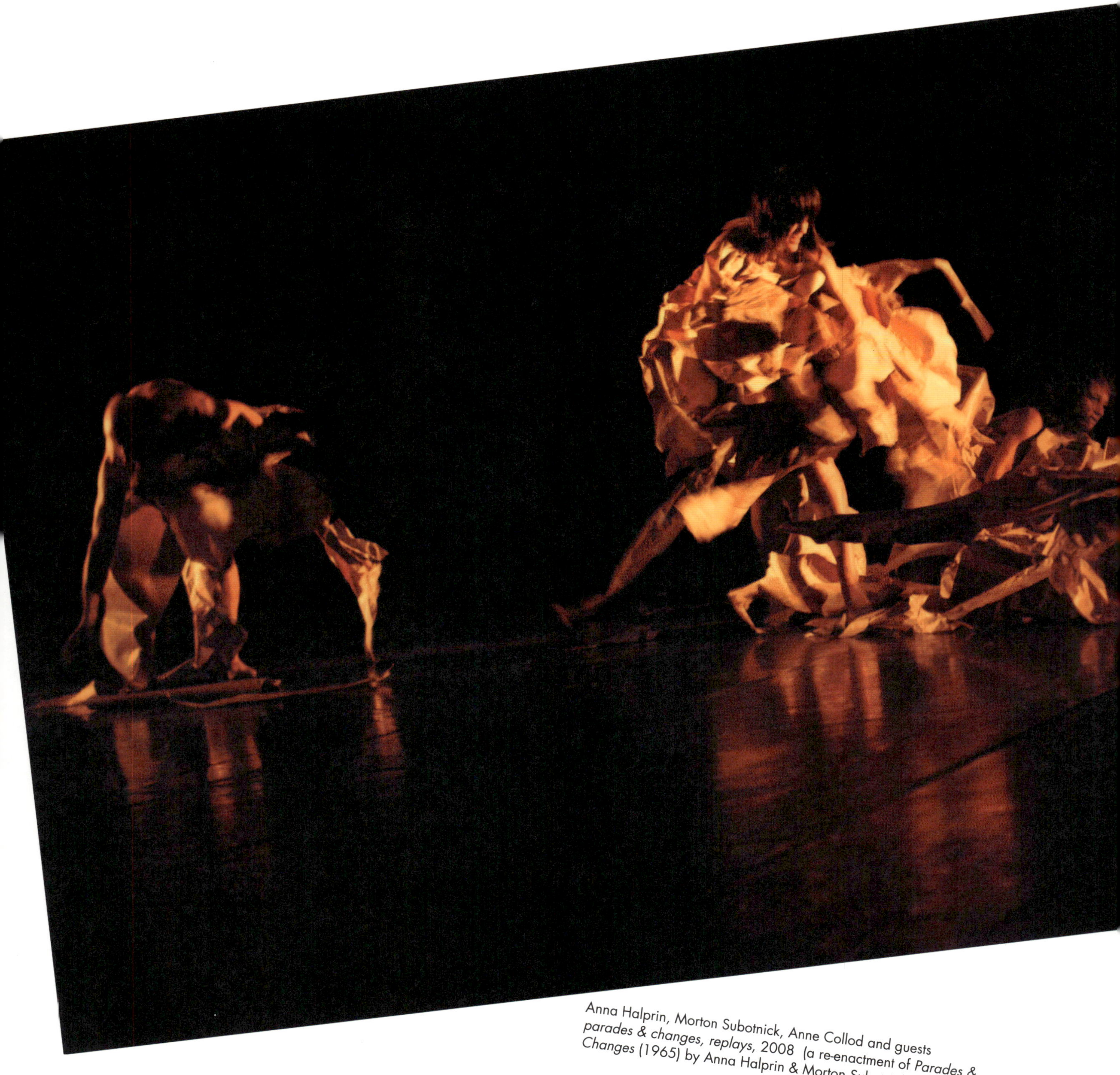

Anna Halprin, Morton Subotnick, Anne Collod and guests
parades & changes, replays, 2008 (a re-enactment of *Parades & Changes* (1965) by Anna Halprin & Morton Subotnick)

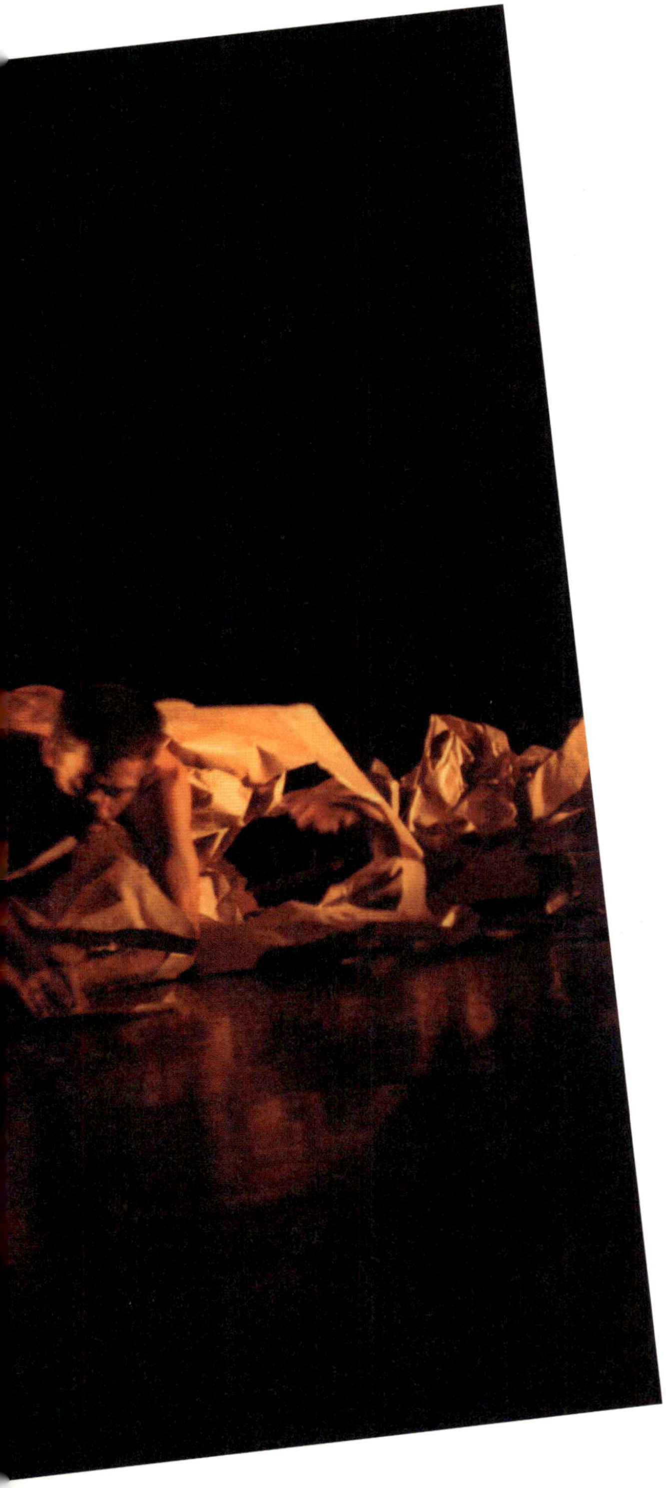

Anna Halprin
Parades & Changes (1965), replays

Anna Halprin has profoundly influenced developments in dance, music and the visual arts for more than 60 years. In 1945, while she was working as a choreographer and soloist with Doris Humphrey, a second-generation American modern dance pioneer, she left New York and settled in California. At this time she was interested in moving away from the individualist styles of artists such as Martha Graham, believing that the next generation of choreographers' work was too derivative. She became focused on finding her own ways of moving and creating, thinking very differently about the source of dance; movement itself. Halprin's work in physical theatre, dance and expressive arts therapy encapsulated the non-conceptual, emotionally driven ethos of the Bay area of the 1960s, where she was one of the co-founders of the San Francisco Dancers' Workshop in 1955. These summer workshops were meeting places for dance artists such as Yvonne Rainer, Trisha Brown and Simone Forti, and just as importantly attracted people from other disciplines, including the sculptor Robert Morris and the composer John Cage. Halprin's approach, and resulting works, subsequently led to a broad redefinition of dance.

In September 1965, Halprin's first 'collective creation' *Parades & Changes* premiered in Sweden, with a further 11 performances taking place in the USA until 1967, when it was banned because of nudity in the piece. To Halprin, the nudity played a crucial role; she has talked about the work as 'the process of undressing, finding your place in space', as well as a 'ceremony of trust'. She referred not only to trust between the performers themselves, but also to that between the performers and the audience.

Parades & Changes exploded what dance could be. The use of improvisation, which was a key element of Halprin's work, as well as that of other choreographers in the early 1960s, was one of the main reasons for this. One consequence of improvised elements was to alter the relationship between performer and spectator, resulting in an enhancement of the spectator's reading of the performers' bodily movements. The work centred on the performers' response to a 'score' that was very specifically task orientated.This forces the performers to examine their intentions – to become aware not only of what is physically taking place, but of how and why they are making specific movements. This in turn exposes the processes of performance to the viewer.

For *Move: Choreographing You*, French choreographer Anne Collod has recreated and reinterpreted *Parades & Changes* in dialogue with Halprin and in collaboration with Morton Subotnick, who composed

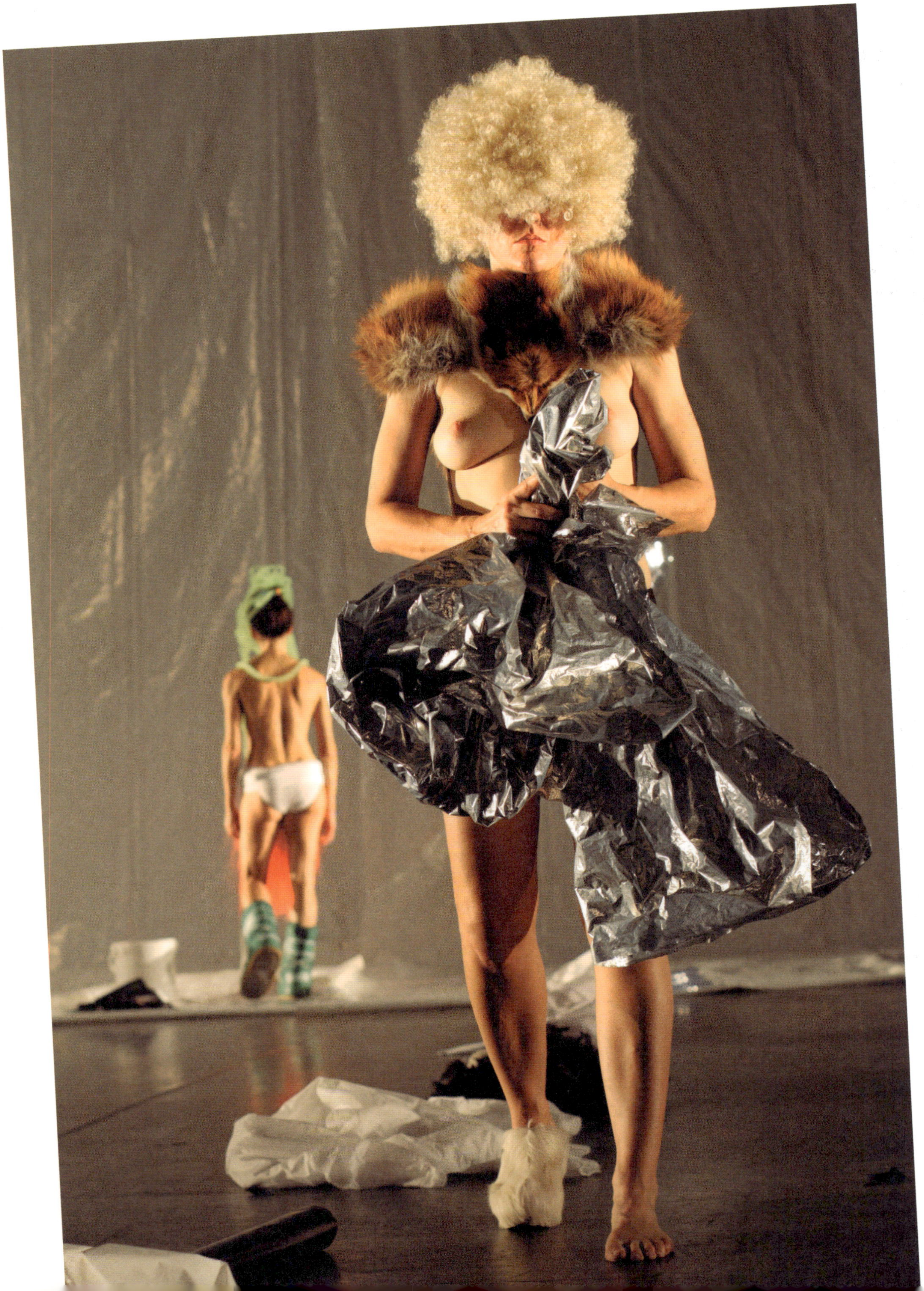

the music for the original. Collod conceived the project as a way of paying tribute to Halprin's achievements and what she made possible for other artists. 'That's why I made this project: to keep it alive', she has commented. The revival was initially seen as revisiting a work that had only historical significance, and the question of how to present it in a contemporary, rather than historical context, had to be carefully considered. However, during the process of experimenting with the score, Collod recognised how relevant to the twenty-first century the questions it asks remain: how to present naked bodies; how to produce sounds with bodies; the semiotic use of costumes; the question of authorship and hierarchical issues when creating work collaboratively. It was also clear that Halprin's influence on dance not only extended to some of the key figures of the Judson Dance Theater (including Rainer and Brown) but also to the continuing evolution of the form we call dance.

Revisiting *Parades & Changes*, particularly due to the collaboration of notable contemporary choreographers and performers such as Vera Mantero and Alain Buffard, allowed the work to be brought into a contemporary context, under the watchful eye of Halprin herself. She first saw the reinvention almost a year after it started touring and she was initially disappointed, feeling that it was too close to her original work. She requested that some sequences from the original version be removed and that other sections should be refined.

Through her art, Halprin wanted to break as many boundaries as she could, moving out of theatres, getting closer to the audience and introducing the language of everyday movement into her work. She has spent her career trying to understand not only how the mind informs the body's movement but also how the body is capable of informing its own movement. In her view, dance is not reserved exclusively for trained professionals, but is an expression of the basic forces within us all.

Nicky Molloy

Anna Halprin was born in Wilmette, Illinois in 1920 and lives and works in Kentfield, California.

This page and opposite: Anna Halprin, Morton Subotnick, Anne Collod and guests *parades & changes, replays*, 2008 (a re-enactment of *Parades & Changes* (1965) by Anna Halprin & Morton Subotnick)

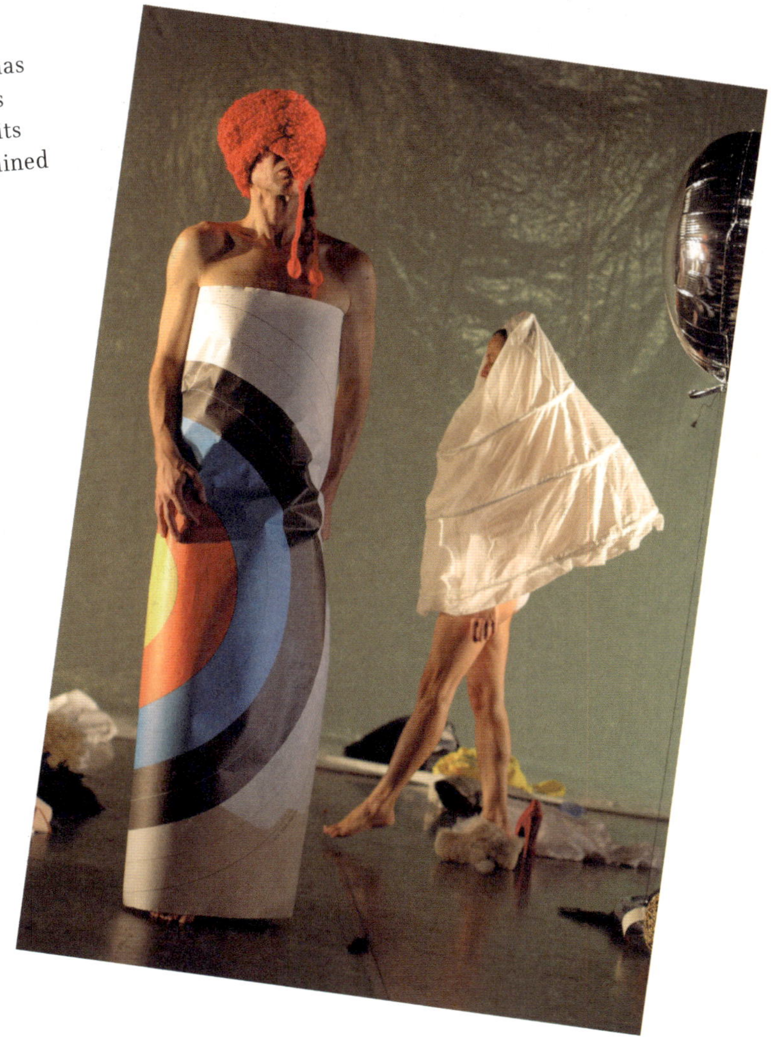

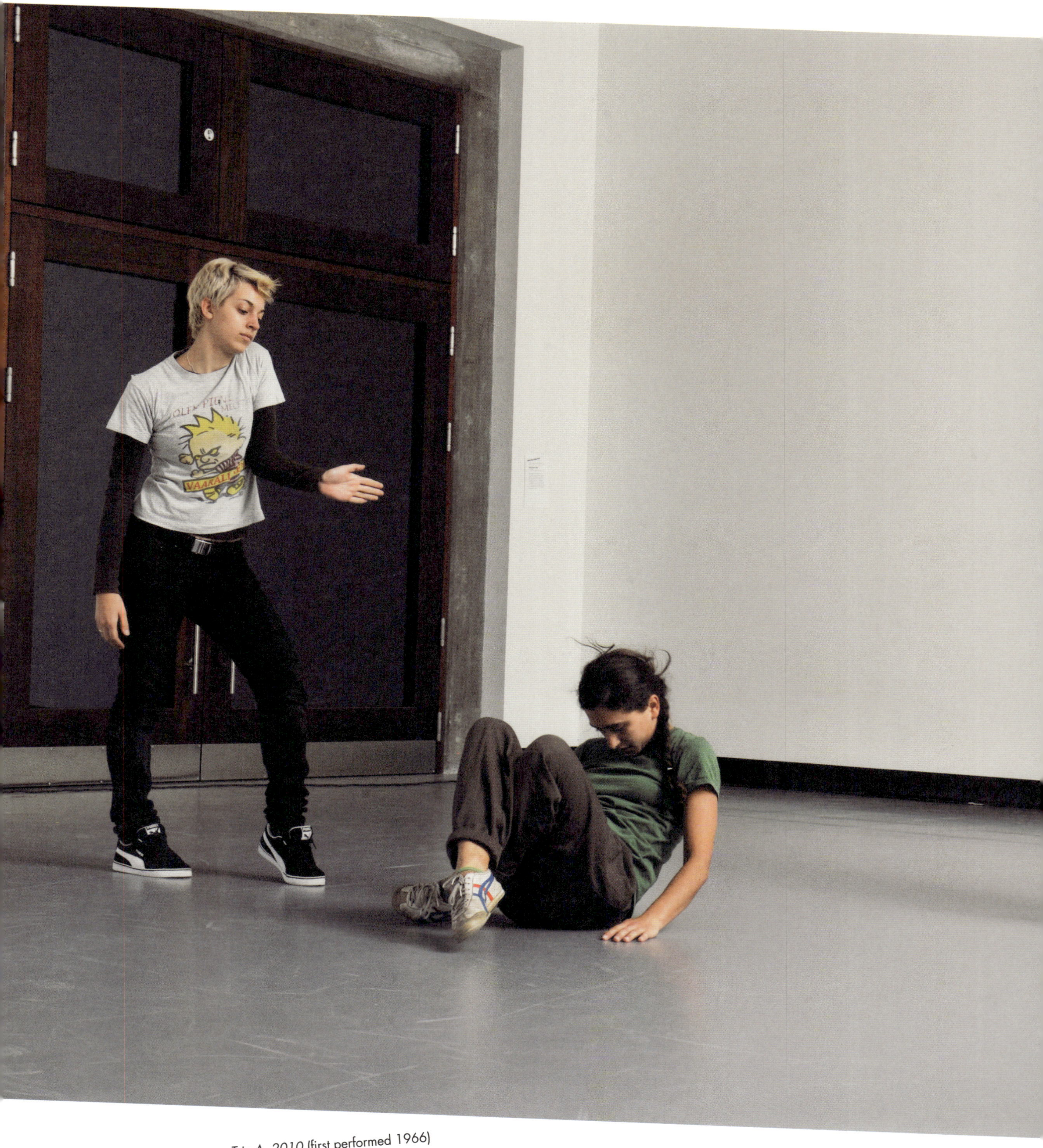

Yvonne Rainer, *Trio A, 2010* (first performed 1966)

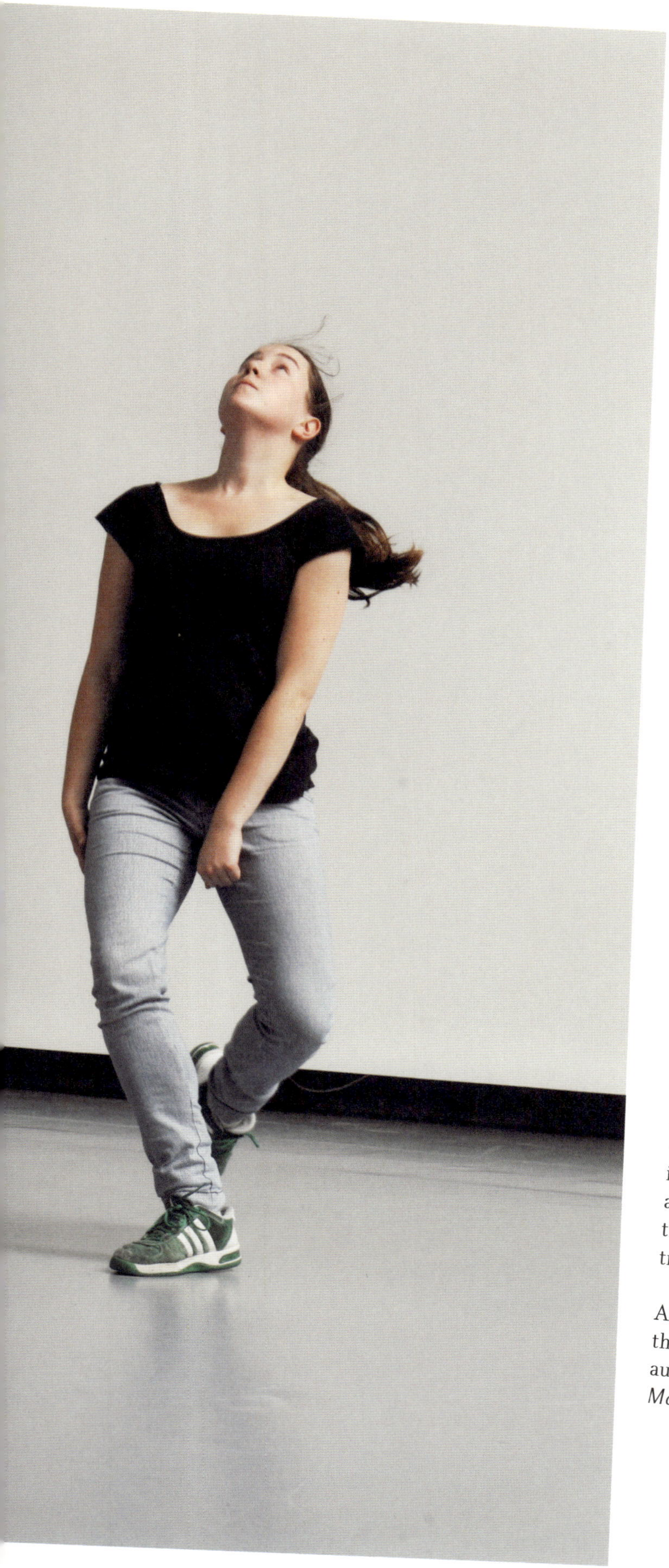

Yvonne Rainer
Trio A (1966)

Trio A is the iconic minimalist dance piece choreographed by Yvonne Rainer. It is a solo performance which lasts approximately four and a half minutes (there is no set time signature, so the dancer finds their own pace). Since the first performance in January 1966, *Trio A* has remained central to Rainer's work and has appeared in many guises, danced by many different people. From the mid-1970s, Rainer focused on filmmaking for twenty years, and her return to choreography in the 1990s was marked by performances of different versions of *Trio A*. In her most recent works, sections from the choreography are lifted directly and placed next to reconstructions of other kinds of physical activity, including vaudeville, stand-up, classical ballet and sports. The programme notes for her evening-length work *The Mind is A Muscle* (1968), which contained *Trio A*, both performed by three men and solo by Rainer in tap shoes, laid out her ambivalent engagement with the lure of the moving body:

> If my rage at the impoverishment of ideas, narcissism, and disguised sexual exhibitionism of most dancing can be considered puritan moralizing, it is also true that I love the body – its actual weight, mass, and unenhanced physicality. It is my overall concern to reveal people as they are engaged in various kinds of activities – alone, with each other, with objects – and to weight the quality of the human body towards that of objects and away from the superstylization of the dancer. Interaction on the one hand; substantiality and inertia on the other.[1]

The object-like presentation of the body is achieved in *Trio A* through a continuous pace that rejects the phrasing and lyricism of traditional dance. There is no repetition of movement or development of themes, and often the top half of the body is performing in a different plane and rhythm to the bottom. It is a challenging piece to perform, as it requires constant concentration and attention to carry out the illogical combination of actions, yet it doesn't look difficult or reveal the skill of the dancer through displays of virtuosic technique. Although it has been called a 'pedestrian' piece, because it doesn't demand years of training or a particular bodily facility to perform (Rainer taught it to non-dancers and ballet dancers alike), it is actually a complex and intricate choreography that requires the dancer to be absorbed in the enactment of precise activity, maintaining a steady tempo whilst tracing an exact floor pattern.

As a filmmaker, Rainer's major concerns were with representation and the relationship between the image on screen and the bodies in the auditorium. Inspired by an engagement with feminist film theory, *The Man Who Envied Women* (1985) stars Trisha Brown but she is never fully on-screen. Rainer directly confronts the conventional cinematic modes of seduction, frustrating the gaze of the spectator through a refusal to display the female body. *Trio A* prefigures this more overtly politicised denial of presentation, in that the dancer never meets the gaze of the audience. In the one moment where the face is looking forward and towards the viewer, the eyes are closed. Just before making *Trio A*, Rainer listed some of her concerns with dance in an essay, as a list of 'no's:

> No to spectacle.
> No to virtuosity.
> No to transformations and magic and make-believe.
> No to the glamour and transcendency of the star image.
> No to the heroic.
> No to the anti-heroic.
> No to trash imagery.
> No to involvement of performer or spectator.
> No to style.
> No to camp.
> No to seduction of spectator by the wiles of the performer.
> No to eccentricity.
> No to moving or being moved.[2]

In the 1960s and 70s, *Trio A* exemplified many of these denials of traditional dance and its inherent narcissistic attempts to attract the attention of the spectator. In the years since the publication of this essay Rainer has revised and corrected her list, noting the impossibility of some of these attempts to redefine how an audience may view dance. Nevertheless, as a statement of purpose written contemporaneous to *Trio A*'s creation, they are useful guides to understanding the complex questions it asks of an audience and how they might relate to the bodies moving in front of them.

Martin Hargreaves

1 Yvonne Rainer, *Work 1961–73*, Nova Scotia College of Art and Design, Halifax and New York University Press, New York, 1974, p. 71.
2 Yvonne Rainer, 'Some retrospective notes on a dance for 10 people and 12 mattresses called *Parts of Some Sextets*, performed at the Wadsworth Atheneum, Hartford, Connecticut, and Judson Memorial Church, New York, in March, 1965', in ibid., p. 51.

Yvonne Rainer was born in San Francisco in 1934 and lives and works in Los Angeles and New York.

Yvonne Rainer, *Trio A*, 1973
(first performed 1966)

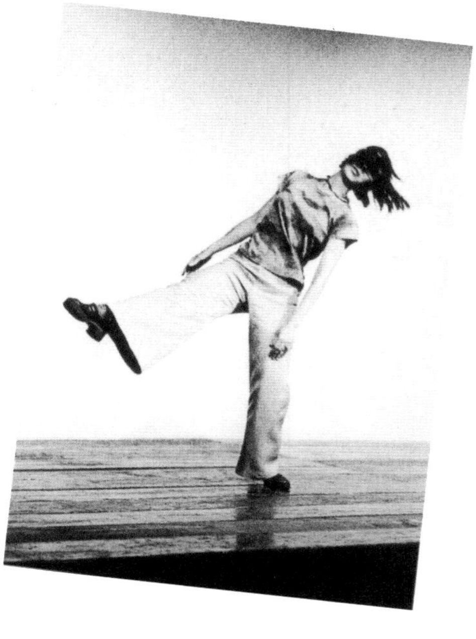

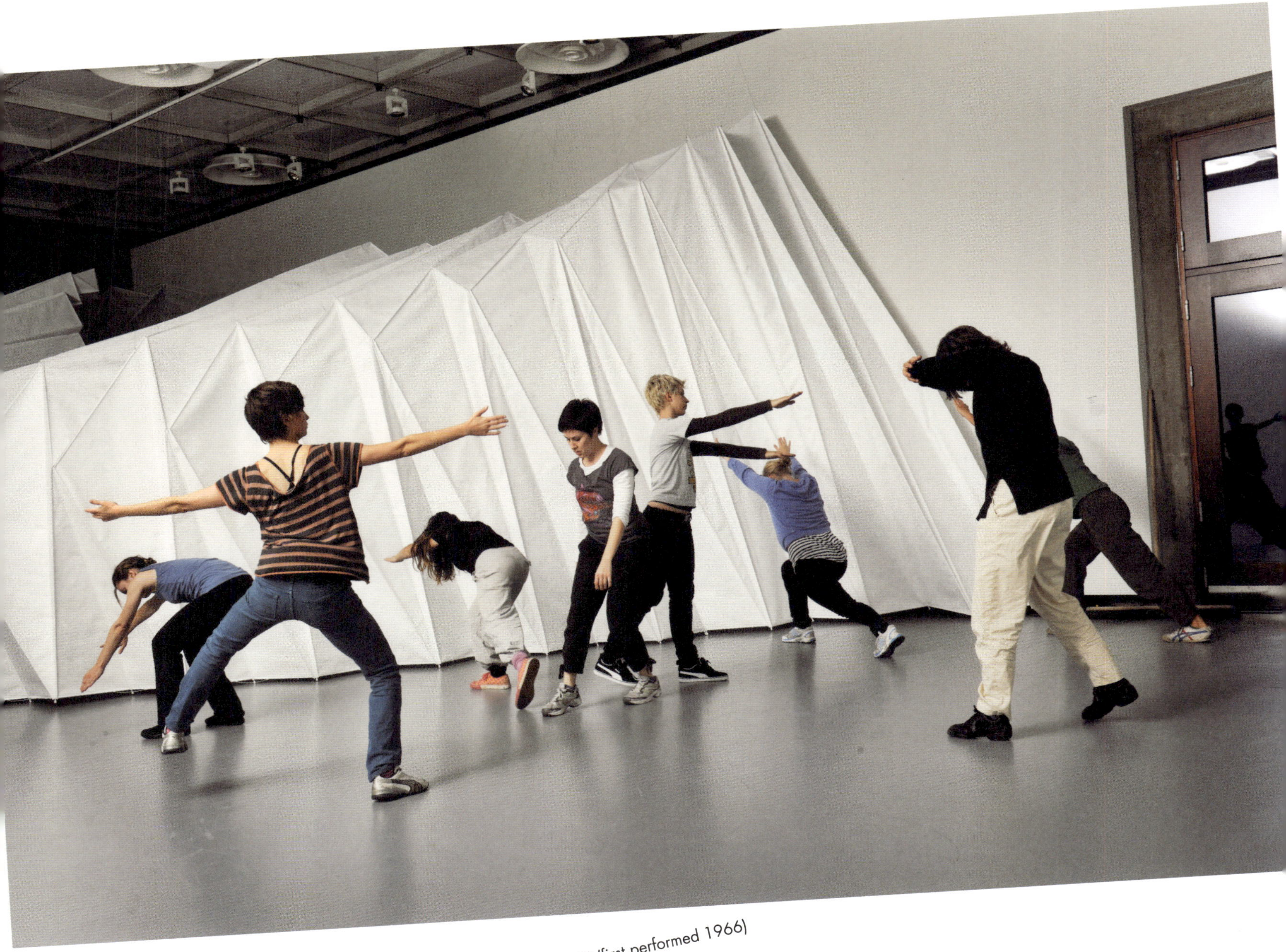

Yvonne Rainer, Trio A, 2010 (first performed 1966)

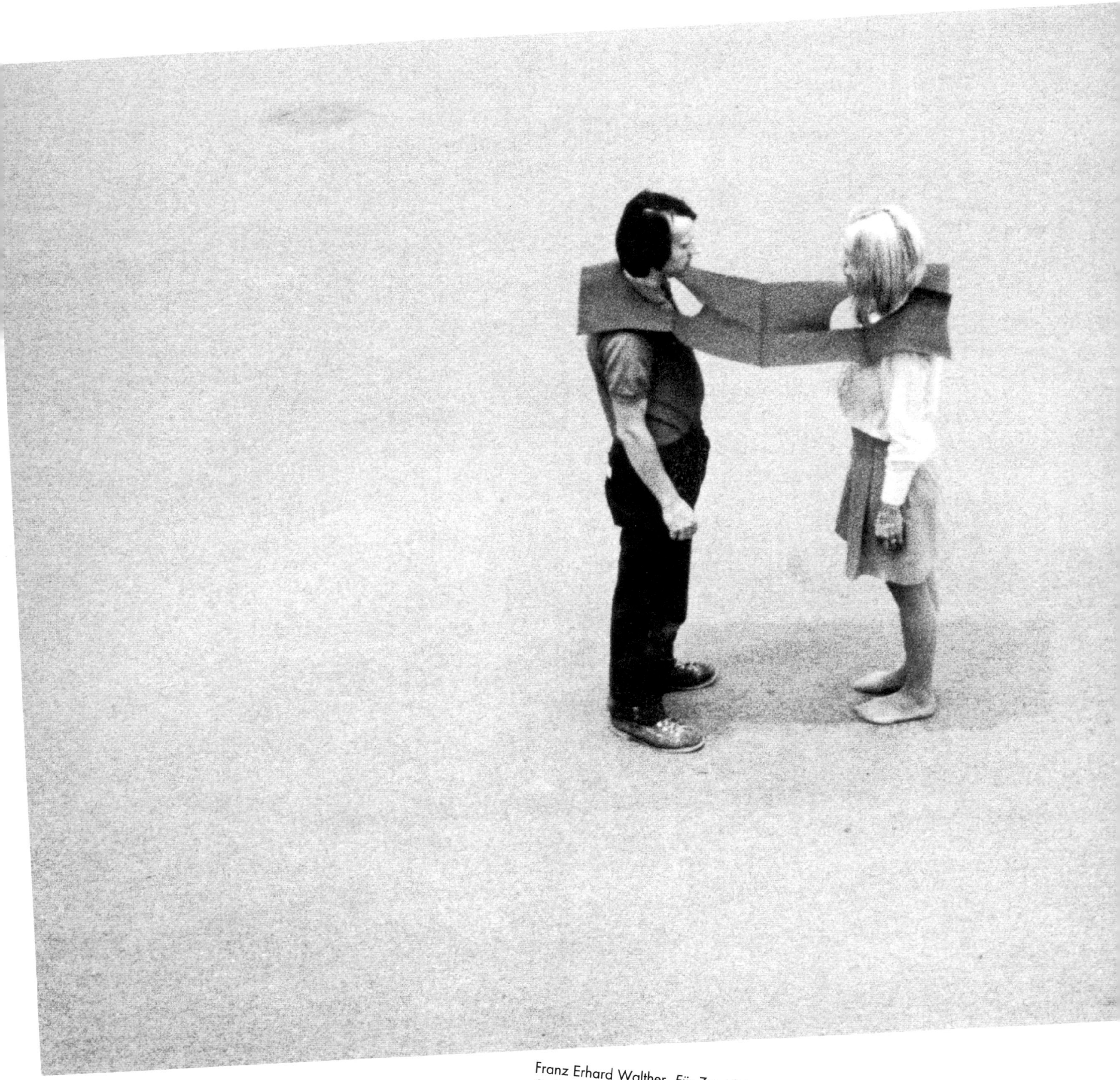

Franz Erhard Walther, *Für Zwei (Nr. 31, 1. Werksatz) (For Two [No. 31, First Work Set])*, 1967

Franz Erhard Walther

First Work Set (1963–69); Standing Piece in Two Sections (1974); Over Head (1984)

Looking at the photographs of Franz Erhard Walther's early works from the *1. Werksatz* (First Work Set, 1963–9) as well as his *Wandformationen* (Wall Formations), created in 1978, it becomes immediately apparent that it is always the artist himself who demonstrates their use. Walther's established term for such works is 'animated sculptures', indicating that the artist's presence brings them to life. To be more precise: he becomes an object in them, making the boundary between the artist and his work appear permeable. The title of a 1985 exhibition by Walther illustrates this transformation of the artist into an art object with particular clarity: *I am the sculpture*, it declares, as though to proclaim the artist's determination to be his own work.

The emphatic reference to life had already been a characteristic feature of the historic avant-gardes, but Walther takes it one step further: any distinction between the artist's life or person and his work is to be effaced. Walther takes this abolition of the boundary between art and personal life upon himself, almost as a form of physical labour; the more so since his objects, such as *Für Zwei* (For Two) (no. 31, *1. Werksatz*) and *Gegenüber* (Counterpart) (no. 28, *1. Werksatz*), are presented as implements for actions – that is to say, the claim is that everyday actions can be performed with them. But we might ask whether the actions Walther proposes for these objects are in fact as ordinary, as drawn from real life, as this suggests.

Let us take, for example, the famous *Stirnstück* (Forehead Piece, 1963), no. 1 of the 58-piece *Werksatz*. It is an object composed of five fabric pillows that promises the possibility of immediate contact with the viewer. Once again, Walther himself demonstrates exactly how this contact is to take place – the viewer lays his forehead against the topmost pillow and then slowly slides down along the object. Quite patently, a form of bodily meditation is considered the correct way to experience this object. Instead of regarding it from a distance, we are literally to immerse ourselves in this pillow, to gain an immediate feel for its material qualities. This privileges the tactile experience, to which visual perception is subordinated. But what is decisive is that Walther by no means forces the visitor to engage in this form of immediate participation. Each viewer is free to decide whether or not to use an object – for instance, the *Zweiteiliges Standstück* (Standing Piece in Two Sections, 1975) – in the way Walther proposes.

The actions the artist demonstrates, moreover, are not ones with which we would be familiar from our everyday lives. As the art historian Gottfried Boehm rightly noted, handling the *Werksatz* means committing to an artificial mode of action. This aspect of artificiality is also characteristic of the postures that Walther demonstrates in engaging his works. When he stands stiffly upright inside one of his *Wall Formations*, for instance, he looks like a man who is trying to squeeze into a wall closet. Instead of taking the stage with a charismatic artist's persona, that is to say, with expressive gestures, Walther chooses a more stoic and humble bodily attitude. And although the pose he strikes suggests ordinariness – he is simply standing there (an attitude that resembles the emphasis on the ordinary in minimalist dance) – we cannot fail to notice that he looks extremely tense, recalling a mummy. The suggestion of life always reverts into an impression of lifelessness; as though he wanted to remind us that becoming an object is not an unmixed pleasure, that the compulsion under which artists labour to exhibit themselves in order to be credible – a compulsion that has grown even stronger since the 1960s – demands extraordinary reserves of strength and discipline.

Körpergewichte (Nr. 48, 1. Werksatz), (Forehead Piece [No. 48, First Work Set]), 1966

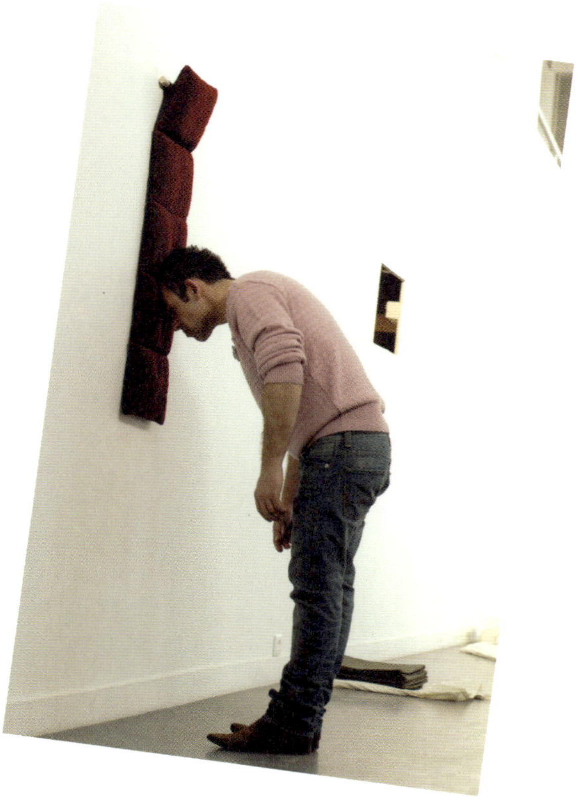

The *Werksatz* as a whole seems to be directed against the personalisation of art. The works are displayed in a state of inertness; like utensils in a gym locker, they sit there, one stacked on top of the other, stripped of their reference to life. At the moment they are staged, however, numerous references to everyday life emerge – they evoke associations, for example, with group activities such as school trips or excursions and the accompanying equipment such as sleeping bags, tents, etc. It is as though art has taken up the ambitions of 1920s *Lebensreform* (Life Reform) movement.

At the same time, these works lay claim to a semantics of formal aesthetics, especially those made since 1978, when Walther began to use colours, primarily red and yellow, in massive amounts, lending these fabric constructions an air of aliveness even beyond the life to which the performer brings them. If Walther to this day insists on an intimate and positively physical relationship with his works, we are confronted with the fact that an artist who turns himself into an object still has an object at his disposal to which he can relate in one way or another. Though this object will be fraught with myths about the artistic subject, it can ultimately supplant – and hence to a certain degree relieve – the artist.

Isabelle Graw

Franz Erhard Walther was born in Fulda, Germany in 1939, where he lives and works.

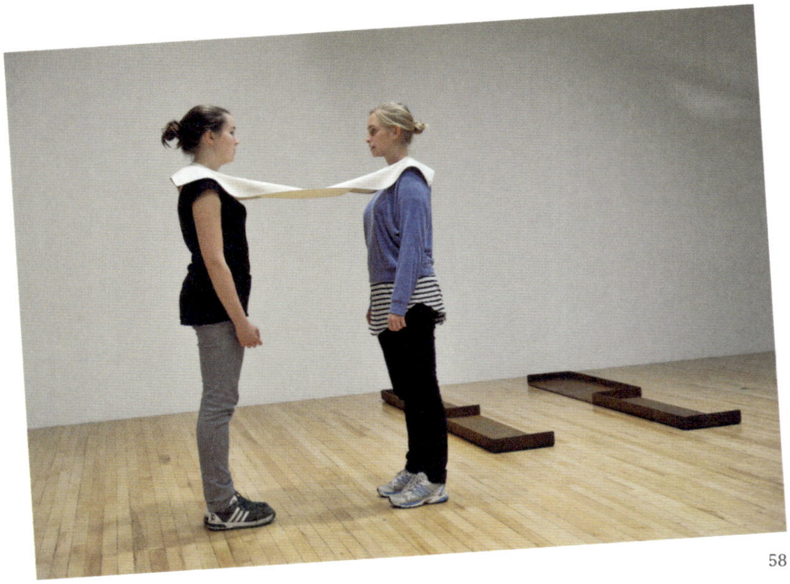

Franz Erhard Walther, Für Zwei (Nr. 31, 1. Werksatz) (For Two [No. 31, First Work Set]), 1967

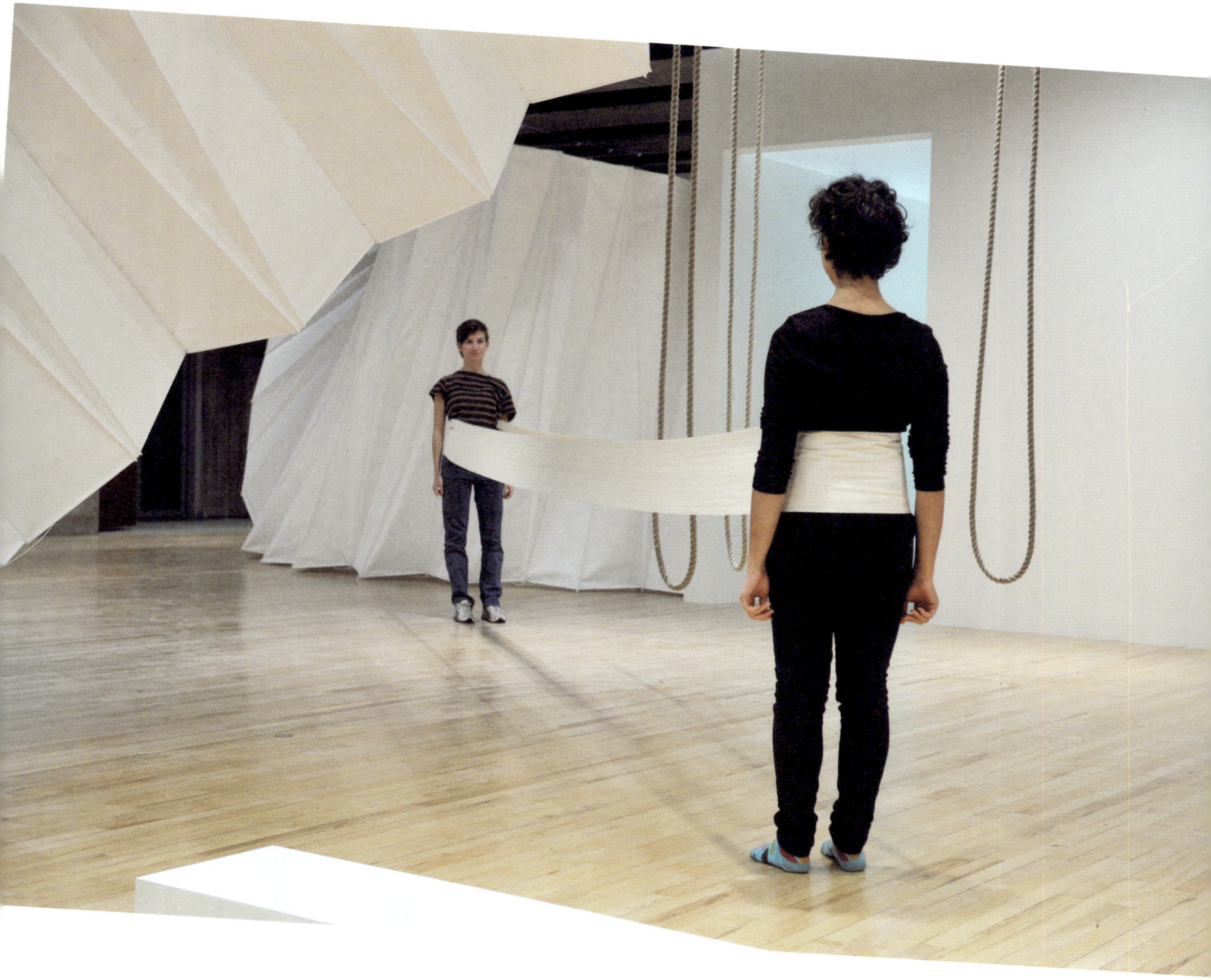

Franz Erhard Walther, Körpergewichte (Nr. 48, 1. Werksatz) (Body Weights [No. 48, First Work Set]), 1966

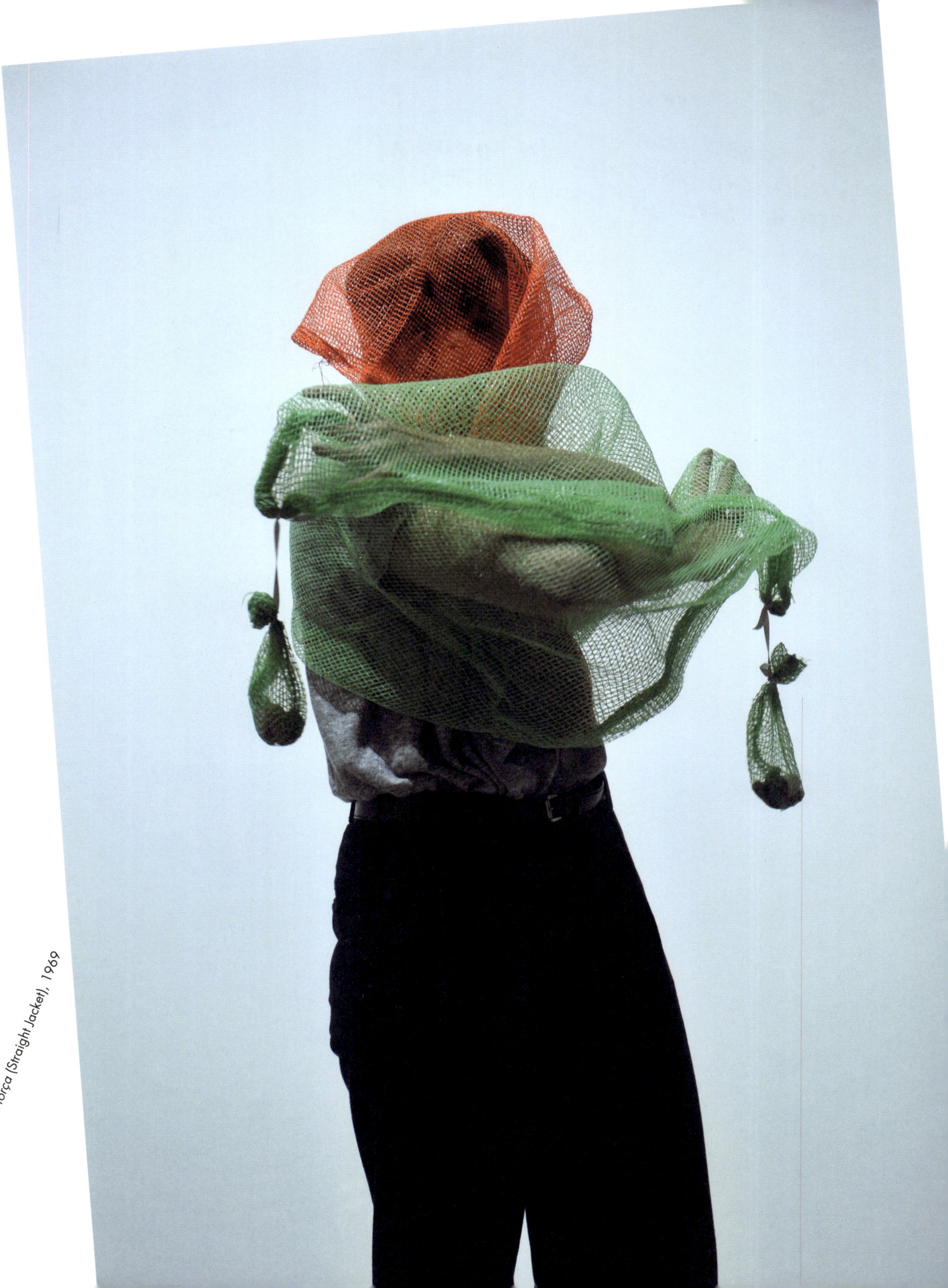

Lygia Clark, *Camisa-de-força (Straight Jacket)*, 1969

Lygia Clark
The House is the Body. Penetration, ovulation, germination, expulsion (1968); Straight Jacket (1969); Elastic Net (1973)

Lygia Clark's artistic career began with an emphasis on visuality: from 1947 to the mid-1960s, she successively made drawings, paintings and sculptures. However, following the creation of *Caminhando* in 1963, Clark's work gradually shifted towards an investigation of corporeality, that involved the making of interactive objects. This meticulous research culminated with her last proposal: the development of a psychophysical therapy entitled *The Structuring of the Self* which she practised until her death in 1988. This shift in artistic matters, materials and modes of operation, was conducted simultaneously on four levels: through a progressive destabilisation of the art object; through a systematic transformation of the spectator into active creator; through the dissipation of the traditional notion of authorship; and through the gradual abandonment of the artistic milieu together with its modes of production and consumption.

Clark worked sequentially: As a realist draughtsman at the beginning of her career. As a geometric abstract painter inventing pictorial procedures such as the 'organic line' and the 'light line', deconstructing the painting's frame and ultimately abandoning the two-dimensional support in favour of the relief's 'active density'.[1] As a cubist sculptor, inviting the public to manipulate interactive objects that she suggestively titled *Bichos* (a noun that in Portuguese means living creatures, animals, insects, or beasts). As a creator of *Sensorial Objects*, masks, clothes and installations to be experienced by participants. As a proponent of actions to be collectively or individually performed by collaborators. Finally, as a therapist who applied *Relational Objects* to the bodies of her patients during private sessions of 'art by appointment'.[2] Moving from the creation of art objects to be viewed, to the creation of practices with objects to be embodied, Clark developed a poetic and ethical dimension in her work where rigid separations between object and body, spectatorship and authorship, aesthetics and healing, art and not-art, were drastically destabilised. Today, due to its sophisticated approach on corporeality, liminality and embodied politics, Clark's oeuvre has influenced contemporary dancers and choreographers – Lia Rodrigues, Meg Stuart, Vera Mantero to cite a few – interested in investigating psychophysical expansion, participatory dramaturgies and organic objecthood.

The three works selected for this exhibition mark critical moments in Clark's process of metamorphosing the art object and of increasing the public's active participation and mobility. *The House is the Body: Penetration, ovulation, germination, expulsion* (1968) is an eight-metre long installation. Clark described the work's mode of operation as follows:

While penetrating into the labyrinth, the visitor confronts several elastics stretched at the entryway thus experiencing a rupturing similar to a complacent hymen. This entrance gives access to the first compartment called 'penetration'. In this cabin, the person steps on a canvas stretched a few inches above the ground and loses equilibrium: in the darkness, the visitor reaches for the walls that, just as the ground, yield. Using the sense of touch to follow the path, the person will then find another passage similar to the entryway. This is the arrival at 'ovulation' a space similar to the previous one, but full of balloons. Proceeding, the visitor then arrives at the big central area where it is possible to see and to be seen from the outside. In this place there is a huge mouth through which the person enters into 'germination' – a space where visitors can accommodate themselves. Back in the tunnel, continuing the path, one penetrates the 'expulsion' compartment, filled with soft little balls on the floor and a forest of hair hanging from the ceiling.[3]

This large-scale but intimate space – designed for an erotic and ludic intertwinement of imagination, memory and actuality, and conceived to offer 'the visitor' a sensorial, symbolic and phantasmagorical experience of the body's interiority, of an intravaginal or uterine life – emphatically weaves together object and subject as well as outsides and insides.

Unlike *The House is the Body*, the work *Straight Jacket* (1969) is not a large structure built in a museum or gallery, but an assemblage of six nylon bags, some stones and elastic bands, that the user can wear anywhere. Clark's description reads: 'One of the bags covers the head. On the backside of the bag, tied up with a rubber band, there is another smaller bag of the same material, containing a stone inside. From each side of the large bag hang two other bags that cover the arms. From these bags hang two other smaller bags with stones inside'.[4] *Straight Jacket* is one of Clark's *Sensorial Objects*, a series of pieces designed to activate and expand sensorial awareness.[5] It is an object that only gains form and function if incorporated and energised by the user's psychophysical response. Clark was inspired to create this piece after watching a documentary about a psychiatric hospital where doctors and nurses, instead of using strait-jackets to control a patient's crisis, would hug the person to calm him or her down. While wearing and moving with Clark's *Straight Jacket*, one experiences a subtle loss of stability thanks to the stones' weight and momentum, and the bags' and elastics' haphazard mobility. This simple object, subtly yet profoundly, disorganises the habitual anatomical architecture of the body, triggering not only postural and kinetic reactions, but also sensorial, imaginary and mnemonic responses. This jacket-mask, which extends the arms and covers the face, activates psychophysical awareness and augments one's capacity to listen to one's body. It is a paradoxical machine: by introspecting, it expands; by constraining, it liberates.

As described by Clark, the manufacture of *Straight Jacket* implies the use of rubber bands to close the bags and to connect them. The use of elastic bands rather than knots to join parts or to tie bags is a common procedure in her work. Knots do not allow the elasticity required to compose her bio-objects; they are not compatible with our organic geometries.

Dozens of interwoven elastic rings are used to build the *Elastic Net* (1973). This work is part of a phase that Clark called the 'Phantasmatic of the Body' or 'Collective Body', a period where she developed several proposals with her students at the Sorbonne in Paris.[6] Unlike *Straight Jacket*, *Elastic Net* is a collective practice, thus raising awareness of, with and through others. According to Clark, in order to create a collective body, the act of assembling the elastics together is as important as the act of incorporating the web, moving it and being moved by it. The creation and experiencing of the collective through the *Elastic Net* involves expansions and contractions of affects and motions, as well as the apparition and sharing of the participants' phantasmatics. This flexible web resembling molecular networks and tissues is an 'objectact' – to cite the inspired concept elaborated by Hélio Oiticica, who suggests that 'the object is the discovery of the world at every instant'. He argues: 'we should not limit ourselves to face academically and comfortably the object as a new category that substitutes painting and sculpture. The conceptualization and formulation of the object is nothing more than a bridge to access the instant, *objectact*'.[7] Lygia Clark is a creator of objectacts that partake in the relational potency and precarious condition of every living body.

The House is the Body, *Straight Jacket* and *Elastic Net* can be experienced as relational machines that one triggers while being triggered by them, that one moves while being moved by them. These works announce a poetics of radical precariousness that manifests itself theoretically and politically: while destabilising strict separations between art and non-art, aesthetics and ethics, object and act, objectivity and subjectivity, they bring elasticity to rigid definitions of spectator, artist, work of art and art itself. Clark's processes generate a 'state of art-without-art',[8] a paradoxical and precarious state-of-things that emancipates aesthetics from rigid frames.

Eleonora Fabião

1 The expression 'active density' is proposed by Paulo Herkenhoff when referring to Clark's *Counter Relief* series. In *A Aventura Planar de Lygia Clark: de Caracóis, Escadas e Caminhando*, Museu de Arte Moderna, São Paulo, 1999, p. 26.
2 Expression used by Lula Wanderley during a talk about Lygia Clark's work delivered at the House of the World Cultures, *In Transit Festival*, Berlin, 2004.
3 In *Lygia Clark*, Funarte, Rio de Janeiro, 1980, p. 33.
4 *Lygia Clark*, Fundació Antonio Tàpies, Barcelona, 1998, p. 242.
5 The *Straight Jacket* is presented as one of the *Sensorial Objects* in the official website of Clark's work: http://www.lygiaclark.org.br/defaultpt.asp.
6 For a detailed discussion of Clark's work phases, see Suely Rolnik's 'Molding a Contemporary Soul: The Empty-Full of Lygia Clark', in *The Experimental Exercise of Freedom*, Rina Carvajal (org.), The Museum of Contemporary Art, Los Angeles, 1999.
7 Hélio Oiticica, *GAM #15*, Galeria de Arte Moderna, Rio de Janeiro, 1968, pp. 26–27.
8 An expression formulated by the Brazilian art critic Mário Pedrosa to describe Clark's operations.

Lygia Clark was born in Belo Horizonte, Brazil in 1920 and died in Rio De Janeiro in 1988. She also lived and worked in Paris on and off for many years.

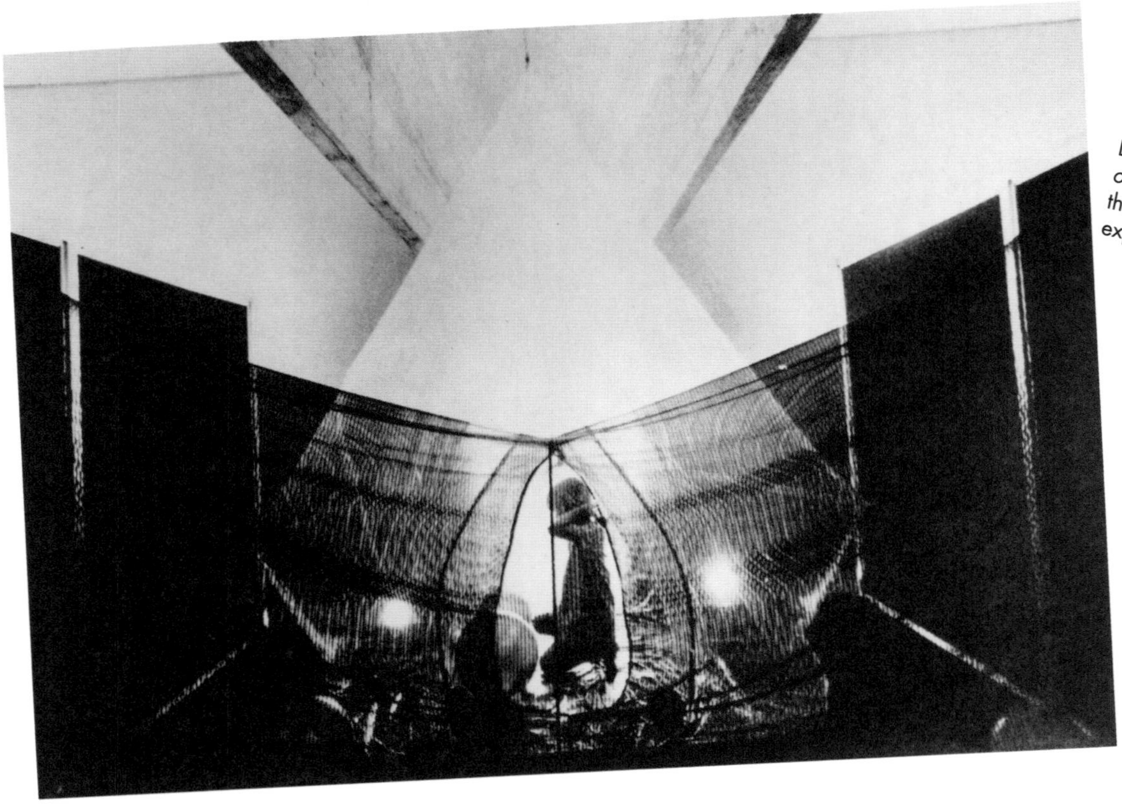

Lygia Clark, *A casa é corpo. Penetração, ovulação, germinação, expulsão* (The House is the Body. Penetration, ovulation, germination, expulsion), 1968

Lygia Clark, *Rede de elástico* (*Elastic Net*), 1973

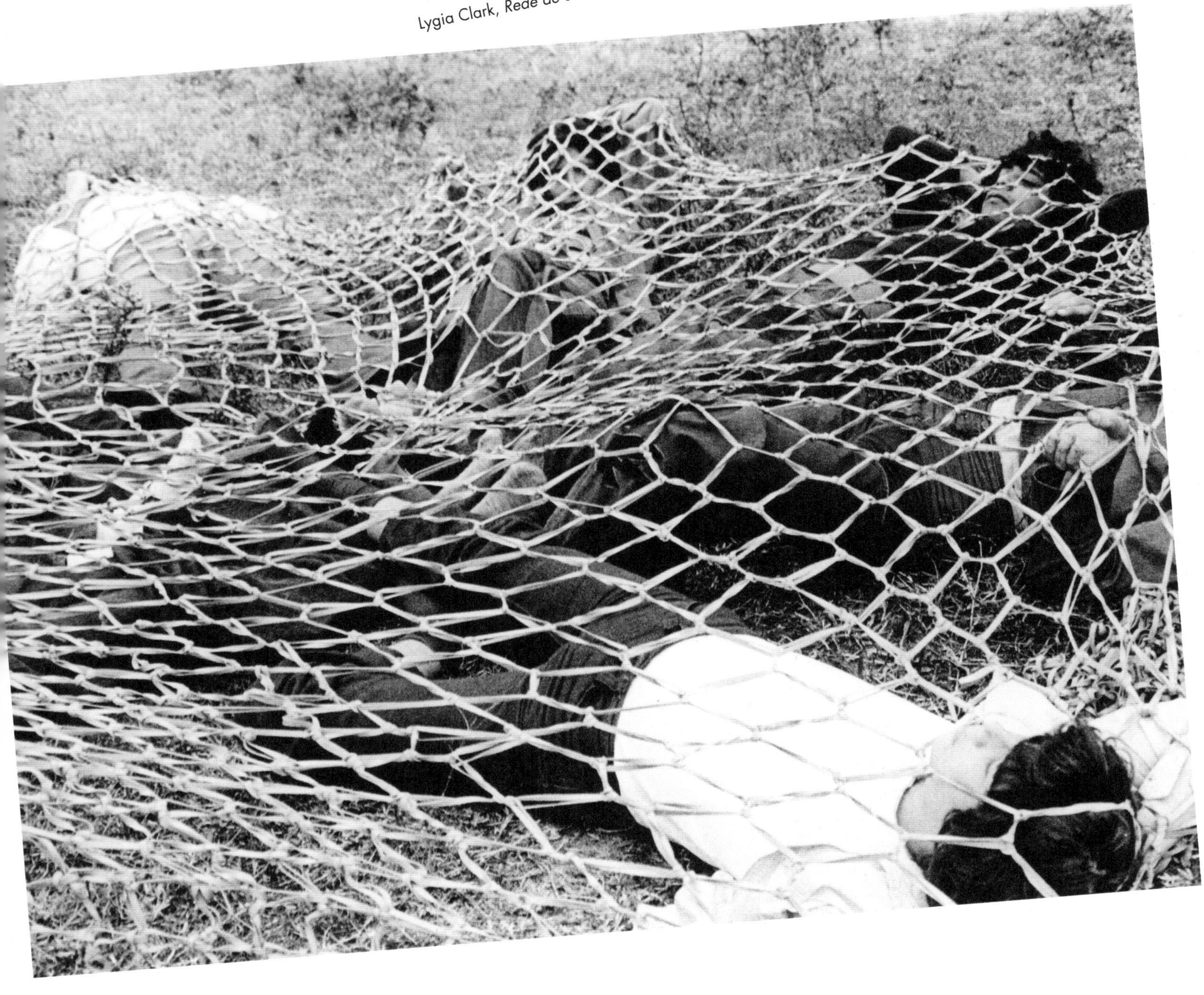

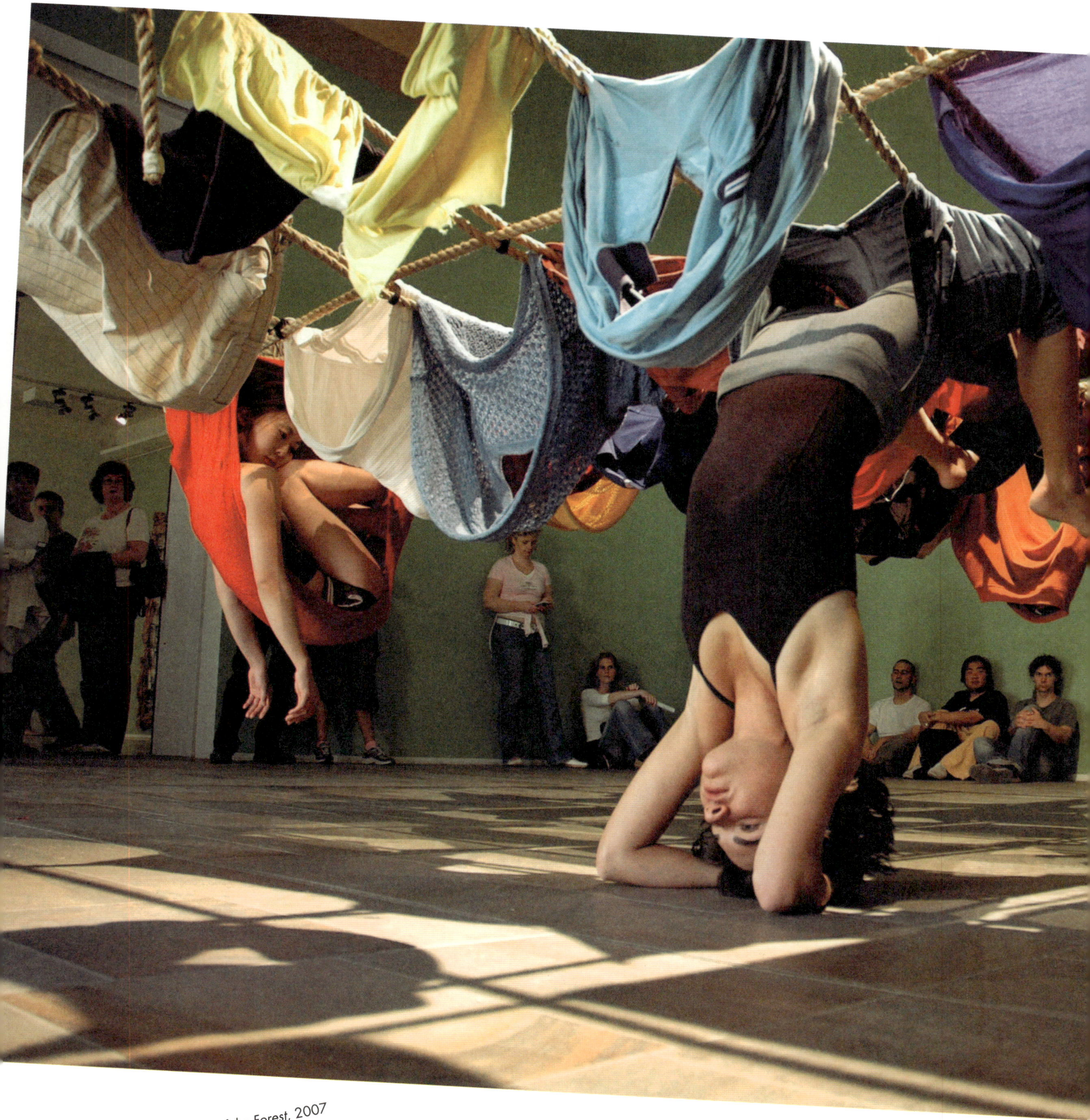

Trisha Brown, *Floor of the Forest*, 2007
(first performed 1970)

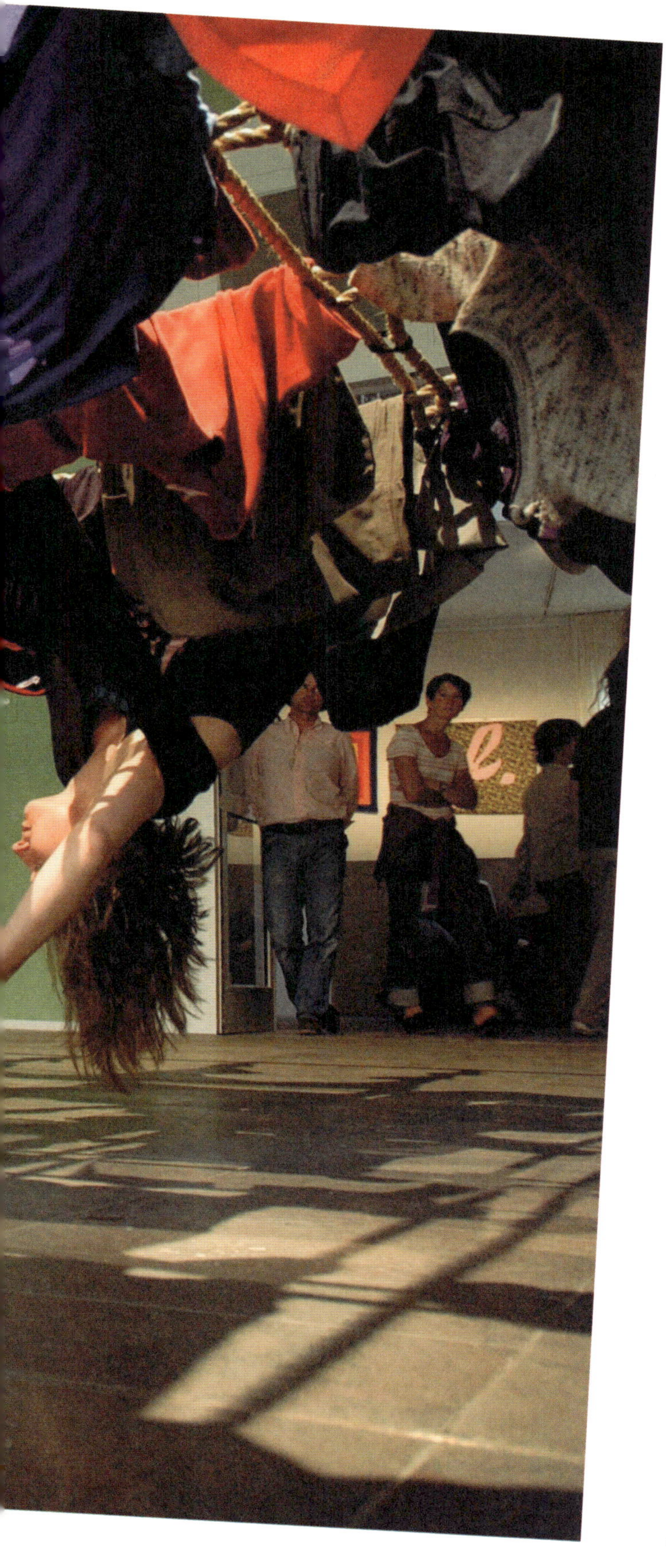

Trisha Brown

The Stream (1970); Floor of the Forest (1970); Drift (1974)

Trisha Brown's choreographic work dates back to the early 1960s. Like Simone Forti and Yvonne Rainer, she developed her training in modern dance through the use of improvisatory techniques explored in summer workshops in California with Anna Halprin. Brown relocated to New York in 1961 and participated in the Judson workshop series, exploring new concepts of composition and performance, inspired in part by John Cage's musical investigations. The results of these workshops were a series of dance concerts that have since been acknowledged as the seedbed for Postmodernism in choreography. Brown's interest at this point was in how improvisation revealed the potential for a different engagement with an audience, away from the heroism of the perfect body replete with the 'glazed-over' look of modern dance: 'At Judson, the performers looked at each other and the audience; they breathed audibly, ran out of breath, sweated, talked things over. They began behaving more like human beings, revealing what was thought of as deficiencies as well as their skills.'[1]

At the close of the 1960s and into the 1970s, Brown took this attention to a more human style of communication into a cycle of works that have become known as her 'Equipment Pieces'. The most iconic of these is perhaps *Man Walking Down The Side of A Building* (1970), which is exactly what the title promises: a man in a harness walking down a seven-storey building in downtown New York. This simple switch in the orientation of an everyday activity was carried into another piece presented the same day in a public space in SoHo: *Floor of the Forest* (1970). Two performers traversed a rope grid suspended from a frame, undressing and dressing again as they climbed. Brown, herself one half of this duet, recounts:

> Two people dressed and undressed their way through the structure [...] It was done as naturally as it could be done. A normally vertical activity performed horizontally and reshaped by the vertical pull of gravity. It was strenuous. Great strain and effort to support the body weight while negotiating buttons and zippers. We rested at times, and when we rested hanging down, an article of clothing became a hammock. The audience ducked down to see the performers suspended or climbing below the frame, or stretched upward to see the activity above.[2]

Here Brown emphasises the key element: an active invitation to the audience to reconsider their habitual perceptions of movement. This invitation arguably persists throughout all of her work, even as she moved into more conventional theatrical spaces in the late 1970s. In these early 'Equipment Pieces', she is playing with the reframing of an activity with which any member of the audience would be

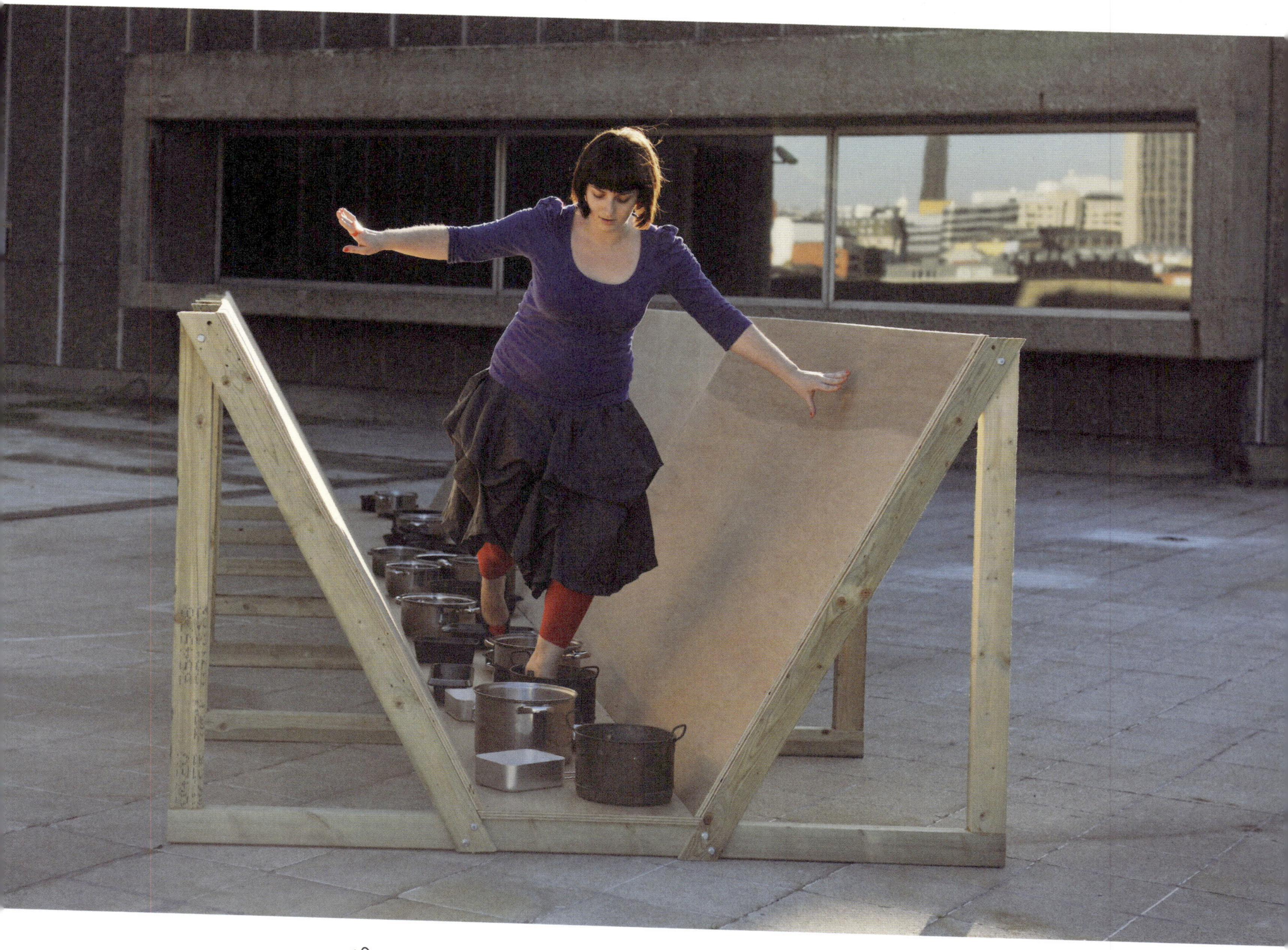

Trisha Brown, The Stream, 1970/2010

familiar – walking, dressing – and using props and environments to reconfigure them, translating them into a performance not through abstraction or representation but through a physical reconsideration of effort and gravity. Another work in this cycle, *The Stream* (1970) is a rare instance where Brown dispenses with any performers other than the audience themselves. The U-shaped structure, filled with pots and pans, seems to hint at domesticity, but Brown's invitation to participants is to defamiliarise themselves with these everyday objects and step into the water if they wish, turning the chore of washing up into a new upside-down experience, their feet rather than their hands dipping into the sink.

Drift (1974) is again concerned with perception. In this choreography, like many others from the period, Brown takes the act of walking and asks what adjustments can be made to this literally pedestrian activity to raise questions about how the body moves and how we see this movement. *From Walking on the Wall* (1971), which had the performers strolling at 90 degrees to the floor along the walls of the Whitney Museum, to the *Leaning Duets* (1970–71), where a pair of pedestrians negotiated each other's weight by inclining away from each other whilst stepping along the street, Brown used gravity to twist an idle perambulation into an act of full-bodied performance. In both cases the dancers had to rethink each step, not taking for granted how it would land and where the next one would take them. *Drift* is more subtle in its reworking of walking. The straight line of dancers shifts ever so slightly and slowly as it progresses, skewing the line of travel and in doing so asking us to skew our thoughts about an action we see all around us as we walk through the city or gallery.

Martin Hargreaves

1 Trisha Brown, in Anne Livet, *Contemporary Dance*, Abbeville Press, New York, 1978, p. 48.
2 Ibid., p. 51.

Trisha Brown was born in Aberdeen, Washington in 1936 and lives and works in New York.

Trisha Brown, The Stream, 1970

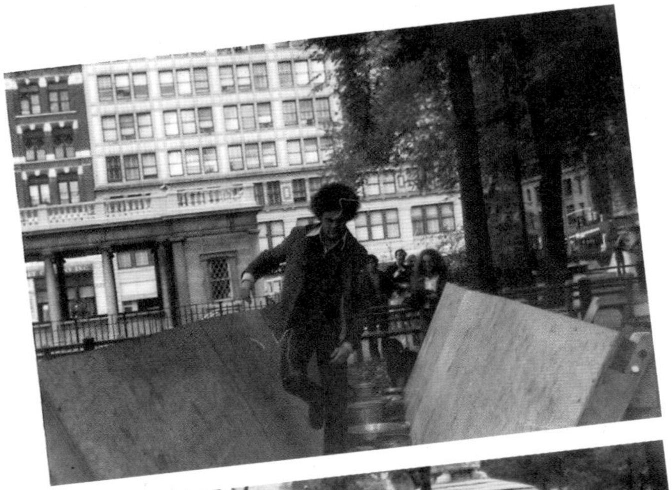

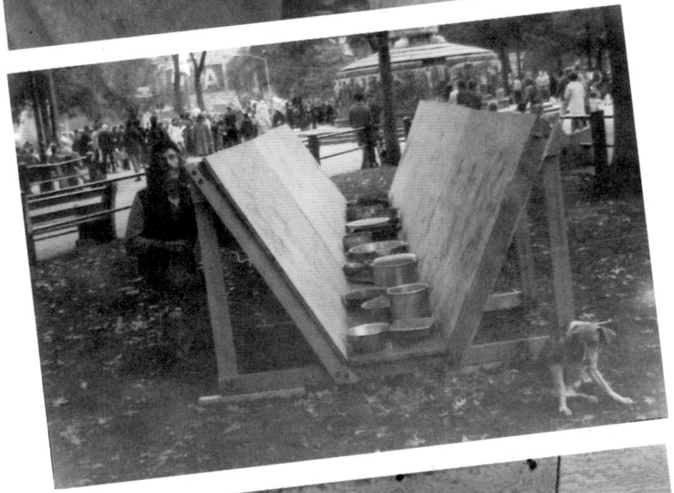

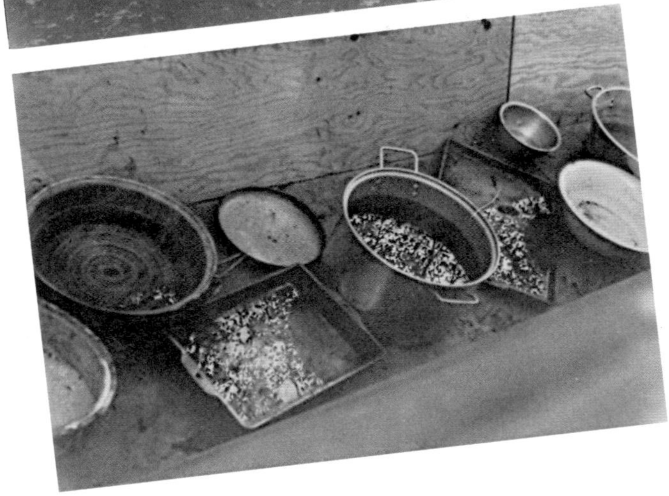

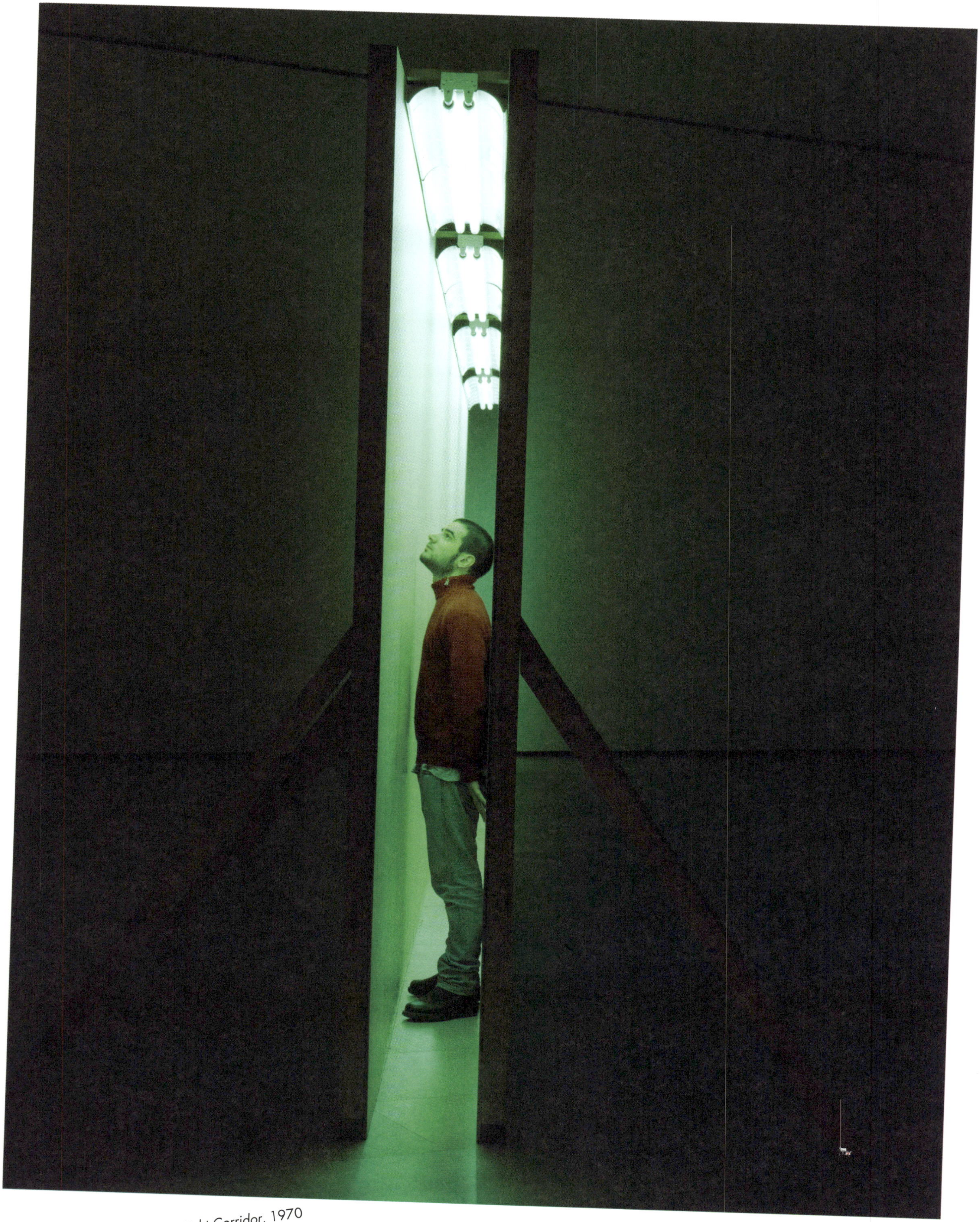

Bruce Nauman, *Green Light Corridor*, 1970

Bruce Nauman
Green Light Corridor (1970)

Green Light Corridor (1970) brings together some of the main concerns of Bruce Nauman's practice that have emerged since he first began making work in California in the mid-1960s. It invites us to experience our individual physical reactions to a narrow structure, saturated with a green neon glow. As a sculpture it does not visually represent an abstracted ideal but instead addresses itself directly to the body of the visitor, who participates in, and completes the work by responding to it, walking through it with a heightened awareness of how it shapes the relationship between the body and space. Nauman has used neon regularly in his work because of the specific experience it creates for the visitor. He has noted that some people find the green colour relaxing, while in others – including him – it creates a tense feeling. The experience, he says, is 'more like being in a liquid at first, so that there [is] a very strong psychological and physiological response involved'.[1]

Writing in *Artforum* the same year as *Green Light Corridor* was conceived, curator and critic Marcia Tucker suggested that Nauman's range of pieces in various media 'defy our habitual esthetic expectations. To encounter one of these pieces is to experience basic phenomena that have been isolated, inverted, taken out of context, or progressively destroyed'. In this scrutiny of sensations there is a re-siting of the work away from the skill or knowledge of the artist and towards the active participatory experience of the viewer: 'Where earlier the artist was the subject and object of recorded situations, now it is the spectator who becomes both the actor and observer of his own activity.'[2]

In this attention to the productivity rather than passivity of the audience, Nauman is building on the democratisation of art promoted by John Cage in the 1950s, which had a widespread influence across all art forms in 1960s America. For Nauman, this relocation of work onto the body of the spectator arose out of investigations centred on his own performing body. He made a series of films in which he carries out instructional movement in his studio, at first in California in 1967–8 and then in New York from 1968–69. A film such as *Walking in an Exaggerated Manner around the Perimeter of a Square* (1967–8) shows him doing just that. A taped square on his studio floor frames the action, and his informal clothing of jeans and t-shirt shifts the emphasis onto the formal completion of the task. The exaggeration promised by the title, however, skews the pedestrianism into an absurd performance, revealing an explicit interest in the reframing of a mundane activity in order to draw attention to a physical process that in everyday life the body has learnt to ignore. At the same time, choreographers such as Trisha Brown and Yvonne Rainer were using dance with precisely these intentions. Nauman has cited his connection with choreographer Meredith Monk as being instrumental in understanding how his attention to bodily awareness can be considered as dance:

> [...] I guess I thought of what I was doing as dance because I was familiar with some of the things that Cunningham had done and some other dancers, where you can take any simple movement and make it into a dance, just by presenting it as a dance. I wasn't a dancer, but I sort of thought if I took things that I didn't know how to do, but I was serious enough about them, then they would be taken seriously, which sort of works if you pick the right things.[3]

Some of Nauman's live works for galleries were sets of instructions to be performed by professional performers. A score called *Dance Piece* (1970) proposes that the gallery should hire a dancer to perform a stooped slow perambulation around an empty room for thirty minutes each day, observed by the audience from an open door. Within the score, Nauman has written a note: 'Manipulation of information that has to do with how we perceive rather than what'; here he is clearly articulating an interest in making performances that attend to the process of sensing and experiencing instead of producing singular meanings or representations.

It is not, however, that Nauman wants to give free reign to the viewer's experience. When talking about his series of corridors, beginning with the film *Walk with Contrapposto* (1968), which led to the first installation piece *Performance Corridor* (1969), he highlights the explicit restrictiveness of these works as a means to inhibit invention or improvisation. He states, 'I mistrust audience participation. That's why I try to make these works as limiting as possible.'[4] The small space and limited scope offered by *Green Light Corridor* allows one to focus on one's particular embodied experience of this intense verdant confinement, personalising the work while engaging with its limitations.

Martin Hargreaves

1 Nauman in an interview with Michele De Angelus (1980), in Janet Kraynak (ed.), *Please Pay Attention Please: Bruce Nauman's Words*, MIT Press, Cambridge, MA, 2005, p. 261.
2 Marcia Tucker, 'PheNAUMANology' (1970), reprinted in Robert C. Morgan (ed.), *Bruce Nauman*, John Hopkins University Press, London, 2002, pp. 21–3.
3 Lorraine Sciarra,, 'Bruce Nauman, January, 1972', in Janet Kraynak (ed.), *Please Pay Attention Please: Bruce Nauman's Words*, MIT Press, Cambridge, MA. 2005, p. 166.
4 Nauman in an interview with Willoughby Sharp (1970), in Janet Kraynak (ed.), *Please Pay Attention Please: Bruce Nauman's Words*, MIT Press, Cambridge, MA, 2005, p. 113.

Bruce Nauman was born in Fort Wayne, Indiana in 1941 and lives and works in New Mexico.

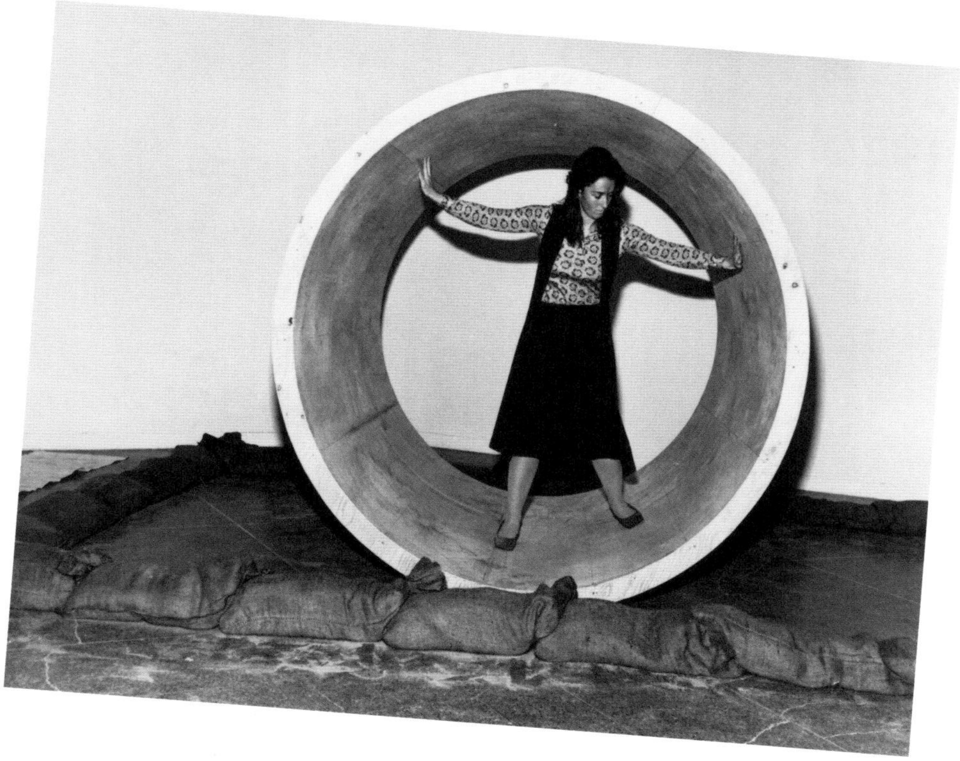

Robert Morris, *Cylinder*, Tate Gallery, London
28 April – 6 June 1971

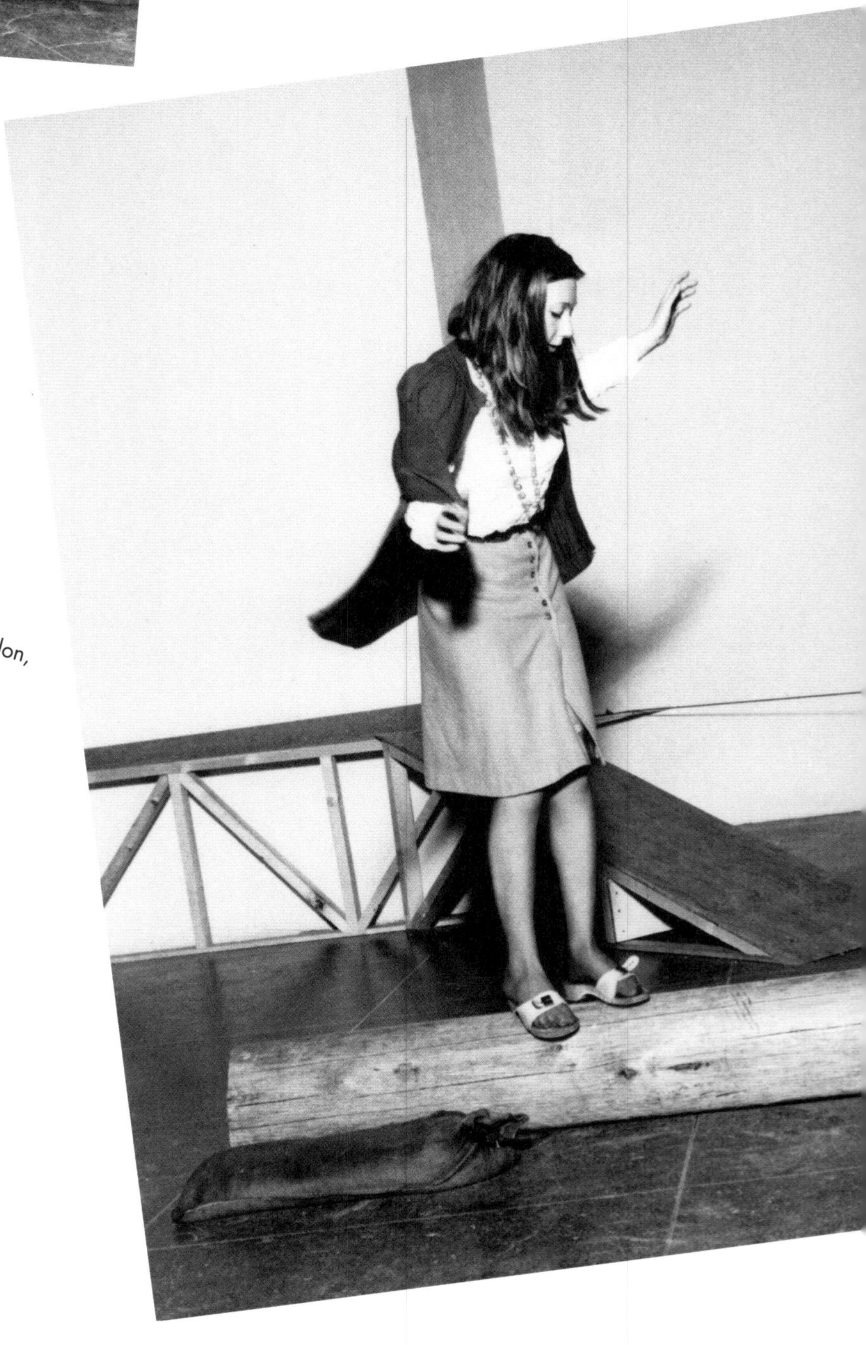

Robert Morris, *Log*, Tate Gallery, London,
28 April – 6 June 1971

Robert Morris
bodyspacemotionthings (1971/2010)

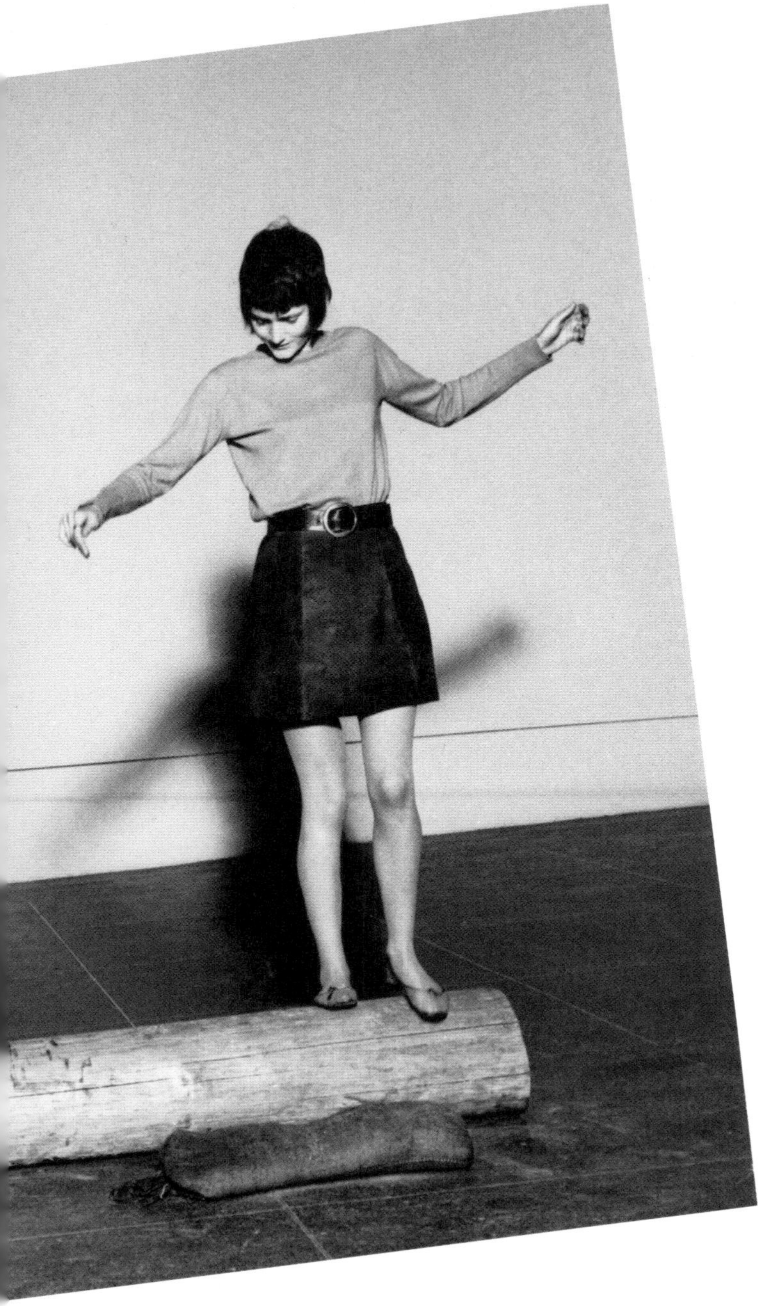

Robert Morris, whose work has embraced many different approaches, techniques and forms of expression, has described his art as 'an investigation'. Having started out as a painter, he made his first sculptures in the early 1960s. One of his earliest sculptural works was *Column* (1961). First presented as part of a concert, rather than in an exhibition, this rectangular, eight-foot high plywood structure was effectively a surrogate dancer and was allocated a seven-minute performance slot. For the first three-and-a-half minutes it stood upright before being toppled, after which it lay prone.

At this period, Morris was also making objects for dancers to interact with in 'task'-oriented performances. He had become interested in dance some years earlier in California when his first wife, Simone Forti, became involved with Anna Halprin's San Francisco Dancers' Workshop. Here, amongst other unorthodox approaches, dancers engaged in physical tasks – such as crawling up a sloping plank and sliding down it headfirst – as a means of exploring improvised movement. In 1959, Morris and Forti moved to New York and shortly afterwards, in the spring of 1961, Forti produced a programme entitled *Five Dance Constructions and Some Other Things* at Yoko Ono's loft studio. In this seminal event, each of the pieces was performed in a different part of the loft and the audience was required to move around to view them. Some of the pieces also involved simple structures which were used to generate movement. These objects, including boxes, a slanting board with ropes and a see-saw, were made by Morris and, as part of Forti's investigations into 'ordinary movement', were to have a profound impact on Morris's own sculptural work. Morris's interest in dance continued after he and Forti separated and he soon became affiliated with the newly-formed Judson Dance Theater. Between 1963 and 1966, until Yvonne Rainer, who became his partner on and off from 1964 to 1971, requested that he stop creating choreographies, Morris choreographed a number of works, including *Arizona* (1963), *Site* (1964) and *Waterman Switch* (1965), in which dancers performed a sequence of everyday actions

Robert Morris, *See-saw*, 1971/2010

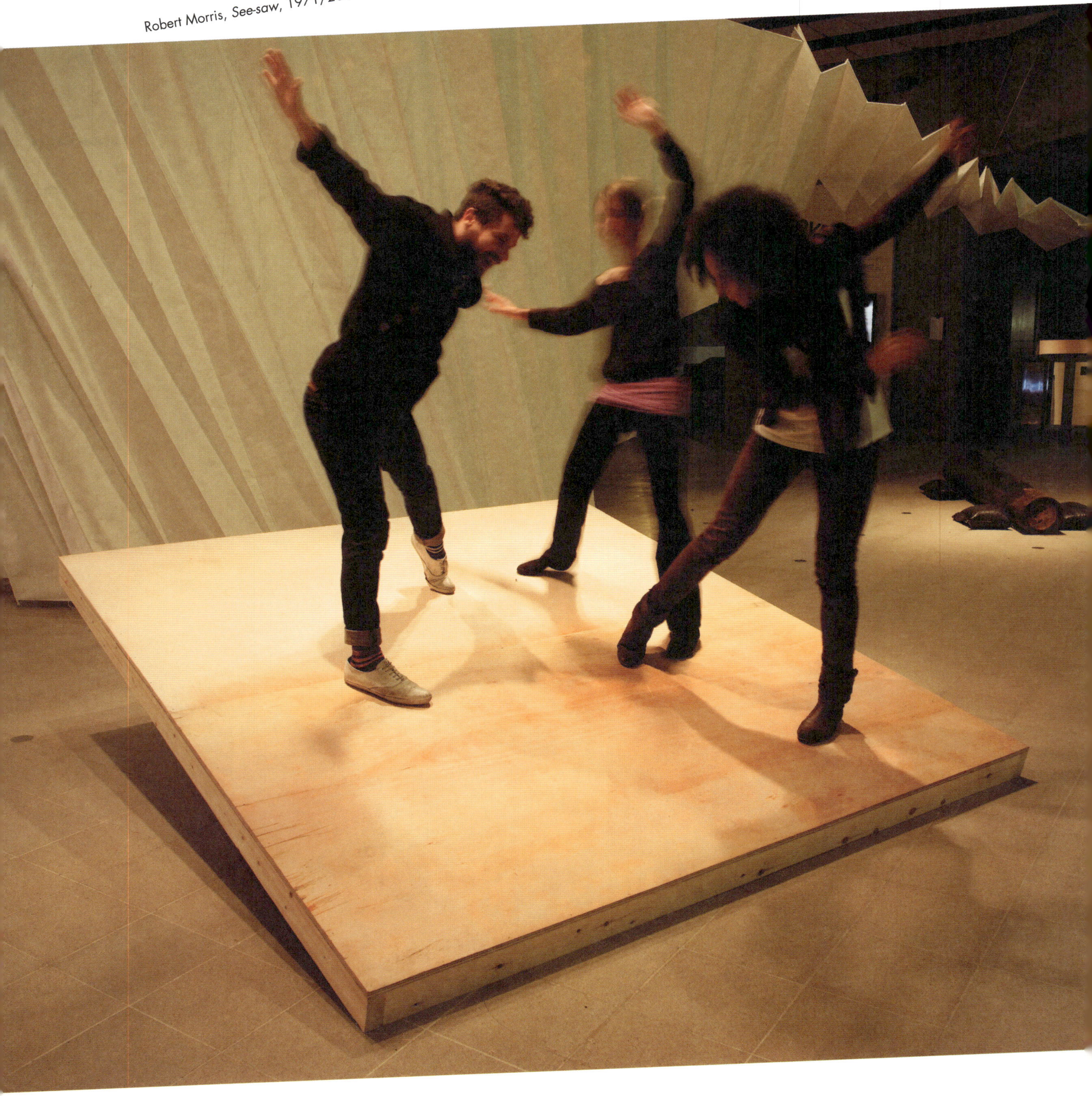

using costumes and props which he devised. During this time, Morris also emerged as an influential theorist and a pioneer of Minimalist sculpture, creating abstract, geometric forms, first in painted plywood and later in fibreglass and metal.

In 1971, at the invitation of the Tate Gallery, Morris produced the gallery's first ever fully participatory exhibition. Originally envisaged by the organisers as a conventional retrospective of his Minimalist sculptures, which though highly acclaimed were little known in Britain at that time, Morris proposed an entirely different project: an exhibition which would be 'more environmental than object-like'; where people became active participants instead of passive spectators and experienced the work with their bodies as well as their eyes. 'We have become blind from so much seeing,' he told the Tate curators. 'Time to press up against things, squeeze around, crawl over [...]' He designed a series of three interactive spaces which occupied the whole of the central Duveen Galleries in what is now Tate Britain. Describing its sequential movement from 'the manipulation of objects, to constructions which adjust to the body's presence, to situations where the body itself is manipulated,' he explained that 'the works were based on progressive physical difficulty as one proceeded toward the end of the space. Objects to handle gave way to things to balance on and then to climb on or in.'

Morris clearly expected that the response of visitors to this participatory exhibition would be similar to that of contemporary dancers, and neither he nor the Tate anticipated the degree of 'exuberant and excited behaviour' which caused the exhibition to be closed after a mere five days. The public had mistaken the project for a playground; there were minor injuries to people and damage to the works, and the worrying possibility of some more serious occurrence. The participatory element was removed and the exhibition eventually reopened as a more or less passive retrospective of static sculpture. Thirty-eight years later, the interactive element of the show was recreated as *bodyspacemotionthings* in the Turbine Hall at Tate Modern. Two of the works reconstructed for *bodyspacemotionthings* are presented here in order that visitors may not only, as Morris hoped, have 'an opportunity to involve themselves with the work, become aware of their own bodies, gravity, effort, fatigue, their bodies under different conditions', but can do so in the context of both similar and dissimilar work by other artists.

Helen Luckett

Robert Morris was born in Kansas City, Missouri in 1931 and lives and works in New York.

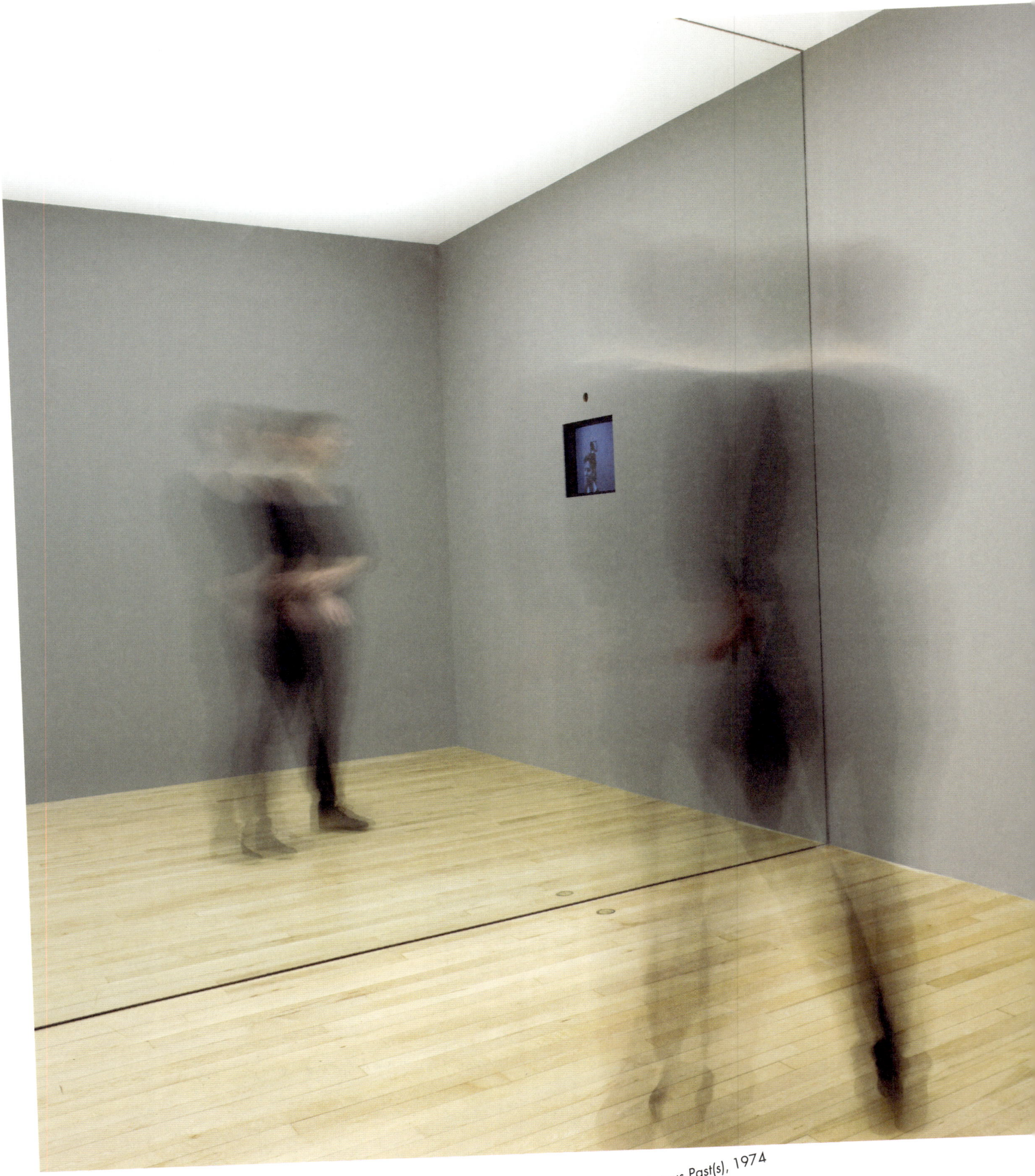

Dan Graham, *Present Continuous Past(s)*, 1974

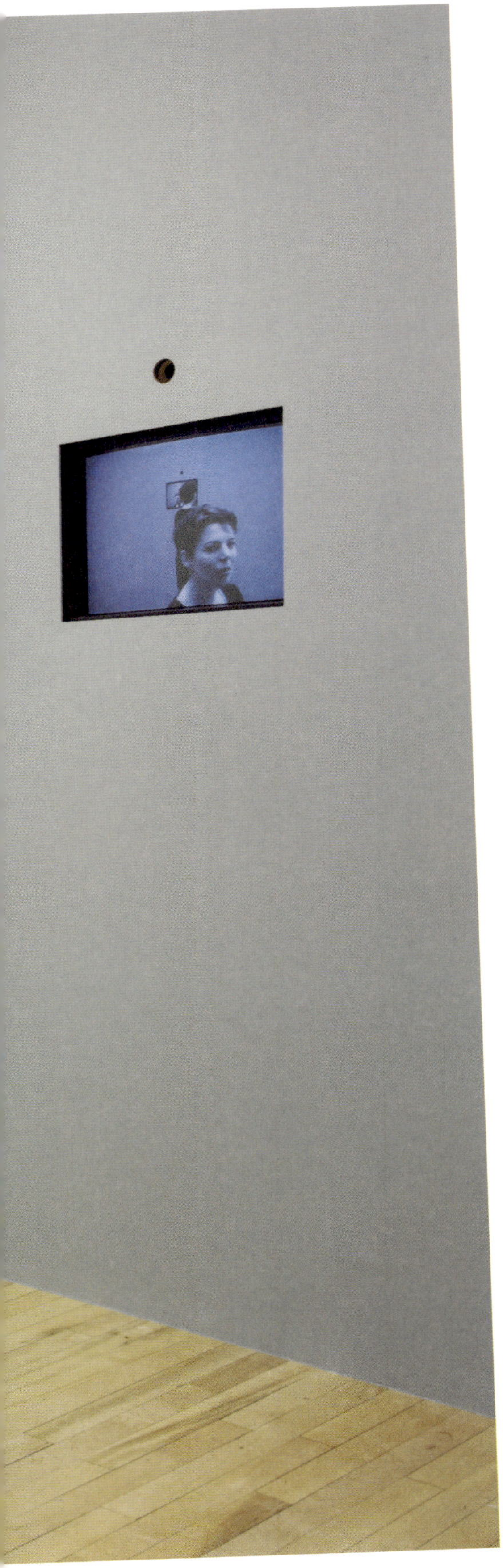

Dan Graham
Present Continuous Past(s) (1974); Two Viewing Rooms (1975)

Mirrors, performers and time-delay video – these are the elements employed in Dan Graham's experiments with perception from the 1970s. One such experiment is *Present Continuous Past(s)* (1974), a work whose title refers to a present experience haunted by not just one but several pasts. The viewer who enters this room with its mirrored walls initially finds himself transmuted into an actor; he is confronted not only with his current mirror image but with an image of himself from the immediate past. More precisely, what he sees on the monitor is his own image recorded eight seconds ago – the interval to which the time-delay is set – as well as the monitor image reflected by the mirror eight seconds ago, an image from sixteen seconds ago. Graham's technique of time-delay owes much to experiments in 1960s minimalist music, when tape-delay devices were first used.[1] In an interview with Benjamin Buchloh, Graham emphasised the significance of the musician Terry Riley's exploration and use of time-delay techniques for his work.[2]

By using mirrors, Graham has recourse to a device that comes close to being an art historical cliché (painting as a mirror onto the world). But the symbolic function of the mirror in painting is transformed by insisting on its literal use (the mirror as an instrument of reflection). Yet large mirrors such as those Graham uses are also part of the apparatus of dance, where they sustain the dancer's control over and evaluation of his or her body. It is only through the mirror image that the dancer learns whether or not a movement has been executed correctly. In the everyday life of a consumer society, mirrors are used in shop windows and changing rooms, where they force consumers to take a hard look at their own appearance. We know, however, from Lacan's famous essay on the 'Mirror Stage' that misrecognition mars the perception of the self in the mirror. According to the psychoanalyst Jacques Lacan, the subject is blind to himself because his mirror image is pervaded by projections, wishful thinking and qualities attributed to him by others.

Present Continuous Past(s) has taken Lacan's metaphor for this self-misrecognition at its word, enacting a literal splitting of the subject by exploding his relation to the present. When the past and current self-images interpenetrate, the subject's unity and self-possession are threatened. The installation insistently reminds us of the psychoanalytic truth that the past cannot be shaken off, that it profoundly interferes with our being and our actions. The time-delay intensifies this irritating experience further by imposing on the viewer an ostensibly objectifying perspective on himself. Whereas the viewer of his own current mirror image is at least able to fashion it, for example by striking a certain pose in front of the mirror, the image on the monitor amounts to an accomplished fact: this recording of myself is history; there's no changing it anymore.

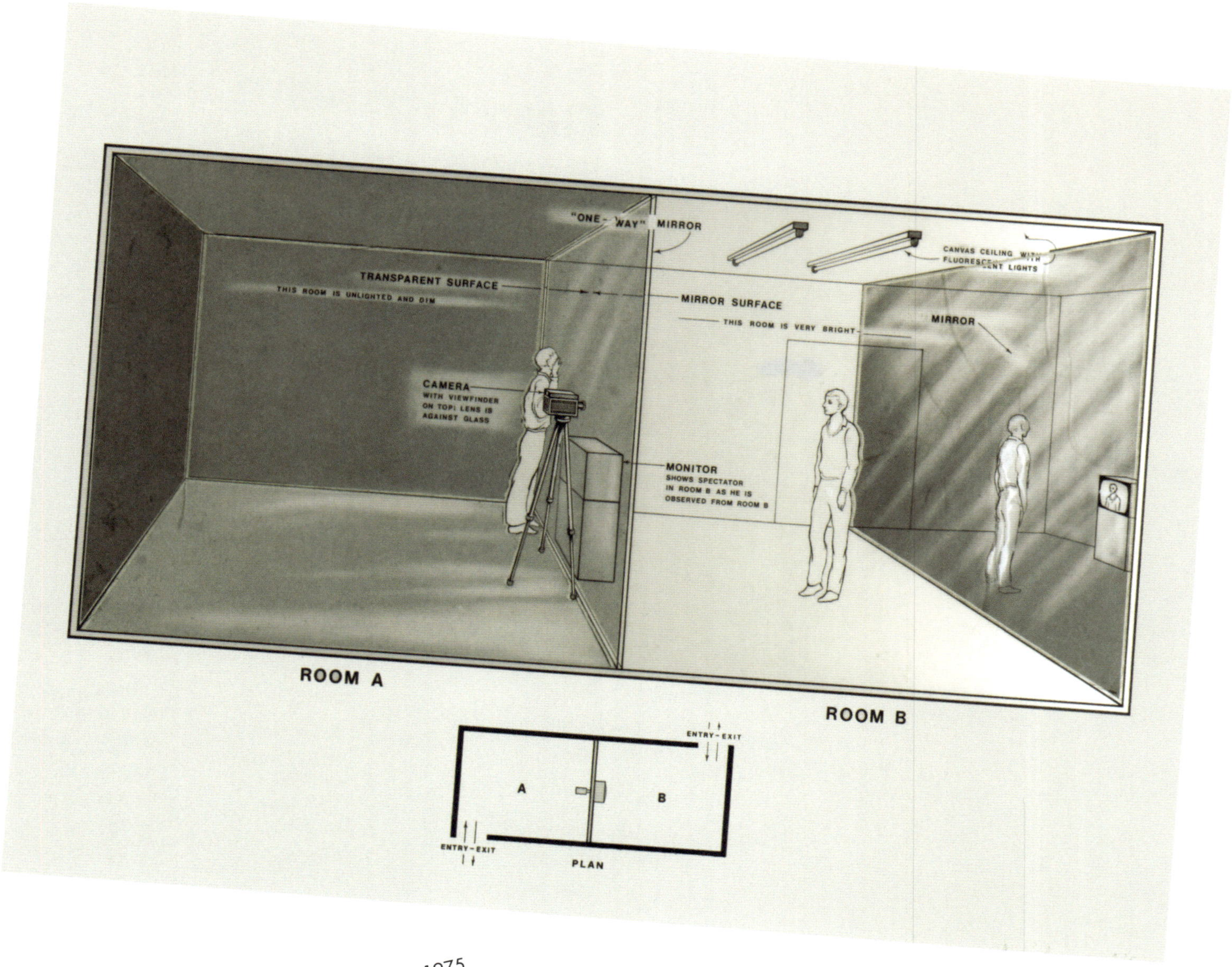

This page and opposite: Dan Graham, *Two Viewing Rooms*, 1975

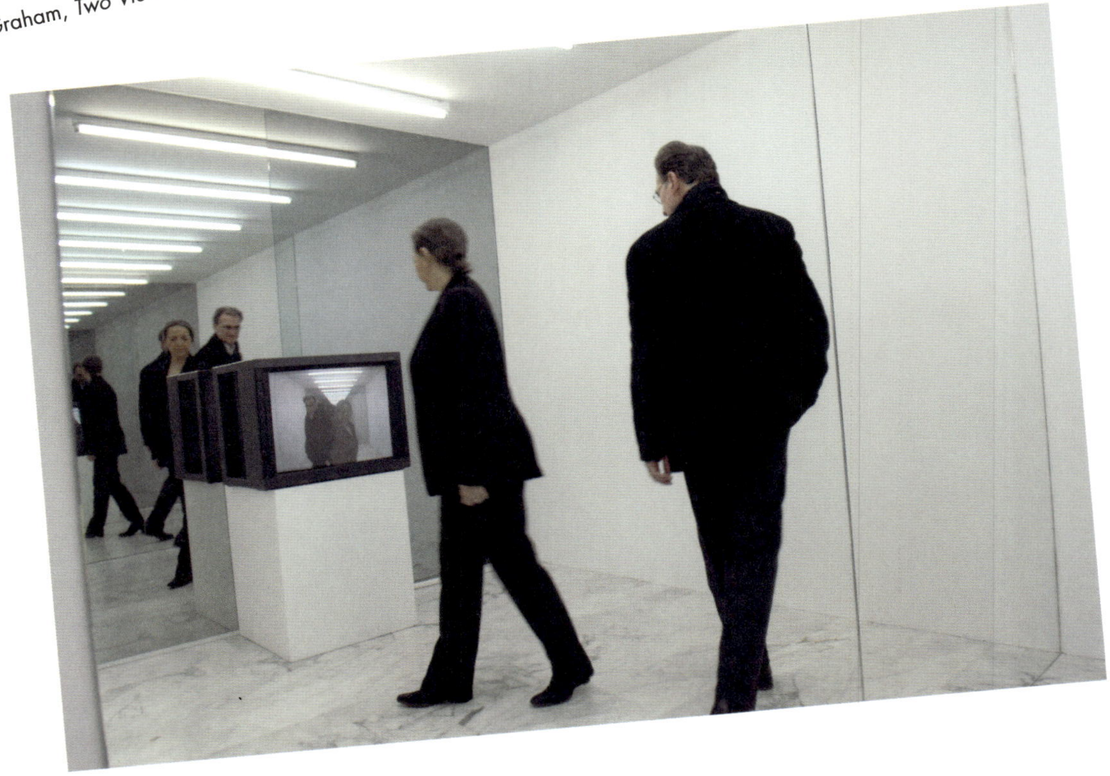

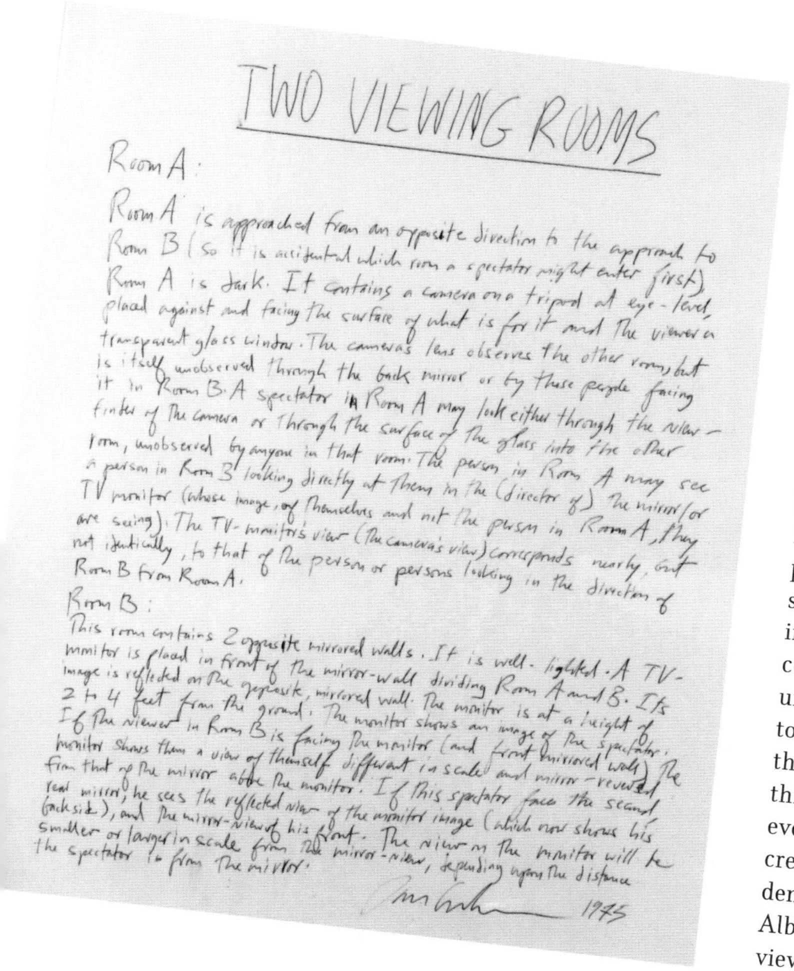

TWO VIEWING ROOMS

Room A:

Room A is approached from an opposite direction to the approach to Room B (so it is accidental which room a spectator might enter first). Room A is dark. It contains a camera on a tripod at eye-level, placed against and facing the surface of what is for it and the viewer a transparent glass window. The cameras lens observes the other room, but is itself unobserved through the back mirror or by those people facing it in Room B. A spectator in Room A may look either through the view-finder of the camera or through the surface of the glass into the other room, unobserved by anyone in that room. The person in Room A may see a person in Room B looking directly at them in the (direction of) the mirror (or TV monitor (whose image, of themselves and not the person in Room A, they are seeing). The TV-monitor's view (the camera's view) corresponds nearly, but not identically, to that of the person or persons looking in the direction of Room B from Room A.

Room B:

This room contains 2 opposite mirrored walls. It is well-lighted. A TV-monitor is placed in front of the mirror-wall dividing Room A and B. Its image is reflected on the opposite, mirrored wall. The monitor is at a height of 2 to 4 feet from the ground. The monitor shows an image of the spectator. If the viewer in Room B is facing the monitor (and front mirrored wall) the monitor shows them a view of themself different in scale and mirror-reversed from that of the mirror above the monitor. If this spectator faces the second real mirror, he sees the reflected view of the monitor image (which now shows his backside), and the mirror-view of his front. The view on the monitor will be smaller or larger in scale from the mirror-view, depending upon the distance the spectator is from the mirror.

1975

We might conclude that Graham wishes to deprive the subject of his illusions – captured by his past, split between his past and present egos, he has long ceased to be master in his own house and has lost control over himself. The problem with this reading is that it passes a little too quickly over the hopes tied in the 1960s and 1970s to works of art that pursued the viewer's participative engagement. At the time, the emphasis was not so much on an experience of compulsions and limitations but rather on the liberating potential ascribed to the viewer's involvement. In Minimal art, for example, the activation of the viewer was intended not as an attack on his integrity but as an attempt to jolt him out of his attitude of passive contemplation, to emancipate him. In *Present Continuous Past(s)*, too, aesthetic experience is conceived as an encounter with the self, and interestingly enough, Graham meant for this encounter to be a group experience rather than a solipsistic one.[3] The ideal form of reception he envisioned was in fact the mass audience of a rock concert.[4] In his large mirrors, the subject was meant to experience not merely himself but himself in relation to others.

Setting aside the fact that even in the exhibition practice of the time such an interactive group experience was an ideal vision rather than a reality, Graham's evocation of a large audience attests to his keen anticipation of the changes that the art world would undergo in the 1990s. By imagining his ideal audience as a mass public, he pre-empted the transformation of the art business: in the 1990s, a small set of insiders would grow into a mass industry manufacturing imagery and meaning. The viewers who in Graham's works are always compelled to exhibit themselves are now being prepared for a life that, under the conditions of celebrity culture, is more and more exposed to public attention, resembling life on the catwalk. It follows that the mise-en-scène of the self is of enormous importance today – and this insight, too, is at the root of Graham's mirror installations. If even during the Renaissance visual artists were required to produce credible public personae by cultivating a convincing habitus – this demand is articulated, for example, in the writings of Leon Battista Alberti – Graham delegates this artistic becoming-an-object to the viewer. The focus is here not so much on the viewers' specific qualities, such as social background or gender. What matters more is that every viewer has to stage herself in front of his mirror. This corresponds to the expectation in celebrity culture – that we are able to develop a convincing image of ourselves. Identity-related differences certainly still matter in such a situation, but they also function as just another factor in the making of our public personae.

Isabelle Graw

1 Branden Joseph, 'The Social Turn', in *Beyond the Dream Syndicate. Tony Conrad and the Arts after Cage*, Zone Books, New York 2008, p. 71.
2 Cf. Benjamin Buchloh, 'Vier Gespräche. Dezember 1999–Mai 2000', in *Dan Graham 1965–2000*, Richter Verlag, Düsseldorf 2002, p. 86.
3 'The spectator is made socially and psychologically more self-conscious: the observer becomes conscious of himself or herself as body as a perceiving subject, and of himself or herself in relation to a group'. Dan Graham, *Rock My Religion. Writings and art projects 1965–1990*, Brian Wallis (ed.), MIT Press, Cambridge, MA. 1993, p. 190.
4 Buchloh, 'Vier Gespräche', p. 75.

Dan Graham was born in Urbana, Illinois in 1942 and lives and works in New York City.

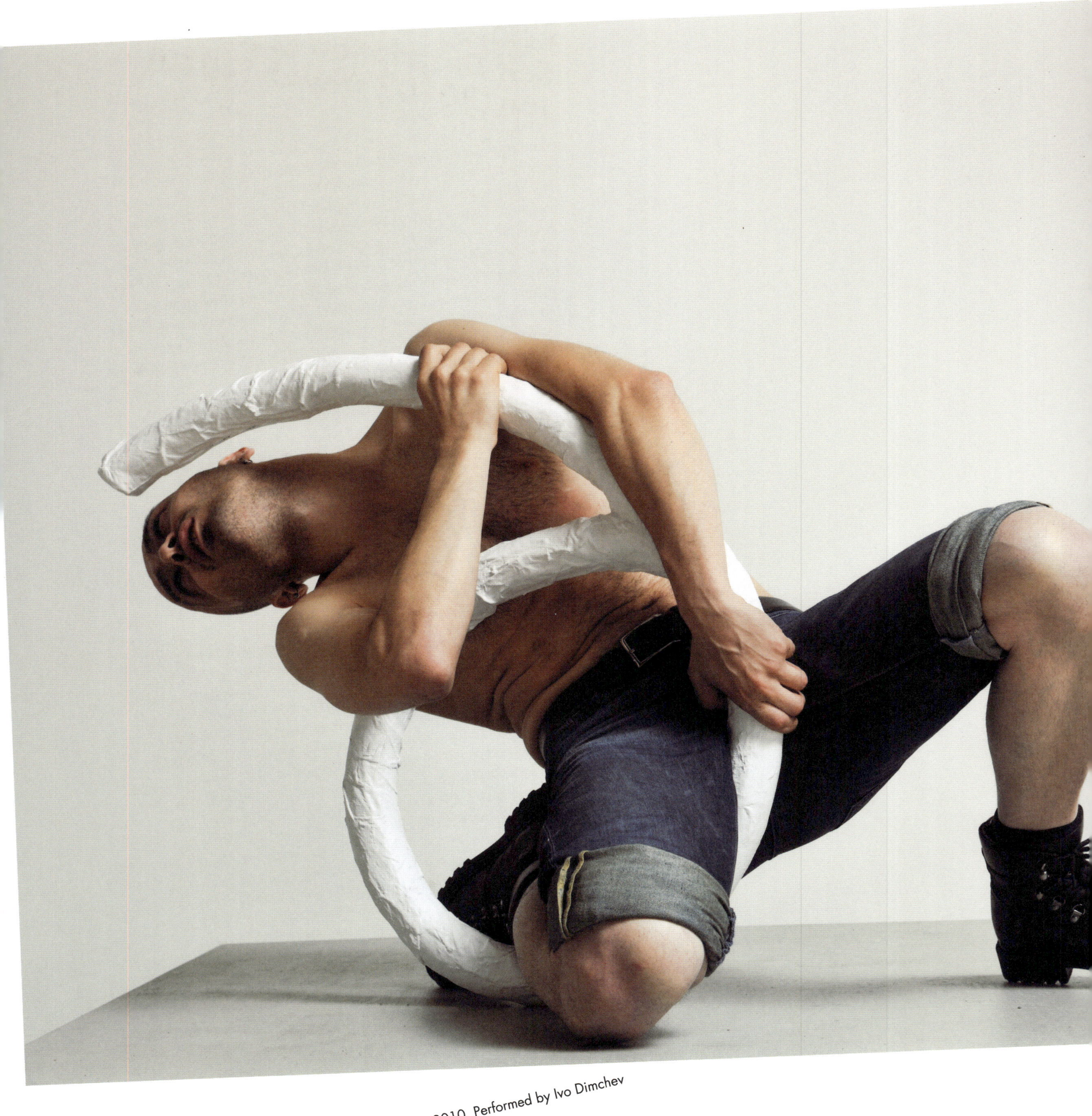

Franz West, *Ion*, 2010, Performed by Ivo Dimchev

Franz West
Self Description (2004); Ion (2010); Diwan (2010)

The Austrian sculptor Franz West began his artistic career in the aftermath of the neo-avant-garde and performance tradition of the 1960s. At this time, in his hometown of Vienna, the Vienna Actionists had performed their visceral Happenings in an attempt to rid themselves of the material, technical and formal filters that they believed created a distance between art and life. They did so by using their bodies and objects from everyday life as their means of expression. Against this background, West reworked elements from contemporaneous American art, operating on the border between Happenings, junk sculpture and Pop. Obvious predecessors are Claes Oldenburg and Jim Dine, as well as Allan Kaprow.

While West may take the moulding of objects as his starting point, these objects are often displayed in an arena or environment that invites the audience to use and interact with them. His works are experienced not only through visual and mental reflection, but also through full phenomenological participation, something that West inherited from Kaprow and Robert Morris, as well as the Fluxus movement. His preference for cheap, leftover and simple materials, such as plaster, lead, tape, nylon ribbon etc, is shared with the Italian Arte Povera artists, not to mention their great role model Joseph Beuys.

West's sculptures, whether the early plaster, wood and metal works that he calls *Paßstücke* (Adaptives or Fitting Pieces), or the more recent painted, welded aluminium sculptures, are biomorphic in form and display an ambiguity that enriches their emotional register and potential for interpretation. In many of the 'Adaptives', a small fragment of functionality is hinted at, such as the handle of a compass saw that sticks out of a shapeless lump of plaster, or two steel loops that are reminiscent of the handles of a bag, where 'the bag' is a compact plaster form moulded from the bottom of a pot. One could subtitle his 'Adaptives' 'How to Do Things with Things', for that is exactly what he sets out to do in these works. An important influence, amongst other philosophers, is the American logician Willard van Orman Quine, much-read amongst the neo-avant-garde. Quine reflects on the relationship between *Word and Object*, the title of the book he published in 1960. Here, he takes a phenomenological approach to how people learn to form and use conceptual terms through objects. He argues that those objects – which he calls 'conceptual firsts'[1] – that are just large enough for the hands to grasp become models for the creation of conceptual terms. In this way, words such as table, chair, play, cup, shoe, and so on, become imprinted early on and lead to the creation of concepts and theories, with the body as the starting point. That West's works fit the body perfectly, like hand in glove, has to do with a societal linguistic consensus that enables us to communicate, even though we all have a unique, individual experience of the world.[2]

Robert Morris had perhaps understood this in his performance, *Site* (1964), where, wearing gloves, a mask and a boiler suit, he dances a *pas de deux* with a sheet of plyboard. While this work is undoubtedly a precedent for the 'Adaptives', West goes further: he places the audience in the role of the artist, inviting us to interact with the objects, both through a dialogue with the sculpture and through mirror image, as well as with other viewers. In this way, he explores the psychological games with mirror reflection and viewing/observation/exhibitionism investigated by Dan Graham in some of his video installations made during the 1960s and 70s.

West's works are built directly on the important linguistic changes that transformed the art of the 1960s and 1970s and he never loses sight of these origins. In his 'Adaptives', he makes us explicitly aware of how an object's meaning depends on how we interact with it. As we touch his works, interact with them and move them, we experience a perceptible, almost existential closeness to the sculptures. In this friendly, inclusive and disarming way, West manages to continue the concerns of the avant-garde art at a time when the tactile, physical and phenomenological encounter between people, objects and their surroundings is threatened by immersion in the virtual world.

Otto Kobalek with *Paßstück (Adaptive)*, 1975

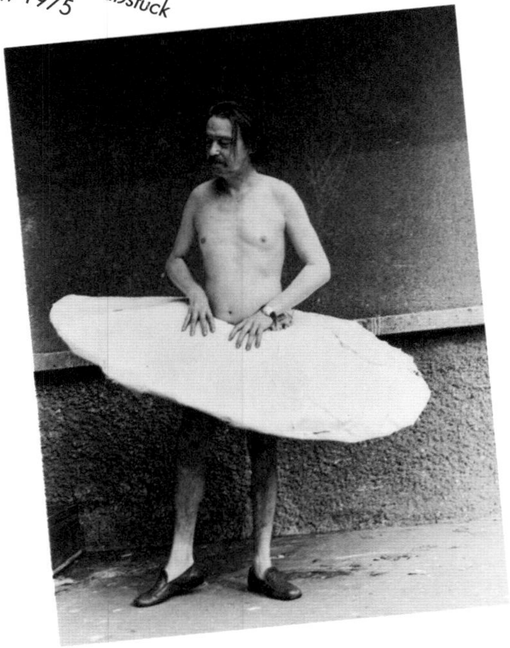

Franz West, *Paßstück (Adaptive)*, 2006

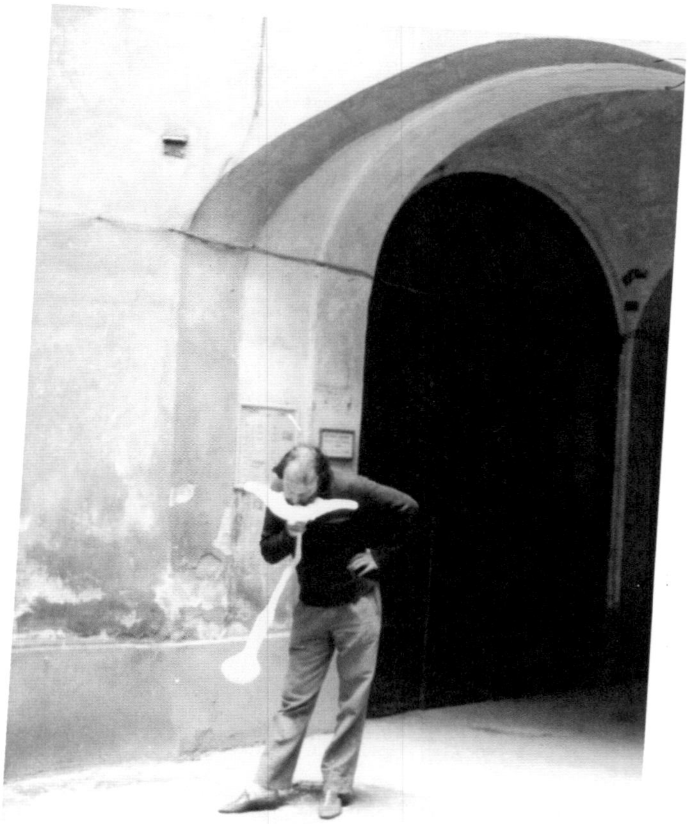

Åsmund Thorkildsen

1 Willard van Orman Quine, *Word & Object*, MIT Press, Cambridge, MA, 1960.

2 A typical example in philosophy is the use and understanding of the word 'pain'. Pain is something each and every one of us can feel, and we don't know whether we feel exactly the same, but we still use the same word for it, and it seems to work well enough in order for us to show compassion or to offer help and consolation. In *Word & Object* Quine puts it in this way about the use of the word 'Ouch', a one-word sentence we express when we feel pain:

> 'Ouch' is a one-word sentence [,] which a man may volunteer from time to time by way of laconic comment on the passing show. The correct occasion of its use are those attended by painful stimulation. Such use of the word, like the correct use of language generally, is inculcated in the individual by training on the part of society; and society achieves this despite not sharing the individual's pain [...] Society, acting solely on overt manifestations, has been able to train the individual to say the socially proper thing in response even to socially undetectable stimulations.'

This is an abridged version of a text originally published in *Franz West – Paßstücke*, Peder Lund, Oslo, 2010.

Franz West was born in Vienna, Austria in 1947, where he lives and works.

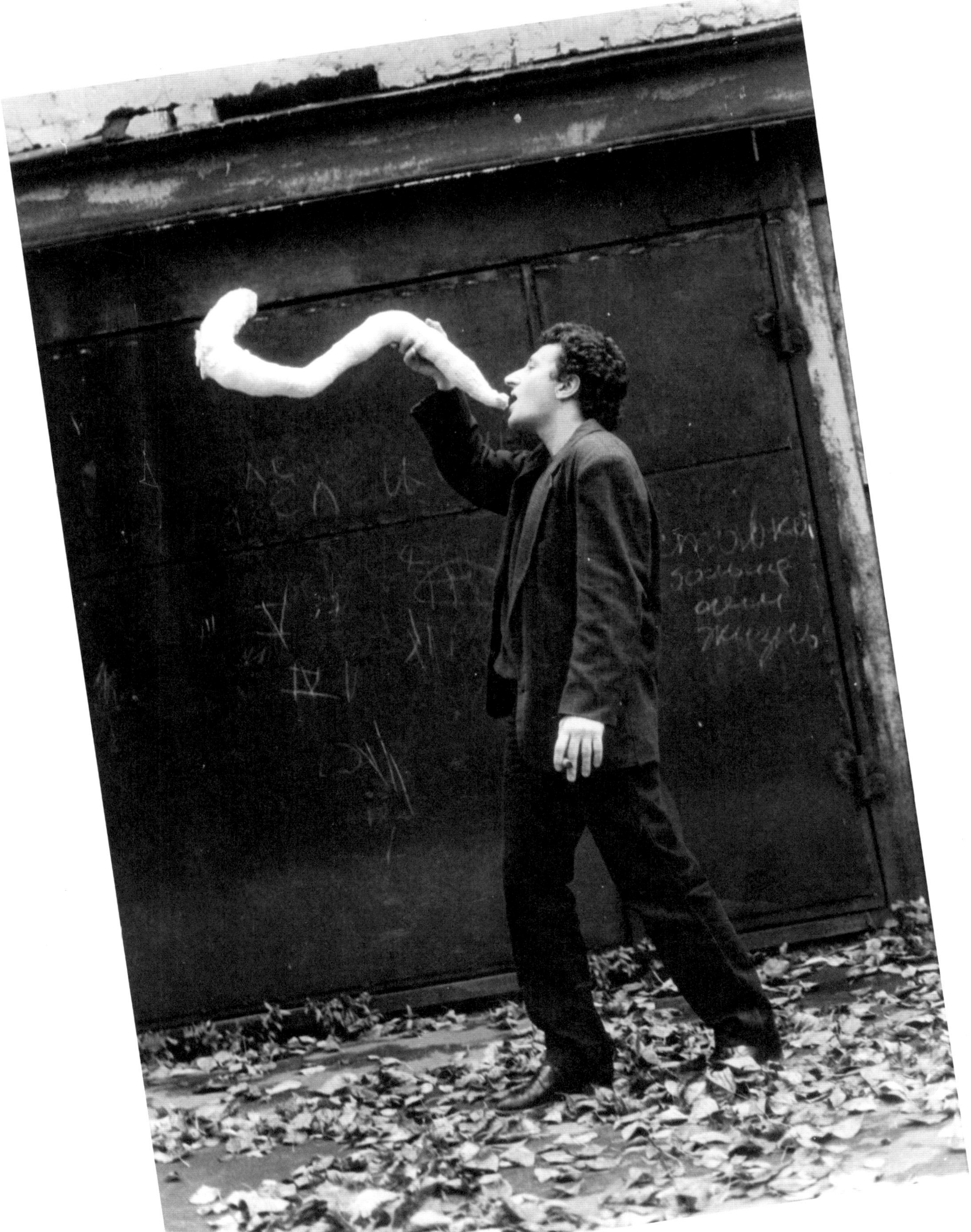

Franz West, *Paßstück (Adaptive)*, 2006

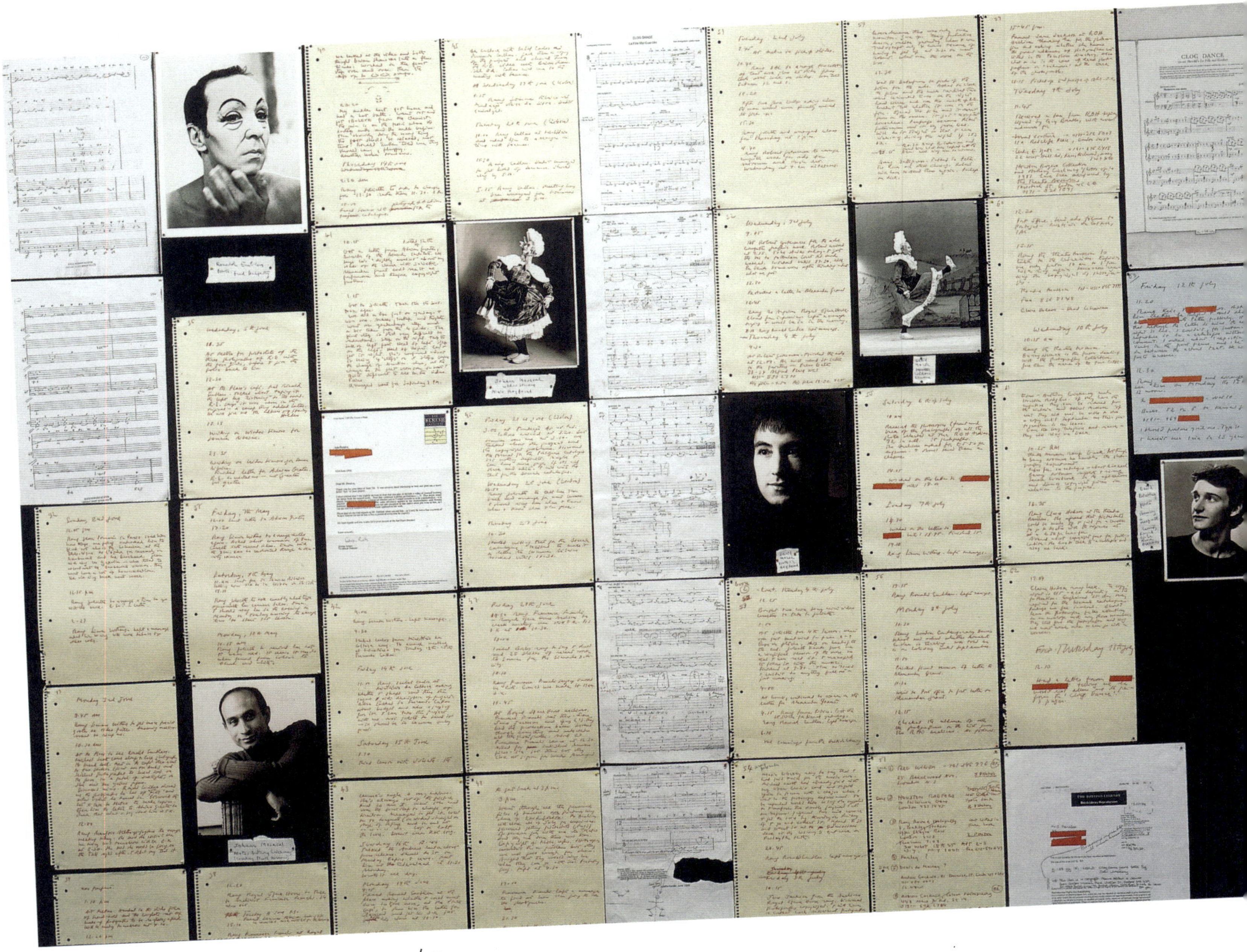

João Penalva, Widow Simone (Entr'acte, 20 years), 1996

João Penalva
Widow Simone (Entr'acte, 20 years) (1996)

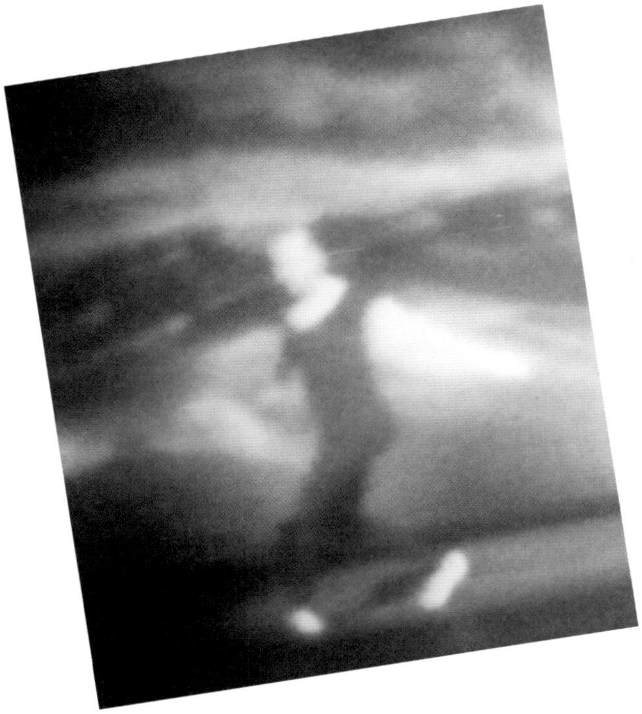

João Penalva
Video still from Unclogged, 1996

Having trained as a dancer at the London School of Contemporary Dance, João Penalva worked with choreographers like Pina Bausch and Gerhard Bohner before entering art school in 1976. Twenty years later, his installation *Widow Simone (Entr'acte, 20 years)* (1996) is his most direct engagement with his past, linking dance and the visual arts. 'Widow Simone' refers to the character role in the ballet *La Fille mal gardée*, originally created in the eighteenth century. Choreographer Sir Frederick Ashton's version of 1960 is undoubtedly the best known: here, the character Simone – a widow trying to marry off her daughter – is played by a man in drag, whose 'Clog Dance' in Act II is a comical but also technically challenging highlight of the ballet.

Penalva took it upon himself to learn this role, despite his 20-year break from dancing. He worked with Royal Ballet dancer Ronald Emblen, who had performed the role in Ashton's ballet over 700 times, as well as dancer and choreologist Juliette Kando, who translated the Benesh notated score of the 'Clog Dance' into steps. After months of physical struggle, however, Penalva's wish to perform the piece was thwarted by the copyright owner. Ironically, Penalva was just the right age for the role. And just like Emblen, had he continued dancing, the steps would have been ingrained in his body and mind.

Accepting the copyright decision, which also prohibited the use of the original music and costume, Penalva rearranged the piano score, changed the costume from a frilly widow's outfit to a plain leotard and tights, and choreographed his own dance. He then performed and taped this new arrangement at the Hackney Empire Theatre. This video became part of the *Widow Simone (Entr'acte, 20 years)* installation, which resembles a dance studio with black lino flooring and ballet bars. Two further videos are shown in the space: The Royal Ballet's performance of Ashton's version of *La Fille mal gardée* and Penalva reading out an account of his experiences. However, it is not Penalva's voice one hears in the video, but, in a direct reference to the role he studied, a female voice. In a further twist, the woman chosen for the voiceover was the photographer who over the years documented the various male performers with the Royal Ballet Company in the role of Simone. The entire, complex process of the project can be found documented in hand-written diary entries and notes, letters, sheets of musical scores and dance notation, archival material, photographs and drawings, neatly pinned onto black boards on opposing walls.

Inviting the viewer into this 'dance studio', a place of rehearsal and learning, Penalva shows his progression during the project step

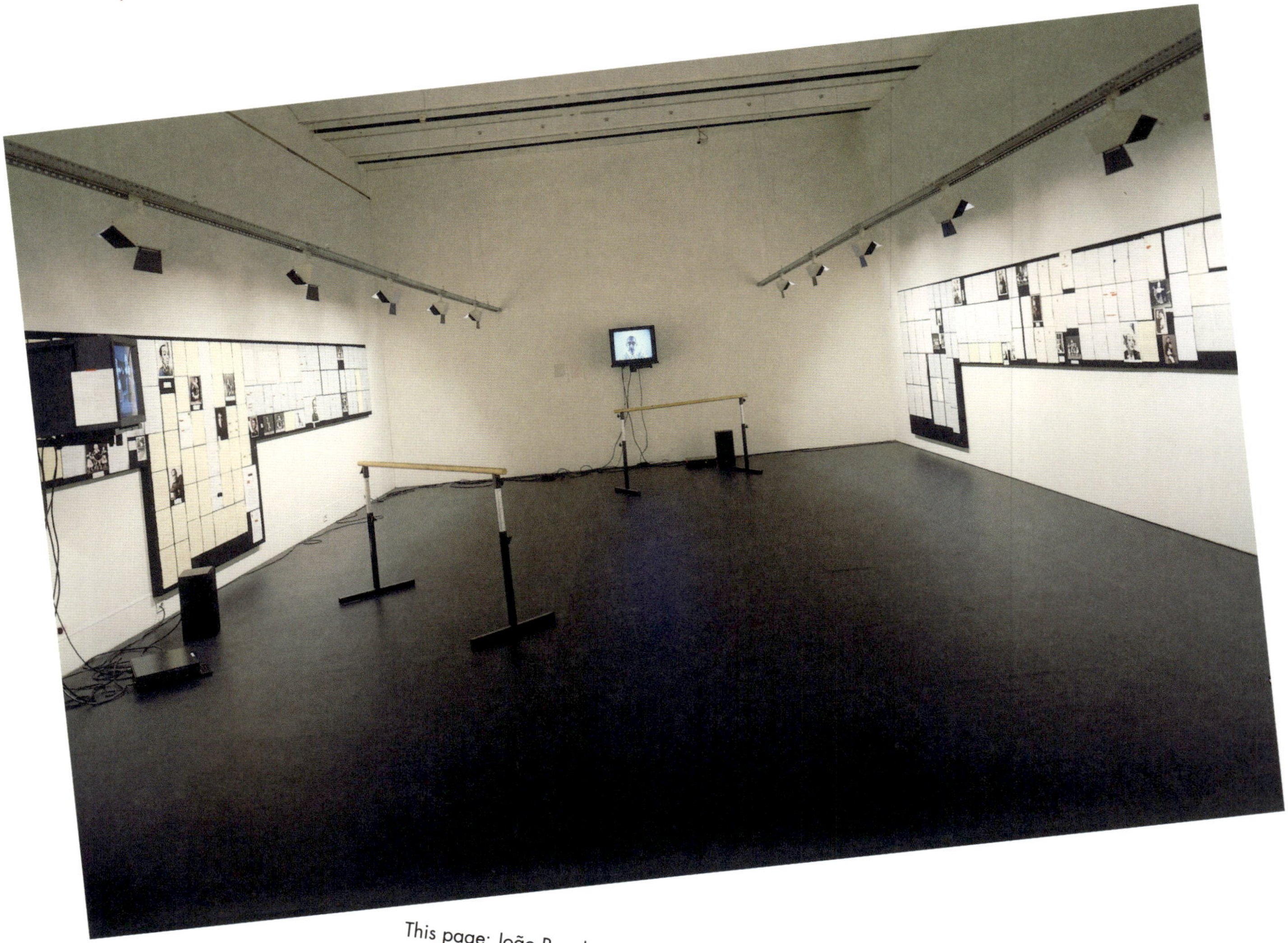

This page: João Penalva, *Widow Simone (Entr'acte, 20 years)*, 1996

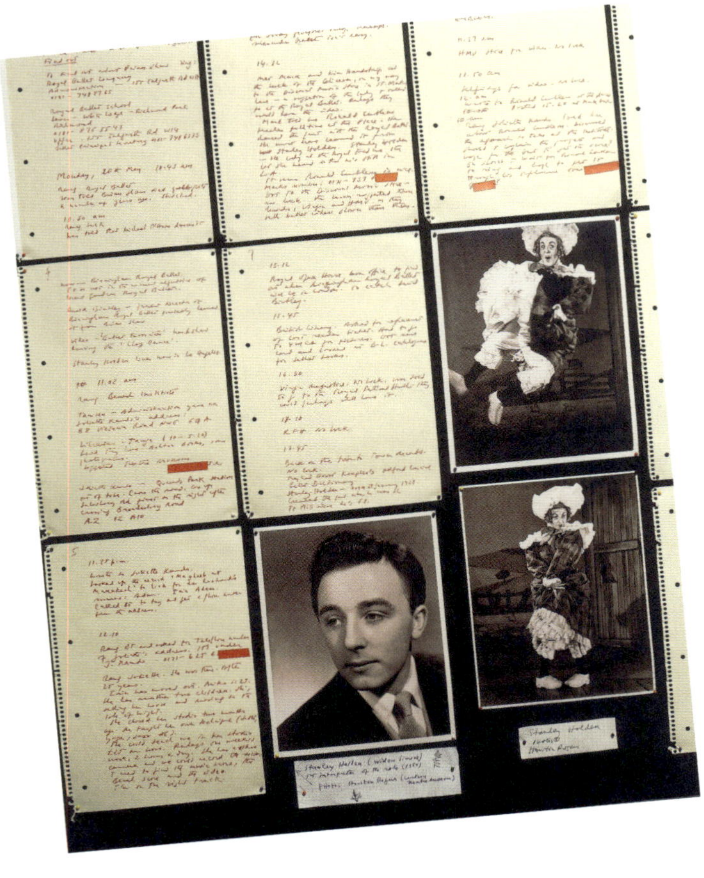

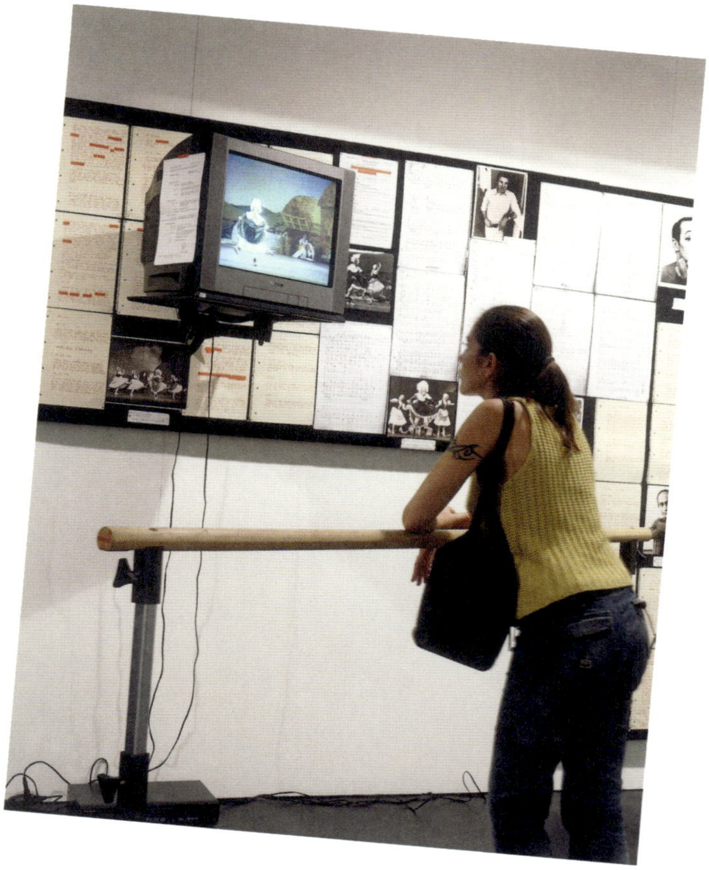

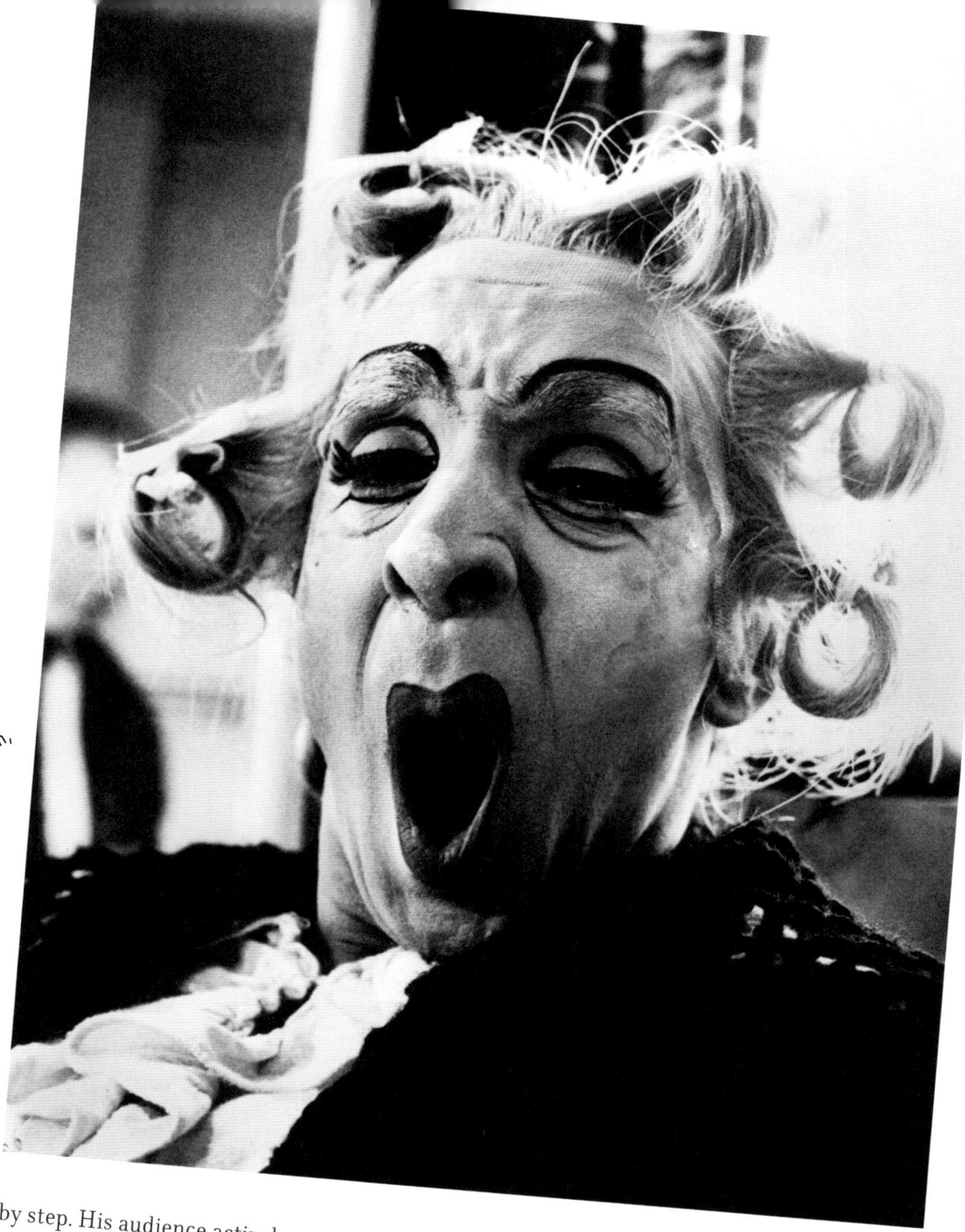

Ronald Emblem as Widow Simone in his Dressing Room, Royal Opera House, London, c. 1964

by step. His audience actively participates in reading, listening, observing, moving: the ballet bars that are placed in front of the video monitors, fixed at just above head height to different walls, turn into physical supports for watching; the lino flooring subtly inspires a more conscious walk; and the extensive documentation encourages an exploration of the space.

As is characteristic of Penalva's works, the different layers of language and imagery merge into a narrative that hovers between a fabricated story and documented facts. It is in the viewer's mind that the various strands converge and a larger picture – whether real or imagined – can arise. Yet one is left with the disturbing thought that if our bodies can be regulated by copyright laws, they do not always completely belong to us.

Julienne Lorz

João Penalva was born in Lisbon, Portugal in 1949 and lives and works in London.

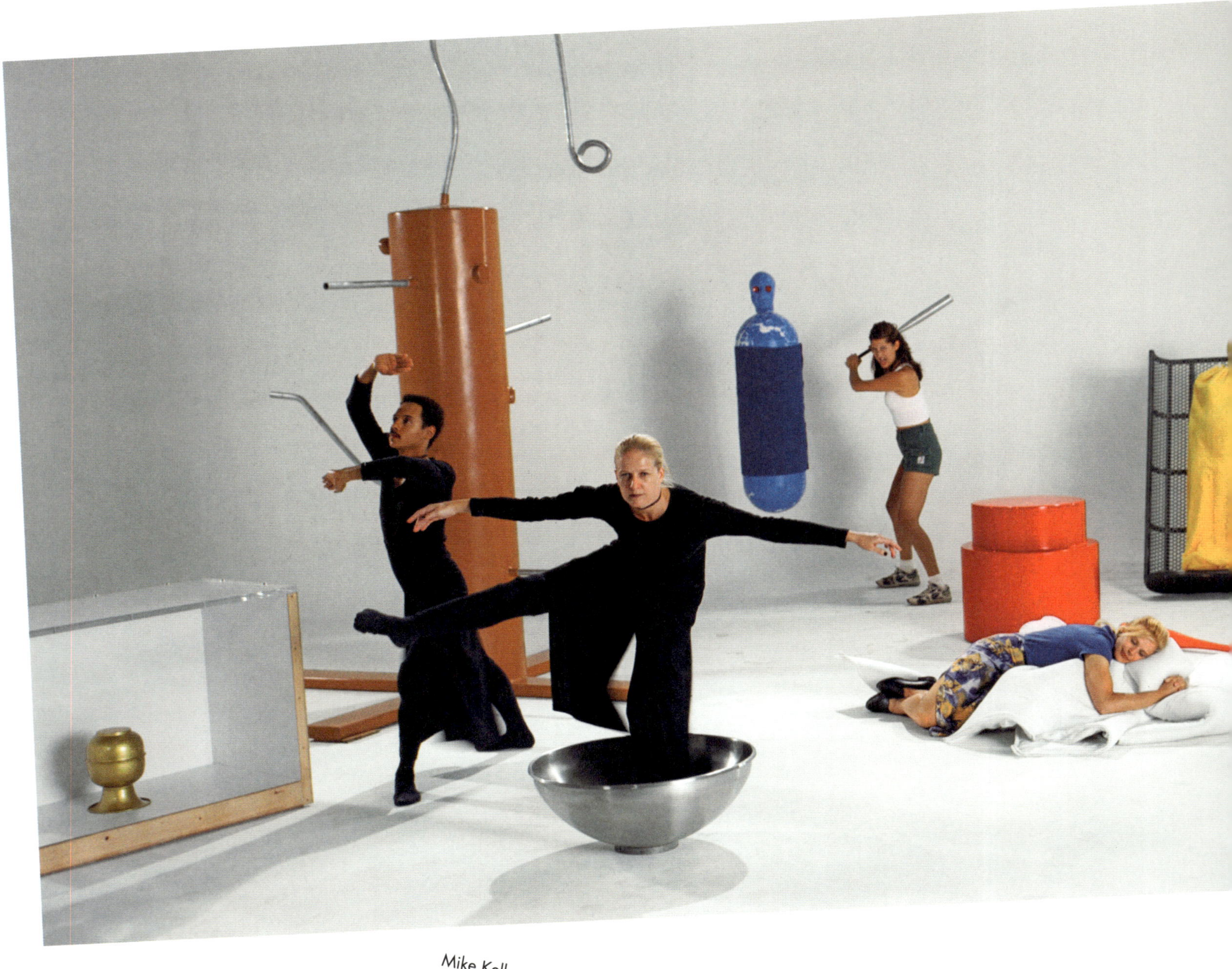

Mike Kelley, *Adaptation: Test Room Containing Multiple Stimuli Known to Elicit Curiosity and Manipulatory Responses*, 1999/2010

Mike Kelley

Adaptation: Test Room Containing Multiple Stimuli Known to Elicit Curiosity and Manipulatory Responses (1999/2010)

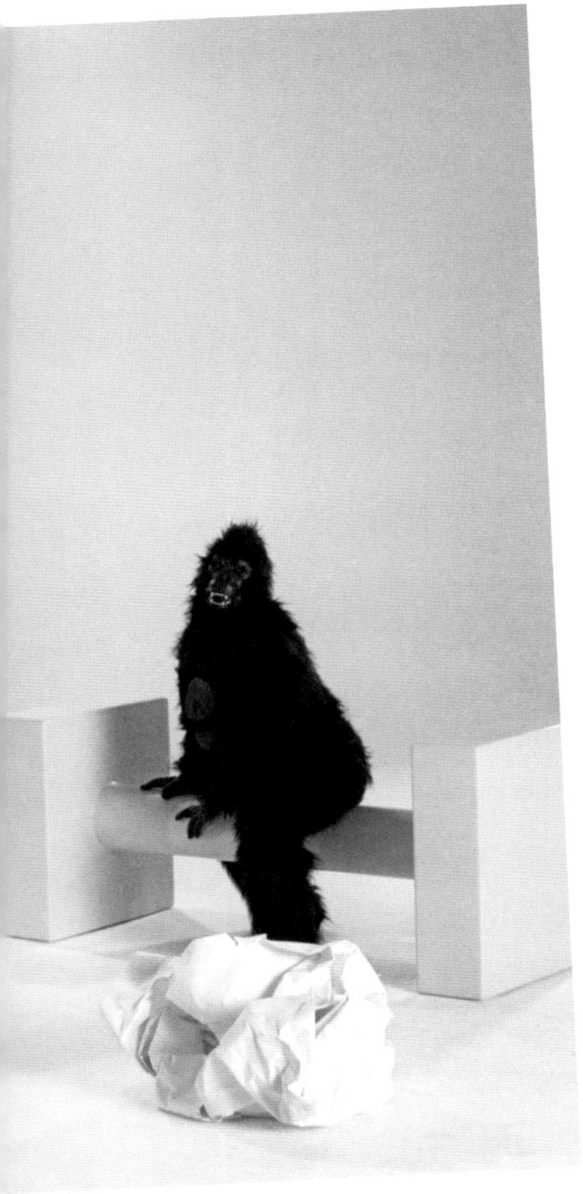

Artistic research has always been a major component in the work of Mike Kelley, who combines it with a modernist aesthetic vocabulary. His *Test Room Containing Multiple Stimuli Known to Elicit Curiosity and Manipulatory Responses* (1999) is a striking demonstration of the fact that what distinguishes artistic from scientific methods is, first and foremost, their more associative and discontinuous progress. Yet it is precisely this unorthodox approach to other fields – whether dance or the natural sciences – that constitutes the aesthetic potential of artistic research, as is emphatically illustrated by the original and entertaining insights that the viewer can gain from Kelley's work. To uncover the contexts to which this work refers means to pursue the artist's idiosyncratic chains of associations, the morphological analogies he constructs and reveals between the most divergent disciplines (behavioural research, modernist sculpture, modern dance).

In the original version, this work was framed by a steel cage equipped with an elevated ramp that enabled visitors to observe what was going on from a central vantage point. Projected on one wall of the cage was video documentation of a dance performance (Anita Pace's choreography, based on a piece by Martha Graham). In the current version, which has, as it were, been let out of the cage and opened up to the viewers, this dance is performed live by dancers in tandem with a presentation of the film. Where the cage represented a symbolic exclusion of the viewer, the new version invites us to imitate the movements performed by the dancers or to invent our own sequences of movements. Exclusion, then, has been supplanted by inclusion, though the question remains whether this solicitation to self-exposure does not also amount to an unreasonable demand that many will justifiably reject. In earlier works, Kelley had already turned away from idealistic models of participation in order to bring out the impertinence, even the sadism, implicit in any solicitation of interactivity.

The cage invoked the association of a zoo while also recalling a panopticon, the surveillance structure described by Foucault. While the panopticon functions in Foucault as a metaphor for a liberal form of government and its mechanisms of control, Kelley's cage was literally an environment of inclusion. The material – steel – communicated with the formal vocabulary of Minimal art, which, as for example in Richard Serra's work, chose industrial materials to create a symbolic link between artistic and industrial work. The cage was also a variation on another fundamental modernist figure, the grid; but the character of the grid as an index of artistic autonomy here receded behind its function. In Kelley, the grid was subservient to a purpose, comparable to a prison cell.

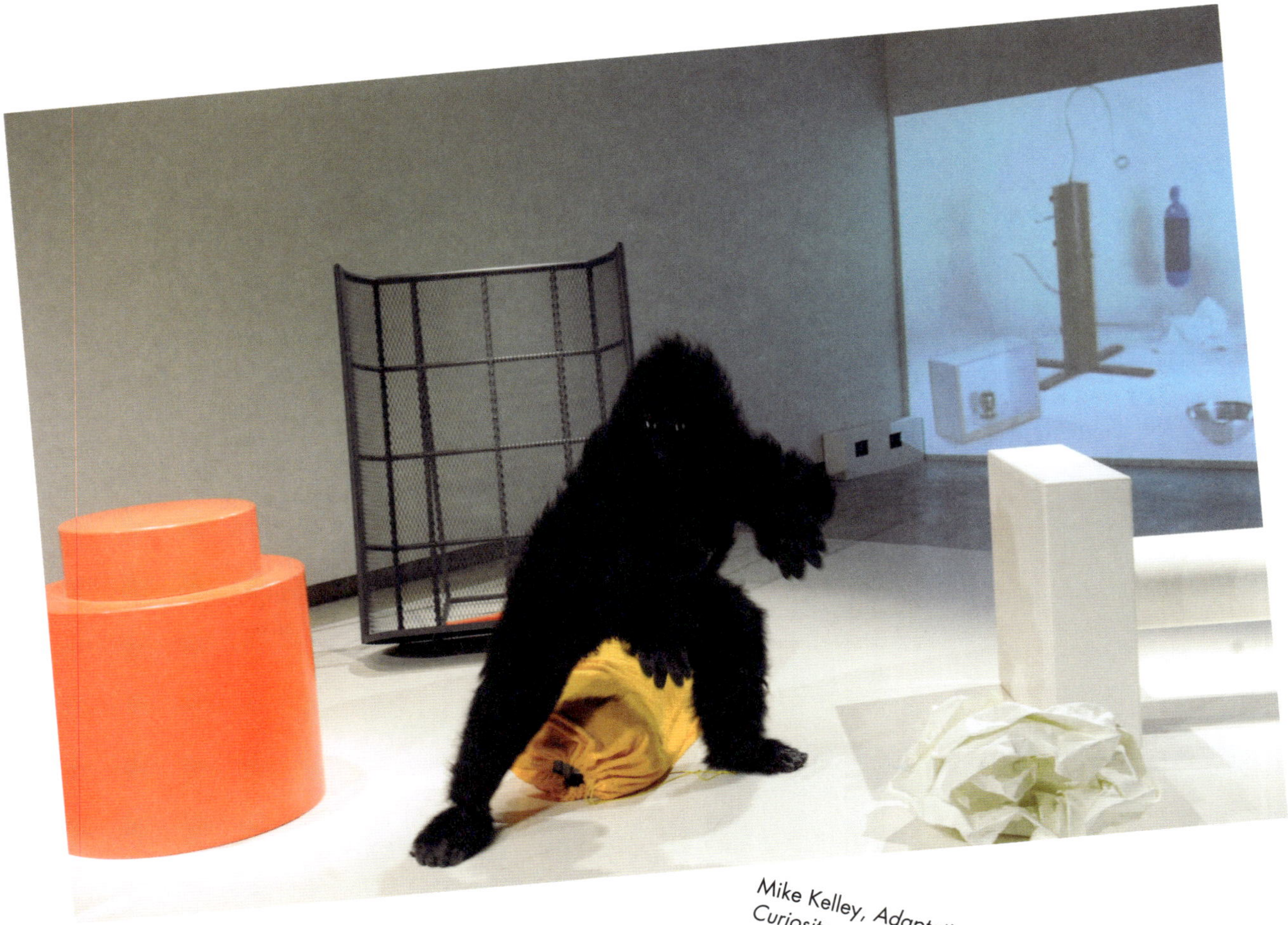

Mike Kelley, *Adaptation: Test Room Containing Multiple Stimuli Known to Elicit Curiosity and Manipulatory Responses*, 1999/2010

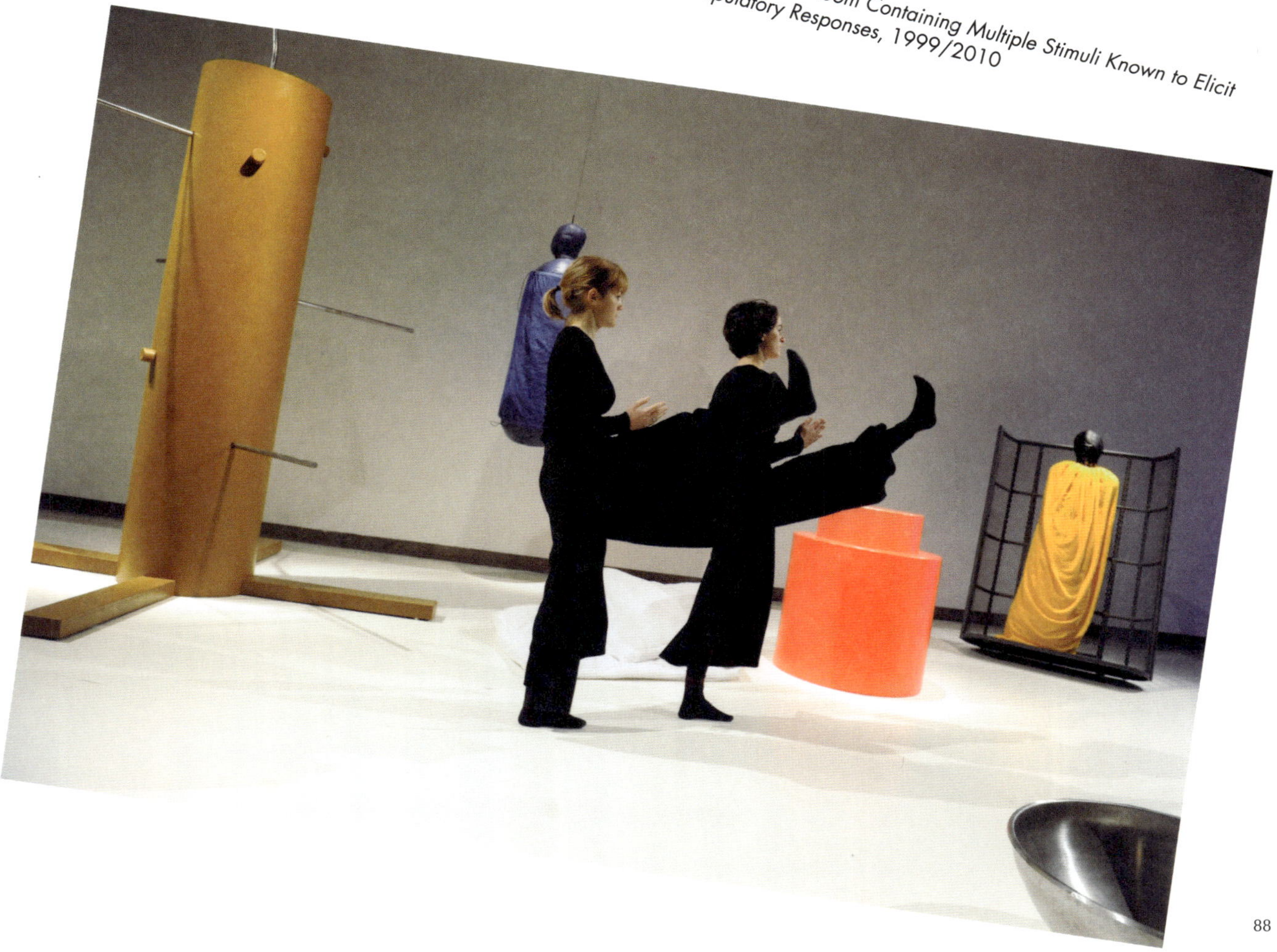

With this work, Kelley killed two birds with one stone, bringing not only classical themes such as surveillance and punishment into play but also, and more importantly, forcing the ostensibly neutral semantics of modernism to deal with explicit content. The objects on display inside the cage were exemplary demonstrations of this double strategy. In formal terms, some were derived from the famous 'surrogate mother' – the dummies that Harry Harlow used in his experiments with rhesus monkeys. Kelley noticed that these objects evince a modernist formal vocabulary, faintly suggesting a Picasso sculpture. At the same time, however, his objects take up the biomorphic formal language of the props that the artist Isamu Noguchi created for Martha Graham's choreographies. Harlow's experiments with monkeys originally served to elucidate the mother-child relationship. The observation that the baby monkeys, rather than preferring a decoy mother who provided milk, cuddled up to a fluffy and soft surrogate who did not offer food, led researchers to recognise the great importance of physical contact to babies. In Kelley's cage, however, another interpretation would seem to suggest itself: that the baby monkeys, rather than following functional criteria, gave preference to aesthetic criteria. They sought out the object they liked better because it evinced a peculiar and non-functional aesthetic. Noguchi's strangely biomorphic objects similarly lay claim to aesthetic autonomy, with a formal vocabulary that seems to emphasise the particular internal logic they obey, even though they served, first and foremost, as props used by Graham's dancers.

If the tension between autonomy and functionality is characteristic of Noguchi's objects, Kelley's work likewise keeps this opposition strictly suspended. For just as the latter's objects appear here as sculptures, the performers also instrumentalise them by using them to act out their emotions, negative as well as positive, in tempestuous interactions inspired, according to Kelley, by Albert Bandura's research on aggression. Kelley's project thus short-circuits two scientific experiments with a dance project. Still, we might also read the appearance of actors who pummel objects, kick them or snuggle up to them as a critique of the interactive premises of 'relational aesthetics', especially since, in Kelley's project, the interactive engagement with these objects does not give rise to a 'better' community founded on communication. Each performer in fact acts mostly alone, performing exaggerated actions that appear so grotesque and meaningless that the experimental arrangement evokes the idea of an emancipatory potential only to reveal it to be hopelessly idealistic. But however various the activities performed by Kelley's actors – some of them wearing monkey costumes – may be, there can be no doubt regarding the objecthood of the elements with which they interact. The concrete use of these props remains inscribed upon them even when they are considered as sculptures, enhancing their value as meta-objects because they also contain a surplus or emotional investment.

Ultimately, however, there was also a social-political dimension to what was going on in Kelley's cage. Both the research projects and the dance by Anita Pace, after all, aim at affect-production – at the observation, generation and control of affect. The fact that we live in an age of biopolitics lends new political urgency to this focus on affect-production. The emotional states that Harlow and Bandura examined and that modern dance seeks to put more immediately onstage have long become an exploitable resource. Artistic production, of course, is likewise a form of affect-production, to the extent that it both aims at sensual experience and extracts the artist's affects. Nonetheless, dance and science must be considered forms of immaterial labour, whereas the traditional artist – and in this sense Kelley is a traditional artist – has a product at his disposal; a product that, while it may be enriched with affects and circumstantial elements of real life, transcends these components. The visual arts thus enjoy a structural advantage over modern dance and behavioural research, and Kelley's work plays to this advantage. For as much as his artistic-experimental arrangement makes a statement about the social production and exploitation of affect, the reality of this work is in no way to be confused with the real conditions of life.

Isabelle Graw

Mike Kelley was born in Detroit, Michigan in 1954 and lives and works in Los Angeles.

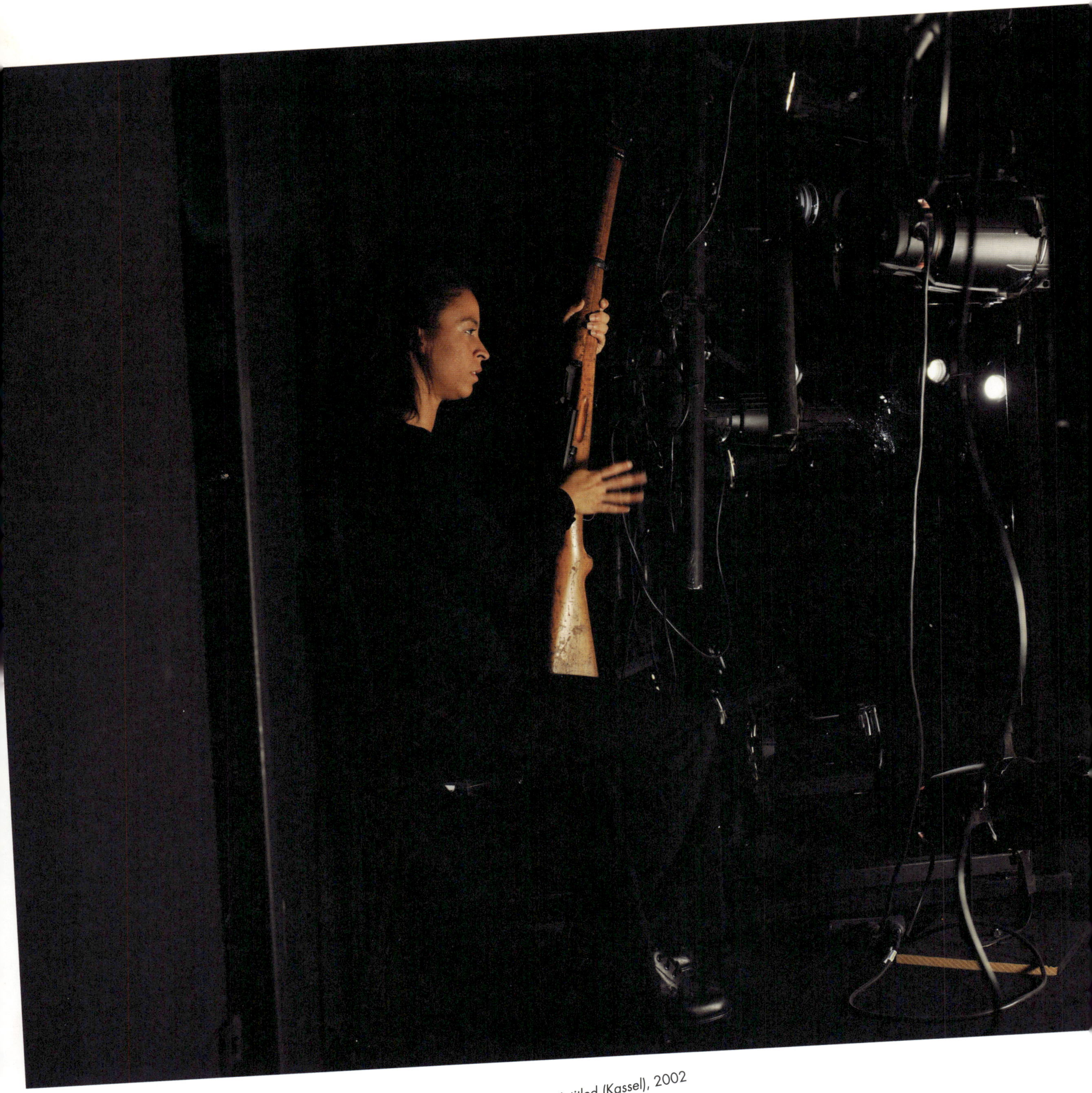

Tania Bruguera, *Untitled (Kassel)*, 2002

Tania Bruguera
Untitled (Kassel) (2002)

Tania Bruguera's early works, made while still in art school in Cuba, were directly in dialogue with the hybrid art of Ana Mendieta (1948–1985). Since then, she has been producing installations and performances where the politics of the body is her main aesthetic material. If Mendieta worked on hybrid forms between sculpture and performance, film and video remained the main media for her intimate art. Bruguera, on the other hand, has always insisted on exploring the tensions underlying a face-to-face relationship between viewers. It is in this realm that Bruguera has proposed her *arte de conducta* ('art of behaviour'), where above all she is concerned with the political. In her pieces, the systems of control that invisibly choreograph our lives are made visible, denounced and put into question. The result is not always the most comfortable experience for audiences.

The installation *Untitled (Kassel)* (2002) is a perfect example of Bruguera's artistic-political project. The work is predicated on a powerful paradox – the more the viewer is exposed to a field of light, the less he or she is able to see. This paradoxical construction at the level of perception has a counterpart at the level of sensation – after viewers have been subjected to a blinding light, the room is plunged into darkness, and the more they linger in this darkness, the more enlightened they become about the nature of absolute, insidious control. As Bruguera wrote about this piece: 'This is a moment of awareness. Awareness of power, of the significance and transcendence of action. It is politics as sensation.'[1]

This 'politics as sensation' is activated in *Untitled (Kassel)* by an uncanny apparatus – scaffolding, planks and 30,000 watts of power beamed directly in the viewer's sightline at regular intervals. In the dark, choreographed performers lock and load rifles in precise rhythms and march ominously around a periphery that functions less as a frame for an artwork than a prison wall or border. A barely visible video projection, appearing like a faint hallucination, lists in red letters sites of political terror, from 1945 (Cheju, South Korea) to the year of the installation's creation in 2002 (Netanya, Israel), interspersed with black and white footage of people running. Fusing the philosopher Gilles Deleuze's call for an aesthetics of sensation that 'is inseparable from its direct action on the nervous system'[2] with Giorgio Agamben's insight that 'the [concentration] camp is the hidden matrix and the nomos of the political space in which we still live',[3] Bruguera's 'politics as sensation' refuses to remain purely descriptive of our current condition. It offers at least one line of flight: the possibility of historical and political awareness. This awareness occurs through the visceral and kinesthetic apprehension of the situation in which we find ourselves. Light and darkness, the stomping sounds on the scaffolding, the locking of the guns, operate in tandem to direct our movement: to freeze, to step hesitantly, haltingly, trying

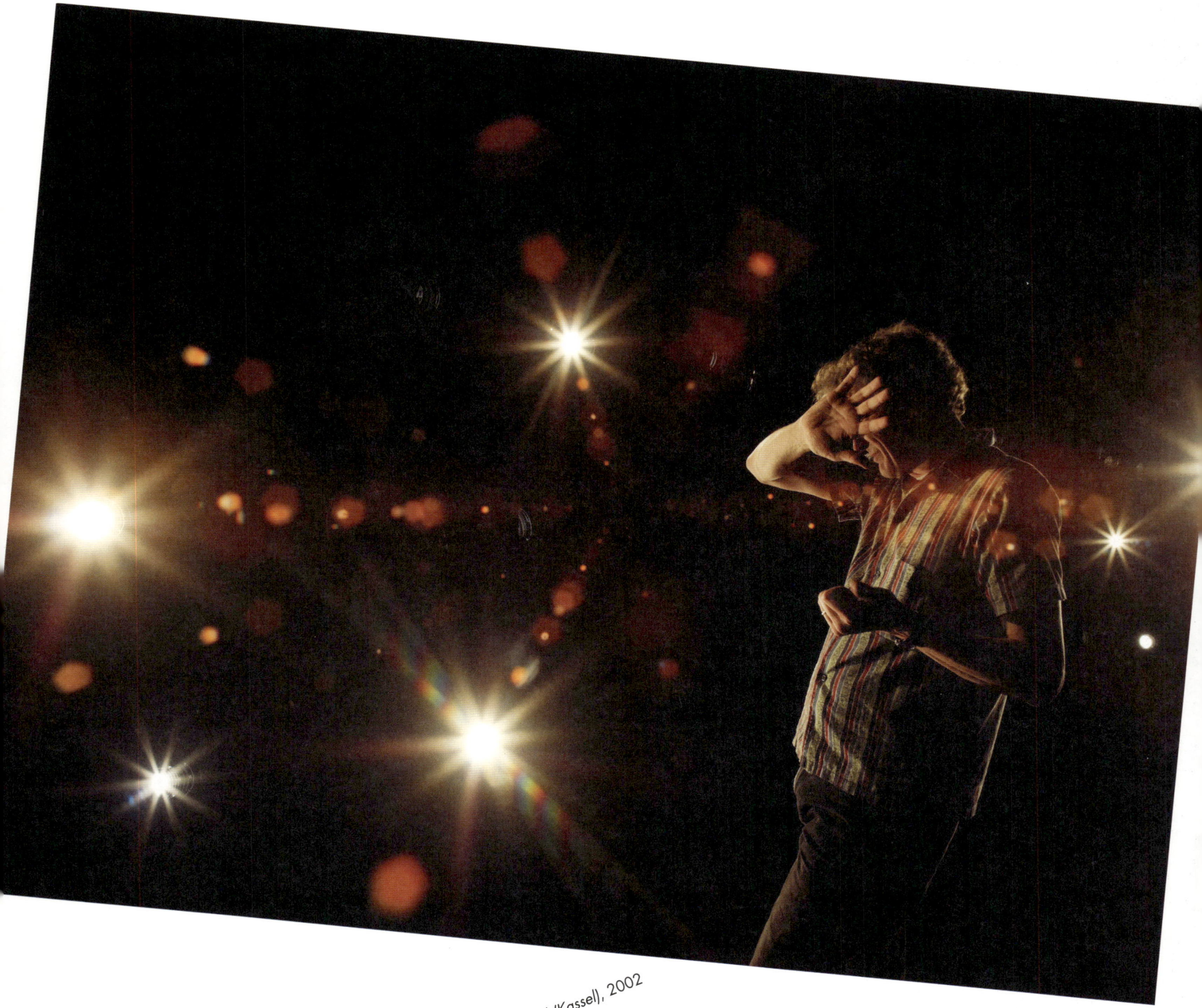

Tania Bruguera, *Untitled (Kassel)*, 2002

not to trip. We cannot help but assess the situation we are in and then carefully determine our next move. Assaulted by menacing sounds and a sense of dizziness and dissolution, moving blindly and slowly in the room, we experience a sensation of disorientation that pushes us into an awareness of our generalised state of emergency – and of our own actions in this condition.

Untitled (Kassel), first presented at Documenta 11, was, as Bruguera wrote, 'a translation' of a previous work: *Untitled (Havana)* (2000). In this earlier installation, which took place in a pitch-black tunnel whose floor was covered with decomposing sugar-cane husks, sounds of skin rubbing against skin revealed otherwise undetectable bodies in the space (every few metres a naked man would be standing along the walls, making these sounds), interspersed with the faintest of lights coming from a TV monitor that hovered at the end of the tunnel showing slowed-down images of Fidel Castro. All this resulted in a visceral apprehension of Cuba's particular historical-political condition, where the nauseating sweetness of the rotting sugar cane was key. In Kassel, Bruguera also used local materials and historical information to link the militaristic connotations of the work to its site, referring to: 'the period when Kassel was a munitions manufacturing center, [the] Allied bombardment of the city [and how] Kassel bordered the socialist East'.[4]

However, it is through its displacement to other venues that *Untitled (Kassel)* (2002) reveals the full force of Bruguera's insight into how political violence rules our daily existence. Whether viewed in early 2010 at the Neuberger Museum of Art, Purchase College, New York, or during this exhibition in London, Munich and Düsseldorf, *Untitled (Kassel)* (2002) gains a universal dimension that grounds it even more firmly in our 'political imaginary'. In the dark, surrounded by a choreographed clockwork of terror, we suddenly sense, viscerally and politically, the truth behind Peter Sloterdijk's aphorism: 'If we ask a modern subject "where were you at the time of the crime?" the answer is: "I was where the crime took place."'[5] Without an alibi, blinking between two kinds of blindness, we receive an illuminating insight: we understand that we can always redefine our choreographed selves and, in doing so, change the rhythms and powers that subjugate us. This is the active side of Bruguera's politics as sensation – an art of behaviour.

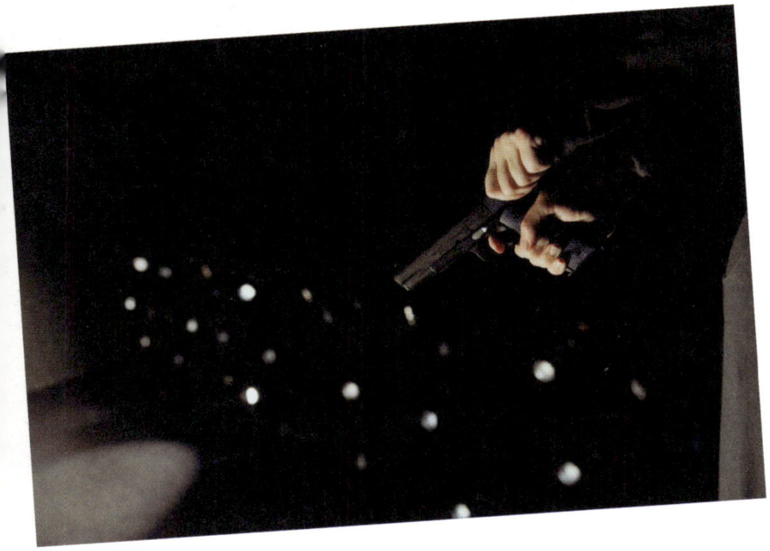

André Lepecki

1 *Documenta 11*, Hatje-Cantz, Ostfildern-Ruit, 2002, p. 555.
2 Gilles Deleuze, *The Logic of Sensation*, University of Minnesota Press, Minneapolis, 2004, p. 34.
3 Giorgio Agamben, *Means Without Ends*, University of Minnesota Press, Minneapolis, 2000, p. 37.
4 *Documenta 11*, p. 556.
5 Peter Sloterdijk, *L'Heure du Crime et le Temps de l'Oeuvre d'Art*, Calmann-Lévy, Paris, 2000, p. 9 (author's translation).

Tania Bruguera was born in Havana, Cuba in 1968 and lives and works in Havana and Paris.

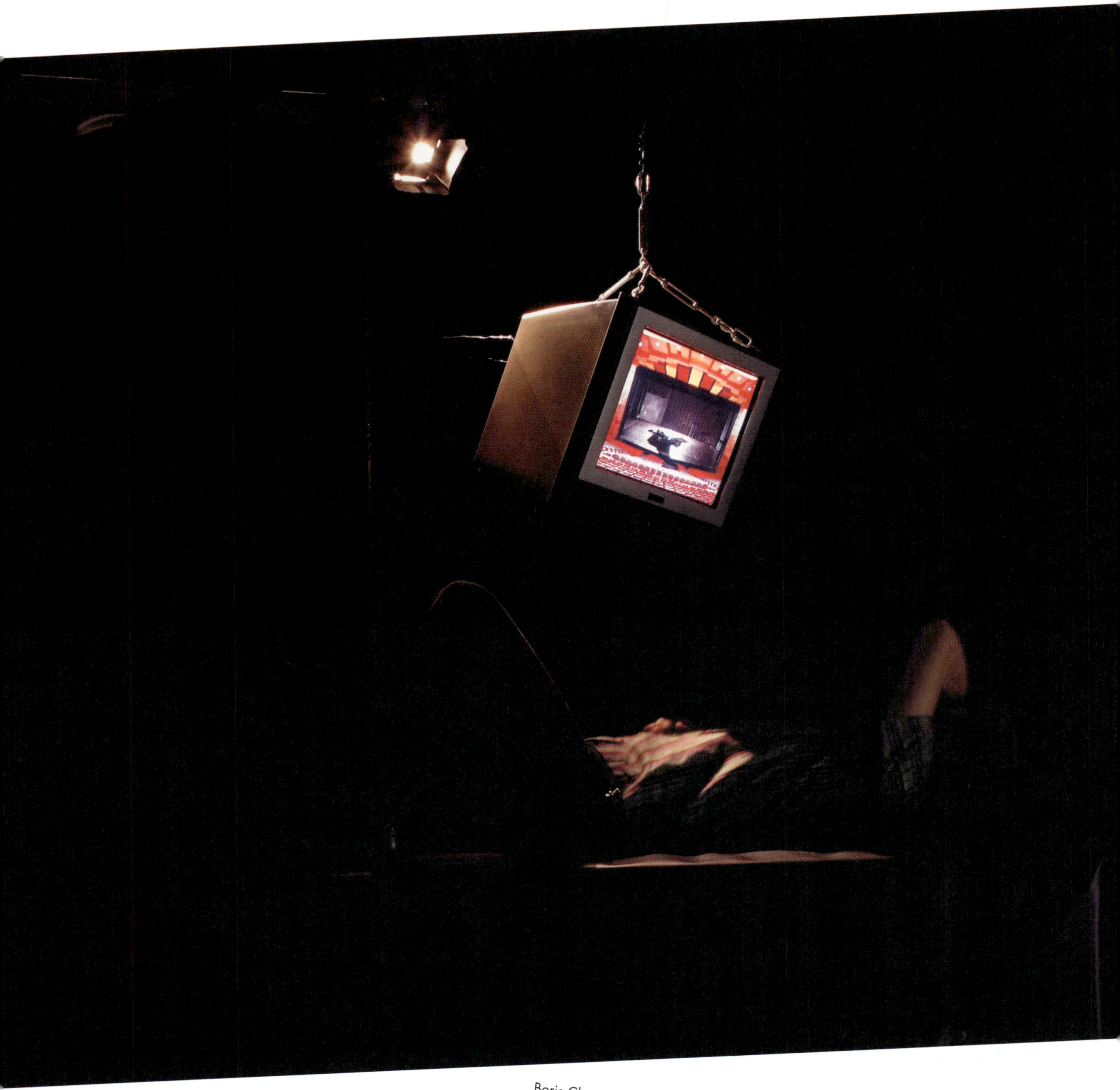

Boris Charmatz, *héâtre-élévision*, 2002/2010

Boris Charmatz/ Musée de la danse

héâtre-élévision (2002)

Héâtre-élévision (2002), by the French choreographer Boris Charmatz, is a 'pseudo-performance' as its subtitle announces: it stages an artificial choreography in which absent dancers are substituted and heightened by pixellated bodies on a television monitor. The spectator, invited to lie on the flat surface of a piano, witnesses on a screen hanging overhead, a series of uncanny tableaux in which the distorted, jolting dancers appear and disappear in circumscribed spaces. This choreographic installation mobilises bodies across a string of nesting boxes (the room, the piano, the television) in the manner of Russian dolls, confining the elusive dance in order to amplify its hypnotic effects. This is a performance reduced to a film; a singular choreographic distillation. Detached from the imperatives of presence, verticality and representation to which the idealised dancing body has been historically and technologically subjected, this virtual dance can begin to resonate with a range of linguistic, social and political issues – as they are inscribed on the spectator's body.

Since the early 1990s, Charmatz has created a series of innovative pieces exploring the parameters of the visible in dance. His work experiments with the deployment of dance in space, reinventing its perceptual limits and redefining its relation to the audience. In each work, Charmatz activates a spatial *dispositif* – or apparatus – that tackles the relation between movement, the body and its surfaces of representation. His first piece, *À bras le corps* (1993), created with Dimitri Chamblas, contains an athletic duet in a rectangle closely bordered by the spectators; *Aatt enen tionon* (1996) is a vertiginous trio performed semi-naked on a three-level metallic platform; *Programme court avec essorage* (1999) takes place on two spinning platforms (designed by the artist Gilles Touyard) that subject the body to an extreme centrifugal force. In *héâtre-élévision*, the spectator becomes the singular stage of the performance: the work choreographs his or her movements, shifting the conventional orientation towards the performer and experimenting with logics of gravity and empathy. The work also seems to prompt the spectator's own thoughts by projecting an intimate stream of movement-images just before one's eyes.

In the fixed shot of the screen, glimpsed choreographies overlap with a test card and its persistent drone. The flattened bodies play with the borders of their confinement: tongues and voices pouring out, limbs pressing on walls, gazes directed far beyond the frame. Here, Charmatz sets up a forceful tension that rarefies dance (where are the dancers?) while showing its very function: the ways in which it organises bodies at the threshold of the visible and the significant. Lying alone in the dark room – whether hypnotized, drifting, drowsy or exhilarated – the spectator encounters a crucial, distant and disorienting dance. There is nothing behind the curtains: the television functions as a mechanical proscenium that displays everything on its surface, exposing a depthless choreography – one that takes form nowhere but in the minds of its witnesses.

Noémie Solomon

Boris Charmatz was born in Chambéry, Savoie in 1973 and lives and works in Rennes.

Boris Charmatz, *héâtre-élévision*, 2002/2005

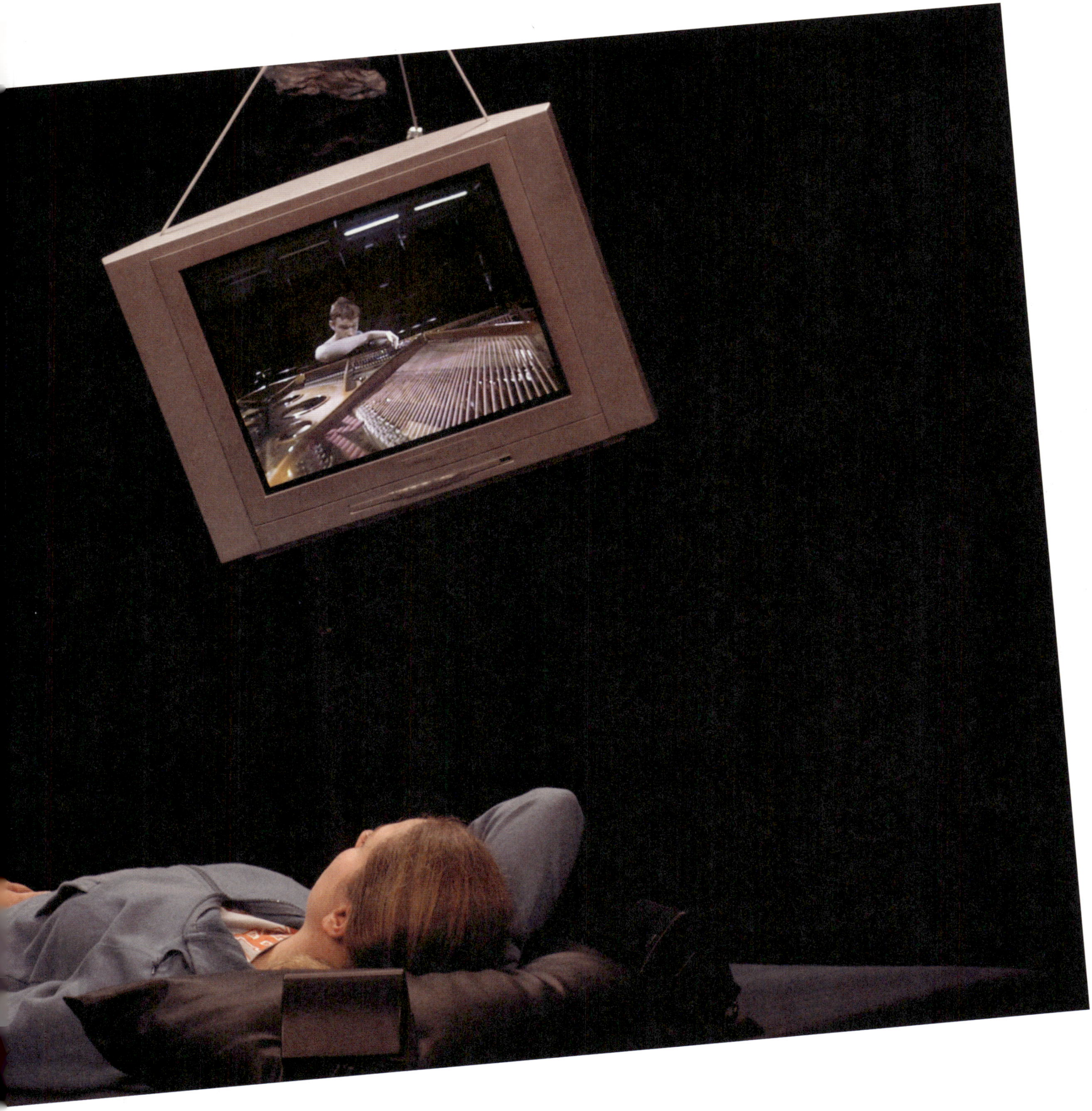

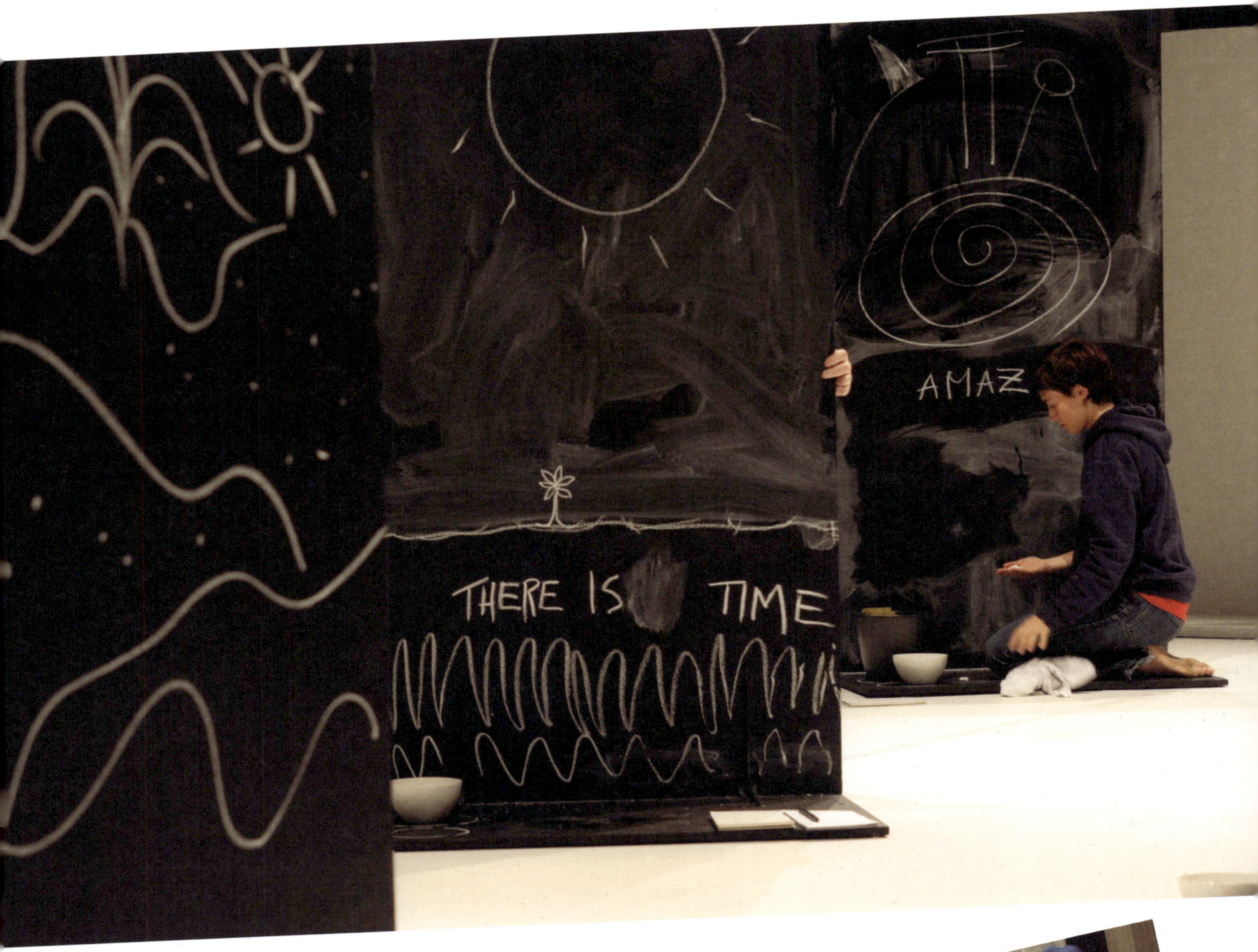

Michael Kliën with Steve Valk, *Choreography for Blackboards*, 2006

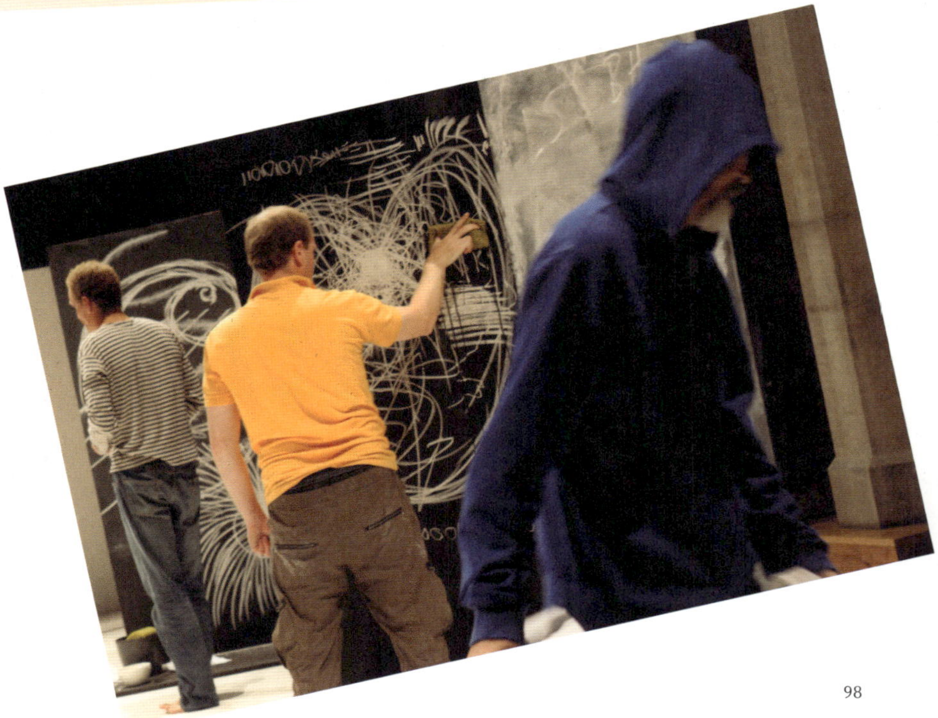

Michael Kliën with Steve Valk
Choreography for Blackboards (2006)

Daghdha Dance Company, one of Ireland's leading dance organisations, is currently under the artistic direction of Austrian choreographer Michael Kliën, whose numerous touring productions and installations include commissions from Ballett Frankfurt (William Forsythe) and the Vienna Volksoper. Noted for a strong programme of activities and a clear focus on generating discourse about choreography, Kliën has developed a theoretical and practical basis for choreography which he sees as 'an autonomous aesthetics, concerned with notions of change, governance and steering'. Together with dramaturg Steve Valk, his work is also associated with new methodologies for dance improvisation and with the development of 'social choreography'. The company's recent repertoire combines thought and practice into productions that set out to 'examine the wider structures that bind us all together'.

For *Move: Choreographing You*, a recent piece by Daghdha Dance Company is presented on the roof of the Hayward Gallery, in an outdoor space. *Choreography for Blackboards* (2006) is a performance installation made specifically for galleries and museums. It is, first of all, a choreographic structure – seven participants, not all professional dancers, and of varying ages and gender – face seven monolithic blackboards spread throughout a large white open space. Each performer actively draws on the blackboards over a set period of time, as the audience surrounds them. The initial silence, marked by the sound of the white chalk on the boards, morphs into an electronic soundscape composed by one of Kliën's long-term collaborators, Volkmar Kliën. Before the space becomes invested with actions, the freestanding boards, only slightly higher than the performers, provide a clear one-to-one performance area for each protagonist. The contrast between the immaculate floor and the intense blackness of the boards creates a strong visual and structural impact. We are told the performers 'follow exact, rehearsed procedures, developing and exchanging insights and individual expressions in various, immediate communicative forms, weaving their relations into a concentrated collective dance of minds'. Notebooks are referred to, and are evidence of preparation, shattering the initial illusion of creative spontaneity. On closer inspection, there are also some words printed on labels next to the blackboards. One reads:' the spontaneous amplitude of a movement'; another reads: ' storing up emotional events'. Are these instructions of some kind? Whose words are these? Once the performance has come to an end, a landscape of drawings is left out on display. The audience is free to walk, sit, converse, as well as read what has been left behind.

Choreography for Blackboards is constructed with the viewer as a central part of the performance. One written instruction: 'observer-created reality', clearly reveals this. Although the observers are not actively taking part in the actions during the performance, the second part of the piece is an invitation to the audience to interact and in doing so complete the piece. The familiar object of the blackboard, with its connotations of bygone school days, is certainly a link to a common experience, an object perhaps soon to disappear in this age of digitalisation. The communal nature of the piece, of bringing the audience in, is important to Kliën, even though the performers seem very much isolated from each other, in a *face à face* with their own black 'mirror'.

This performance brings forth the legacy of a certain choreographic history to the exhibition, where the use of the trace and markings are constant motifs and preoccupations common to dance makers and visual artists. These preoccupations take on an altogether different significance as the everyday and pedestrian movement invades the choreographic and performance field, from the pioneering work of Allan Kaprow onwards, with domestic objects making an appearance too. The intention of *Choreography for Blackboards* draws on ritualistic qualities and the need for audience members to bear witness to the events, to create a collective 'third space'.

Eva Martinez

Michael Kliën was born in Vienna, Austria in 1973 and lives and works in Limerick, Ireland.

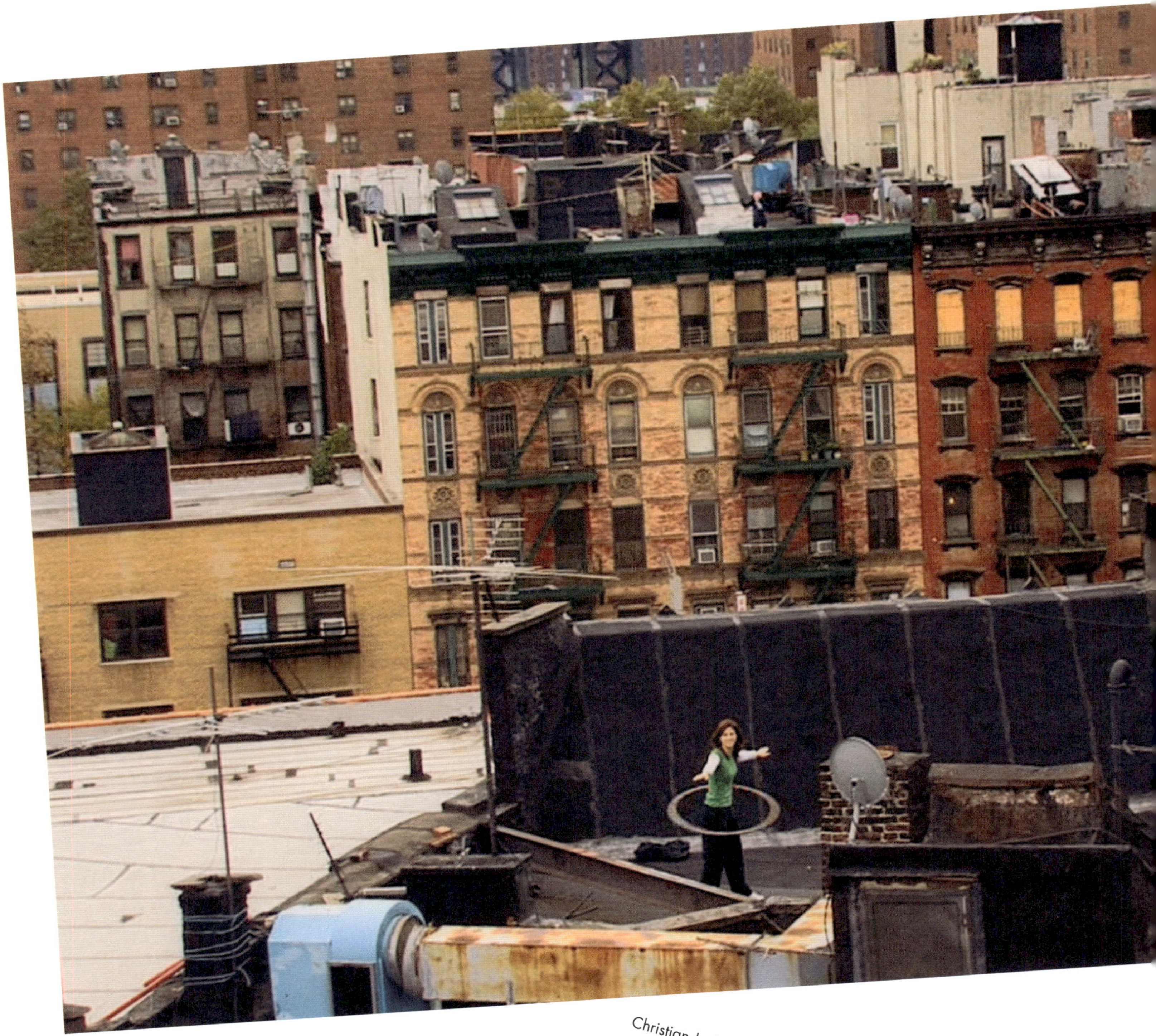

Christian Jankowski, *Rooftop Routine*, 2008

Christian Jankowski
Rooftop Routine (2008)

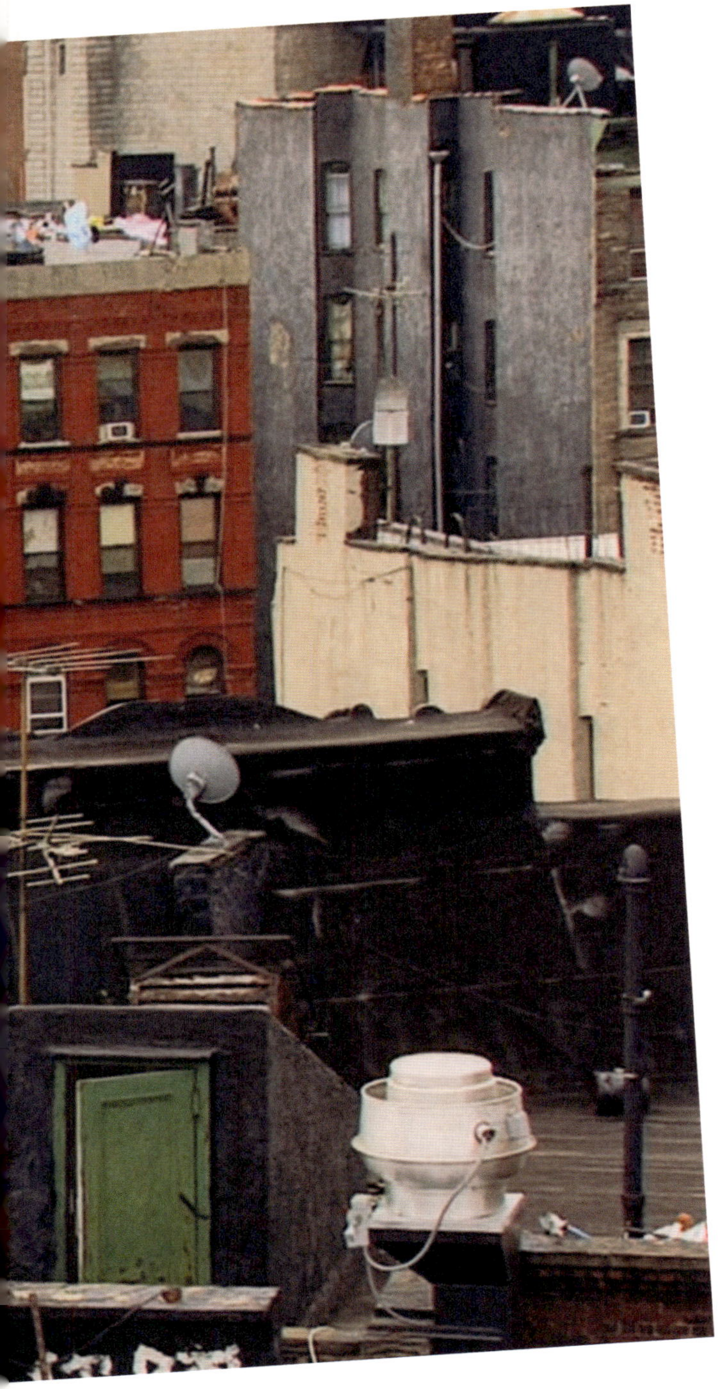

Christian Jankowski's work can be characterised as one-part performance and one-part event, situated within an unrepeatable moment. The artist employs mass-media formats such as mainstream cinema and popular TV programmes as vehicles for his own films, videos and installations. Through humorous exploitation of popular entertainment formats, Jankowski puts himself and his audience in unlikely scenarios, thereby shifting subject positions from artist to entertainer, from creator to collaborator and from passive viewer to engaged actor.

Jankowski's cast of witting and unwitting collaborators has included psychics, magicians, televangelists, living sculptures, horror-movie aficionados and special-effects artists. He comments: 'I like collaborating with these other powerful image creators [...] and find[ing] out what happens when you enter their formats. How much space do they give you?' Through humorous appropriation or direct intervention, Jankowski deliberately blurs the boundaries between art, popular entertainment and everyday life. Through re-framing mass-media conventions or popular-culture clichés, he exposes the choreography ingrained in diverse situations.

Rooftop Routine (2008) is Jankowski's clever and playful reinvention of Trisha Brown's seminal performance work *Roof Piece* (1973). Brown's original work consisted of fourteen dancers dressed in red, spread across a series of New York rooftops. Brown performed an improvised movement, transmitting it to the nearest dancer, who would in turn mimic the movement, passing it on to the next dancer, so that the choreography was transmitted in a telegraphic chain over the rooftops and back again. The dance was akin to a game of Chinese whispers, the artist exploring the transformation or (mis)translation of movement across distance and duration.

Thirty-five years later, Jankowski's *Rooftop Routine* was performed in New York as part of the Performa Biennial in 2007. The artist was inspired after spotting his neighbour Suat Ling Chua doing her daily hula-hoop exercise routine on an apartment rooftop. Jankowski explains: 'There was something very peaceful in this movement, something hypnotic almost [...] Within boxes of the city, you had this circular hula hoop.' The artist asked his neighbour to collaborate on a hula-hoop performance. The resulting work features a troupe of 25 brightly dressed hula-hoopers spread out across the rooftops, with Chua taking the lead role. She narrates her routine, gives tips on technique and shows new moves, while the other dancers copy her movements. Though humorously referencing Brown's performance, *Rooftop Routine* features key aspects of Jankowski's own practice, such the importance of exchange: an exchange of roles, creative exchange between the artist and his collaborators, and the literal exchange of movement across rooftops.

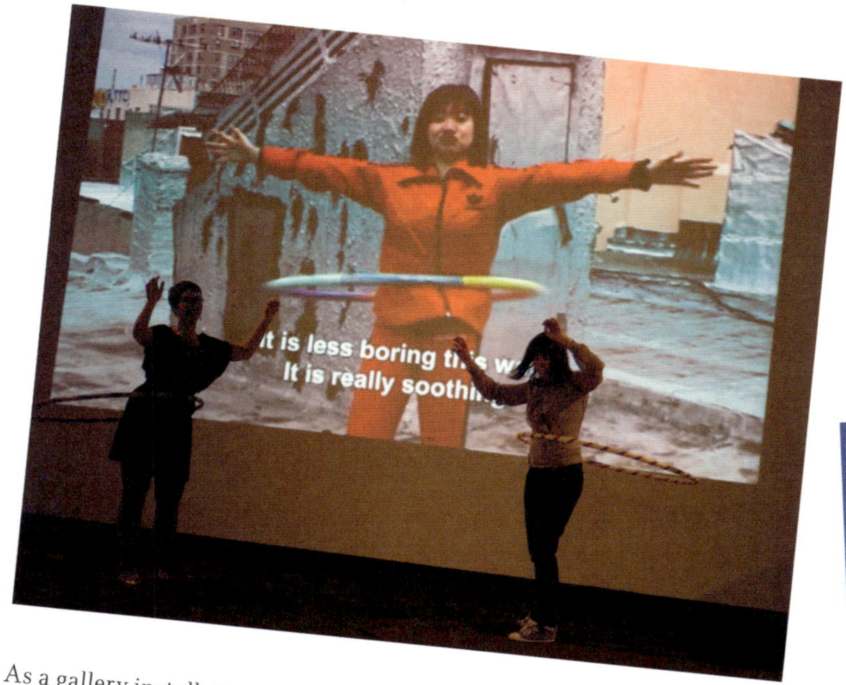

As a gallery installation, *Rooftop Routine* continues the exchange, in this case from video screen to gallery-goer. The effect is equally animated – cheesy pop music blaring, hula-hooper hips gyrating, colourful hoops on display and Suat Ling Chua's direct address to the viewer. Jankowski engages the viewer in multiple senses: visually, aurally and physically. The gallery spectator is invited to transcend viewership, becoming a performer by picking up a hula hoop in the gallery space and taking part in the action. In this way, Jankowski's work references an instructional fitness video or a dance-along videogame. Instead of a virtual hula hoop offered by the technology of Wii in the comfort and privacy of your own home, however, the artist challenges you to have fun and be silly in the slightly less comfortable and more public surrounds of an art gallery. He states: 'It's important to make things slightly uncomfortable and challenging – to be somehow unclear where you're supposed to stand in relation to the work.' In this way Jankowski constructs a space for open collaboration in the attempt to carry on the chain of movement.

Siobhan McCracken Nixon

Christian Jankowski was born in Göttingen, Germany in 1968 and lives and works in Berlin.

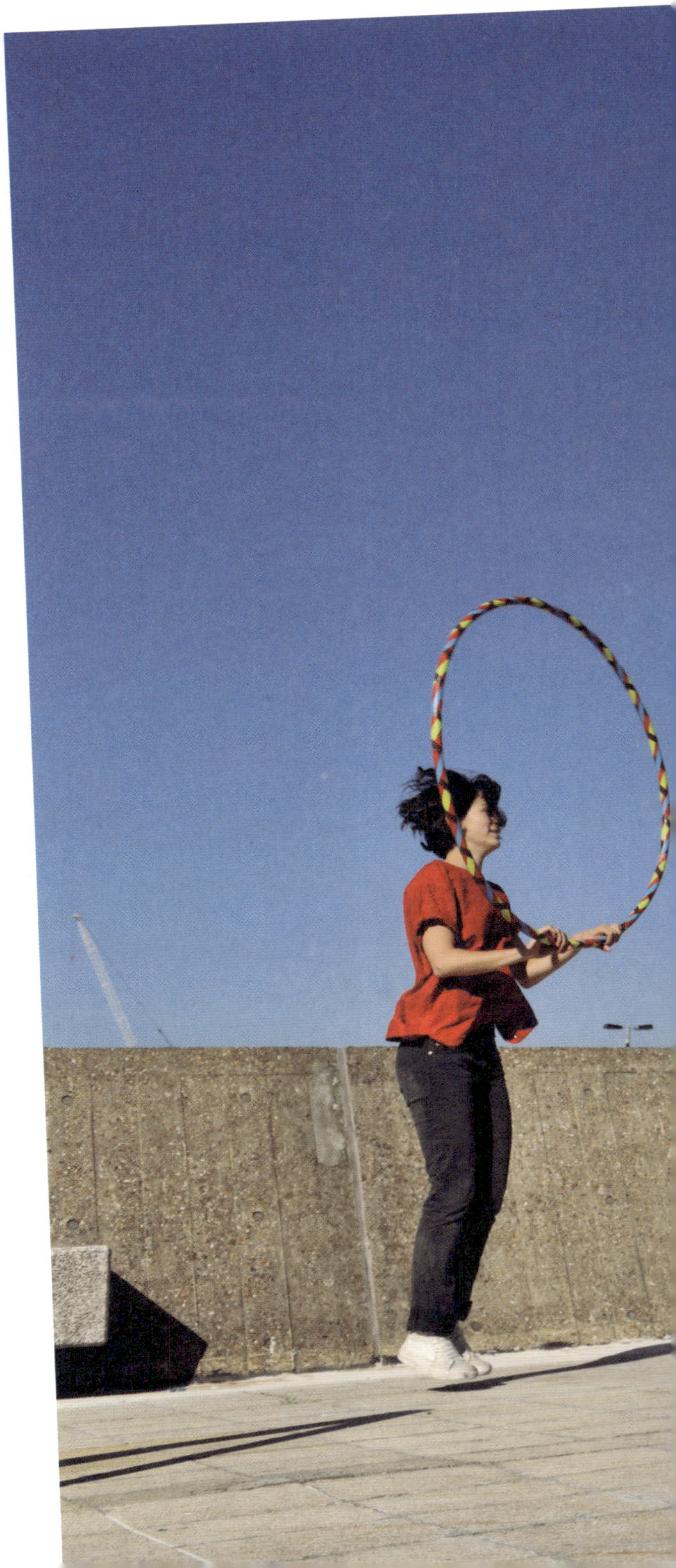

This page and opposite: Christian Jankowski, *Rooftop Routine*, 2008/2010

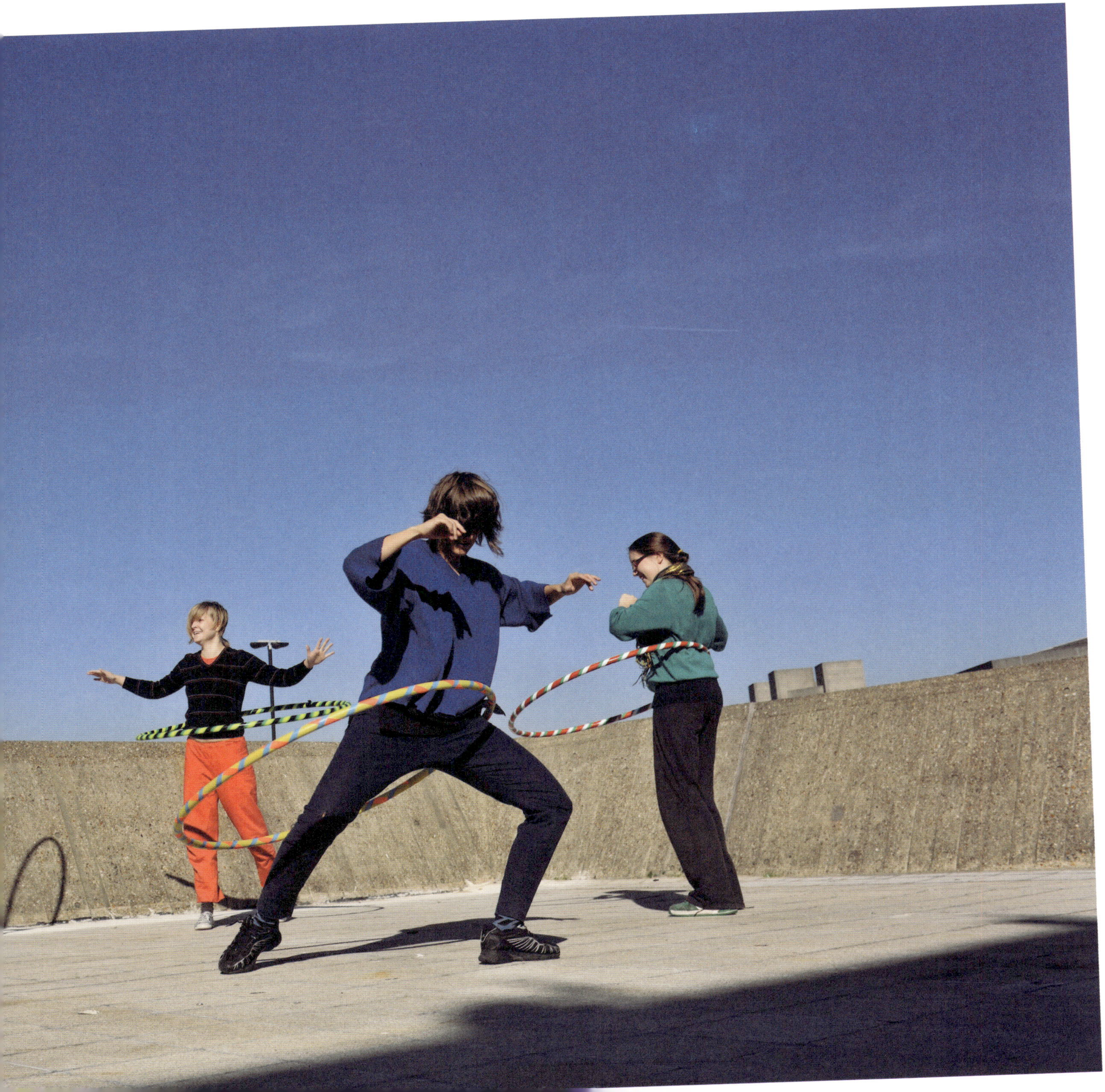

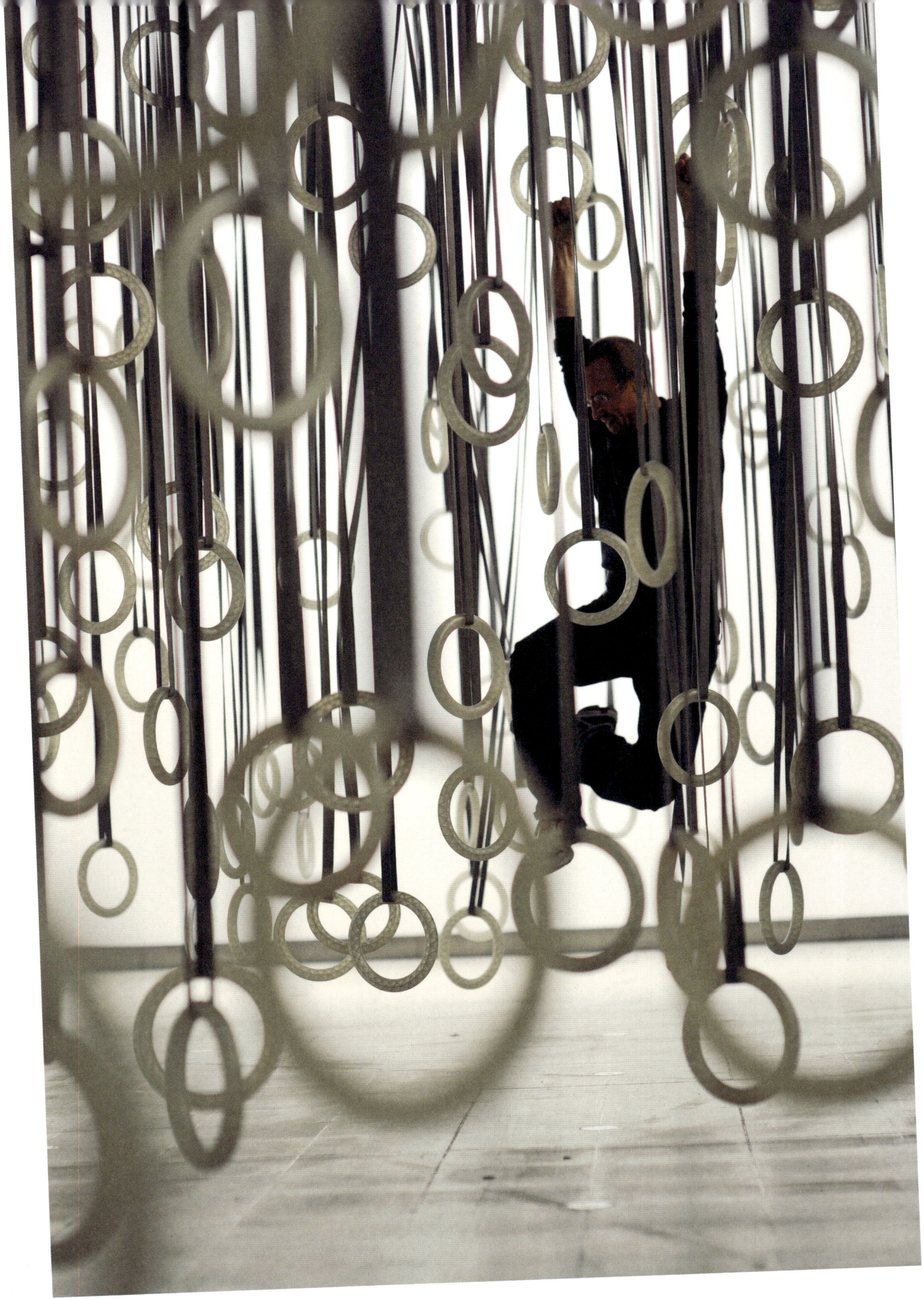

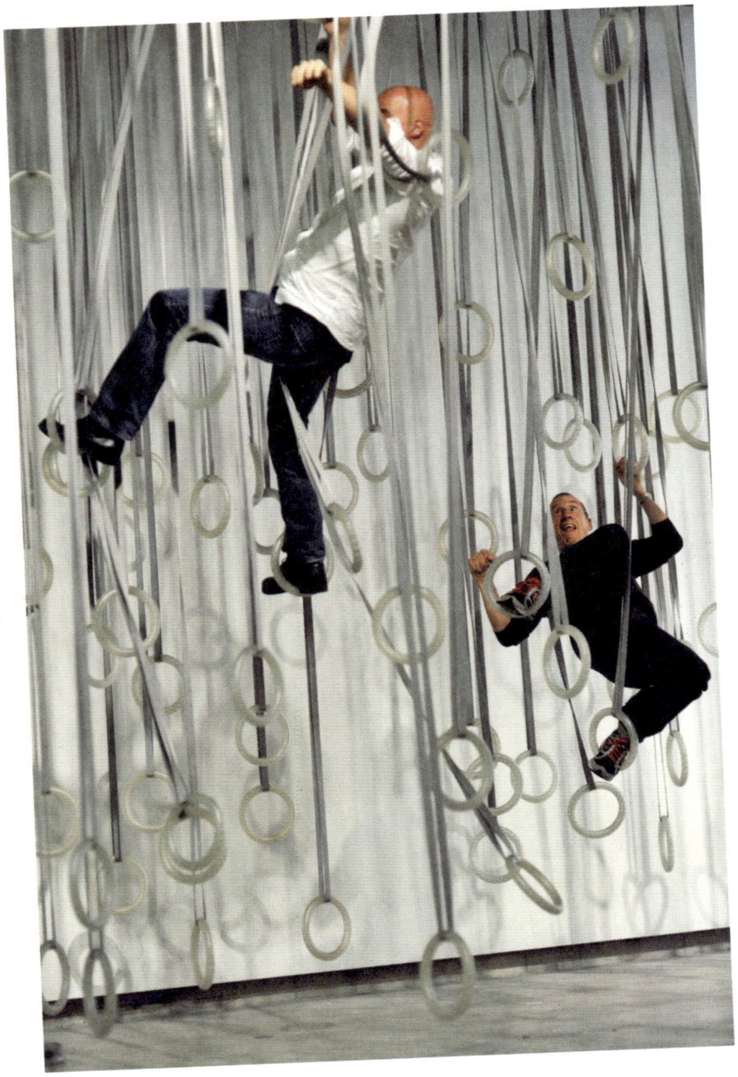

William Forsythe, *The Fact of Matter*, 2009

William Forsythe

City of Abstracts (2000) and The Fact of Matter (2009)

In his ballets and choreographic installations, William Forsythe aims 'to facilitate dancing that shows the body's own experience of itself.'[1] Trained in classical dance in Florida and New York, Forsythe left America to join the Stuttgart Ballet in 1973 and has lived in Germany ever since. From Stuttgart, where he became resident choreographer, he went on to direct the Frankfurt Ballet for twenty years and then launched the Forsythe Company, a 'choreographic collective' based in Frankfurt and Dresden, in 2005. Throughout his career he has challenged conventional assumptions about how ballet should be staged, and has radically changed the way we look at, and think about, classical dance. His ballets often involve text, image, innovative lighting, experimental music and sound, and reflect his interest in science, architecture, mathematics, philosophy and literature. Since the late 1990s, he has extended his choreographic enquiries beyond theatrical dance into other areas, such as environments and installations for galleries and public places, video and film, digital media, and publications; experimenting with new ways to experience movement, both physically and mentally.

Forsythe points out that choreography and dance are two very different and distinct practices, which can (and often do) exist independently of each other: 'choreography is not necessarily bound to dance, nor is dance bound to choreography, for that matter – you can just get up and dance. It doesn't have to be what is traditionally known as dance; you can set crowds of people into action, inadvertently, without them knowing.'[2] While he has defined dancing as 'a conversation with gravity', he describes choreography as a 'curious and deceptive term; the word itself, like the processes it describes, is elusive, agile, and maddeningly unmanageable.'[3] At its most basic, choreography is about engendering, ordering and composing movement; about 'organising bodies in space, or organising bodies with other bodies, or a body with other bodies in an environment that is organised.'[4]

Since the dissolution of the Frankfurt Ballet, which had been based at the city's Opera House, and the Forsythe Company's subsequent move to smaller, more industrial premises, Forsythe has increasingly moved away from the confines of the conventional stage and has explored other environments as sites for choreographic experiments. Though his various 'Choreographic Objects' take disparate forms, each is designed to initiate encounters between the human body and physical space. The earliest, made in collaboration with dancer Dana Caspersen and composer Joel Ryan in 1997, is the 'White Bouncy Castle', a giant inflatable that provides a choreographic space in which there are no spectators and everyone becomes a participant. As Forsythe remarks, 'as soon as someone steps inside the castle, the dance has already begun.'[5] Within it, the experience is one of complete physical destabilisation and momentary weightlessness; on returning

William Forsythe, City of Abstracts, 2000

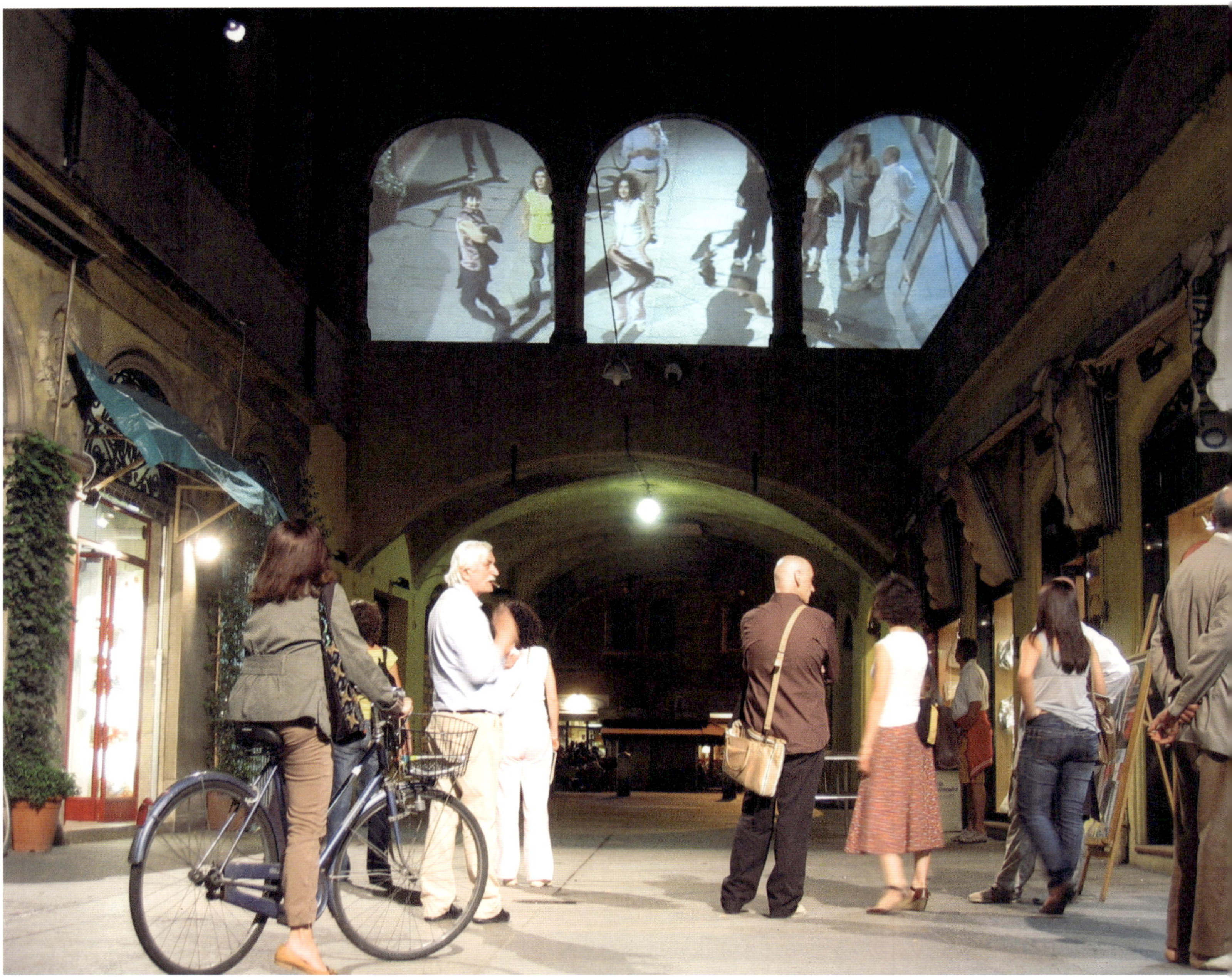

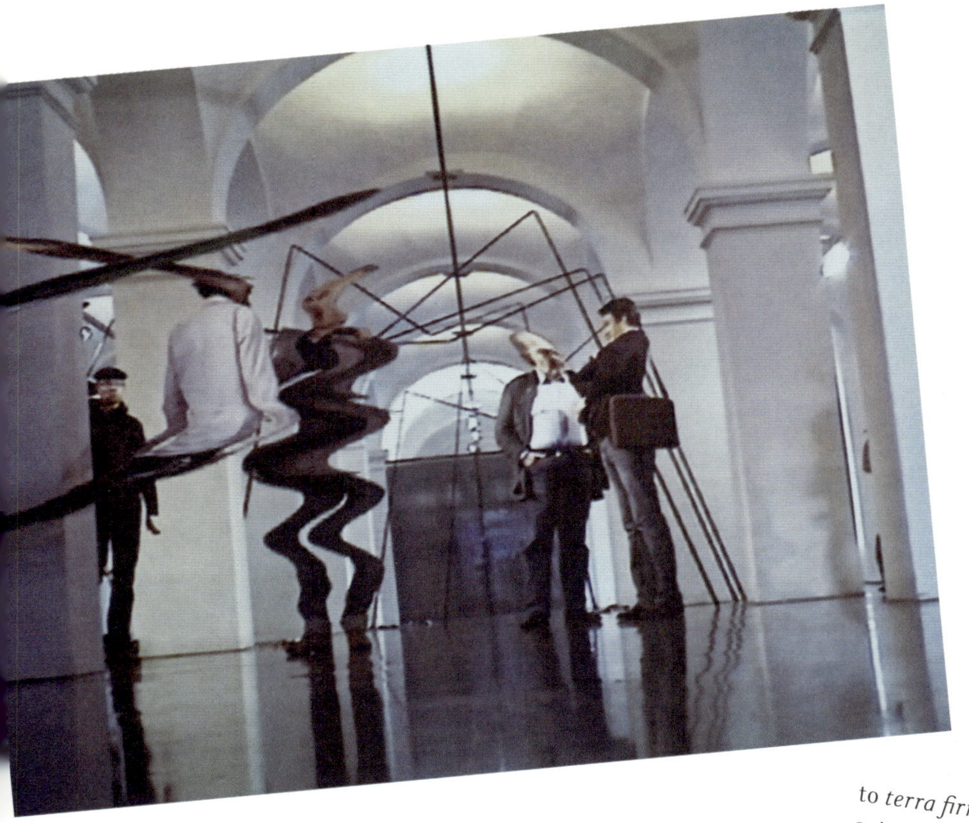

William Forsythe, City of Abstracts, 2000

to *terra firma*, participants suddenly become aware of the body's actual heaviness and mass. Visitors to *Move: Choreographing You* will discover that in the case of *The Fact of Matter* (2009) the opposite is true. This choreographic object consists of a thicket of dangling gymnastic rings which invite visitors to stretch and swing their way across space. Though it may look easy, in practice the traversal becomes a test of physical and mental agility which makes the user acutely conscious of their body, its weight and its limitations and, when accomplished, leaves a feeling of weightlessness. As Forsythe stresses, 'the object is not so much there to be seen, as to be used. An engagement with the object offers the user a possible re-assessment of their mass, strength, and coordination skill as a unified system.'[6]

Forsythe's second contribution to this exhibition is *City of Abstracts* (2000), an outdoor video installation that captures the movements of passers-by As people approach the wall-sized screen, hidden cameras and time-delayed projections gradually distort their actions, turning them into fairground-mirror images in a dance of rippling, slithering, stretching and spiralling forms. Enticed into interaction, they begin a sort of *pas de deux* with themselves, making what are in effect drawings with their own bodies. 'As you move, you get these snaky versions of yourself,' Forsythe comments. 'People learn it very quickly.'[7]

Helen Luckett

1 William Forsythe in Roslyn Sulcas, 'The Continuing Evolution of Mr. Forsythe', in *Dance Magazine*, January 1997.
2 William Forsythe, in video interview for Dance-Tech.Net, http://www.dance-tech.net/video/interview-with-william (my transcription).
3 William Forsythe, 'Choreographic Objects', http://www.williamforsythe.de/essay.html.
4 William Forsythe, in conversation with Dana Caspersen and Peter Cook at the Royal Geographical Society, London, 7 March 1997.
5 William Forsythe, quoted in http://contemporaryperformance.com/2010/07/26/highlights-2010-international-hamburg-summer-festival-hamburg-germany/.
6 William Forsythe, http://www.williamforsythe.de/installations.html?&no_cache=1&detail=1&uid=29.
7 William Forsythe in Sarah Compton, 'Interview with William Forsythe', *The Daily Telegraph*, Tuesday 7 April 2009.

William Forsythe was born in New York City in 1949 and lives in Frankfurt and Dresden.

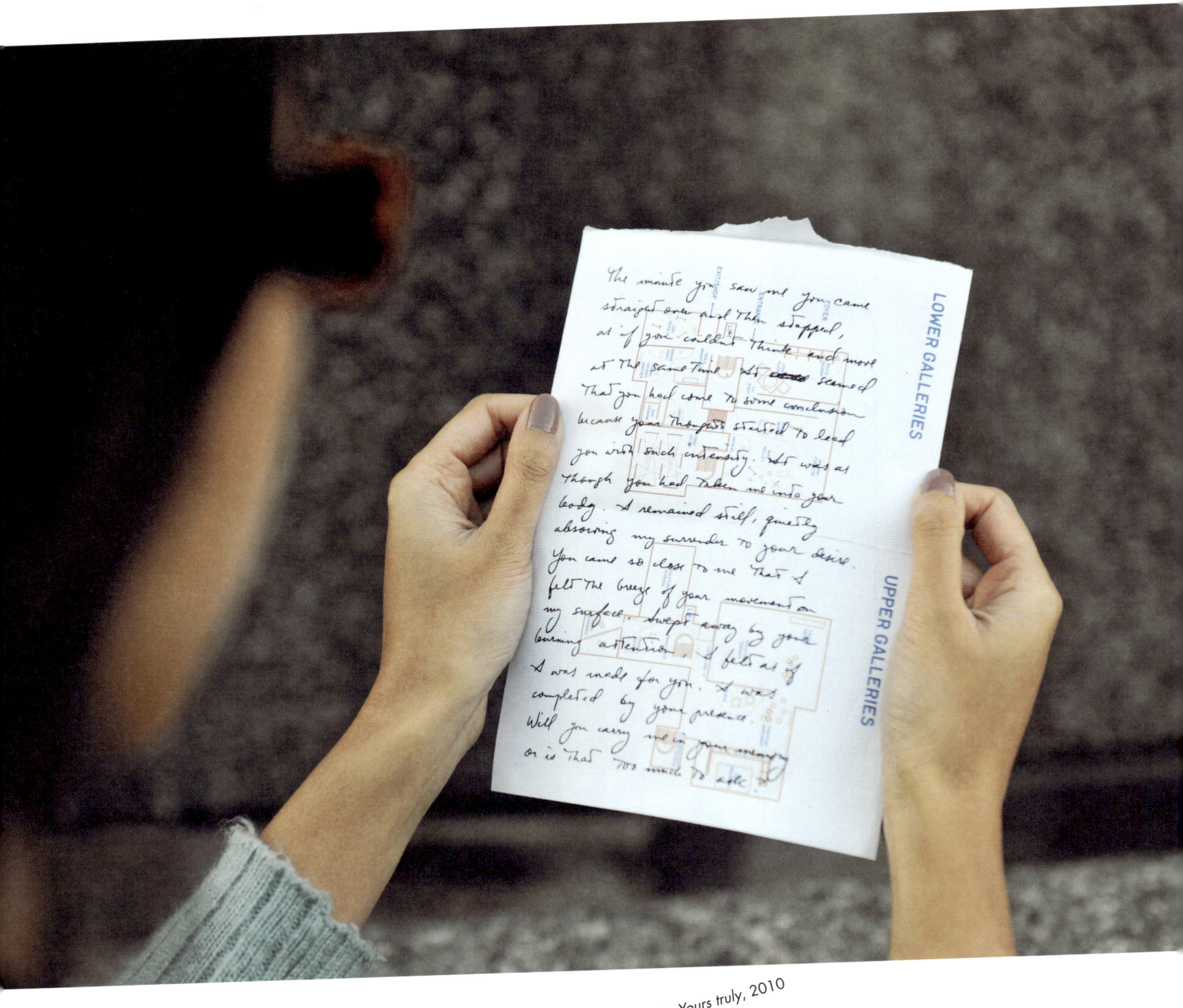

Janine Antoni, *Yours truly*, 2010

Janine Antoni
Yours truly, 2010

In 1959, the artist Lygia Clark wrote in a letter to Piet Mondrian, who was by that time deceased: 'If I exhibit it is to transmit to someone else "this moment" stopped within the cosmological dynamics which the artist captures.'[1] The honesty of her language is reminiscent of a diary entry. Expressing her innermost battles, she closes the letter with the words 'Mondrian, today I love you.'[2]

Inspired by the intimacy of Clark's words, addressed to a person only encountered through his art, Janine Antoni conceived *Yours truly* (2010), her contribution to *Move: Choreographing You*, in the form of a letter addressed to the exhibition visitor. Scribbled on a page from the exhibition guide and written from the perspective of a fictional work in the show, this love letter is smuggled into the belongings of visitors and left there as a surprise to be discovered later.

The letter speaks of an encounter between a visitor and an artwork that supposedly took place during a trip to the exhibition. It describes the intensity and intimacy of the moment, as if portraying the exchange between two lovers – conflating sexual attraction with attraction to art. By endowing an artwork with the ability to feel and to be touched by the gaze of the viewer, Antoni is planting a seed in the reader's consciousness that may change the way in which he or she approaches art in the future. Yet the discourse around attributing human qualities to artworks is not a new one. As Michael Fried wrote in his seminal critique of Minimalism, 'Art and Objecthood': 'being distanced by such objects is not, I suggest, entirely unlike being distanced, or crowded by the silent presence of another person.'[3]

Antoni accepts the fact that not everyone will be the wiser for this subtle intervention. Depending on an intricate chain of events, the work may go unnoticed for many, making the experience for visitors who find the letter all the more distinctive. Her partners for this intimate *pas de deux* are chosen at random, and the ephemeral and secretive nature of the piece allows it to take on a life outside of the frame of the exhibition.

Antoni likes to observe people's behaviour in exhibition spaces. She often talks to the guards in the galleries, gathering information like a field researcher on how people interact with the works. She envisions the audience's reaction to her work in great detail, anticipating their every step, wondering where they pause, what draws them in, what touches them. Movement is an essential aspect of her practice, which originates from dance. In playing with the multiple meanings of the word 'move' in this work, which describes both physical action and emotional reaction, she is retrospectively directing the movement of the viewer, who is suddenly aware that the tables have been turned: they themselves are the object of attention. The duet that Antoni is choreographing here generates a mild form of paranoia in the visitor, influencing their behaviour after the fact. In a form of self-conscious *déjà vu*, the viewer retraces his or her steps, revisiting every move in the exhibition in an attempt to trace the origin of the letter.

While sticking to familiar Antoni turf by situating itself 'between object, performance and relict',[4] *Yours truly* is in many ways a departure from her previous work. Here, Antoni is abandoning the extreme acts and elaborate material constructions of her early installations and performances, choosing instead to create an unmediated physical experience that involves the viewer directly: 'I'm [...] interested in the viewer empathizing with my process. I do these extreme acts because I feel that viewers can relate to them through their bodies.' Performance is a strategy that has allowed her to achieve this, as well as reconciling her interest in process with the object. In pieces such as *Loving Care* (1993), in which she mops a gallery floor with her hair soaked in dye, or *Gnaw* (1992), where she bites away the corners of a 600-pound perfect cube of chocolate, her body becomes a stand-in that allows the viewer to unlock personal experiences through the act of witnessing and to relate to the work through their own body memories. Antoni longs for an intimate contact with the viewer and feels a great connection with her audience through the simple fact that they are engaging with her work. In that sense, *Yours truly* is the pinnacle of the ambitions she has had all along.

Anna Gritz

1 Lygia Clark, *Letter to Mondrian*, 1959, in *Lygia Clark*, Fundacio Antoni Tapies, Barcelona. 1998, p 114.
2 Ibid., p. 116.
3 Michael Fried, 'Art and Objecthood' (1967), in *Art and Theory: 1900-1990*, Wiley-Blackwell, Oxford, 1992, p. 826.
4 Janine Antoni, 'Escape Hatch. Janine Antoni in Conversation with Douglas Dreishpoon', *Art in America*, No. 9, October 2009, p. 128.

Janine Antoni was born in 1964 in Freeport, Bahamas and lives and works in New York.

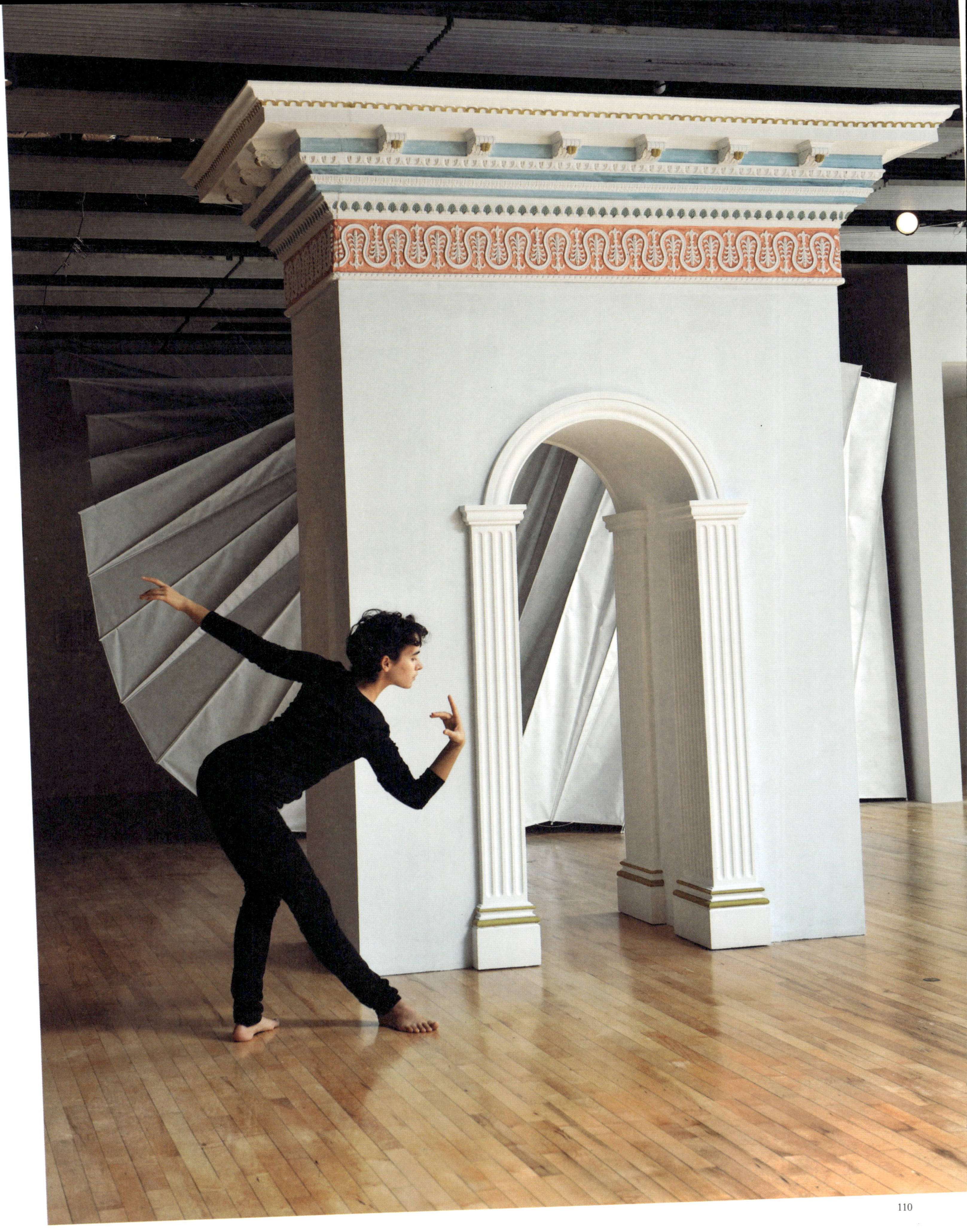

Pablo Bronstein, *Magnificent Triumphal Arch in Pompeian Colours*, 2010

Pablo Bronstein
Magnificent Triumphal Arch in Pompeian Colours (2010)

Pablo Bronstein borrows from the language and forms of architecture, insisting he is 'ultimately interested in people's relation to architecture, and not in architecture per se [...] in the way architecture constructs, or helps to construct, images of power and control, and ways in which it fails to do so.' His varied output, including paintings, drawings, performances and installations, features a common interest in how public space can function as a form of theatre.

In his performances and installations, Bronstein intervenes in physical space and makes a connection between it and the performed or choreographed body. Dance, for him, as with drawing or architecture, can demarcate space: 'it is another way of drawing [...] you mark space out, you mark territories out, and dimensions and volumes with gestures, positions of people on a plane'. His live performances and installations respond to or construct a specific environment, which sets the stage for heavily directed or theatricalised movement. As the artist notes: 'façades [...] are created by particular ideologies'. Within Bronstein's work, these ideologies and their physical manifestations are unveiled or embodied.

For *Move: Choreographing You*, Bronstein has created within the galleries a reincarnation of a monumental arch. *Magnificent Triumphal Arch in Pompeian Colours* (2010) dominates the space, standing three metres tall, complete with decorative supporting pilasters, colourful façade and cornice moulding. The archway functions as both a grand thoroughfare in the gallery and stage for a solo performance by a dancer that takes place at regular intervals. A performer's pedestrian movements transform into a stylised Baroque *sprezzatura* gesture as they move through the arch. The arch, alongside columns, obelisks and public plazas, is a recurring motif in the artist's work, as is his interest in the neoclassical and the baroque in general; particularly their association with theatricality, movement, pomp, discipline and ornamentation. Classicism and Postmodernism often meet in the artist's work – detailed ink drawings imagine Postmodernist buildings embellished with baroque ornamentation in a type of fantasy architecture. His installations introduce fake or overbearing architectural fragments within pristine white cube spaces to disruptive ends. The performance works infuse elements of baroque dance with the everyday movements of Post-minimalist dance.

Bronstein's installation for *Move* sits incongruously within its gallery surroundings, looking as if it has been plonked down from a far-off age or aesthetic. Visitors are forced to engage with it physically and visually – as a setting for the exhibition's resident dancers, thereby theatricalising a visitor's ordinary movements, as if they were walking through a stage set or into their own performance piece. The work functions as a literal and figurative passageway towards a heightened awareness of one's own movement and behaviour in public space. *Magnificent Triumphal Arch* imposes a setting within which the dancer's or the visitor's everyday movements become exaggeratedly staged, theatrically framed or highlighted. Bronstein acknowledges architecture's performative aspect, whereby buildings govern or express how we organise ourselves, control and mediate both public space and public action – and where we perform roles as citizens, consumers, bystanders or workers on a daily basis. Playing with the motifs of historical buildings or settings, he creates a highly formal and artificial-looking space to direct and then dramatise the everyday movements of visitors, revealing the choreography in the act of walking, looking and watching in particular spaces.

Magnificent Triumphal Arch prompts both physical and cognitive transformation. Gallery goers must navigate through the work, but its theatrical look and stage set function creates the sense that they too are performing their own dance of sorts. Just as Bronstein treats the body as sculpture in his live performances, and utilises dancers to mark out space through gesture and movement, here the pedestrian body becomes aestheticised and directed. Visitors could be another performer, or stand-ins for statues or ornamentation, to be likewise admired or watched. But it is not an entirely unrestricted performance: other bodies, the limits of the space and the conventions of etiquette, restrict, direct and codify movement. Bronstein's installation suggests that public space can be its own form of stage set, with its own props and certainly its own choreography.

Siobhan McCracken Nixon

Pablo Bronstein was born in Buenos Aires in 1977 and lives and works in London.

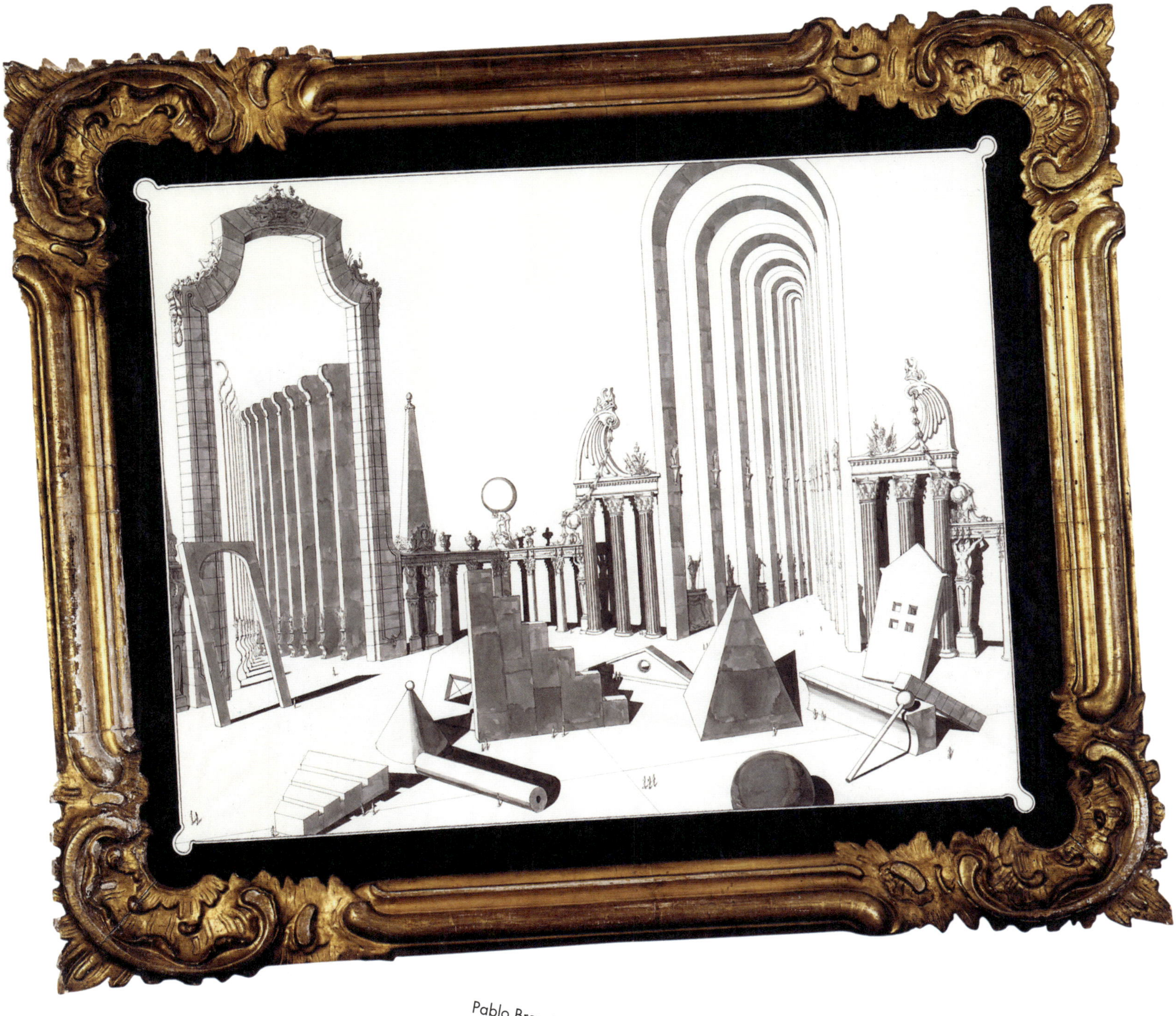

Pablo Bronstein, *Magnificent Plaza*, 2007

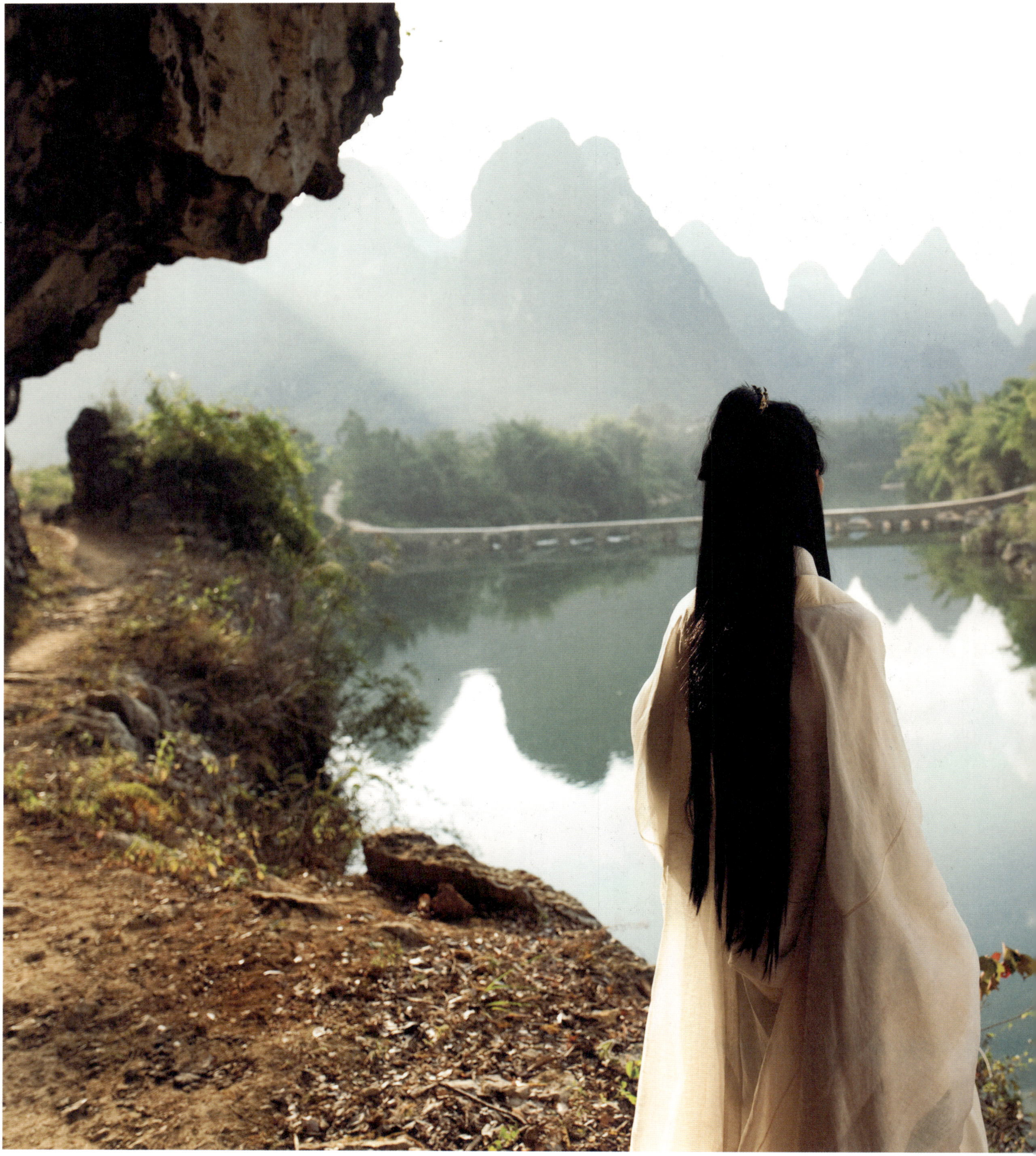

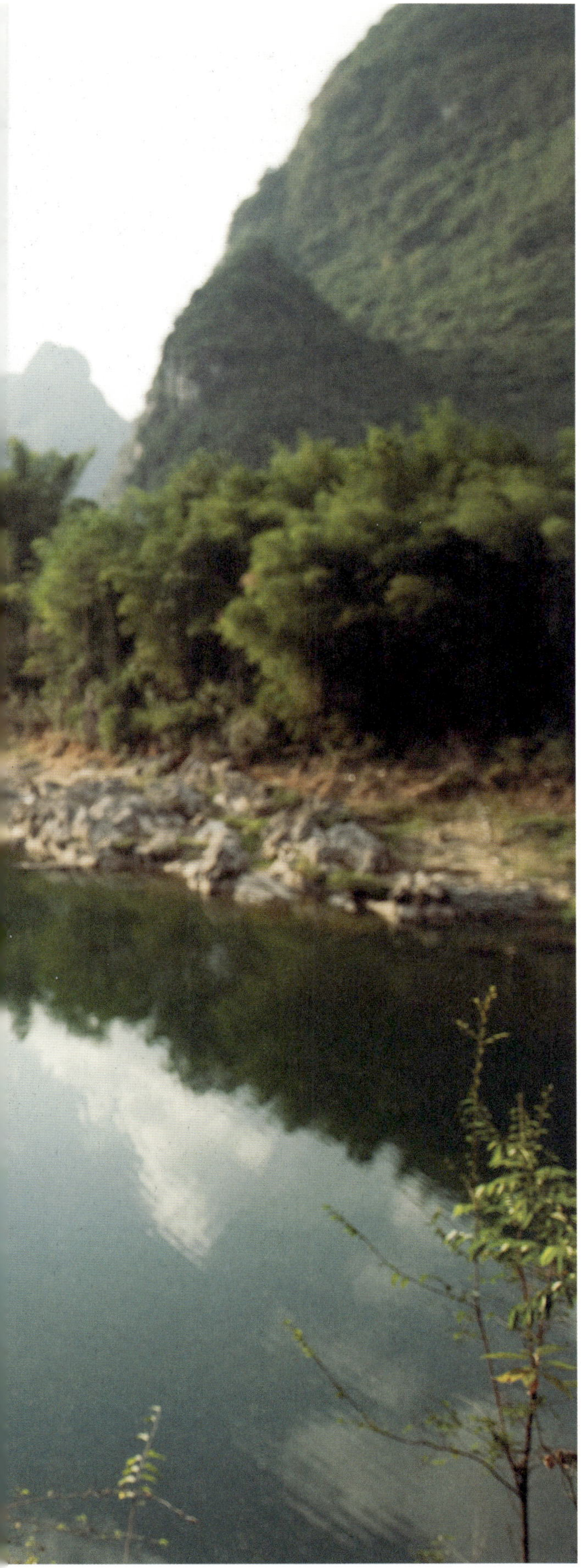

Isaac Julien, *TEN THOUSAND WAVES*, 2010

Isaac Julien
TEN THOUSAND WAVES (2010)

Isaac Julien's multi-screen film installations create cinematic experiences in which art, architecture, dance, sound and movement intermix. In these 'gallery films', which he has made over the past decade, the audience enters into an active relationship with the image through what Julien calls the 'choreography of the gaze'. While some of his films have involved collaborations with choreographers and dancers (mostly recently with Stephen Galloway in *Fantôme Afrique* (2005) and in 2007 with Russell Maliphant in *WESTERN UNION: Small Boats*), Julien's work is itself inherently choreographic in terms of editing, its use of montage and multiple screens, and its articulation of space.

Emphasising that 'film and dance are different languages', Julien explains that his interest in movement, which stems from his teenage involvement with the London Dance Youth Theatre, is fundamental to the composition of his works. As an artist and maker of film installations, his concern is to expand the concept of cinema; to break away from the convention of a passive audience that sits in front of a single screen, watching a linear narrative with a controlled start and finish. In his recent installations – most particularly *TEN THOUSAND WAVES* (2010) – the moving image requires a moving audience, since spectators are encouraged not to view the works from a single fixed position and must negotiate constantly changing lines of sight. Although each work has a definable beginning and end, the films are shown continuously in looped presentations and their narratives constructed in a way that takes account of the fact that the audience may enter and leave at any point in the journey

TEN THOUSAND WAVES, which is being shown for the first time in the UK in this exhibition, is Julien's most complex film installation to date. An extended contrapuntal meditation on migration, physical and cultural dislocation and unfinished journeys, it weaves together three separate stories which are presented as a montage of moving images oscillating between nine free-hanging screens suspended at angles to each other. Viewers enter an immersive and frequently disorienting environment in which they are compelled to make their own experiential journeys, both in physical and psychological terms.

The original impetus for *TEN THOUSAND WAVES* was the disaster that occurred in north-west England in 2004 when 23 Chinese cockle-pickers were drowned in Morecambe Bay. Having travelled from the other side of the world in search of a better life, these men and women were exploited by unscrupulous gangmasters and found themselves working in appalling conditions, exacerbated by their lack of local knowledge and the fact that they spoke almost no English.

An account of this tragedy, told through documentary audio and video footage, is intertwined with the ancient Chinese legend of the goddess

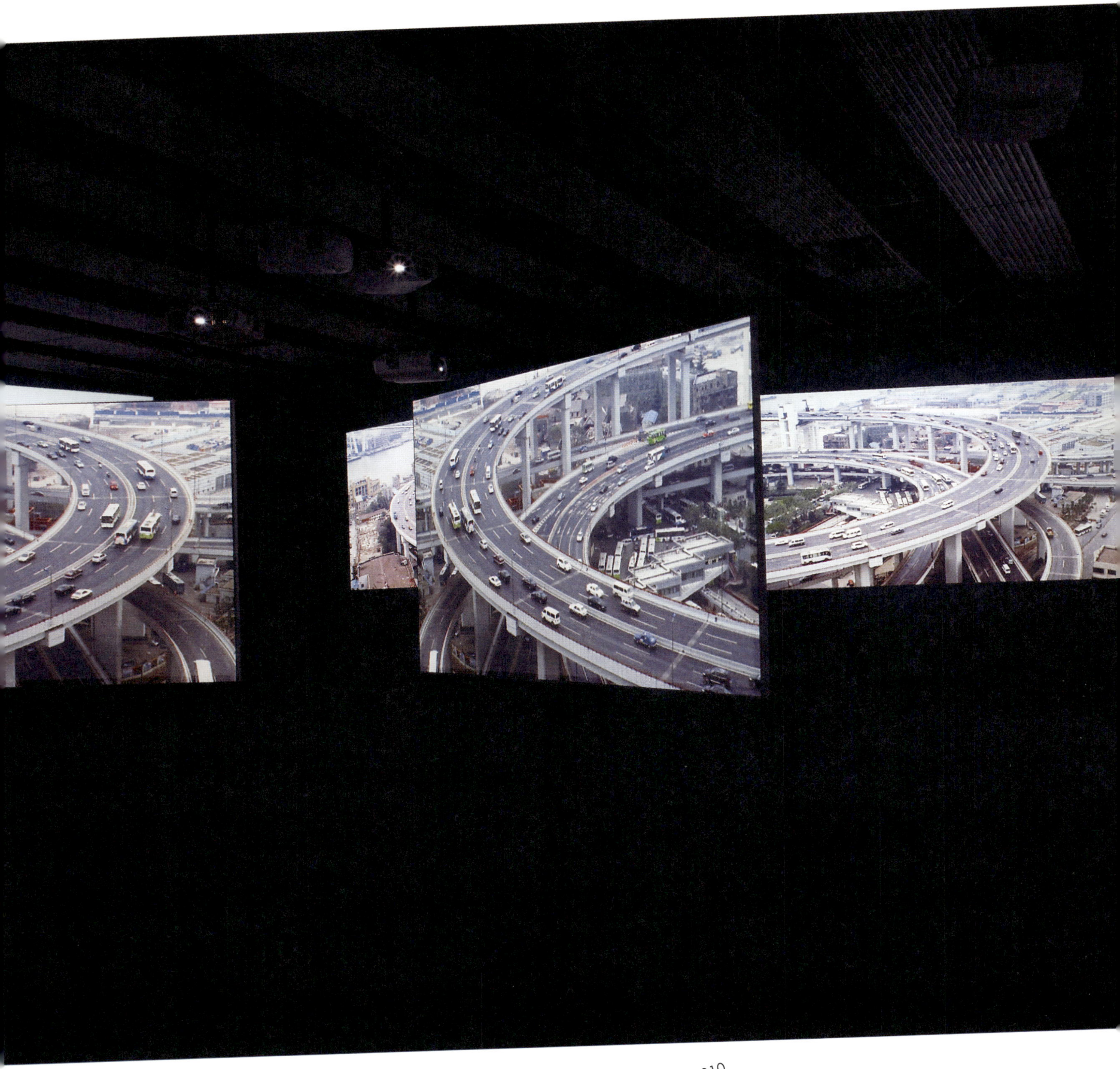

This page and opposite: Isaac Julien, *TEN THOUSAND WAVES*, 2010

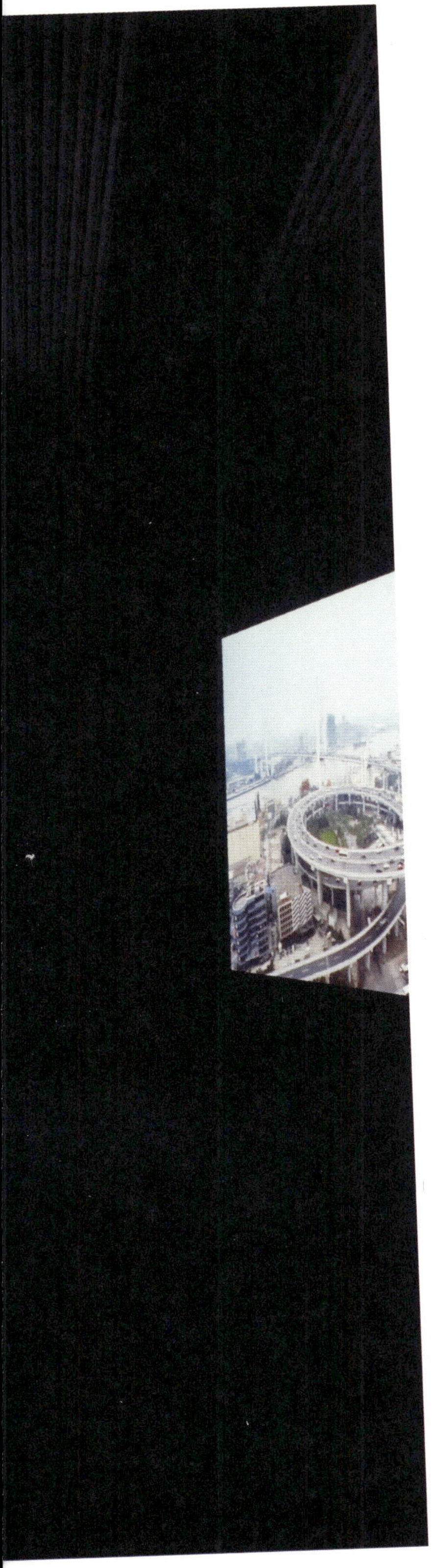

Mazu (played by Maggie Cheung), protector of seafarers who, in one especially lyrical sequence, rescues fishermen from drowning and brings them to a safe haven. A third narrative strand is provided by the re-enactment of scenes from *The Goddess* (1934), a classic Chinese film about a young woman who 'has no choice but to struggle in the whirlpool of life' and resorts to prostitution in order to support her small son. The Blue Goddess figure (played by Zhao Tao) both mirrors Mazu and acts as a ghostly guide to old and new Shanghai, travelling through the Shanghai Film Studios (a place of illusions) and around the modern city. In a separate twist, the mechanics of film are exposed and illusions unravelled as Mazu is shown being filmed on a green screen in the studio (the backgrounds were added later). Julien points out that this revelation is 'really just a form of deconstruction that exposes the choreographic work behind creating film.'

The various strands are brought together visually through the use of 'parallel montage' in which several screens are edited at once to form an architectural space. Alongside the repetition, mirroring, doubling and interchanging of individual shots, Julien also uses the visual technique of bricolage, bringing together thermal search video taken by British police, computer-generated imagery, footage from a Hong Kong-made documentary about the victims' families, and 35mm film. Sound is used in a similar way, with 'found' sound co-existing with commissioned music, while the use of multi-channel surround sound means that music, the spoken word and incidental noise are localised and, as with the separate screens, help to direct movement through the space. Throughout the work, the overriding themes of migration, the restless sea, and lost souls are voiced in poems by Wang Ping, which are themselves interlaced with Mazu's repeated summons '*Hun xi gui lai!*' [Come home Soul!] and a recurring cry from the telephone call made to the emergency services from Morecambe Bay: 'just people [...]'

Helen Luckett

Isaac Julien was born in London in 1960, where he lives and works.

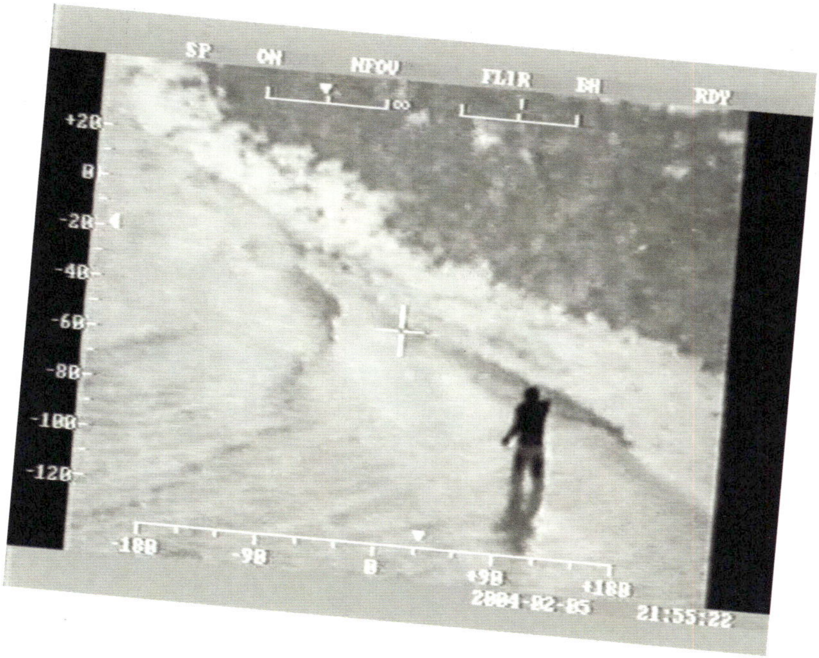

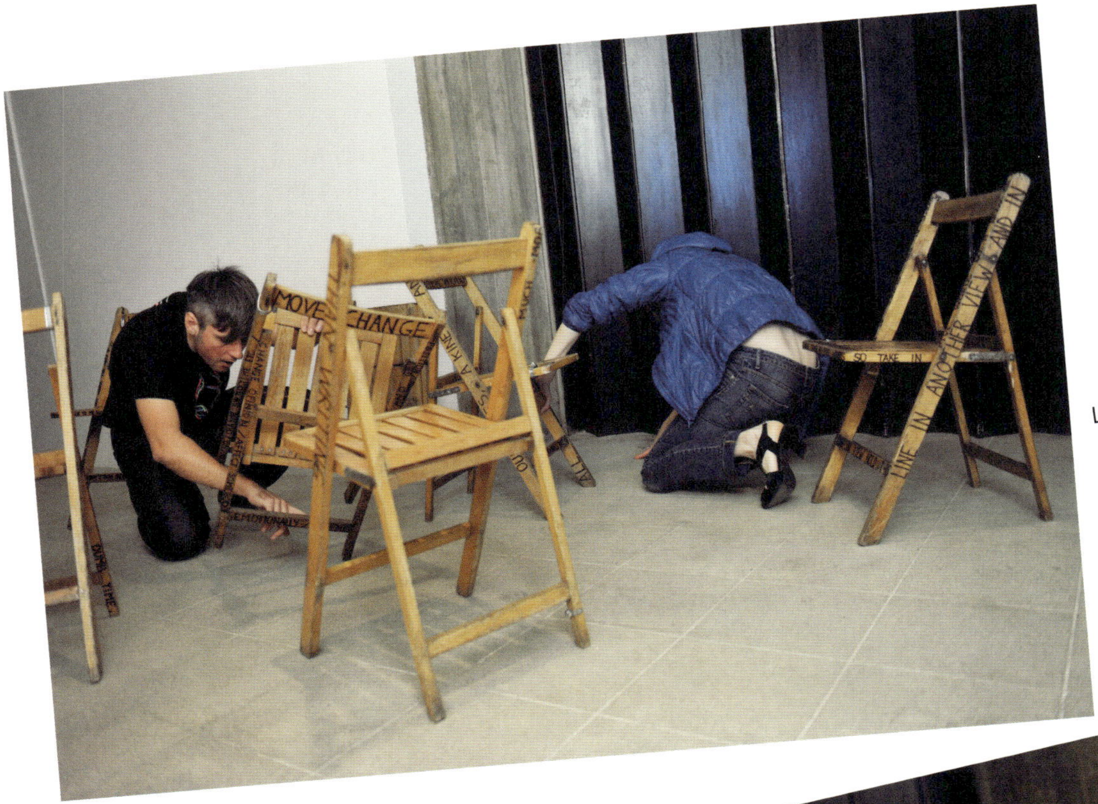

La Ribot, *Walk the Chair*, 2010

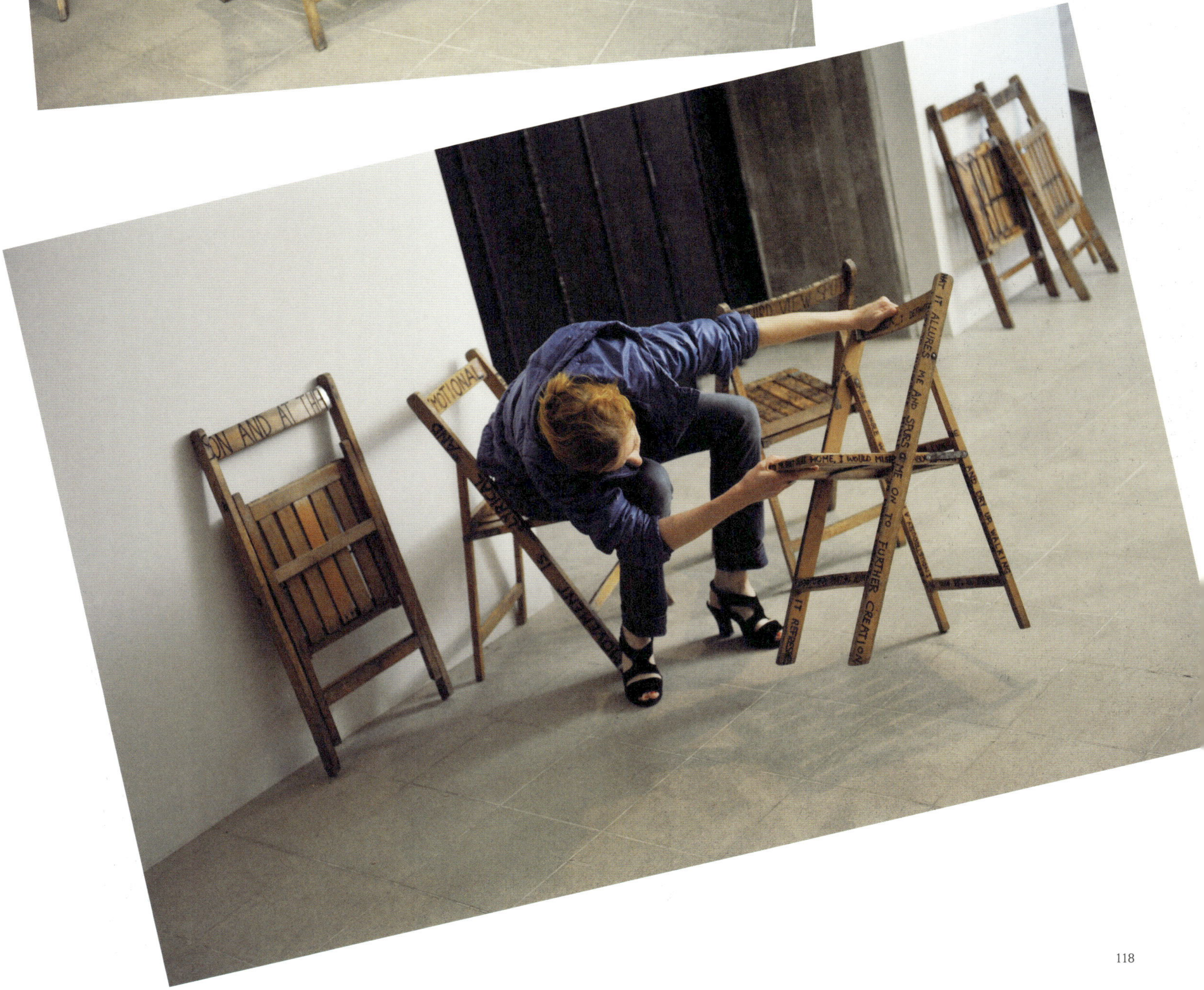

La Ribot
Llámame Mariachi (2009); Walk the Chair (2010)

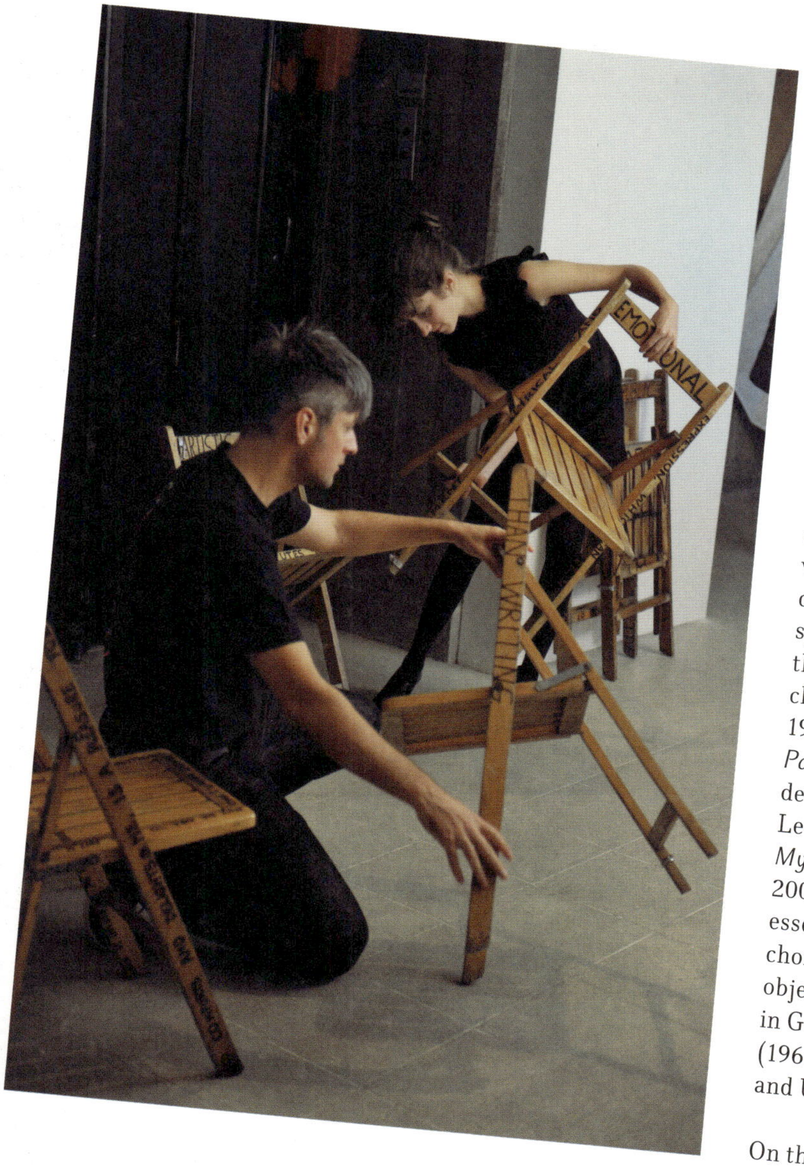

Since the Spanish choreographer La Ribot initiated her series of short works entitled *Distinguished Pieces* in 1993, she has walked a fine line between dance and the visual arts. Systematically investigating stillness in live performance, utilising a variety of objects to create miniature tableaux-vivants, occupying galleries, creating videos, exploring the durational and deploying an acute sense of plasticity, La Ribot creates work where 'dance, performance and the plastic arts all unfold on a common plane'.[1]

In *Walk the Chair* (2010) the resonances of the chair in the recent history of dance, Conceptual and performance art emerge. The historian Siegfried Giedion has suggested that the chair has defined our mode of living in the modern age.[2] Due to its function of supporting a resting body, however, a chair's presence in theatrical dance performances disrupts the usual association of dancing with verticality, stepping, leaping, moving around. In this context, chairs should properly belong to, and define, the passive realm of spectatorship, as opposed to the active realm of dancing. But in the radical reformulation of the imperative to move as the defining characteristic of dance initiated by choreographers since the early 1960s, we find chairs taking a crucial role. Key examples include Steve Paxton's *Flat* (1964), Pina Bausch's *Café Müller* (1978), Anne Therese de Keersmaker's *Rosa Danst Rosas* (1983), and more recently Xavier Le Roy's *Self Unfinished* (1998), Juan Dominguez's *All Good Spies Are My Age* (2003) and most of La Ribot's *Distinguished Pieces* (1993–2000). In all of these works, chairs and the sitting position appear as essential partners, and even as the main subjects, in the redefinition of choreography and dance. Similarly, the chair has been the subject and object of some crucial pieces in Conceptual and performance art, as in George Brecht's *Three Chair Events* (1961) or *Chair with a History* (1966), Joseph Kosuth's *One and Three Chairs* (1965) and Abramovic and Ulay's *Nightsea Crossing* (1981–87).

On the first day of *Walk the Chair*, the public will find 50 folded wooden chairs (the same type that La Ribot has used in all of her previous pieces) lined up along the gallery walls. The title of the piece is an explicit instruction to the public, and as the days go by and the public engages in this task, the chairs will remain in whatever place they have been left after their walk. To perform this humorous score is to disrupt the social contract of spectatorship – animating that which is supposed to remain inanimate. By moving the chairs, the audience literally 'creates the piece', as La Ribot emphasises. But if the title asks for one to walk the chair, the modes and pathways of each walk remain undetermined. La Ribot has stated her wish not to direct the spectator's actions in any way: 'It will be different from one day to the next, from one place to the next'. People may want to take chairs for a walk, or they may want simply to sit on them and watch others moving the chairs; they may want to pile them up, or arrange them in rows. Eventually, all the chairs will have been 'walked' – some perhaps through the whole exhibition. In this way, the social space of the art gallery is redefined. (See also Vlatka Horvat's *This Here and That There* (2007), presented in the Archive section of this exhibition (p. 156), where possibilities of socialisation are defined by an endless choreography of chairs.)

Since the title/score remains vague in its demand, the spectator also remains free to resist it and simply look at the chairs. This looking, however, still demands a supplemental activity, since while sitting on a chair one can literally read it: the chairs are also surfaces of inscription where a whole history of thoughts about mobility has been written in fire. La Ribot has pyrographed her chairs with quotes from Isadora Duncan, Gordon Craig, Roland Barthes, Peter Sloterdijk, Gilles Deleuze and many others. She has called this writing with fire an 'act of vandalism', but it is an act that frees spectators, things and words from the strict choreographies commanding how they should move, behave and be – in museums as well as in life.

La Ribot's more theatrical piece *Llámame Mariachi* (2009) is premised on the sharp division between filmic image and live performance. Part one of the work is a 20-minute-long single-shot sequence filmed at belly height by three dancers, who pass the camera between themselves as they move about an empty old theatre. The kinetic film is an experiment in how handling a camera choreographs a film's perception. In the second half of the piece, the same three dancers appear on stage, walking as slowly and as deliberately as possible – always on the edge of falling, as if in a low-gravity environment. Slowing down movement to almost an aberrant point, the three women sit on a table and proceed to read aloud from dozens of books, pamphlets and papers. The humour of the piece (between Buster Keaton and Samuel Beckett) creates a suspension between gravity and gravitas, creating a truly airy and light dance, which is nevertheless slowed down and highly verbal.

André Lepecki

1 Christophe Kihm, 'Chaises et jeux de positions', in www.laribot.com/spip.php?article1009, accessed Sept., 2010.
2 Siegfried Giedion, *Mechanization Takes Command*, W.W. Norton, New York and London, 1969, pp. 389–508.

La Ribot was born in Madrid in 1962 and lives and works in Geneva.

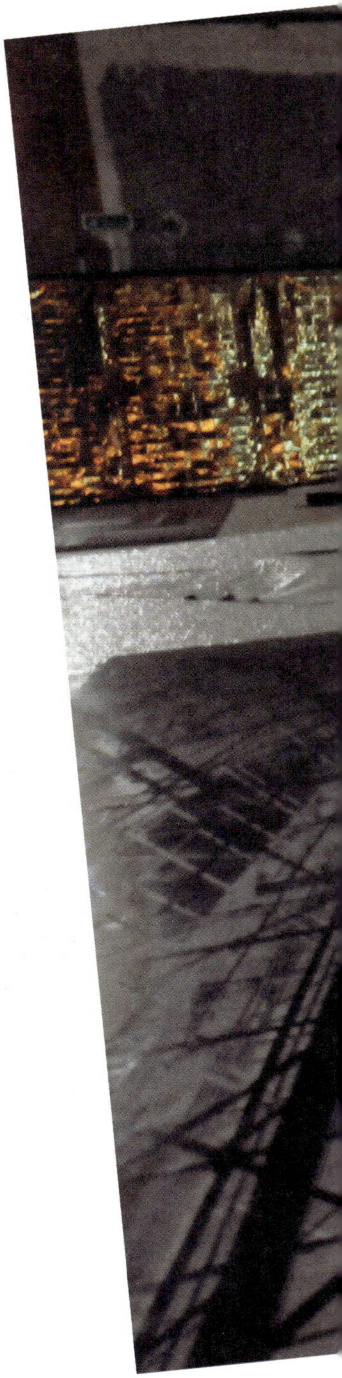

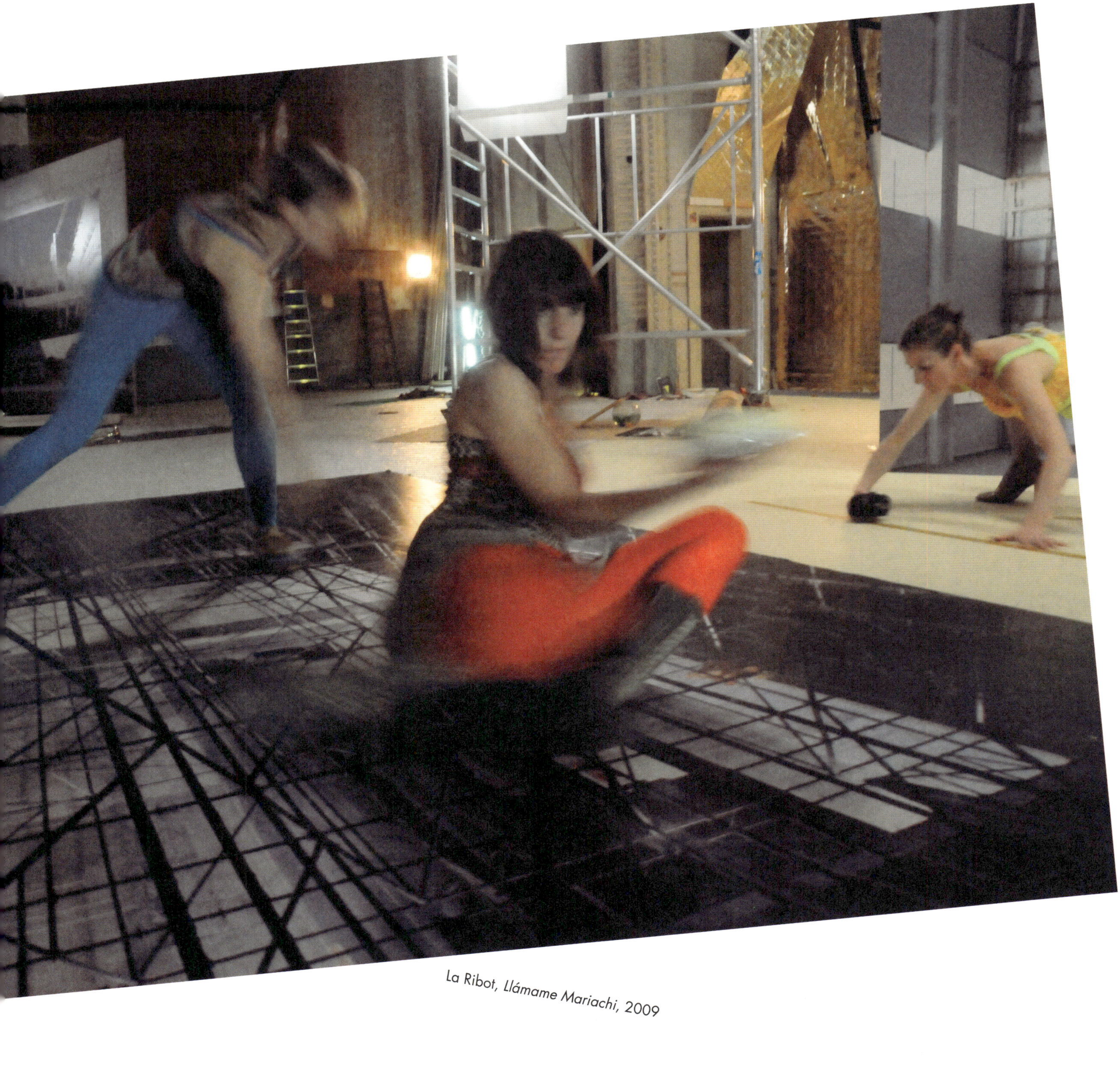

La Ribot, Llámame Mariachi, 2009

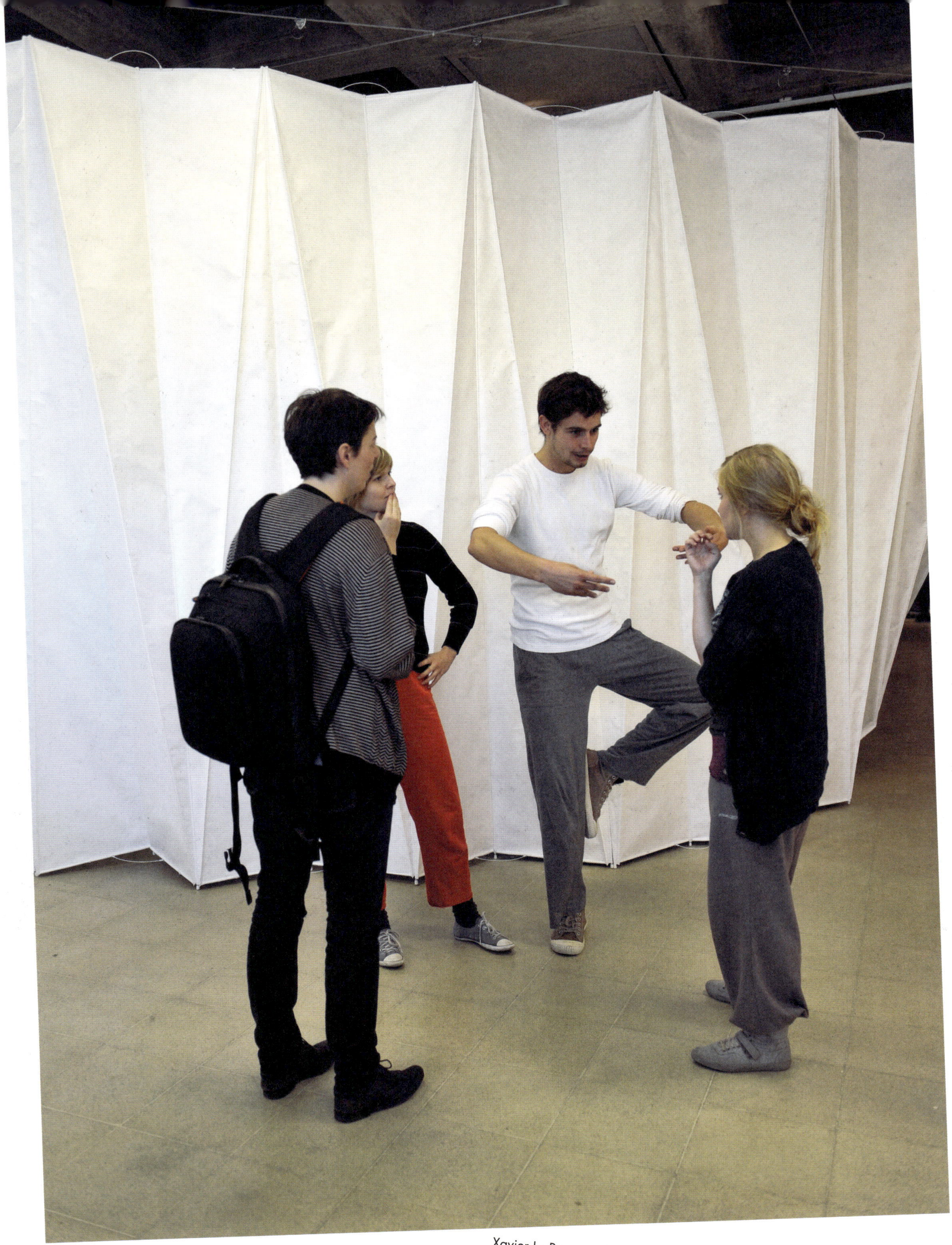

Xavier Le Roy, *production*, 2010

Xavier Le Roy and Mårten Spångberg
production (2010)

Over the last 15 years, the French choreographer Xavier Le Roy has experimented with the artistic, social and political functions of choreography. By proposing acute and affective explorations of the moving body, Le Roy created a series of groundbreaking works that have profoundly transformed the European dance scene, such as *Self-Unfinished* (1998), *Product of Circumstances* (1999), *Project* (2003), *Mouvements für Lachenmann* (2005), *Le Sacre du Printemps* (2007), or *Low Pieces* (2010). Incorporating both everyday and idiosyncratic gestures and an emphasis on research and process, Le Roy's work thoroughly investigates the field of dance in relation to its conventions, its modes of audience address and the movements it produces at the intersection with theatre, music, performance and visual arts.

production (2010) emerges from the motivation to work with 'human resources' that activate the exhibition space through specific modes of engagement, where the activity itself is understood as production. Conceived with the participants in charge of actuating some of the pieces that compose *Move: Choreographing You* (works by Simone Forti, Mike Kelley and Pablo Bronstein), *production* experiments with a range of conventions around work, representation, knowledge production and enjoyment. *production* initiates a series of 'artificially staged actions and/or situations' – to take up Le Roy's provisional definition of choreography – which organise and mediate bodies, movement and signification in order to redistribute and diversify the use of the museum space. As *production* engages the visitor in mobile and indeterminate situations, traditional notions of interpretation and contemplation are cast aside by these active and affective exchanges. Here, two dynamics take place simultaneously: the participants and the visitors engage in the formation of social constellations, while the participants elaborate a range of activities that might be said to be without end, as their actions take place even when the exhibition space is unoccupied, producing a series of 'practices of the self'. As such, *production* not only exposes the moving body as labour and spectacle, but it destabilizes notions of production and representation by allowing the participants to spend time rehearsing for themselves.

production is developed in collaboration with the artist Mårten Spångberg, whose engagement with dance and architecture, particularly in International Festival (an interdisciplinary practice Spångberg initiated), has extended understandings of choreographic practices over the last decade. Together, they set up an apparatus that tackles the function of the museum and dance/choreography as institutions. Developed closely with the group of participants, the work appropriates material from the archive of the exhibition, giving the participants opportunities to develop their individual practices. The work might be said to be empowering for the individual since it enables the making of lateral decisions, the production of social relations and processes of becoming. By considering the museum space a site of labour and rehearsal – of movement practices – *production* dislocates the material conditions in which choreography usually takes place. As a forceful exploration of the museum's ecology, the work foregrounds movement as a dynamic yet sustained way of producing knowledge. What this work effectively proposes, then, is an ethico-choreographic paradigm: it incessantly re-composes the moving body and its relations, re-imagining the structures of power in which it operates.

Noémie Solomon

Xavier Le Roy was born in Juvisy sur Orge, France in 1963 and lives and works in Montpellier. Mårten Spångberg was born in Stockholm in 1968 where he lives and works.

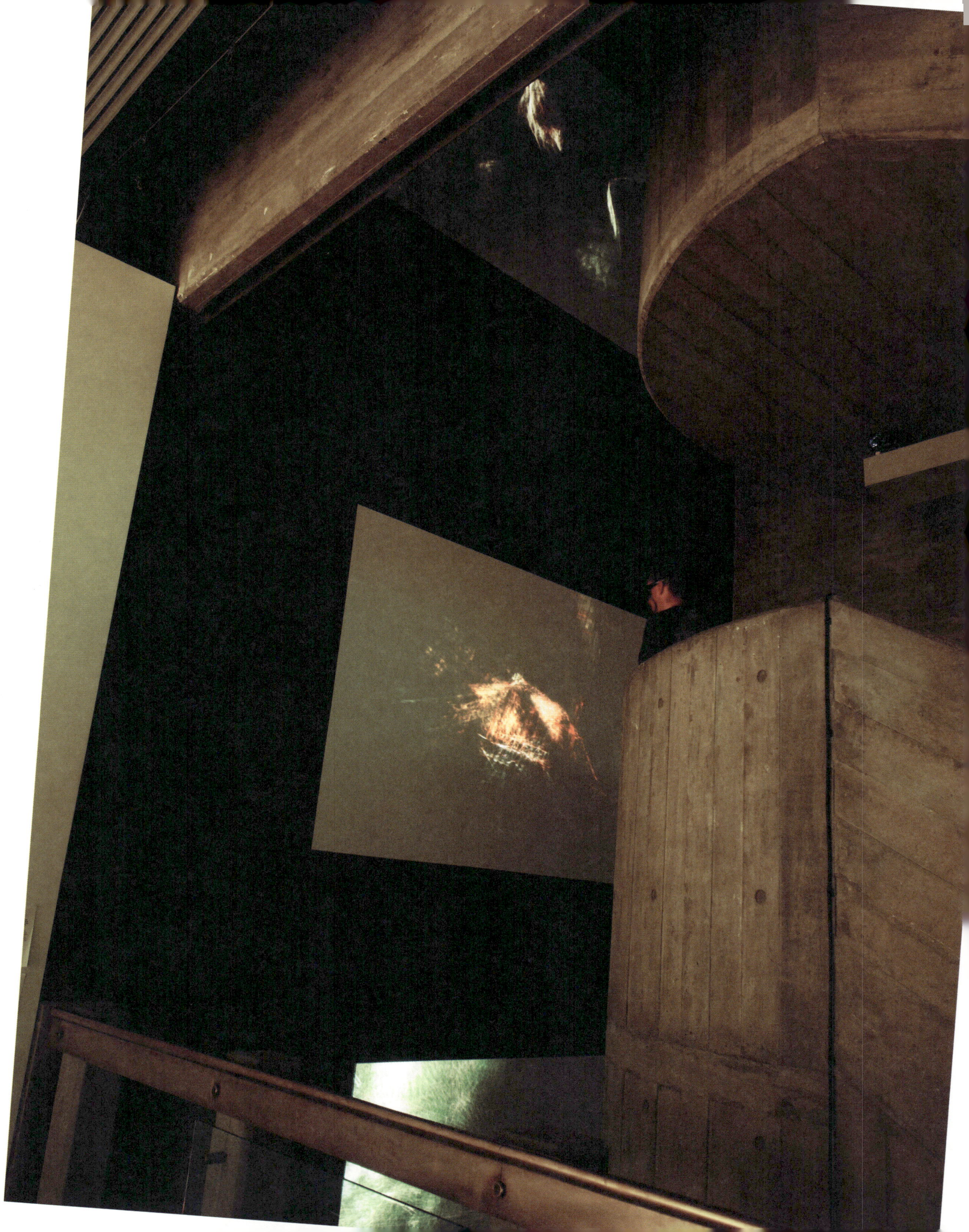

The OpenEnded Group with Wayne McGregor

Stairwell (2010)

The OpenEnded Group with Wayne McGregor, Stairwell, 2010

In *Stairwell* (2010), viewers are plunged into a complex perceptual realm where they can experience the dancing of British choreographer Wayne McGregor as never encountered before. With the three-dimensional imagery of the work floating in space as if within hand's reach, their eyes seem almost to touch the contours of McGregor's motions. These motions, they soon recognise, were performed on the gallery stairs on which they now find themselves; they then realise that it is his continual re-orientation to the awkward angles and corners of that stairwell that constitute his dance.

The three-dimensional capture of McGregor is itself oddly elusive, with the imagery always striving – but often failing – to cast his figure as a solid sculptural form for each instant of his movement. There is a perceptual battle to tell figure from ground, for a curvature of the architecture is easily mistaken for that of a limb, the angle of a knee or elbow for that of a stair. In the ongoing effort to reconstruct three-dimensional forms, surfaces lurch towards and away from solidity in the most startling fashion, and it is only through its movement that the dancing body separates itself from its fixed surrounding, lifting into clear articulation before subsiding into the visual flux again.

Stairwell arose from a close collaboration between McGregor and The OpenEnded Group: three digital artists – Marc Downie, Shelley Eshkar and Paul Kaiser – who create works for stage, screen, gallery, page and public space. In this concurrent project, The OpenEnded Group and McGregor have been working together in a process more typical of their collaborations – a long-term, carefully considered undertaking. They have been seeking out ways to perturb and extend McGregor's choreographic practice through the development of a software tool the group calls the 'Choreographic Language Agent'. A sort of spatial-geometric calculator, the program enables McGregor to experiment with complex visual equations of motion that he has then been setting on his dancers to create *FAR*, the forthcoming production of Wayne McGregor | Random Dance.

When the opportunity arose to make *Stairwell* at the Hayward Gallery, the collaborators made good use of the trust they had already established to take a faster, more risky, improvisatory approach. The OpenEnded Group had just devised a new device for three-dimensional capture to allow them to do fieldwork so to speak, rather than being confined to a motion-capture studio. Thus Downie, Eshkar and Kaiser could use the site of the Hayward Gallery stairwell itself as the stage on which to capture the dance and, as a result, deployed the full system there for the first time one evening in July 2010.

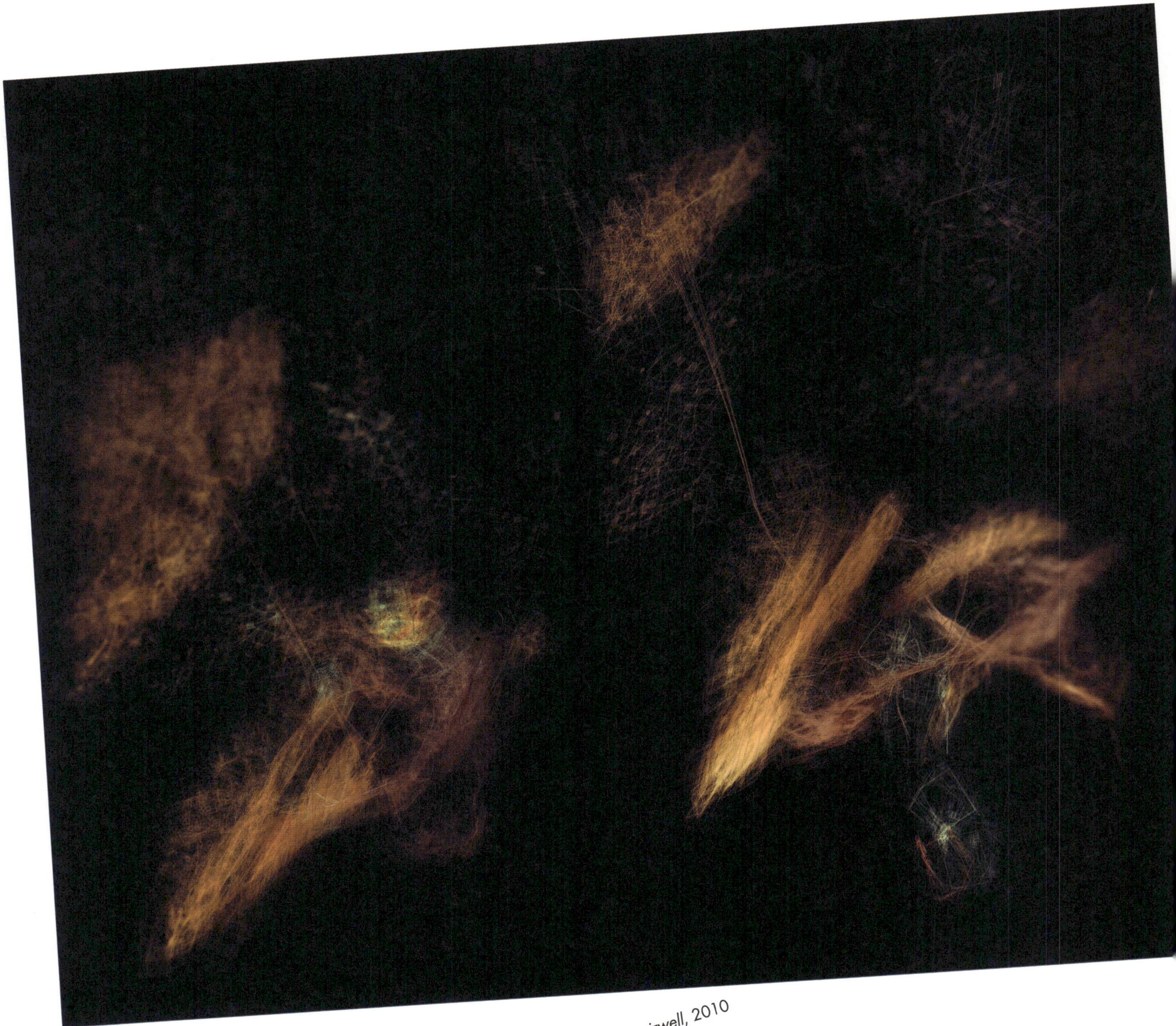

The OpenEnded Group with Wayne McGregor, *Stairwell*, 2010

In an earlier meeting in New York, The OpenEnded Group had suggested that McGregor perform the new dance himself rather than directing one of his dancers. From previous work with Merce Cunningham, Trisha Brown and Bill T. Jones, they found that the signature motion of a choreographer has its own secrets to tell, so McGregor's enthusiastic assent was a big step forward. It meant that when the time came the collaborators could all move forward fast. Literally so in McGregor's case, for his movements kept accelerating to speeds that challenged the group's ability to capture them. Meanwhile, though, he was taking his time to shape his dancing to the eccentric spaces he was discovering on the stairs. As he did so, the group kept finding new ways to frame that moving body in space from the re-orienting angles that would give rise to the final three-dimensional compositions rendered for the finished piece.

McGregor's intuitions about the space were made visible to the group (and their cameras) through the movements of his thinking body. And after each improvisation, he was able to see The OpenEnded Group's visual thinking in the take that was immediately played back for him. McGregor's response to the filmic response led him to his next move, and then his to theirs, forming the back-and-forth exchange that ended up generating *Stairwell*.

Paul Kaiser

Wayne McGregor was born in Stockport, England, in 1970 and lives and works in London. The OpenEnded Group (Marc Downie, Shelley Eshkar and Paul Kaiser) live and work in New York.

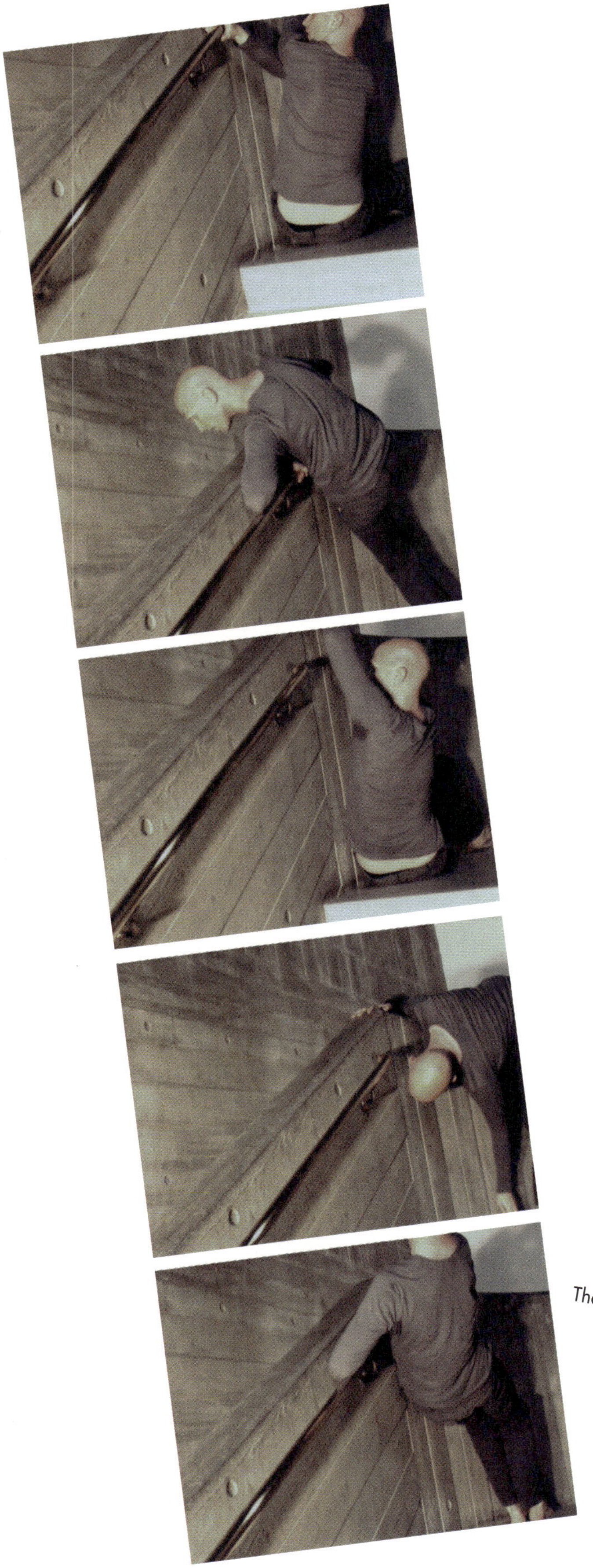

The OpenEnded Group with Wayne McGregor, Stairwell, 2010

Tino Sehgal

Instead of Allowing Some Thing to Rise Up to Your Face Dancing Bruce and Dan and Other Things (2000); This is Good (2001)

Tino Sehgal's background in both dance and economics is detectable in all of his works, which despite their apparent lack of materiality, operate within the economic context of the art market and the museum. Sehgal's ephemeral situations are sold to collectors and museums in much the same way as more tangible works, although his process of involving a solicitor in the negotiations sets up a more elaborate set of relationships. Even here, Sehgal insists on immateriality: the contract between the artist and buyer is verbal and the money is paid in cash.

In *Instead of Allowing Some Thing to Rise Up to Your Face Dancing Bruce and Dan and Other Things* (2000) (shown at Haus der Kunst in Munich), a performer dressed in everyday clothing lies in the corner of an empty space, completely self-absorbed, writhing and rolling slowly along the wall, into the space and back again. The endless loop of movements changes subtly, depending on the age and size of the performers, who alternate every couple of hours.

In its title and content, the piece refers to seminal works by Bruce Nauman and Dan Graham, who were both influenced by New York's Judson Dance Theater movement in the late 1960s and early 1970s. In Nauman's video *Wall-Floor Positions* (1968), the artist positions his body somewhat awkwardly in relation to the wall in 28 different ways, while in the videos *Elke Allowing the Floor to Rise Up Over Her, Face Up* and *Tony Sinking into the Floor, Face Up and Face Down* (both 1973), two actors, one after the other, lie on their backs on the ground, hardly moving at all, trying to fulfill the exercises described in the works' titles. In Graham's two-part projection *Roll* (1970), one Super-8 film shows, from a distance, the artist rolling on an autumnal forest floor, while the other relays his simultaneously recorded personal viewpoint as he rolls – the camera thus replacing Graham's own eyes. For *Instead of Allowing...* Sehgal selects movements from all four of the above works, but only those originally published as film stills. He makes use of this layering of media, where real-life movements are first translated into video or film and then into photographic reproductions. Sehgal, however, does not allow his own works to be recorded or documented in any way. He intermingles these recognisable moments from Nauman and Graham with his own choreography in a manner that always steers clear of a conventional performance and instead takes on the appearance of a fluid sculpture in space. Far from being performed for, the viewer is a witness to a seemingly private act.

In *This is Good* (2001) (shown at Kunstsammlung Nordrhein-Westfalen in Düsseldorf), however – part of a series concerned with the museum as an institution – the viewer is approached directly. When the unsuspecting visitor enters an otherwise empty room, he or she is personally addressed by a museum guard, who skips from one leg to the other with circling arms, ending the choreography by speaking the words of the label that museum visitors would normally find on the wall next to a work: 'Tino Sehgal, This is Good, 2001. Collection: Museum Ludwig'. The normally 'invisible' guard, discreetly watching the viewers' behaviour, becomes the artwork and is now in the vulnerable position of being observed and evaluated, although the title of the piece apparently preempts any criticism. The setting of a museum already presupposes an object's value, since this institution is bestowed with the authority to set standards of quality and worth, even if the object in question is experienced as a transient moment. In contrast to concrete exhibits, *This is Good*, like all other works by Sehgal, is one that every viewer can take home – by committing it to memory.

Julienne Lorz

Tino Sehgal was born in London in 1976 and lives and works in Berlin.

Archive

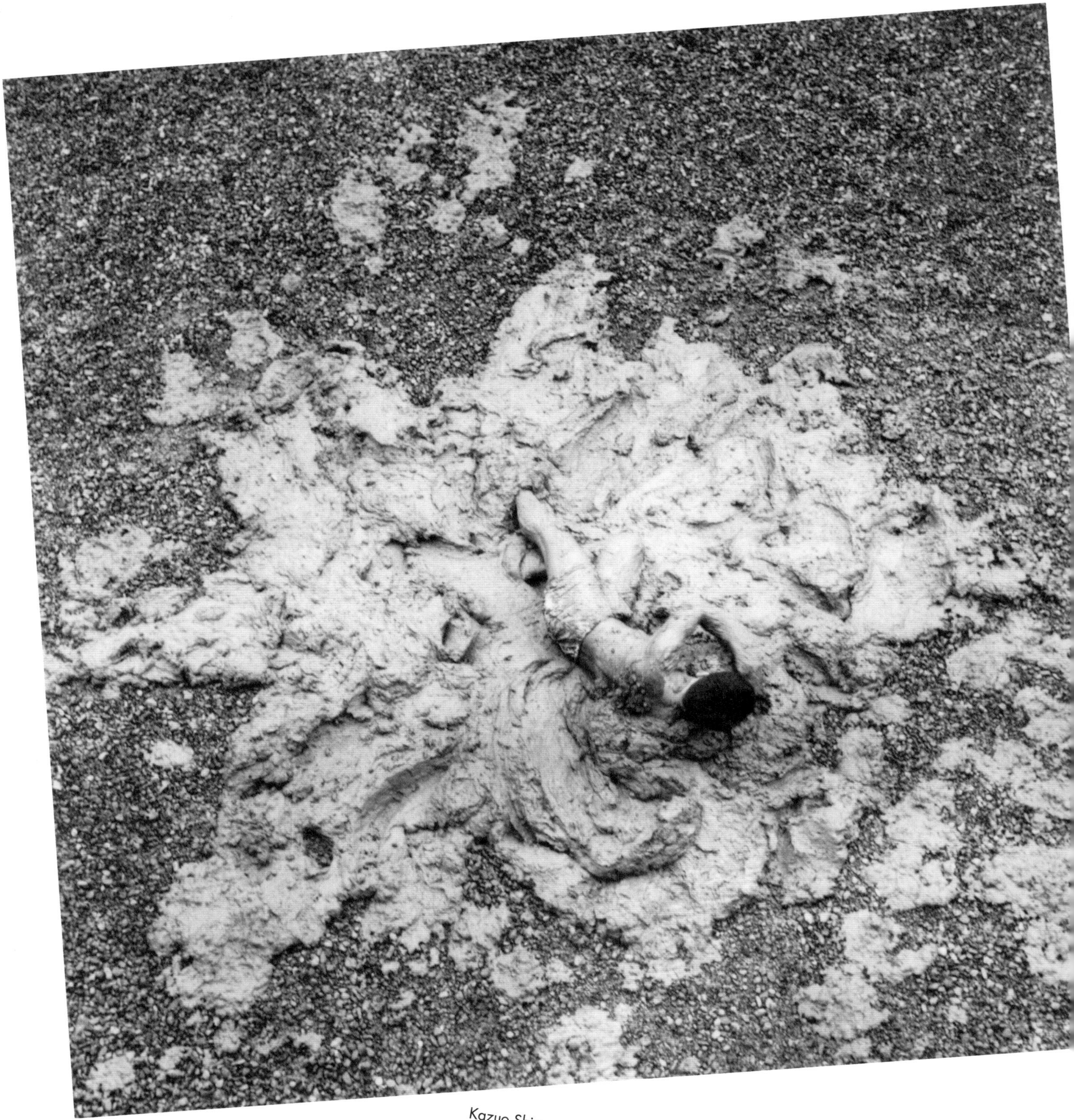

Kazuo Shiraga, *Challenging Mud*, 1955

Introduction

André Lepecki and Stephanie Rosenthal

The contextual archive for *Move: Choreographing You* gathers together 140 works by visual artists and choreographers to propose a dynamic vision of what choreographer Yvonne Rainer called the 'concurrent' history of visual arts and dance since the 1960s.

The archive contains film documentation of artworks that make explicit how dance and the visual arts have entered into a dynamics of mutual formation over the past half century. The following pages contain photographs, film stills and scores from selected performances held over the last fifty years.

The exhibition *Move* focuses primarily on installation and sculpture, which has made it necessary to find a different way to represent the dance pieces, performances and happenings that have been a crucial part of this 'visual art-dance' relationship since the late 1950s. The archive offers an opportunity to explore the history of art and dance in an individual, active and playful way.

By placing the works in an open and dynamic structure, this archive is a transformative machine: identifying artistic, historical, conceptual and disciplinary crossings between past and present uses of the choreographic and the visual in dance and art. A transformative archive is a 'border of time that surrounds our presence'. In the exhibition, this border is represented as a Möbius strip (a tri-dimensional object with only one side) and distributes images of the artworks on its surface, often in unexpected contact with one another. Visitors to the exhibition can choreograph the interactive archive screens and can browse the archive intuitively, choosing a work to view by selecting an artist's name or decade, or can access a work via nine categories that cluster the works thematically.

The archive pages in this book also show this vast range of possible links between the two art forms. The selection of works and the way they are presented, scrambles linear historical narratives to produce unexpected constellations, revealing powerful connections between works – thematic, material, political and aesthetic. Despite the works being set out thematically, it is important that many of them could conceivably belong in several other categories.

The themes, as well as the images of the films, invite and trigger many connections – different threads and layers that link the arts visually and content-wise can be discovered. The archive does not attempt to present itself as complete, but asks to be completed by the reader who nominates the works that are important to him. The categories show common fields of interest including engagement with the use of the human body, with space, time and gravity.

The complete archive of films is held within nine categories:

CHOREOGRAPHING THINGS
People making things move and things making people move.

TRANSFORMING THE BODY
The body as a perpetual, unfinished and open project.

TRANSFORMING TIME
Duration, repetition, accumulation, acceleration and slowing down.

TRACING MOVEMENT
The tracking of the body's imprint in space and time.

MAKING SPACE
How the body is not in space, but of space.

GRAVITY/FALLING
A primary force harnessed and explored in painting, sculpture and dance: The gravitational pull.

SCORING/COMMANDING/ CHOREOGRAPHING
How formalism and conceptual precision require submission to the commands of a score.

SCULPTING DANCES
The paradoxical dialogue between dance and sculpture.

DANCING
Dancing as visual arts material.

CHOREOGRAPHING THINGS

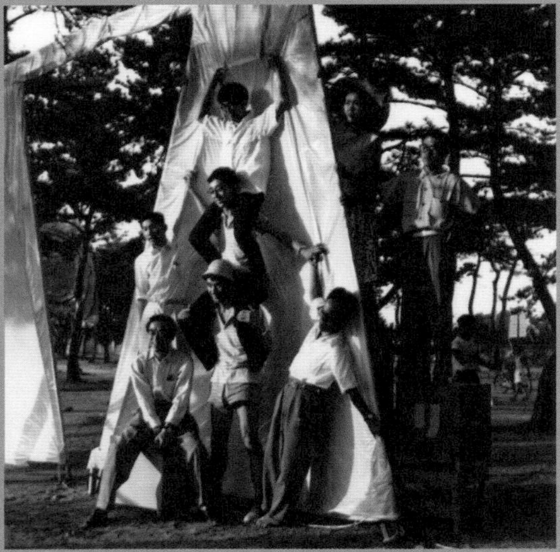

1

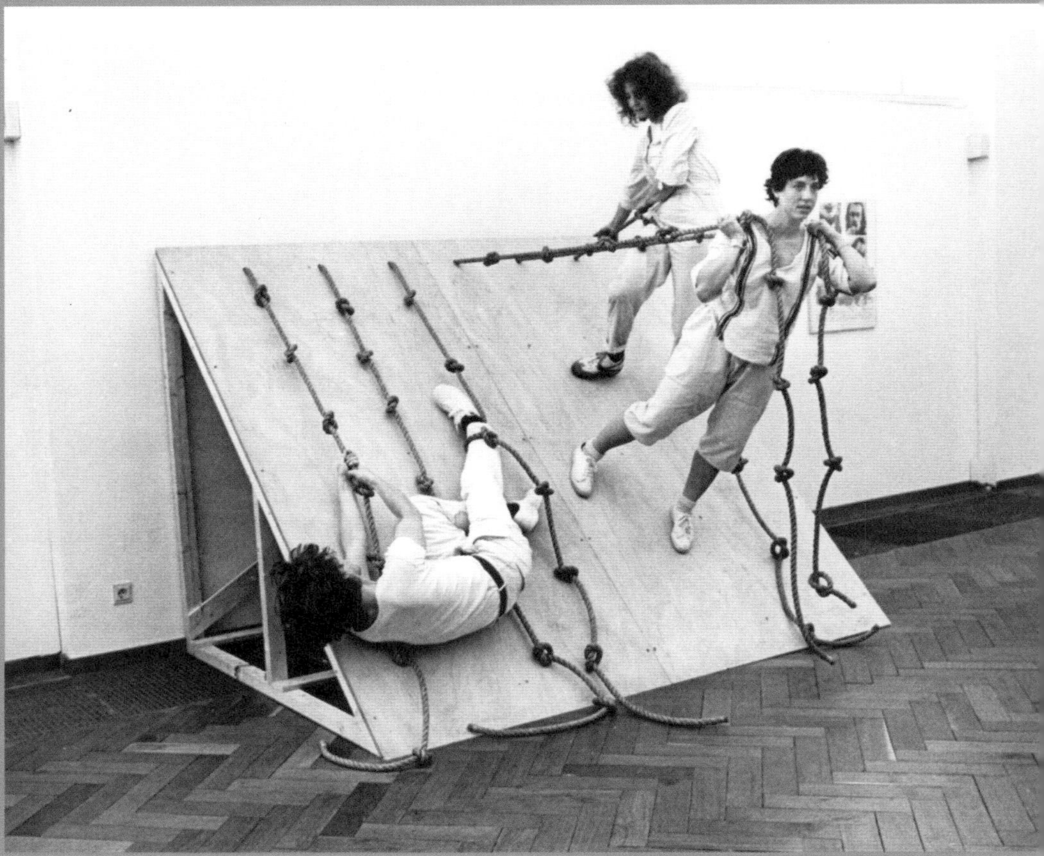

2

Charles Atlas
Nevada, 1958
Film, b&w, silent
2 mins. 53 secs.
Courtesy the artist and Vilma Gold, London

João Fiadeiro
Esto Corpo Que me Ocupa, 2008
Video documentation, colour
1 hr. 1 min. 25 secs.
Courtesy RE.AL, Lisbon

Simone Forti
See-saw, 1960, 2004
Video (performance documentation), colour
9 mins. 10 secs.
Courtesy the artist and ARTPIX

2 Simone Forti
Slant Board, 1960/2004
Video (performance documentation), colour
4 mins. 44 secs.
Courtesy the artist and ARTPIX

Gutai
2nd Gutai Art Exhibition, 1956
Film, b&w, silent
3 mins. 40 secs.
Courtesy Ashiya City Museum of Art & History

1 Gutai
Outdoor Gutai Art Exhibition, 1956
Film, colour, silent
3 mins. 22 secs.
Courtesy Ashiya City Museum of Art & History

Gutai
Gutai on the Stage, 1957
Film, colour, silent
8 mins. 28 secs.
Courtesy Ashiya City Museum of Art & History

Anna Halprin
Parades & Changes, 1965
16mm film transferred to DVD, b&w
37 mins.
Courtesy the artists and the Jerome Robbins Dance Division, The New York Public Library for the Performing Arts

Vlatka Horvat
This Here & That There, 2007
Digital photographs of performance
Courtesy the artist

Gilles Jobin
Steak House, 2005
Video, colour
1 hr. 10 mins.
Courtesy the artist

La Ribot
Panoramix rushes, 2003
Video (performance documentation), colour
2 hrs. 29 mins.
Courtesy the artist

3 Susanne Linke
Im Bade Wannen, 1980
Video excerpt, colour
15 mins.
Courtesy the artist and Deutsches Tanzfilminstitut Bremen

Vera Mantero & Rui Chafes
Eating the Heart Out, 2005
Video, colour
14 mins.
Courtesy the artist and O Rumo do Fumo-Edifício, Lisbon

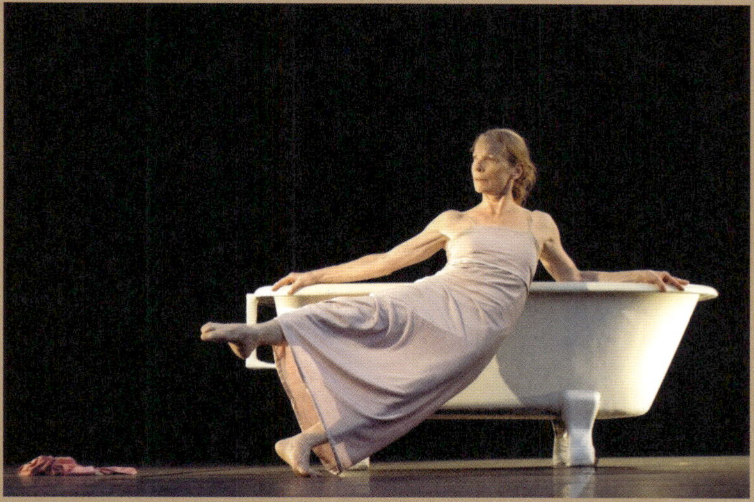

3

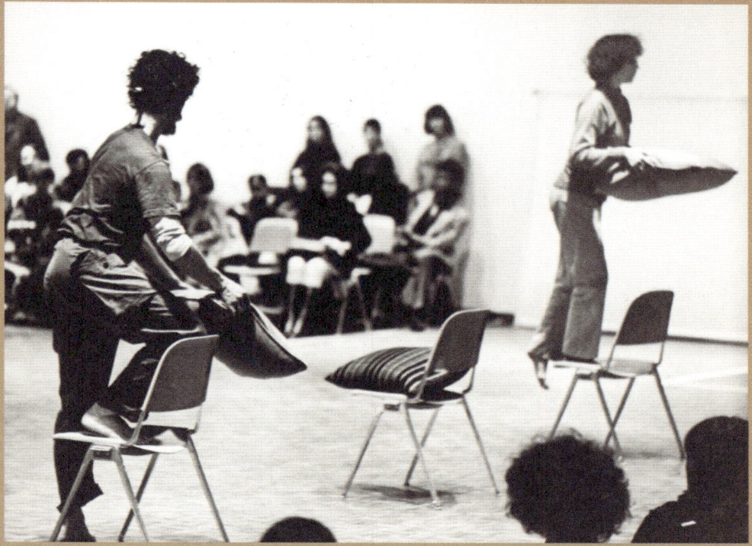

4

Robert Morris
Neo Classic, 1971
Film, b&w, silent
13 mins. 39 secs.
Courtesy the artist, Sonnabend Gallery, New York and Spruth Magers, Berlin London

Robert Morris & Babette Mangolte
Site, 1964
Film, b&w, silent
5 mins. 11 secs.
Courtesy the artists, Spruth Magers, Berlin London, and Broadway 1602, New York

Yvonne Rainer
Volleyball (Foot Film) and *Trio Film* from *Five Easy Pieces*, 1967–1968
16mm film, b&w, silent
10 mins. and 13 mins.
Courtesy Video Data Bank, Chicago

4 Yvonne Rainer
Continuous Project - Altered Daily, 1969–1970
16mm film, b&w, silent
32 mins.
Courtesy the artists and the Jerome Robbins Dance Division, The New York Public Library for the Performing Arts
Photo by Peter Moore © Estate of Peter Moore/ VAGA, NYC

Robert Rauschenberg
Pelican, 1963
Film, b&w, silent
2 mins. 24 secs.
Courtesy of the Estate of Robert Rauschenberg/Licensed by VAGA, New York, NY

Robert Rauschenberg
Map Room II, 1965
Film, b&w, silent
4 mins.
Courtesy of the Estate of Robert Rauschenberg/Licensed by VAGA, New York, NY

Christian Rizzo
et pourquoi pas: "bodymakers", "falbalas", "bazaar" etc, etc...?, 2001
Beta SP video (performance documentation), colour
56 mins.
Filmmaker: Jean-Gabriel Périot
Courtesy l'association fragile / christian rizzo, Paris

Marco Schuler
Bypass, 2009
Video, colour
2 mins. 55 secs.
Courtesy the artist

Marco Schuler
Türmen, 2009
Video, colour
2 mins. 41 secs.
Courtesy the artist

Taldans Company
Dolap, 2000
Video (performance documentation), colour
33 mins.
Choreography: Mustafa Kaplan in collaboration with Filiz Sizanli
Courtesy Taldans Company, Istanbul

TRANSFORMING THE BODY

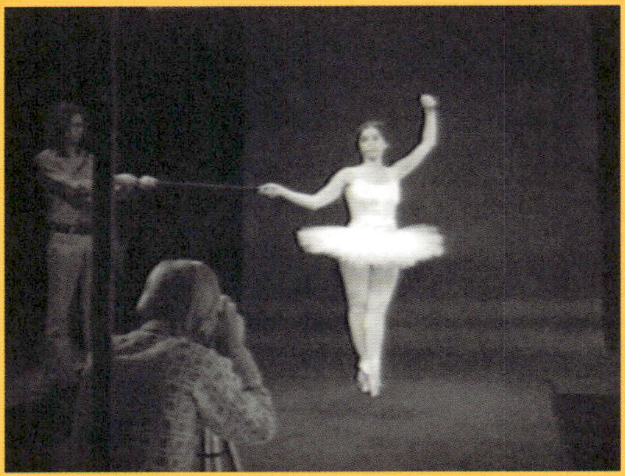

6

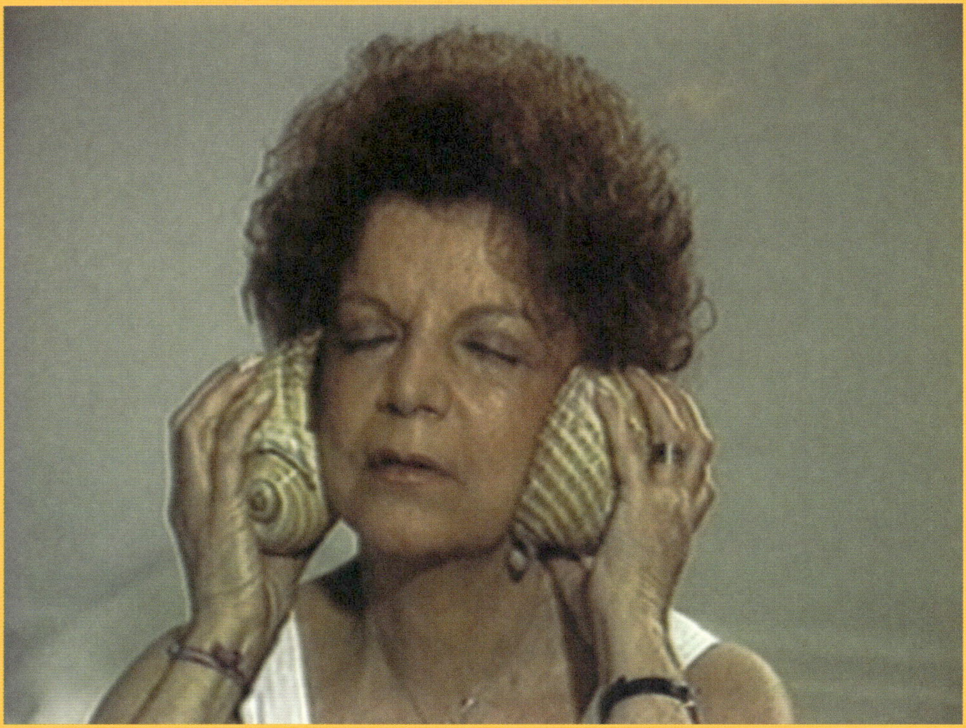

5

Vito Acconci
Conversions I–III, 1971
Super-8 film, b&w, silent
1 hr. 5 mins. 30 secs.
Courtesy Electronic Arts Intermix (EAI), New York

6 Eleanor Antin
Caught in the Act, 1973
Film, b&w
36 mins.
Courtesy Electronic Arts Intermix (EAI), New York

5 Lygia Clark
Memoría do Corpo, 1984
Video, colour
29 mins.
Courtesy of the artist and 'The World of Lygia Clark' Cultural Association, Rio de Janeiro

Michael Clark
Heterospective, 1989
Video (performance documentation), colour
7 mins. 13 secs.
Courtesy Michael Clark Company

Michael Clark
Ludd Gang, 1988
Video, colour
5 mins. 40 secs.
Courtesy Michael Clark Company

Michael Clark
Venus in Furs, 1988
Video, colour
4 mins. 46 secs.
Courtesy Michael Clark Company

Dan Graham
Performer/Audience/Mirror, 1975
16mm film transferred to DVD, b&w
22 mins. 55 secs.
Courtesy Lisson Gallery, London

Emio Greco, Pieter Scholten & Erik Lint
FRA, 2004, 1999
Video transferred to DVD, colour
10 mins.
produced in collaboration with Eyeworks Egmond and the NPS (Dutch Programming Trust).
Courtesy ICKamsterdam – Emio Greco | PC, Amsterdam

Tatsumi Hijikata
Hosotan [The story of smallpox], 1972
Film, b&w
25 mins.
Courtesy the Hijikata Archives, Keio University, Japan

Tatsumi Hijikata
Rebellion of the Body, 1968
Film, b&w
14 mins. 40 secs.
Courtesy the Hijikata Archives, Keio University, Japan

Rebecca Horn
Performances II, 1968–70
Film, colour
36 mins.
Courtesy the artist and Holzwarth Publications GmbH, Berlin

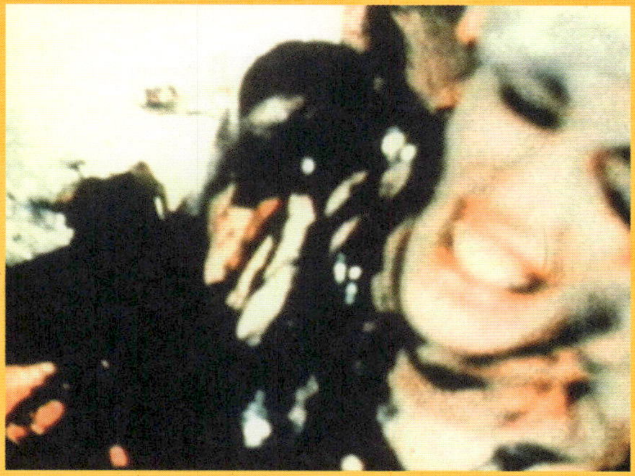

8

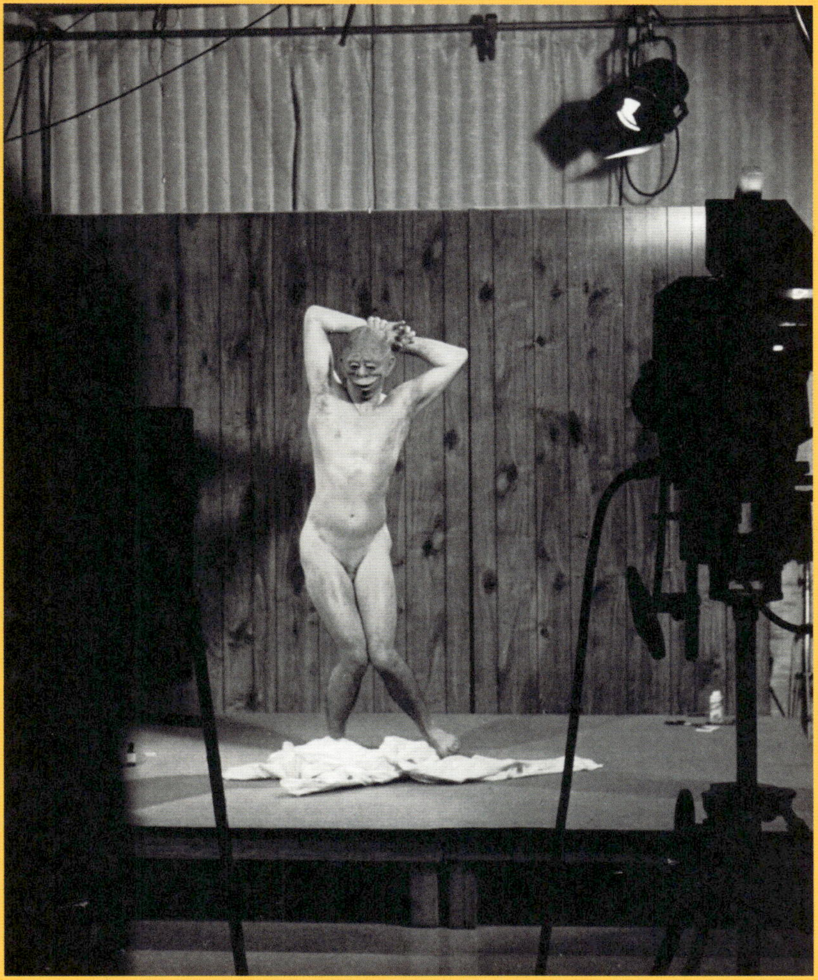

7

Katarzyna Kozyra
The Rite of Spring documentation, 1999–2002
Video, colour
4 mins. 30 secs.
Courtesy the artist and Żak Branicka, Berlin

Xavier Le Roy
Self Unfinished, 1998
Video (performance documentation), colour
53 mins. 40 secs.
Courtesy the artist

7 Paul McCarthy
Experimental Dancer, Edit #1, 1975
Video, colour
4 mins. 35 secs.
Courtesy the artist and Hauser & Wirth

Ana Mendieta
Ocean Bird Washup, 1974
Super-8 colour, silent film transferred to DVD
4 mins. 35 secs.
Courtesy the Estate of Ana Mendieta Collection and Alison Jacques Gallery, London

Eszter Salamon
Reproduction, 2004
Video (performance documentation), colour
1 hr. 1 min. 53 secs.
Courtesy the artist

8 Carolee Schneemann
Meat Joy, 1964
Film on video, colour
10 mins. 35 secs.
Courtesy Electronic Arts Intermix (EAI), New York

TRANSFORMING TIME

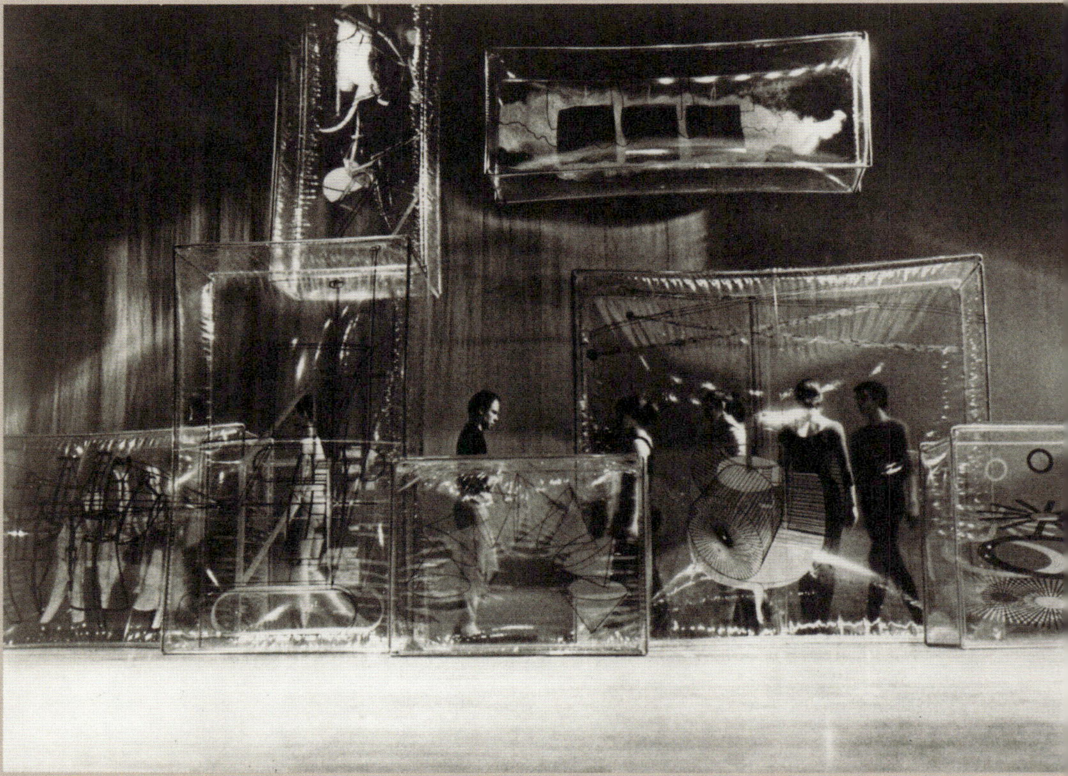

10

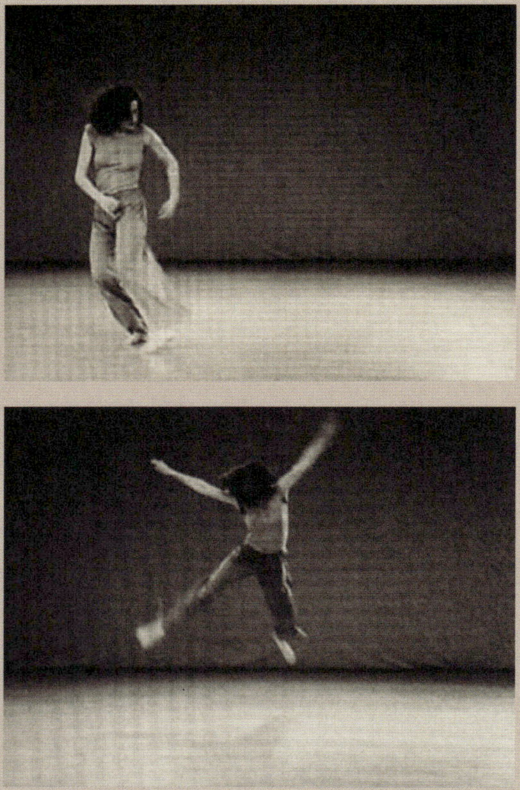

9

Ty Boomershine
Gluttony, 2008
Video, colour
7 mins. 10 secs.
Courtesy the artist

9 Trisha Brown & Babette Mangolte
Watermotor, 1978
16mm film, b&w
7 mins. 52 secs.
Courtesy the artists, Trisha Brown Company, ARTPIX and Broadway 1602, New York

Trisha Brown
Accumulation with Talking Plus Watermotor, 1979
Film, colour
11 mins. 49 secs.
Courtesy Trisha Brown Company, and ARTPIX

Rosemary Butcher
Touch the Earth, 1987
Video (performance documentation), colour
43 mins.
Courtesy the artist

Lucinda Childs
Dance, 1979/2007
Film, b&w and colour
1 hr.
Set design & filmmaker: Sol Lewitt
Music: Philip Glass
Courtesy Lucinda Childs Dance Company and Pomegranate Arts Inc., New York

10 Merce Cunningham & Charles Atlas
Walkaround Time, 1968
Film, b&w, silent
48 mins.
Set design: Jasper Johns after Marcel Duchamp
Courtesy Merce Cunningham Foundation, New York

Merce Cunningham & Charles Atlas
Fractions I, 1977
Film, colour
52 mins.
Courtesy the artists and Merce Cunningham Foundation, New York

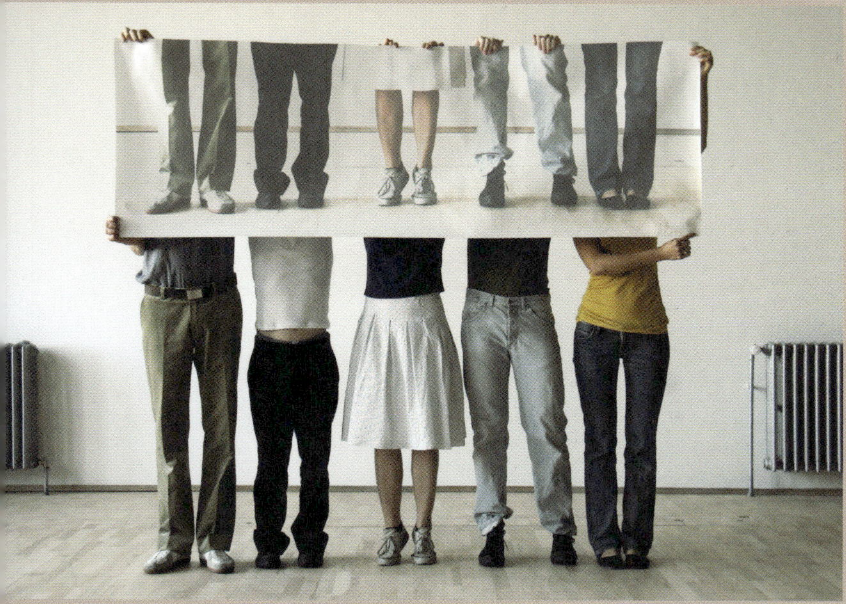

11

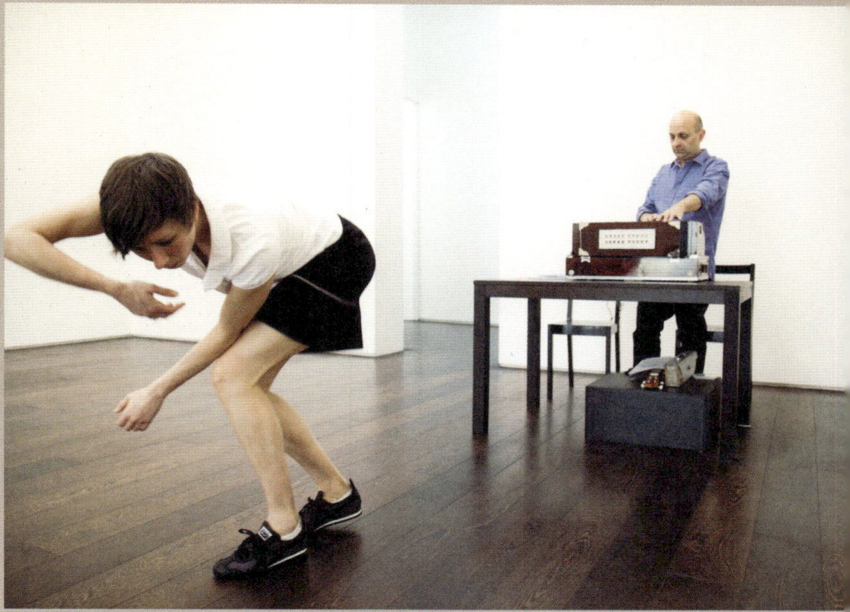

12

Siobhan Davies
Different Trains, 1990/1993
Video, colour
28 mins. 33 secs.
Courtesy Siobhan Davies Dance and Coventry University

12 Siobhan Davies
Minutes, 2009
Video, colour
57 mins. 7 secs.
Courtesy Siobhan Davies Dance and Coventry University

Ed Emshwiller
Thanatopsis, 1962
Film, colour
5 mins. 12 secs.
Courtesy the artist and Anthology Film Archives, New York

Jan Fabre
The Sound of One Hand Clapping, 1990/1993
Video (performance documentation), colour
1 hr. 31 mins. 13 secs.
Courtesy Troubleyn/Jan Fabre, Antwerp

Anne Teresa de Keersmaeker & Thierry de Mey
Rosas Danst Rosas, 1997
Video, colour
57 mins.
Courtesy the artists and Rosas, Brussels

Anne Teresa de Keersmaeker & Thierry de Mey
Fase, Four Movements to the music of Steve Reich, 1982/2002
Video, colour
57 mins.
Courtesy the artists and Rosas, Brussels

Mathilde Monnier
Tempo 76, 2007
Video, colour
1 hr. 5 mins.
Réalisatión: Valérie Urréa
Courtesy the artist

11 Ivana Müller
While We Were Holding It Together, 2006
Video (performance documentation), colour
1 hr. 7 mins.
Courtesy the artist

Kelly Nipper
Weather Center, 2009
Film, b&w
1 hr. 2 mins. 10 secs.
Courtesy the artist

TRACING MOVEMENT

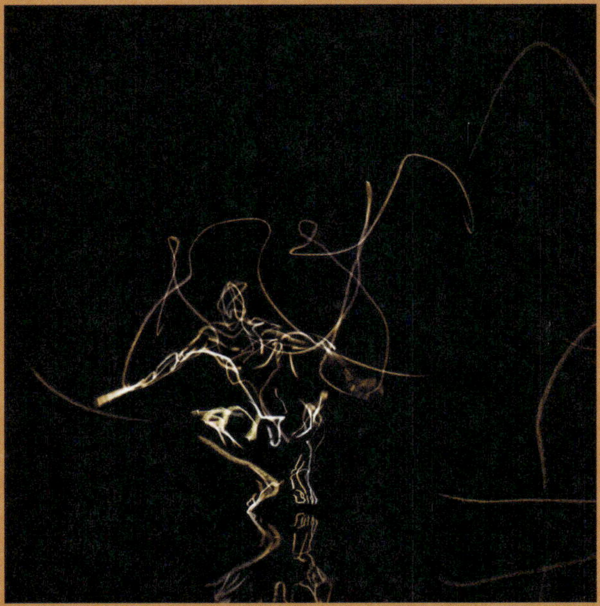

14

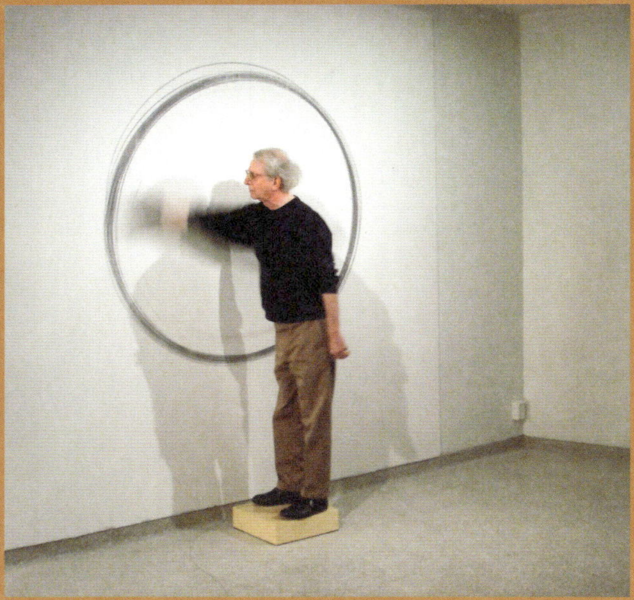

13

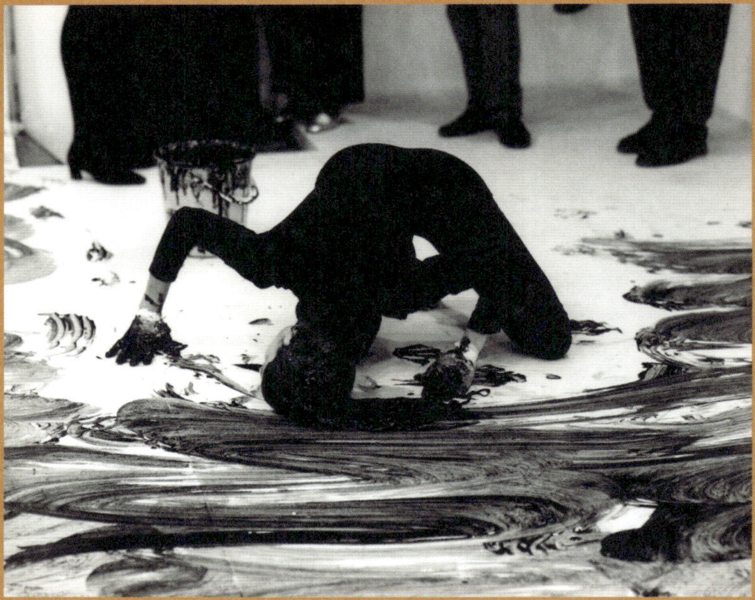

15

Francis Alÿs
Paradox of Praxis 1 (Sometimes Making Something Leads to Nothing), 1997
Video, colour
5 mins.
Courtesy the artist and David Zwirner, New York

15 Janine Antoni
Loving Care, 1992
Video documentation, colour
35 mins. 50 secs.
Courtesy the artist and Luhring Augustine, New York

Trisha Brown
It's a Draw, 2002
Video, colour
20 mins.
Filmmaker: Hugo Glendinning
Courtesy the artists

Merce Cunningham and Charles Atlas
Biped, 1999
Video, colour
48 mins.
Courtesy Merce Cunningham Foundation, New York

João Fiadeiro
I am Here, 2003
Video (performance documentation), colour
40 mins.
Courtesy RE.AL, Lisbon

14 Bill T. Jones, Shelley Eshkar, Paul Kaiser
Ghostcatching, 1999
Video, colour
7 mins.
Courtesy the artists

17 Yves Klein
Anthropometries of the Blue Period and Fire Paintings, 1960
Film, b&w, silent
6 mins. 58 secs.
Courtesy the Yves Klein Archives, Paris

Richard Long
A Line Made by Walking, 1967
Digital photograph, b&w
Courtesy Haunch of Venison, London

13 Tom Marioni
Circle Drawing on Prepared Wall, 2000/2007
Video (performance documentation), colour
17 secs.
Courtesy the artist and Margarete Roeder Gallery, New York

Tom Marioni
Running and Jumping with a Pencil, Marking the Paper while Trying to Fly, 1972/2007
Video (performance documentation), colour
1 min. 35 secs.
Courtesy the artist and Margarete Roeder Gallery, New York

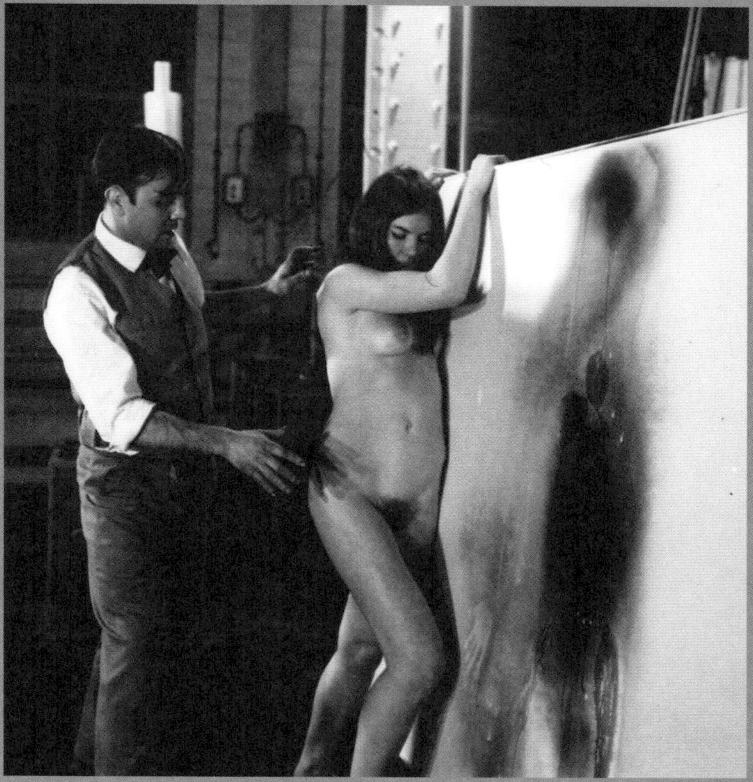

17

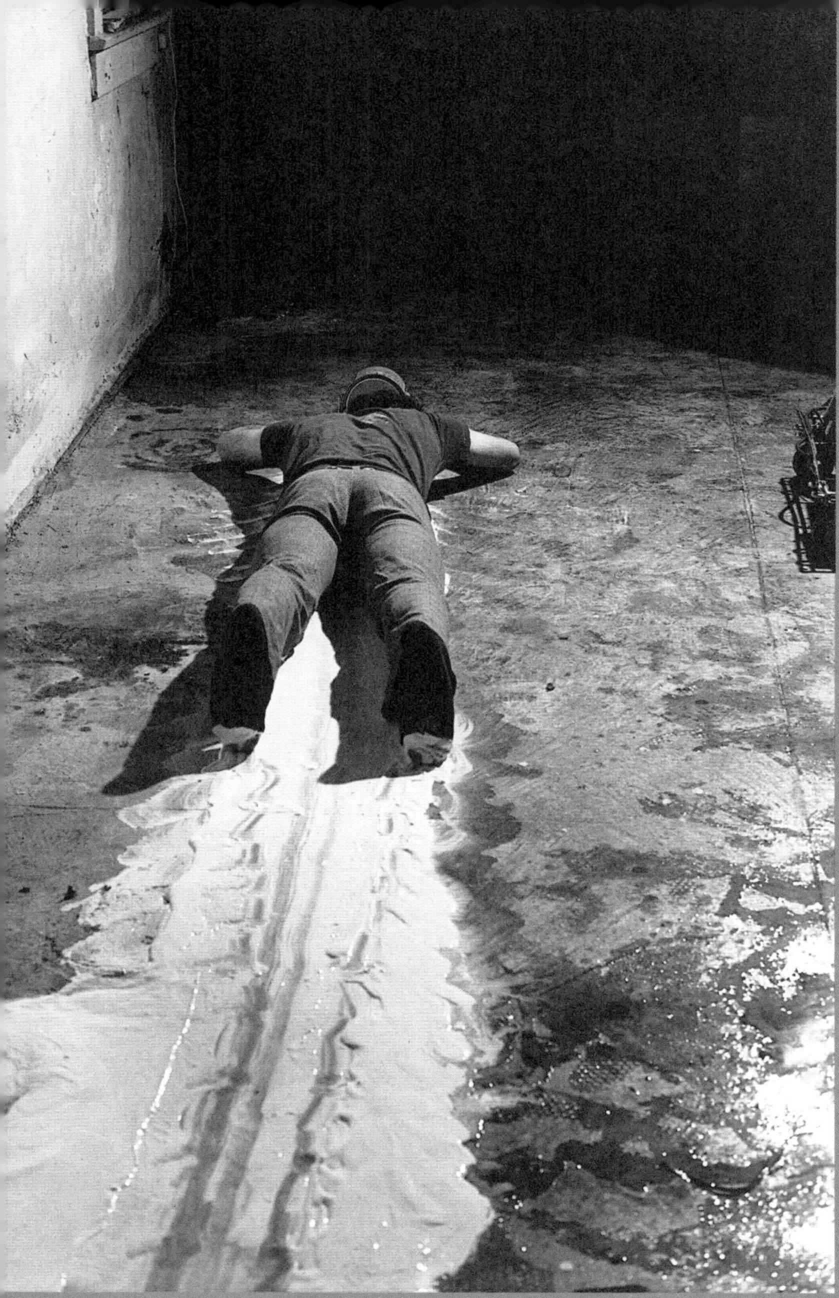

16

George Mathieu
George Mathieu making Toyotomi Hideoshi ['Home to General Hideyoshi'], 1957
Digital photograph
Courtesy Ashiya City Museum of Art & History

16 Paul McCarthy
Face Painting - Floor, White Line, 1972
Film, b&w
2 mins.
Courtesy the artist and Hauser & Wirth

Ana Mendieta
Untitled aka Body Tracks (Blood Sign #2), 1974
Super-8 colour, silent film transferred to DVD
edition of 6
1 min. 10 secs.
Courtesy the Estate of Ana Mendieta Collection and Alison Jacques Gallery, London

Josef Nadj, Miguel Barcélo & Augusti Torres
Paso Doble, 2006
Video, colour
41 mins.
Courtesy the artists and Les Poissons Volants, Paris

Hans Namuth & Jackson Pollock
Jackson Pollock
51, 1951
Film, colour
10 mins.
Courtesy Museum of Modern Art, New York

Robin Rhode
Untitled (Air Guitars), 2005
16mm film on DVD, b&w
7 mins. 15 secs.
Courtesy the artist and Perry Rubenstein Gallery, New York

Robin Rhode
Frequency, 2007
Video (performance documentation), colour
25 mins.
Performed by Jean Baptiste André
Courtesy the artist and Perry Rubenstein Gallery, New York

Carolee Schneemann
Water Light/Water Needle (St. Mark's Church in the Bowery), 1964
16mm film, b&w, silent
3 mins. 48 secs.
Courtesy Electronic Arts Intermix (EAI), New York

MAKING SPACE

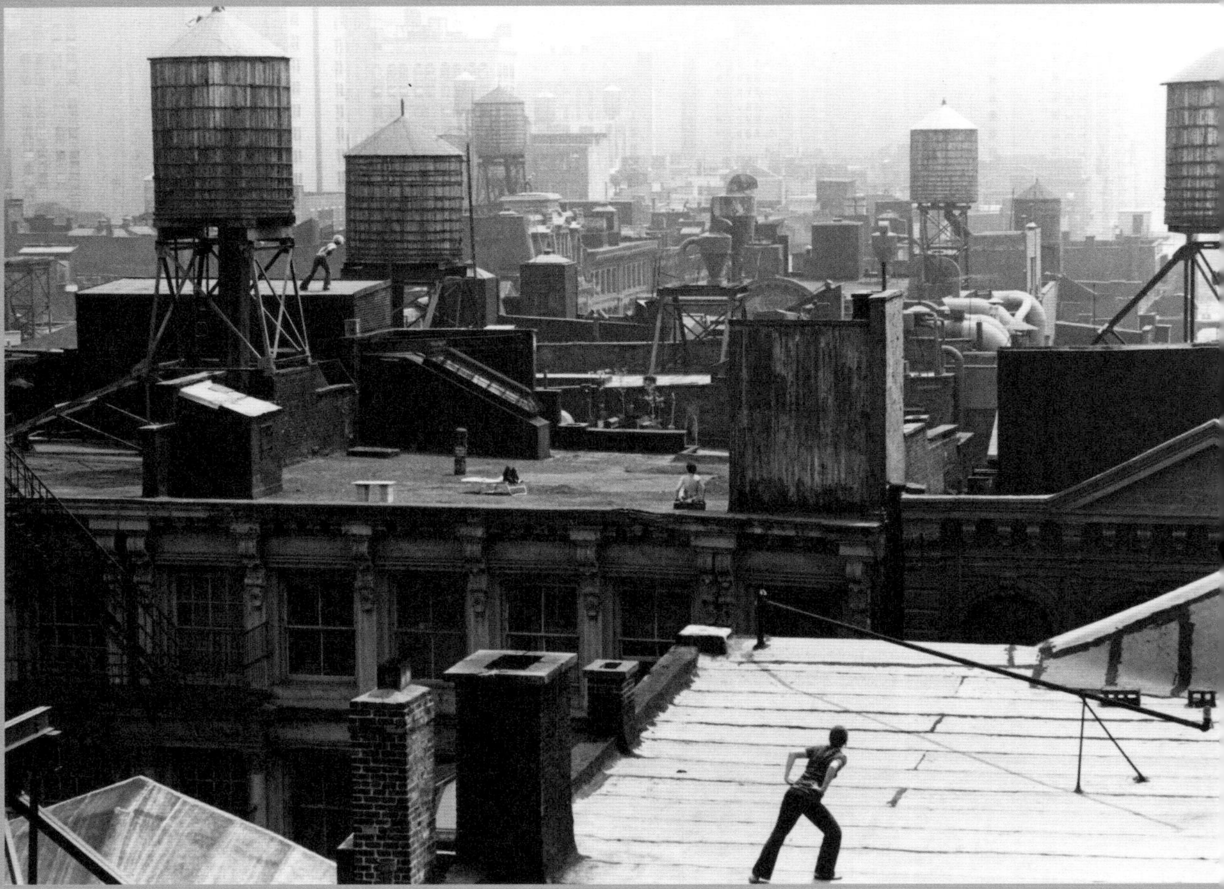

18

Samuel Beckett
Quadrat I and II, 1982
Film, colour
15 mins.
Courtesy SWR Media Services GmbH, Stuttgart

Trisha Brown
Group Primary Accumulation, 1973
Film, colour
8 mins. 34 secs.
Courtesy Trisha Brown Company and ARTPIX

18 Trisha Brown & Babette Mangolte
Roof and Fire Piece, 1973
Film, colour
32 mins.
Courtesy the artists, Trisha Brown Company, ARTPIX, and Broadway 1602, New York

21 Rosemary Butcher with Jon Groom
5-Sided Figure, 1980
Digital photographs
Courtesy the artist

Rosemary Butcher
The Site, 1980
Video (performance documentation), colour
30 mins.
Courtesy the artist

Boris Charmatz / Musée de la Dance
Horace-Benedict, 2001
Digibeta on DVD, colour
38 mins.
Courtesy Musée de la Danse, Rennes

Gustavo Ciríaco & Andrea Sonnberger
Here Whilst We Walk, 2006
Digital photographs
Courtesy the artists

Merce Cunningham
Space, Time and Dance, 1952
Sound recording
8 mins. 11 secs.
Courtesy Merce Cunningham Foundation, New York

Merce Cunningham
Further Thoughts, 1967
Sound recording
9 mins. 22 secs.
Courtesy Merce Cunningham Foundation, New York

Siobhan Davies
This Side to Body, 2002
Video, colour
14 mins. 58 secs.
Courtesy Siobhan Davies Dance and Coventry University

Eiko & Koma
Event Fission, 1980
Video, colour
42 mins. 40 secs.
Courtesy the artists

Eiko & Koma
Husk, 1987
Video, colour
9 mins.
Courtesy the artists

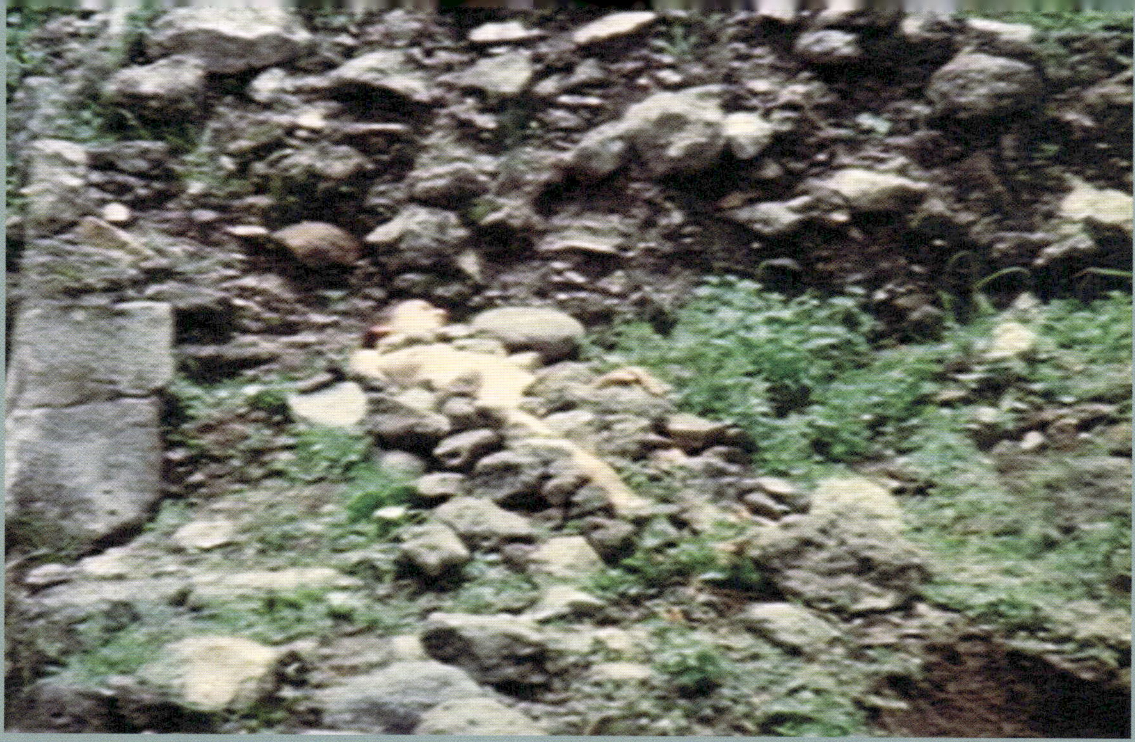

20

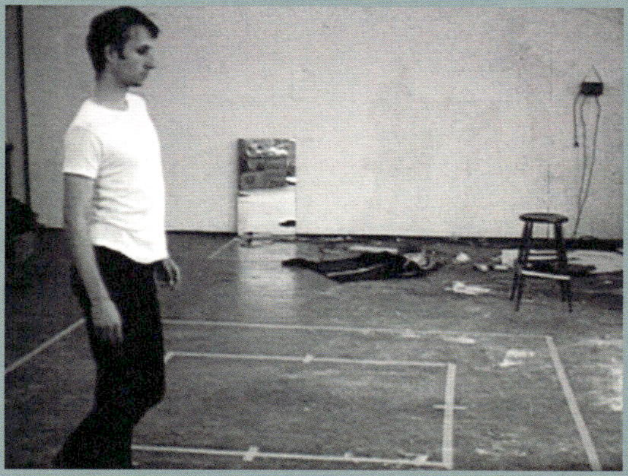

19

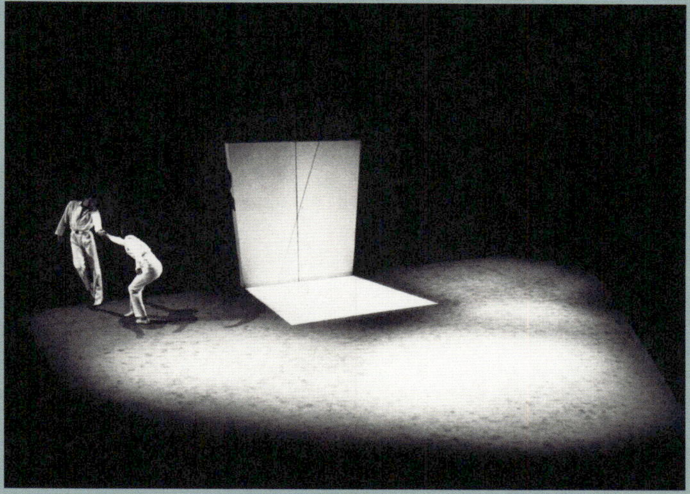

21

Amy Greenfield
Tides, 1982
Film, colour
12 mins
Courtesy the artist

Allan Kaprow
How to Make a Happening, 1966
Sound recording
25 mins.
Courtesy Allan Kaprow Estate, Hauser & Wirth and Primary Information

Akram Khan
Kaash, 2002
Video (performance documentation), colour
57 mins.
Courtesy Akram Khan Company, London

Ralph Lemon
Freedom Bus Rides, 2003
Video, colour
2 mins. 22 secs.
Courtesy the artist

20 Ana Mendieta
Burial Pyramid, Yagul, Mexico, 1974
Super-8 colour, silent film transferred to DVD
2 mins. 14 secs.
Courtesy the Estate of Ana Mendieta Collection and Alison Jacques Gallery, London

Saburo Murakami
Tsuuka ['Passing Through'], 1956
Digital photograph
Courtesy Ashiya City Museum of Art & History

Martin Nachbar & Martine Pisani
One Shared Object PROFIT AND LOSS, 2009
Video (performance documentation), colour
50 mins.
Courtesy the artist

19 Bruce Nauman
Walking in an Exaggerated Manner Around the Perimeter of a Square, 1967–68
Film, b&w
10 mins.
Courtesy Electronic Arts Intermix (EAI), New York

Meg Stuart
Revisited, 2007
Video, colour
2 mins. 9 secs.
Production: Damaged Goods, Time Festival (Ghent), Kunstencentrum Vooruit (Ghent)
Courtesy Britt Mesdagh

GRAVITY/FALLING

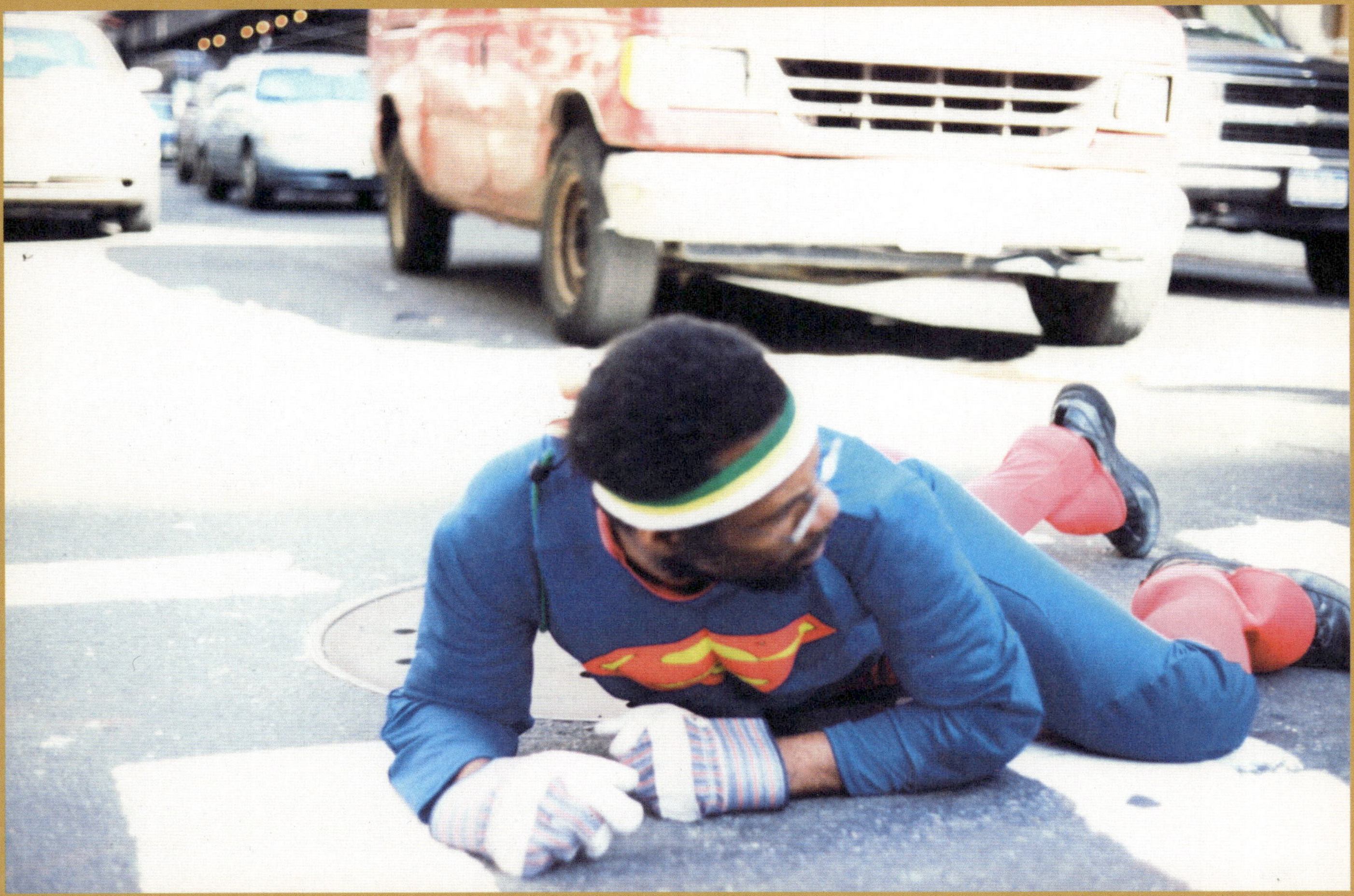

22

23 Bas Jan Ader
Fall 1, Los Angeles, 1970
16mm film on DVD, b&w, silent
34 secs.
Camera: Mary Sue Ader-Andersen
Courtesy of the Bas Jan Ader Estate and Patrick Painter Editions

Bas Jan Ader
Broken Fall (organic), Amsterdamse Bos, Holland, 1971
16mm film on DVD, silent
1 min. 36 secs.
Camera: Peter Bakker
Courtesy of the Bas Jan Ader Estate and Patrick Painter Editions

Trisha Brown
Walking on the Wall, 1971
16mm film, b&w, silent
5 mins. 4 secs.
Courtesy Trisha Brown Company and ARTPIX

24 Trisha Brown
Man Walking Down the Side of a Building, 1974
16mm film, b&w, silent
2 mins. 56 secs.
Courtesy the Trisha Brown Company and ARTPIX

Deborah Hay
Will They or Won't They?, 1963
Film, b&w, silent
1 min. 37 secs.
Courtesy the artist

Deborah Hay
Victory 14, 1964
Film, b&w, silent
2 mins. 28 secs.
Courtesy the artist

Mette Ingvartsen & Jefta van Dinther
It's in the Air, 2008
Video (performance documentation), colour
47 mins.
Courtesy the artists

KATHY
Day Dream, n.d.
Film
20 mins. 10 secs.
Courtesy the artists

Yves Klein
Leap Into the Void, 1960
Digital photograph, b&w
Courtesy the Yves Klein Archives, Paris

Li Wei
Li Wei falls to the Red Square, 2002
Video, colour
7 mins. 58 secs.
Courtesy the artist

Gordon Matta-Clark
Tree Dance, 1971
16mm film, b&w, silent
9 mins. 41 secs.
Courtesy Electronic Arts Intermix (EAI), New York

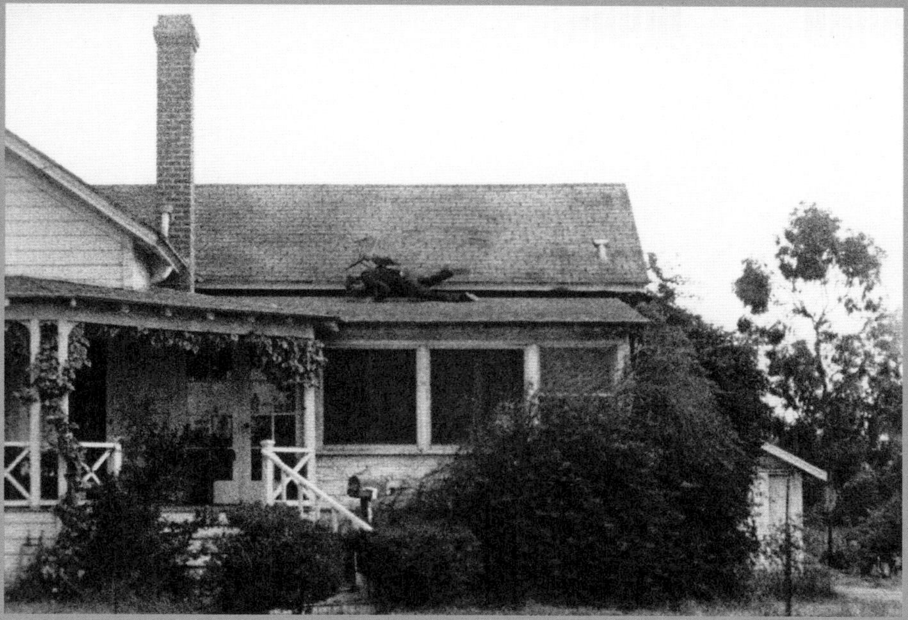

23

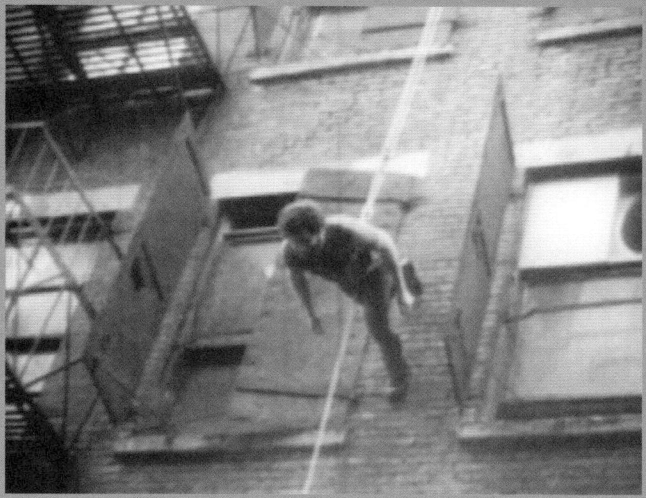

24

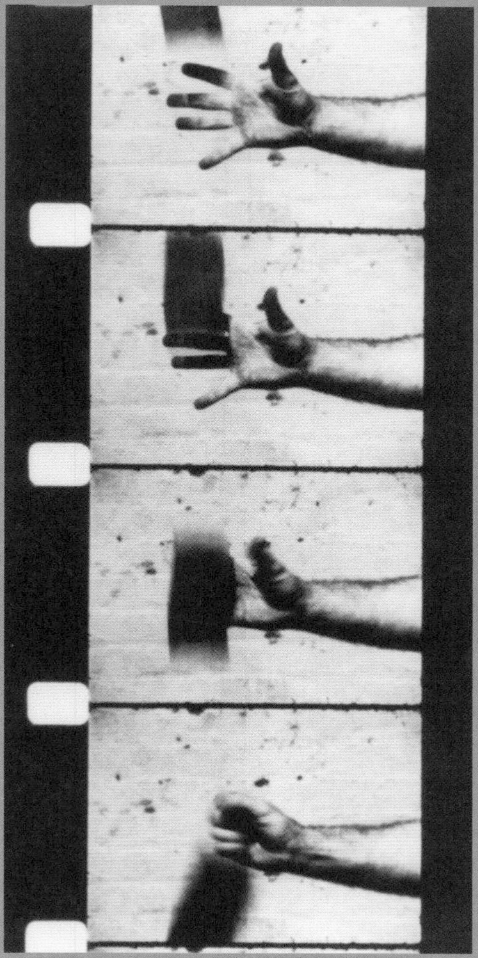

25

Bruce Nauman
Bouncing in the Corner No. 2: Upside Down, 1969
Film, b&w
1 hr.
Courtesy Electronic Arts Intermix (EAI), New York

Steve Paxton
Fall After Newton, 1987
Video, colour
23 mins.
Courtesy the artist and Videoda

22 William Pope.L
The Great White Way, 2001
Video, colour
6 mins. 41 secs.
Courtesy the artist

Marco Schuler
Well, blow me down, 2009
Video, colour
1 min. 6 secs.
Courtesy the artist

25 Richard Serra
Hand Catching Lead, 1968
Film, b&w
3 mins.
Courtesy the Museum of Modern Art, New York

Kazuo Shiraga
Challenging Mud, 1955
Digital photographs, b&w
Courtesy Ashiya City Museum of Art & History

David Weber-Krebs
Robert Morris Revisited, 2009
video documentation, colour
11 mins. 14 secs.
Courtesy the artist

SCORING/COMMANDING/ CHOREOGRAPHING

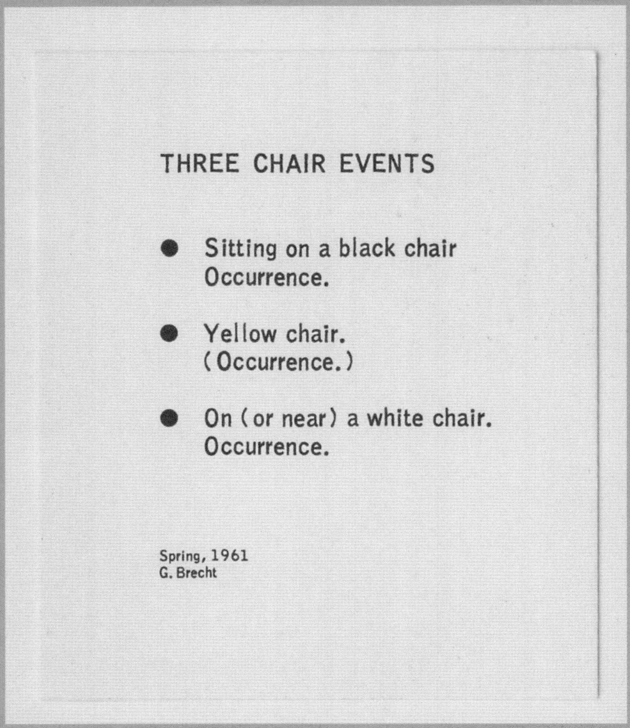
THREE CHAIR EVENTS

- Sitting on a black chair
  Occurrence.
- Yellow chair.
  (Occurrence.)
- On (or near) a white chair.
  Occurrence.

Spring, 1961
G. Brecht

26

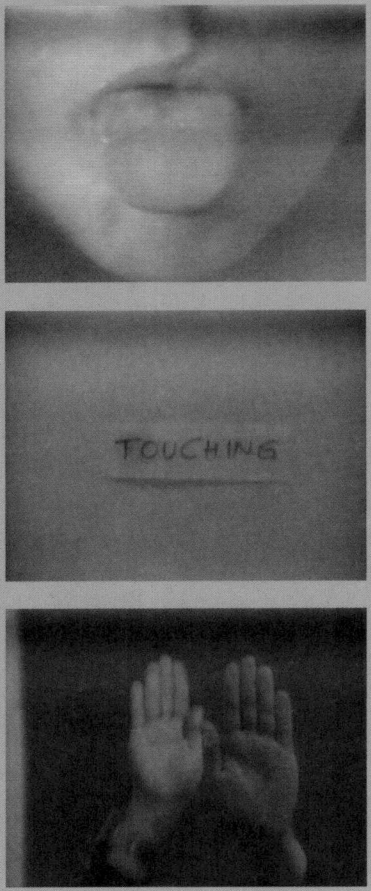

27

Vito Acconci
Command Performance, 1973
Film, b&w
56 mins. 40 secs.
Courtesy Electronic Arts Intermix (EAI), New York

Sasa Asentic
My Private Bio-Politics. A Performance on a Paper Floor, 2006–2008
Score
Courtesy the artist

Antonia Baehr
Laugh, 2006
Video (performance documentation), colour
42 mins. 30 secs.
Courtesy the artist

26 George Brecht
Water Yam (events) - Three Dances, Three Dances, Bed Event, Three Chair Event, Cork Thunder, Window Event, Ladder, 1959–1966
Digital photographs of cards
Each: 13 x 18 x 3 cm
Courtesy Arts Council Collection, Southbank Centre, London

Jonathan Burrows, Matteo Fargion & Adam Roberts
Both Sitting Duet, 2003
Score and video, colour
44 mins.
Filmmaker: Adam Roberts
Courtesy the artists

28 Tania Bruguera
Tatlin's Whispers #5, 2003
Video (performance documentation), colour
6 mins. 23 secs.
Courtesy the artist and Tate New Media

27 Valie Export
Body Tape, 1970
Film, b&w, silent
3 mins. 48 secs.
Courtesy Electronic Arts Intermix (EAI), New York

Félix González-Torres
Untitled, 1994
Score
Courtesy the Félix González-Torres Foundation, New York

Jesse Aron Green
ärztliche zimmergymnastik, 2008
video, colour
1 hr. 20 mins.
Courtesy the artist

Tatsumi Hijikata
Notational Butoh, 2007
DVD, colour
27 mins. 41 secs.
Courtesy the Hijikata Archives, Keio University, Japan

Mart Kangro
Out of Functions, 2004
Video (performance documentation), colour
48 mins.
Courtesy the artist

Allan Kaprow
18 Happenings in 6 Parts – Cast and Instructions, Event and Casts, Movement Score Room 1 Set 1, 1959
Scores
Courtesy Allan Kaprow Estate and Hauser & Wirth
Courtesy Research Library, The Getty Research Institute, Los Angeles

Allan Kaprow
Level, 1970
Score
Courtesy Allan Kaprow Estate and Hauser & Wirth
Courtesy the Research Library, The Getty Research Institute, Los Angeles

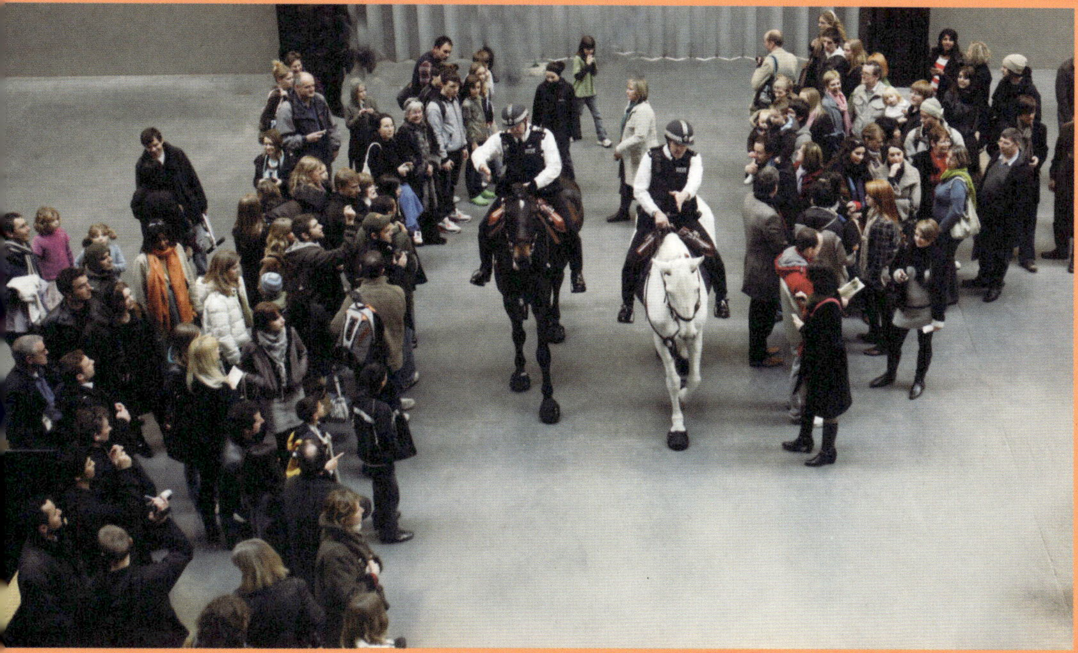

28

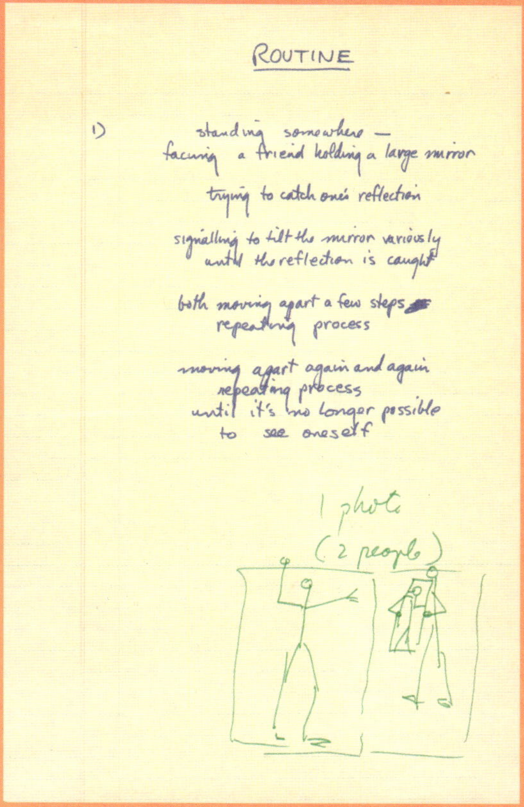

29

Allan Kaprow
Round Trip, 1970
Score
Courtesy Allan Kaprow Estate and Hauser & Wirth
Courtesy the Research Library, The Getty Research Institute, Los Angeles

29 Allan Kaprow
Routine, 1970
Score
Courtesy Allan Kaprow Estate and Hauser & Wirth
Courtesy the Research Library, The Getty Research Institute, Los Angeles

Allan Kaprow
Taking a Shoe for a Walk, 1970
Score
Courtesy Allan Kaprow Estate and Hauser & Wirth
Courtesy the Research Library, The Getty Research Institute, Los Angeles

Thomas Lehmen
Funktionen, 2004
Digital photographs of toolbox of score cards
Performer: Margaretha Lehmen
Photos: Thomas Lehmen
Courtesy the artist

Ligna
Radioballet, 2004
Video, colour
11 mins. 23 secs.
Courtesy the artist

Sharon Lockhart
Goshogaoka, 1997
16mm film excerpt, colour
10 mins. 23 secs.
Courtesy of the Artist, Gladstone Gallery, New York, Blum & Poe, Los Angeles and Neugerriemschneider, Berlin

Brian O'Doherty
Structural Play #3, 1967
Score
Courtesy the artist

Yoko Ono
Cough Piece, 1953
Score
Courtesy the artist and Shoshana Wayne Gallery, Santa Monica

Yoko Ono
Laugh Piece, 1961
Score
Courtesy the artist and Shoshana Wayne Gallery, Santa Monica

Yoko Ono
Smell Piece, 1963
Score
Courtesy the artist and Shoshana Wayne Gallery, Santa Monica

Yoko Ono
Fly Piece, 1963
Score
Courtesy the artist and Shoshana Wayne Gallery, Santa Monica

Yoko Ono
Falling Piece, 1964
Score
Courtesy the artist and Shoshana Wayne Gallery, Santa Monica

Steve Paxton
Satisfyin' Lover, 2001
Video (performance documentation), colour
7 mins.
Courtesy the artists and the Jerome Robbins Dance Division, The New York Public Library for the Performing Arts

Richard Serra
Verb Lists compilation: actions to relate to oneself, 1967
Score
Courtesy Gagosian Gallery, London

SCULPTING DANCES

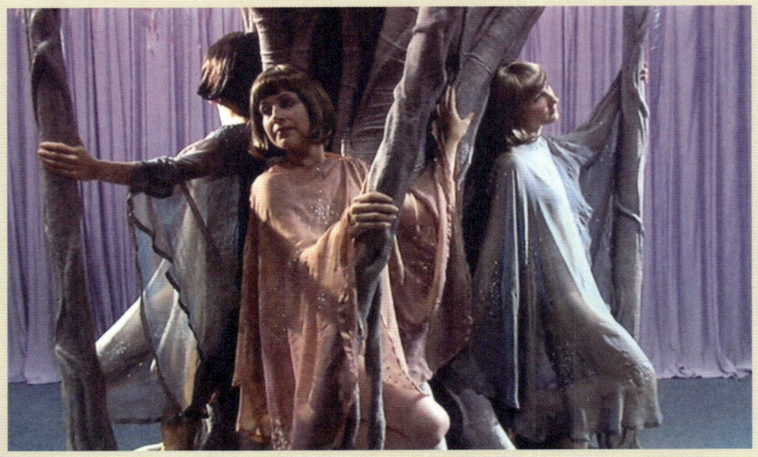

31

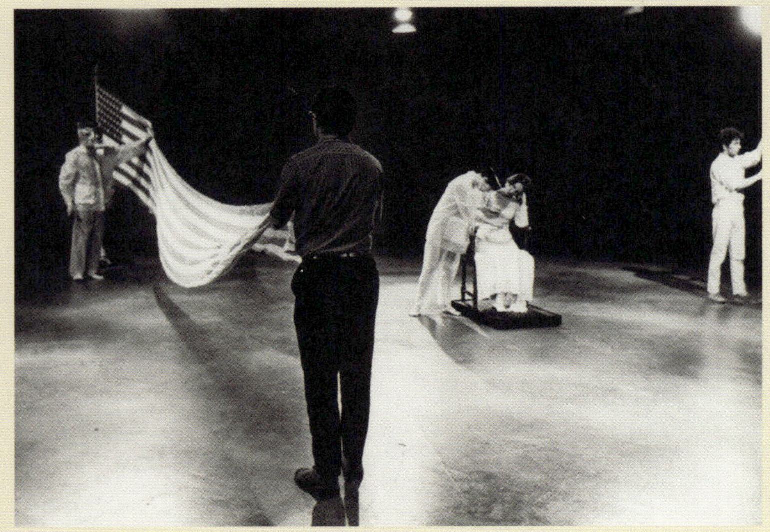

30

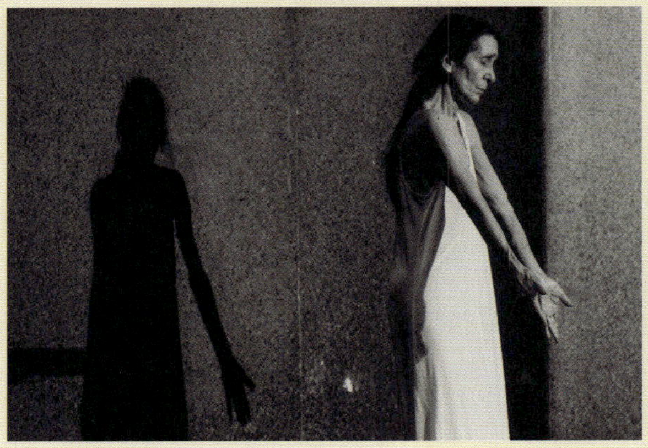

32

32 Pina Bausch
Cafe Müller, 1978
Video, colour
50 mins.
Courtesy L'Arche Editeur, Paris

Rosemary Butcher & Heinz Dieter Pietsch
Spaces 4, 1981
Video, (performance documentation), colour
20 mins.
Courtesy the artist

Boris Charmatz / Musée de la Danse
Ascension after *Aatt enen tionon*, a choregraphy by Boris Charmatz, 1996
video, colour
40 mins.
Director: Alain Michard
Courtesy Musée de la Danse, Rennes

Jae Eun Choi
Anger, Pleasure, Sorrow, Comfort, 2007
Video installation : 4 screens, DVD, 3 mins. (loop); Anger: 3 mins. 52 secs.
Pleasure: 3 mins. 49 secs.; Sorrow: 3 mins. 33 secs.; Comfort: 3 mins. 25 secs.
Courtesy the artist

Michael Clark
BBC Old Grey Whistle Test, 1984
Video, colour
5 mins. 40 secs.
Courtesy Michael Clark Company

DD Dorvillier
Nottthing is importanttt, 2007
Video (performance documentation), colour
57 mins. 11 secs.
Courtesy the DD Dorvillier / human future dance corps

William Forsythe
The Loss of Small Detail, 1991
Video documentation, colour
1 hr. 5 mins.
Courtesy the Forsythe Company, Frankfurt

William Forsythe
Solo, 1997
Video, b&w
6 mins. 54 secs.
Courtesy the Forsythe Company, Frankfurt

Simone Forti
Huddle, 1961/2004
Video (performance documentation), colour
11 mins. 16 secs.
Courtesy the artist and ARTPIX

Simone Forti & Anne Tardos
Statues, 1976
Film, b&w
12 mins. 50 secs.
Courtesy the artist

Raimund Hoghe
Bolero Variations, 2007
Video, (performance documentation), colour
2 hrs. 15 mins.
Courtesy the artist

Joan Jonas
Wind, 1968
Film, b&w, silent
5 mins. 37 secs.
Courtesy Electronic Arts Intermix (EAI), New York

Akram Khan
Zero Degrees, 2005
Video, (performance documentation), colour
1 hr. 5 mins.
Courtesy Axiom Films and Akram Khan Company, London

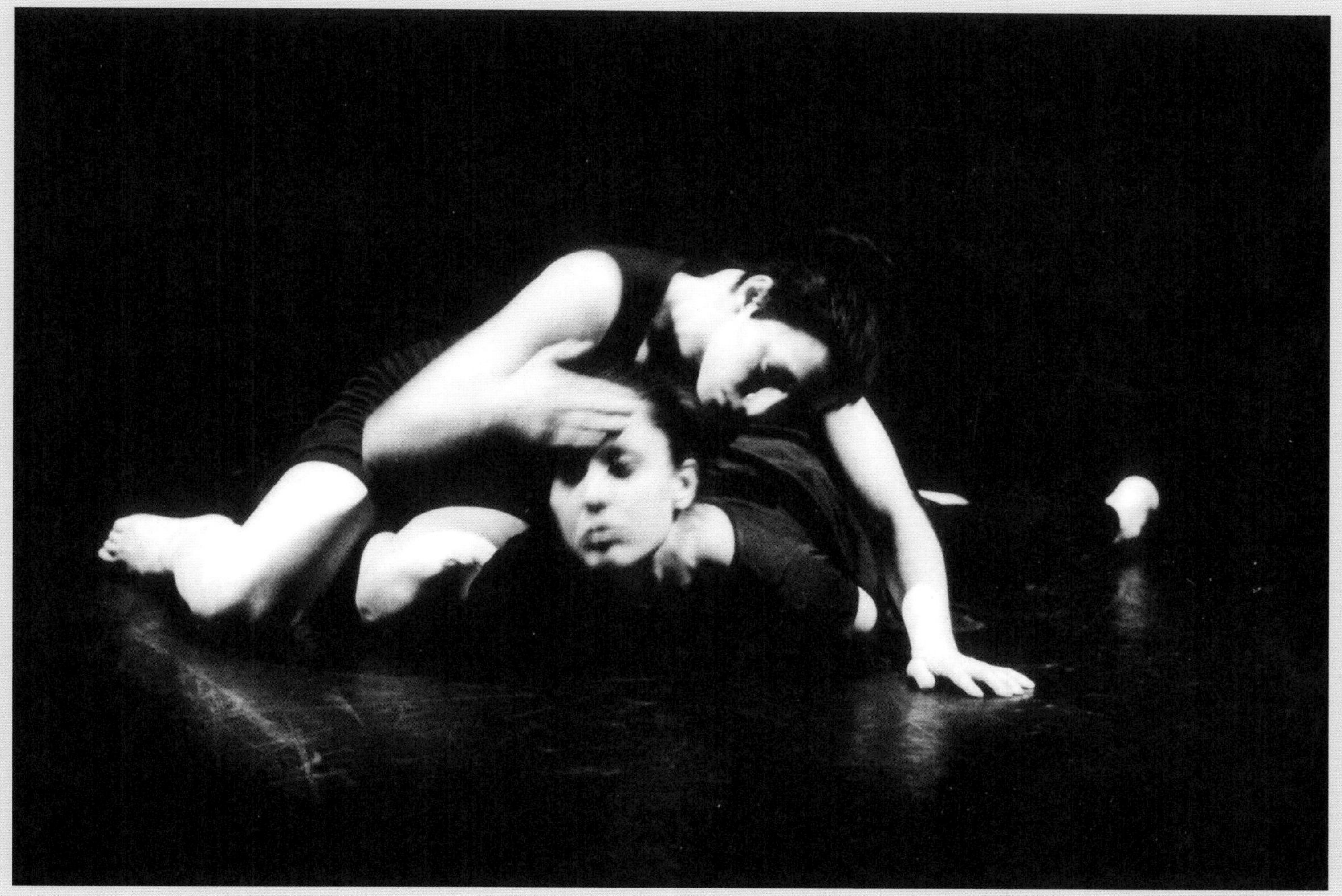

33

Daria Martin
In the Palace, 2000
16mm film transferred to DVD, colour
7 mins.
Courtesy Maureen Paley, London

Daria Martin
Birds, 2001
16mm film transferred to DVD, colour
7 mins. 30 secs.
Courtesy Maureen Paley, London

Meredith Monk
16 Millimeter Earrings, 1966/1980
Film, colour and b&w
25 mins.
Director: Robert Withers, Documentary 1980
Courtesy Meredith Monk/The House Foundation for the Arts

Yvonne Rainer
Trio A, 1966/1978
16mm film, b&w, silent
10 mins. 30 secs.
Courtesy Video Data Bank, Chicago

30 Robert Rauschenberg
Linoleum
1966
Film, b&w, silent
13 mins. 41 secs.
Courtesy of the Estate of Robert Rauschenberg/Licensed by VAGA, New York, NY

Eszter Salamon
What a Body you Have, Honey, 2001
Video (performance documentation), colour
45 mins.
Courtesy the artist

Hooman Sharifi
Once Upon a Time Country, 2009
Video (performance documentation), colour
1 hr. 10 mins.
Courtesy the artist

31 Jim Shaw
The Whole: A Study in Oist Integrated Movement, 2009
Film transferred to DVD, colour
16 mins. 43 secs.
Courtesy Simon Lee Gallery, London

33 Meg Stuart
Disfigure Study, 1991/2002
Video (performance documentation), colour
1 hr. 10 mins. 15 secs.
Courtesy Meg Stuart/Damaged Goods

Meg Stuart & Philipp Gehmacher
Maybe Forever, 2006
Video (Trailer), colour
6 mins. 17 secs.
Courtesy Meg Stuart/Damaged Goods

DANCING

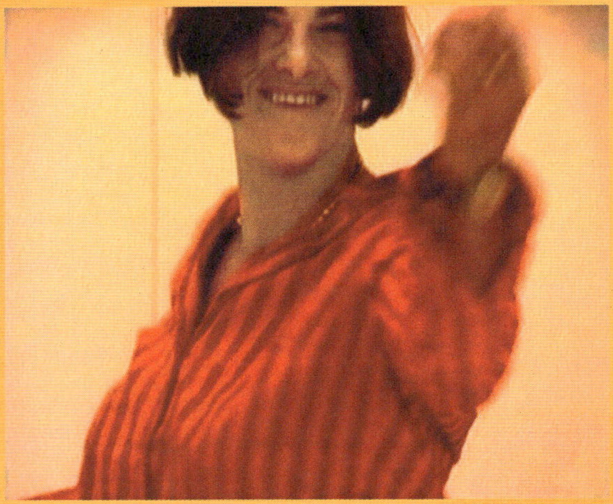

34

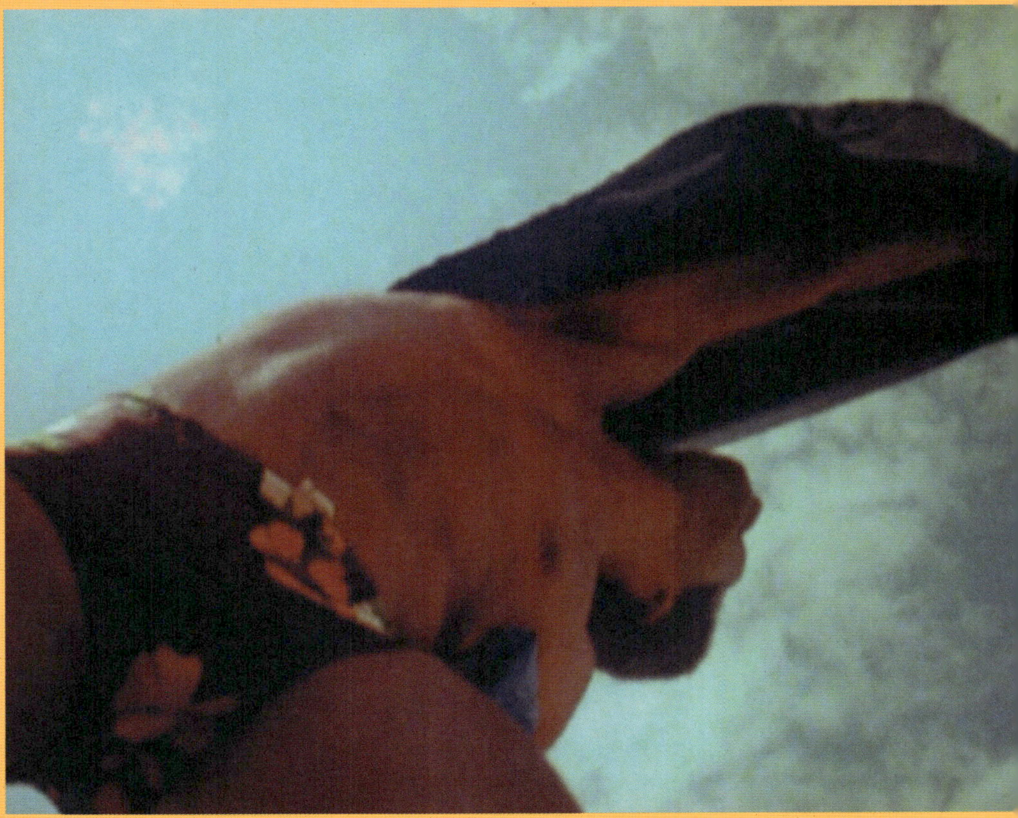

35

Nevin Aladağ
Familie Tezcan, 2001
Video, colour
6 mins. 40 secs.
Courtesy the artist

36 Nevin Aladağ
Raise the Roof, 2007
Video, colour
9 mins.
Courtesy the artist

Ann Carlson & Mary Ellen Strom
Sloss, Kerr, Rosenberg, and Moore, 2007
Video, colour
4 mins. 18 secs.
Courtesy the artists and Alexander Gray Associates LLC

34 Tracey Emin
Why I Never Became a Dancer, 1995
Betacam SP video, colour
6 mins. 40 secs.
Courtesy Arts Council Collection, Southbank Centre, London

Evil Knievel
I Love America, 2006
Video, colour
16 mins. 40 secs.
Courtesy the artist

Daniel Guzmán
New York Groove
2008
Video transferred to DVD, colour
3 mins. 42 secs.
Courtesy the artist and Harris Lieberman Gallery, New York

37 Mike Kelley
Pole Dance, 1997
Video, colour
31 mins. 18 secs.
Courtesy Electronic Arts Intermix (EAI), New York

Katarzyna Kozyra
Cheerleader, 2006
Video, colour
4 mins. 30 secs.
Courtesy the artist and Żak Branicka, Berlin

35 Hélio Oiticica & Ivan Cardoso
H.O., 1979
Film, subtitled in English, colour
6 mins. 58 secs.
Courtesy the artist

Adrian Piper
Funk Lessons, 1983
Video, colour
15 mins.
Courtesy the Adrian Piper Research Archive Foundation, Berlin

Pipilotti Rist
I'm Not the Girl Who Misses Much, 1986
Video, colour
7 mins. 46 secs.
Courtesy Electronic Arts Intermix (EAI), New York

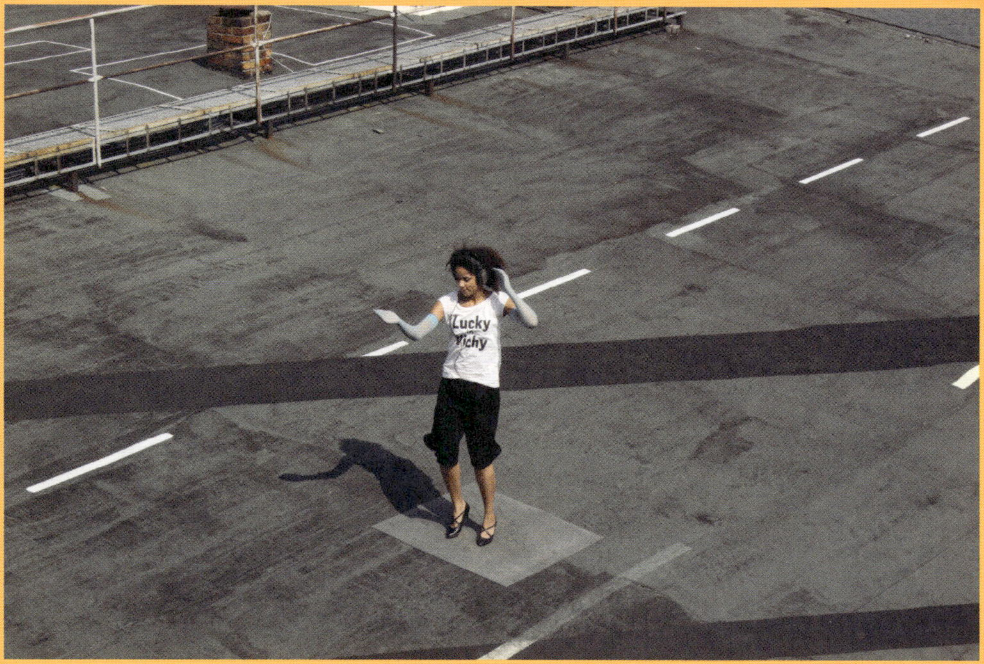

36

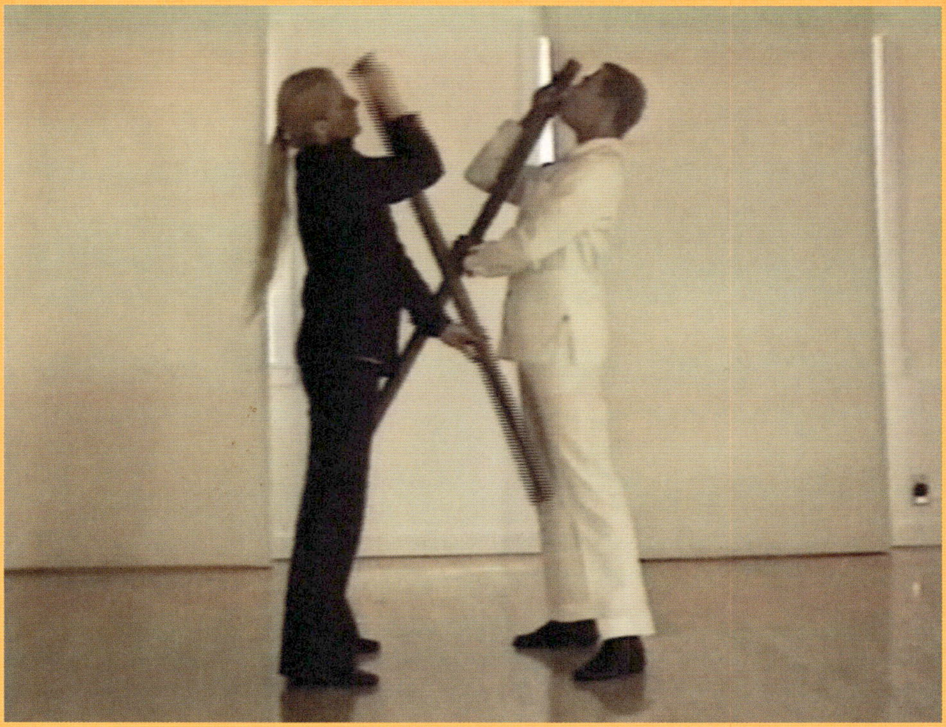

37

Zones of Resonance

Mutual formations in Dance and the Visual Arts Since the 1960s

André Lepecki

Left and right: Xavier Le Roy, Self Unfinished, 1998

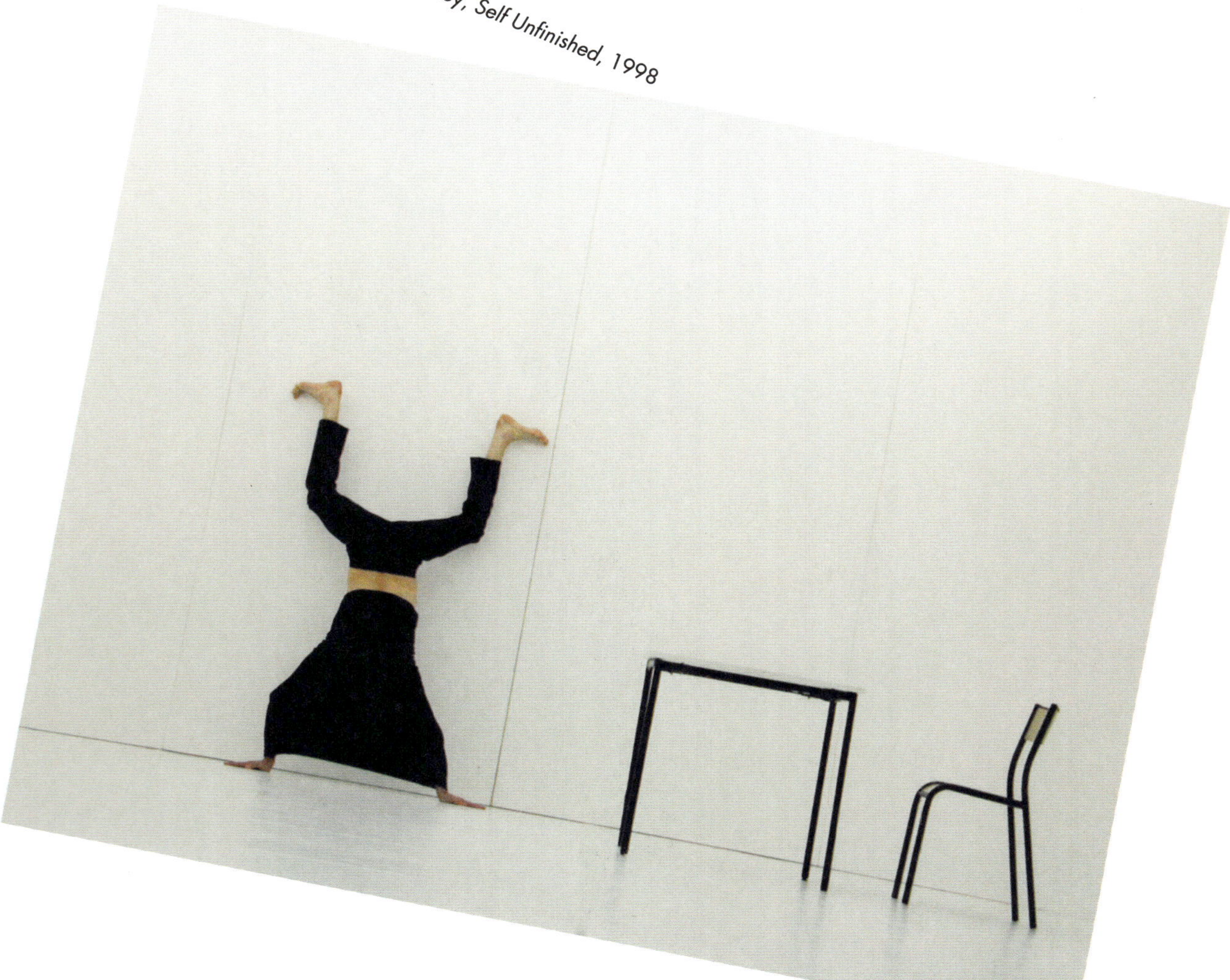

1. CORRESPONDENCES

In the summer and early autumn of 1959, visual artist Allan Kaprow meticulously put down on paper an almost second-by-second movement notation for the six performers (including himself) who would activate his seminal piece *18 Happenings in 6 Parts* (pp. 40–3). Kaprow's detailed scores – based on series of stick figures representing human bodies accompanied by verbal descriptions of each performer's actions – prescribed gestures, steps and timings for each 'Happening'. They revealed a surprising and counter-intuitive fact: the compositional tool that allowed the first happening to exist was literally choreography – the writing down of movements for their future and exact execution.[1]

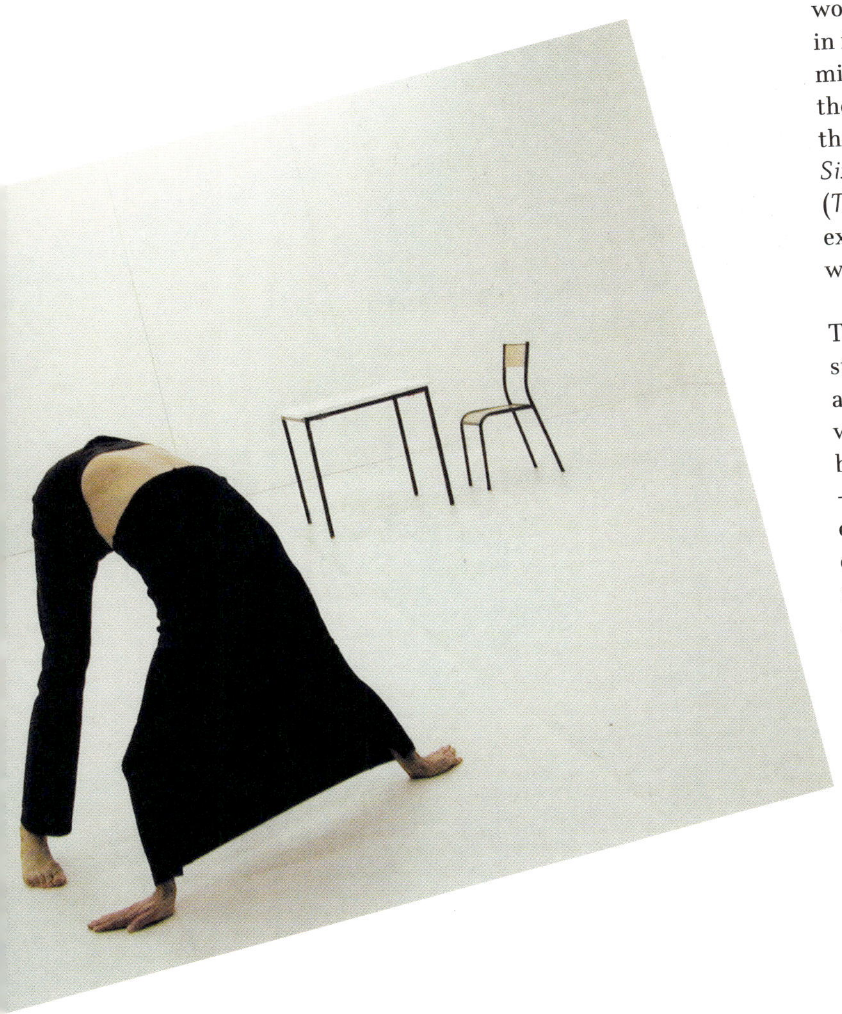

Four years previously, in 1955, Saburo Murakami, a Japanese artist associated with the Gutai group, built a series of tall rectangular wooden frames covered with sheets of paper. After placing each panel in front of the other, Murakami stood at one end of his precarious minimal sculpture and, with energetic decisiveness, rammed through the layers of paper, transforming his sculpture's serial elegance into the register of a catastrophic event. Titled *At One Moment Opening Six Holes*, and repeated in 1956 under the name *Breaking Through* (*Tsuuka*),[2] this action-sculpture (or perhaps 'objectact', to use the expression that Brazilian artist Hélio Oiticica coined to define his own works of the late 1960s[3]) lasted less than a minute.

Through Murakami's simple, fast and irreversible act, an important statement was being made regarding the solidity of sculptural objects and the very nature of objecthood in the visual arts. The moving body was now perceived as that necessary conjugation of forces that could both supplement and shatter traditional surfaces of representation – paper, canvas, a beautiful serial sculpture. Just as with Kaprow's choreographed scores, Murakami had created an object that could only exist thanks to the establishment of a very direct and clear relationship between sculptural elements and those that had been deemed constitutive of (and exclusive to) dance as an art form. If in *18 Happenings in 6 Parts* that element had been choreography, in the case of Murakami, those elements were corporeality, movement and ephemerality.

Throughout the 1960s and the 1970s, we find with increased frequency examples of visual artists using compositional elements that had defined for two centuries the aesthetic regime of theatrical dance. In 1960, at *Galerie Internationale d'Art Contemporain* in Paris, Yves Klein drags across a large paper surface spread on the floor the naked body of a woman drenched in International Klein Blue paint. Part of Klein's *Anthropometries* series (p. 141), this particular performance was accompanied by a live music ensemble, whose presence pushed this event even further into the explicit realm of a dance event. Amelia Jones remarked how in this piece Klein 'becomes a conductor whose role was to orchestrate the individuals making his paintings for him in a spectacle of artistic direction'.[4] But since Klein physically pulled around a naked body in order to leave traces of its motions on paper to the sound of live music, one could argue that his 'artistic direction' was not so much that of a conductor than of a choreographer. Klein called the naked bodies he manipulated 'living brushes', but by grabbing and pulling them in front of an audience

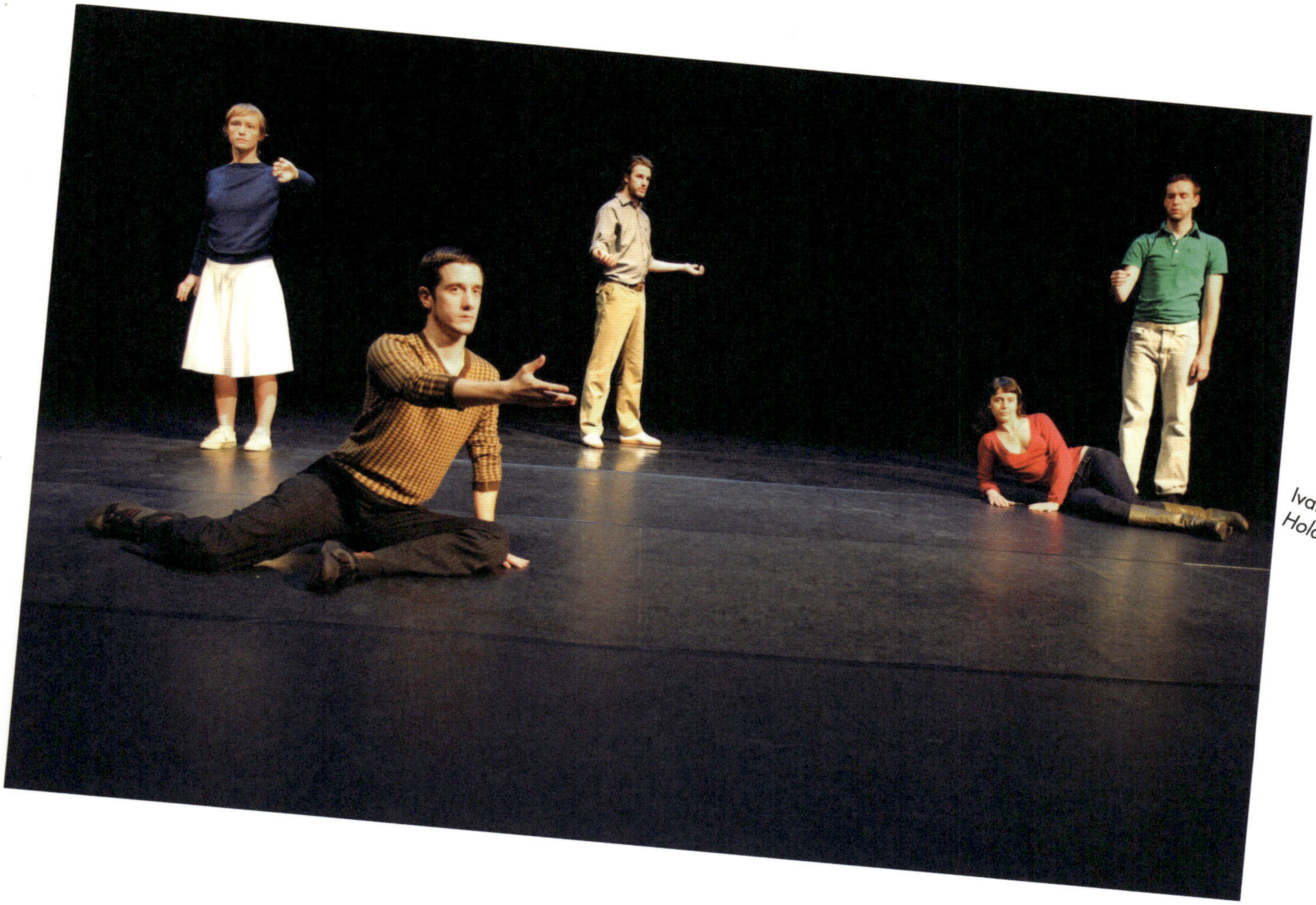

Ivana Müller, While We Were Holding It Together, 2006

he also turned these 'brushes' (and himself) into dancers. Equally, by placing paper on the floor, and having a music ensemble playing next to it, he turned the painting's surface into a stage.

As an operation of inscription, *Anthropometries* established an isomorphic correspondence between paper and stage, which is the exact operation that informs one of the earliest dance notation systems, invented by Raoul-Auger Feuillet and predicated on an overlapping between dance floor and book page.[5] By adding a music ensemble next to this paper dance floor, Klein cast the labour of painting as a choreographic spectacle. And in its manipulation of passive women, *Anthropometries* also reminds us of Heinrich von Kleist's famous association between choreographer and puppeteer, authorial and godlike figures whose power to pull and push bodies under their control would define dance as a brushing of the floor by a body dragged by the compositional will of the choreographer/puppeteer.[6]

Further probing of functional equivalences between the painter or sculptor and the dancer or choreographer define the works of some influential visual artists in the 1960s. It is telling that Robert Morris published his 'Notes on Dance' in 1965, one year before the publication in *Artforum* of his influential 'Notes on Sculpture'. Morris's short essay on dance articulates how live action and choreographic scoring (what he called 'rules or tasks') would enter into compositions with objects in order to reveal 'the coexistence of the static and the mobile'.[7] In the same year that Morris published his 'Notes on Dance', Hélio Oiticica, whose sculpture and painting in the 1950s was still informed by the Brazilian concretist and neo-concretist schools, jotted down his own notes on dance in his diary. As opposed to Morris's 'rules or tasks' (denoting a concern with the choreographic), Oiticica was interested on the impact of improvised dance on his sculptural work. He saw dance as expressing 'the immanence of the act' that leads to a 'new discovery of the image'.[8] This capacity for dance to help discover a renewed visuality in art was to become crucial not only to Oiticica's work, but to the development of the visual arts at large over the next half century.

As visual artists turned to dance, choreographers also started to explore transversal articulations with the visual arts. The choreographer Merce Cunningham stated as early as 1952: 'A prevalent feeling among many painters that lets them make a space in which anything can happen is a feeling dancers may have too.'[9] With this wish for dance to make a space where anything can happen, some choreographers started questioning dance's traditional allegiance to compositions based on movement performed by hyper-trained bodies concerned with the display of their virtuosity. Writing in 1966, choreographer Yvonne Rainer stated it clearly: 'This particular kind of display has finally in this decade exhausted itself, closed back on itself, and perpetuates solely by consuming its tail.'[10]

One of the alternative modes that choreographers found was the creation of 'pedestrian' dances – where the display of technical skill became secondary to the capacity to simply fulfill tasks that were

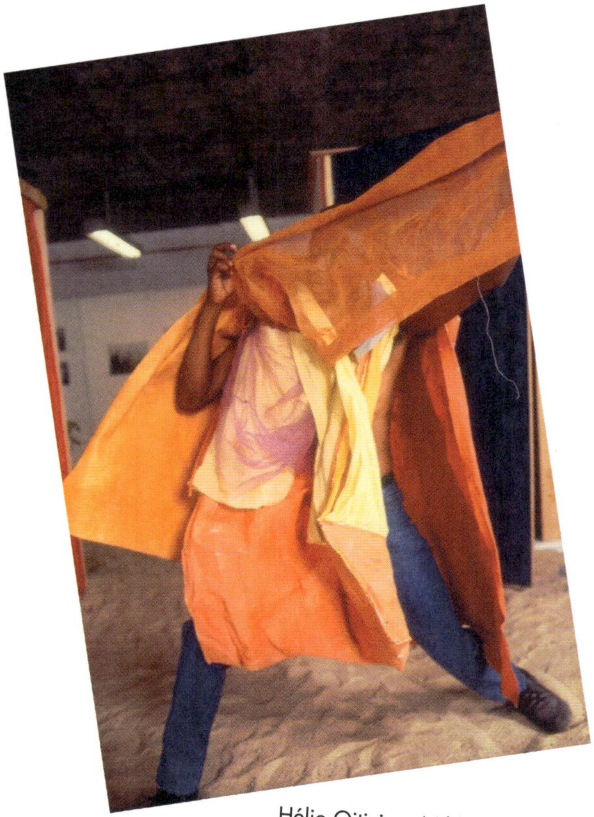

Hélio Oiticica, *Nildo of Mangueira with Parangolé P4 Cape 1*, 1964

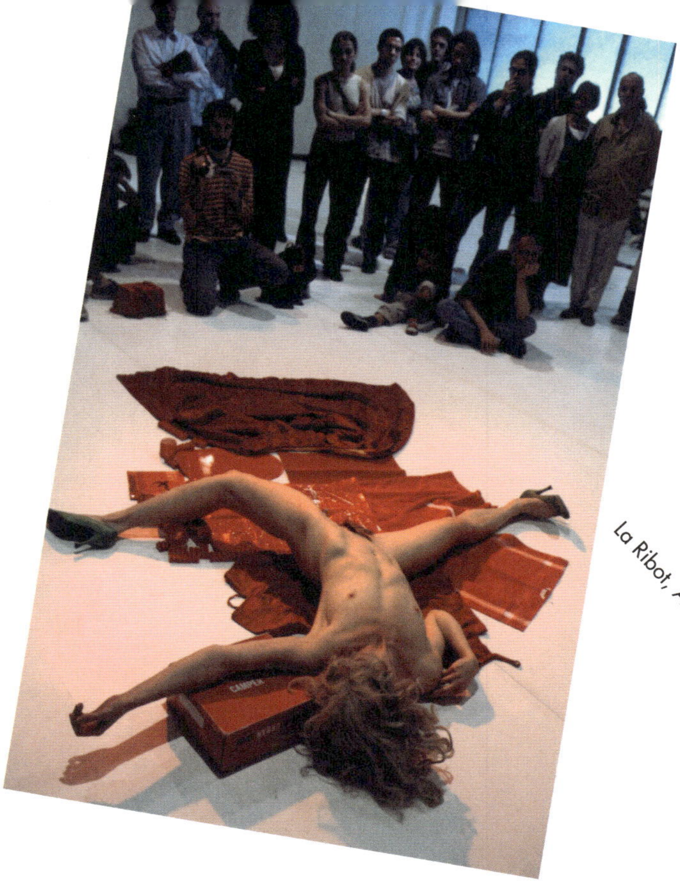

La Ribot, *Another Bloody Mary*, 2000

essentially non-technical. According to Rainer: 'the alternatives [to renew dance] are obvious: stand, walk, run, eat, carry bricks, show movies, or move or be moved by some *thing* rather than by oneself.'[11] Searching for pedestrian or everyday gestures, desiring to be moved by a *thing*, dance was drawing from (as well as expanding) Marcel Duchamp's notion of the readymade. Just as the readymade had been essential for Duchamp's critique of the 'retinal' in visual arts, pedestrian moves and task-oriented choreographies would become essential for dance to critique its unconditional alignment with 'ongoing movement'.

Paul Taylor, who collaborated with visual artists such as Robert Rauschenberg and Jasper Johns, was one of the first choreographers to explore everyday movements on a consistent basis (and not only as incidental narrative necessity, as in ballet), as well as stillness as a compositional strategy – anticipating in this way both the Judson Dance Theater choreographers and the early Happenings. In 1957, Taylor created *Duet*, a choreography of stillness for a music score by John Cage. Wearing street clothes, Taylor and Toby Glanternik (dancer Anita Dencks was replaced in the last minute) appear on stage, one assuming a standing position, the other lying down, and remain absolutely still. After four minutes they exit and the piece ends. A few years later, Steve Paxton, one of the Judson Dance Theater group choreographers, created pieces using stillness and everyday behaviours such as *Flat* (1964) or *Smiling* (1969).

In the past two decades, but most prominently over the past ten years, dance and choreography have become inescapable forces in contemporary art. In the archive to this exhibition, we can see how since the mid-1990s dance and visual arts have become profoundly imbricated. It is as if dance starts to be perceived not only as providing a renewed visuality to the visual arts (as Oiticica wanted), but as being a practice able to provide the necessary tools for rearticulating social-political dimensions of the aesthetic. In this move, dance reinvents itself deeply, shedding its modernist identity as 'the art of movement', while embracing its capacity to critically decode forces already choreographing our gestures, habits, language, thoughts, tastes, desires (even our desire to dance and to see dances). Since 1994, the extraordinary work of French choreographer Jérôme Bel has consistently enacted such decodings, from the function of authorship (*Nom donné par l'auteur*, 1994 and *Jérôme Bel*, 1995) to the politics of theatrical visuality, labour, and the representation of difference in dance (*The Last Performance*, 1998, *Veronique Doisneau* 2004, *Pichet Klunchun and Myself*, 2005). Randy Martin noted in 1998: 'dance displays [and performs], in the very way that bodies are placed in motion [or rest], traces of the forces of contestation that can be found in society at large.'[12] At a moment when the political in art rearticulates the whole field of the aesthetic, dance finds itself in a unique position to offer practices, techniques, corporealities and affects that disclose forces of manipulation – while also demonstrating before our eyes, that it is possible to activate counter-forces of invention to empower our own movements. By moving (or by opting to remain still), dance demonstrates how its decodings are not mere conceptual propositions but actual *possibilities* for action. We can see the enactment of possibilities in the works of Kelly Nipper, Daniel Guzmán, Robin Rhode, Kataryna Kozyra, Pipilotti Rist, Jesse Aron Green, Matthew Barney, Tino Sehgal, Isaac Julien, William Forsythe, Vera Mantero, La Ribot, Jérôme Bel, Eszter Solomon, DD Dorvillier, Meg Stuart, Xavier Le Roy and Boris Charmatz, to mention just a few.

Without producing a durable object, dance offers a few other elements relevant to a contemporary politics in art. Since it

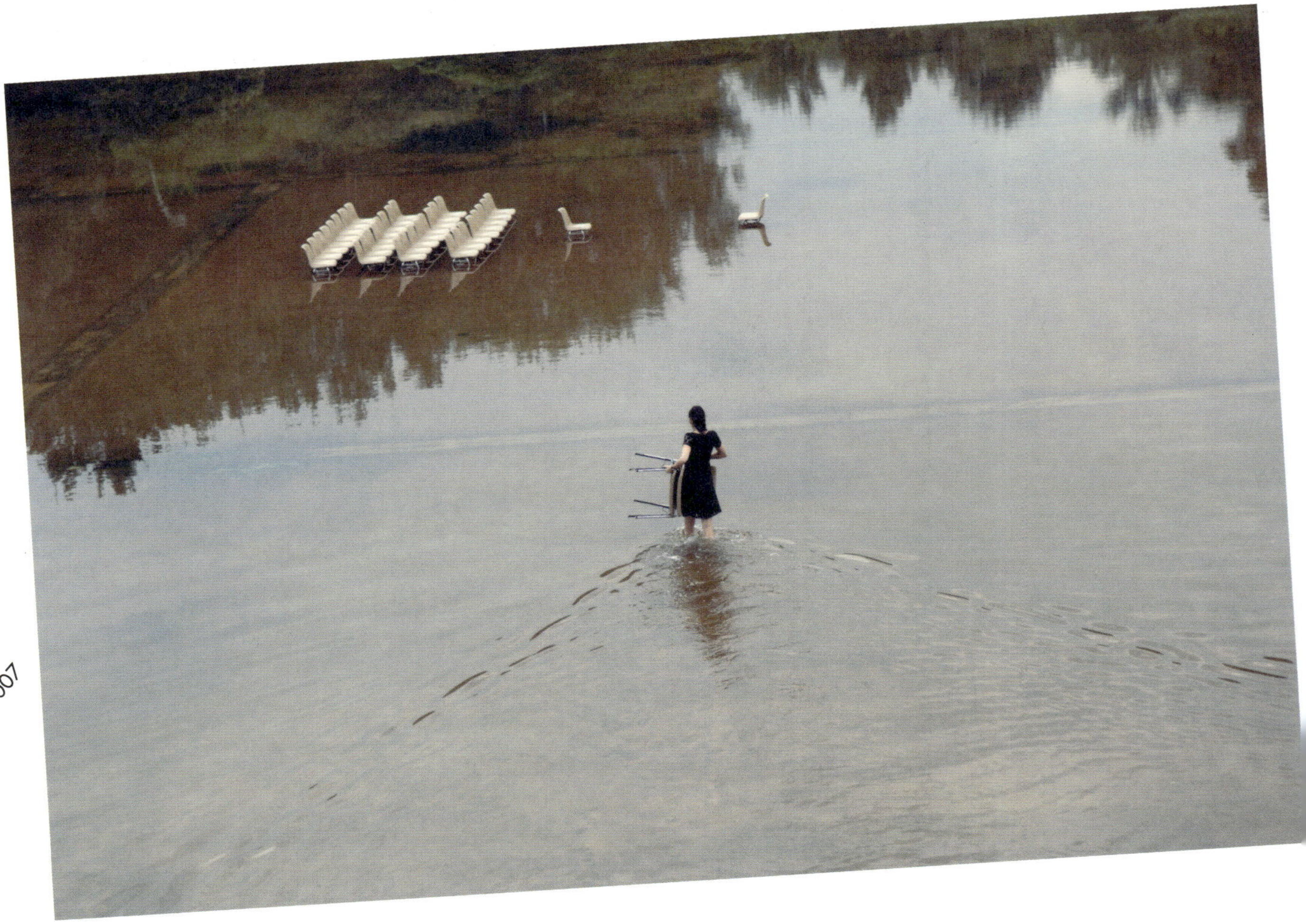

Vlatka Horvat, *This Here & That There*, 2007

inevitably appears to its audience both as spectacle and as labour, dance foregrounds the often hidden links between labour and aesthetics. In Croatian-Dutch choreographer Ivana Müller's *While We Were Holding It Together* (2006), dancers remain still for an hour. The effort of this forced stillness for the sake of representation reveals an excruciating effort. But if dancers can endure, dance itself is ephemeral. The current attraction to its dematerialised materiality reinforces, politically and aesthetically, Michael Newman's insight that Conceptual art was not a mere desire for 'ideas' but 'an attempt to free materiality from a "objecthood" that has become aesthetically and politically compromised.'[13] Dance's dematerialisation as ephemerality offers ways to create works that resist, or bypass, politically compromised notions of the art object as commodity, fetish, or surplus-value. Thus the visual artist must become a choreographer. In *Untitled (Go-go Dancer Platform)* (1991) Félix González-Torres used dance (and its absence) to evoke the political dimension of the ephemeral. On a white platform surrounded by light bulbs, a male go-go dancer occasionally performs during a gallery's regular exhibition hours. As the work alternates between the ephemerality of a dancing presence and the palpability of a dancer's absence, it creates a powerful statement on the precariousness of life – particularly in the context of the AIDS pandemic during which the piece was created, and which eventually took González-Torres's life. British-German artist Tino Sehgal has taken the fusing of sculpture and dance to an extreme in works such as *Kiss* (2003), where a male and a female dancer revolve around each other without stopping, to create a dynamic montage of famous kissing sculptures. In *Instead of Allowing Some Thing to Rise Up to Your Face Dancing Bruce and Dan and Other Things* (2000), we find a perfect justification for naming Sehgal's works 'dancesculptures' – they enact a new space of possibility for a moving image to linger and for movement, corporeality and presence to redefine the links between visuality and choreography, while complicating the problematics of the object and its place in the realm of the visual. In works such as these, exclusively displayed live in museum spaces, dance is what allows art to escape from its deathtraps.

2. A CONCURRENT ARCHIVE

What if we postulate that the history of dance and the visual arts in the past half-century is essentially a co-formative one? Such a history would bypass narratives of how generational lines of influence are more or less pedagogically transmitted within discrete disciplines, and would propose instead the identification of resonating zones of co-articulation and mutual correspondence between visual arts and dance. To propose such a mutual co-formation means surpassing the diagnosis made by Rosalind Krauss on the condition of sculpture after 1945, when 'a large number of postwar European and American sculptors became interested both in theater and in the extended experience of time which seemed part of the conventions of the stage. From this interest came some sculpture to be used as props in productions of dance and theater, some to function as surrogate performers, and some to act as the on-stage generators of scenic effects.'[14] As we saw, there was much more going on than the desire of visual artists to create 'props', 'surrogates' or 'scenic effects' – and much more than choreographers simply wanting to surround their dances with objects.

Yvonne Rainer articulated this co-formative hypothesis as early as 1966, when she wrote: 'What is perhaps unprecedented in the short history of the modern dance is the close correspondence between concurrent developments in dance and the plastic arts.'[15] 'Correspondence' implies not only a notion of communality but also of deep dialoguing. Correspondence is a back and forth that is unconcerned with claims of originary precedence. A genealogy of correspondences in dance and visual arts since the 1960s would reveal the mutual co-formation of concurrent zones of compositional and thematic concerns and practices. It would also reveal mutual interests in certain materials, procedures and modes of display. As Oiticica proposed, this would lead to a renewed political and aesthetic critique of the visual in art; similarly, we could add that it would lead dance to engage in a political and aesthetic critique of dancing.

Those resonating zones of compositional tactics scramble neat divisions between dance and the visual arts, and may be provisionally identified under the following headings, which also structure the archive for this exhibition: 'Choreographing Things'; 'Transforming the Body'; 'Making Space'; 'Transforming Time'; 'Tracing Movement'; 'Scoring/Choreographing/Commanding'; 'Gravity/Falling'; 'Sculpting Dances' and 'Dancing'.

3. ZONES
Choreographing Things

In her essay on minimalism in dance, written in 1966, Rainer proposed that the dancer should: 'be moved by some *thing*, rather than by oneself'. A few years earlier, in 1960, at the Reuben Gallery in New York, choreographer Simone Forti, anticipating Rainer's call, had presented a groundbreaking work titled *See-saw* – a piece where the capacity for things to move dance was deeply explored. Forti placed an oscillating plank in the middle of the gallery and had Morris and Rainer climb on it and try to find their balance. In Forti's *Slant Board* (1961), 'the inclined plane' also 'structured the actions'.[16] Recent choreography has similarly turned its attention towards objects and things as the main activators and protagonists of dances. It is as if the organic and the inorganic have re-found a possibility for intimate partnering. In this partnering, things reveal their subjectivity, while humans reveal their thingness, to the point where it becomes hard to say who moves whom, who choreographs whom, and who is choreographed by whom. In her series of thirty-four short pieces titled *Distinguished Pieces* (1993–2003), which La Ribot presented sequentially as a long-durational performance at Tate Modern, London and at the Museo Nacional Centro de Arte Reina Sofía, Madrid, under the title *Panoramix* (2003), the Spanish choreographer explores the intimacy and indetermination between things and subjectivity, composing and recomposing her body by using objects as varied as a folding chair, a glass of water, a radio, a rubber chicken, a piece of cardboard, a bottle [...] Croatian artist Vlatka Horvat's office chairs transported to different locations (corridors, a pond, a terrace) and rearranged in different patterns for eight consecutive hours in *This Here and That There* (2007), investigate how the mere disposition of things in the world already choreographs our most minute daily behaviours.

Sculpting Dances

If dance evokes the fleeting, the moving, the ephemeral, while sculpture evokes the solid, the stable and the concrete, then why have dance and sculpture enjoyed such an intimate and prolific inter-relationship over the past five decades? The question is not only one of sculpture serving as a background (set-design) for dances; nor of dances (or dancers) serving as occasional inspiration or as extraneous corporeal frisson for sculptures. The question is: how dance and sculpture could be, at a much more fundamental level, one and the same art – 'dancesculpture', an art whose main concern would be to harness invisible forces (political, physical, affective) and make them visible through kinetic assemblages of bodies and matter. Rainer's *Trio A* (1966) (pp. 52–5), enacted the choreographer's explicit interest in Minimalist sculpture by distributing and dispelling the dancer's 'energy investment'[17] across a choreographic through-line that structures the piece as if it were an 'uninterrupted surface'. This even distribution of energy within the dancer's body and across his or her movements is the kinetic equivalent to that 'unitary form' in sculpture proposed by Morris and other Minimalists.[18] In Robert Raushenberg's *Linoleum* (1966) dancers and non-dancers created, if not an even energetic distribution, at least a formal one between bodies (human and animal) and objects (sculpted and found). For this even distribution, everyday movements and things became essential choreo-sculptural elements.

Recent examples of a sculpting mode of choreography can be found in the works of Meg Stuart. Since the 1990s, she has created dances that are less interested in orchestrating displacements of bodies than in chiseling on those bodies an intense image aimed directly at the viewer's nervous system. *Disfigure Study* (1991) (p. 149) displays almost impossible positions for a human body, elegant distortions reminiscent of Francis Bacon's figures. Raimund Hoghe's *Bolero Variations* (2007) takes choreographic language into a delicate plasticity where symmetry, colour, line, and a quiet formalism compose a dancing that is as scored as it is sculptured.

Transforming the Body

Common ground of exploitation and of liberation, central agent in an era defined by the effects and after-effects of so many bio-political horrors, the body has been invested by visual arts and dance as an agent for renewed aesthetic-political explorations. Approached not as a theme, not as a subject, but as an artist's primary and direct material, the body reveals itself to be in an ongoing and unending fugitive state. French choreographer Xavier Le Roy has been working on the premise that the body's 'borders, edges and contours are "osmotic"' and 'have the remarkable power of incorporating and expelling outside and inside in an ongoing interchange'. The activation of this premise can be seen in his solo *Self-Unfinished* (1998) as well as in his more recent group experiments such as *Low Pieces* (2010) (pp. 122–3). Brazilian artist Lygia Clark also based the later part of her work on this 'osmotic' or fluid capacity of the body to enter into powerful aesthetic-political-clinical becomings. In *Baba Antropofágica* (Anthropophagic Drool, 1973) or in her practices in the 1980s known as *Structuring of the Self*, Clark re-imagines and re-assembles body-parts and their systems of sensations by combining them with other bodies and things (pp. 60–3). Clark's work reveals how the transformative capacity of the body is never only a matter of assuming unexpected shapes: it also requires intensification of energy flows, so that aesthetics, politics and corporeality may fuse in the formation of more potent subjectivities. Similarly, some works by Vito Acconci (*Conversions I–III*, 1971), or by Paul McCarthy (*Experimental Dance, Edit #1*, 1975) (p. 137) explore the political implications of the body's metamorphic capacities. Experimenting with gender dynamics, sexuality, corporeality and desire, dance appears in these artists' works as a subtle yet essential force.

Transforming Time

When hyper-accelerated and regimented modes of experiencing temporality take over the pace of labour and leisure and over-determine the rhythm of life itself, time becomes 'essential' – as Kaprow said in act one of *18 Happenings in 6 Parts*. How do visual arts and dance exchange between each other modes for extending, compressing and distorting temporality? Nancy Spector noted how Post-minimalist art 'incorporated temporality and ephemerality in its vocabulary as a way to foreground the experiential nature of its aesthetic experience'.[19] The systematic use of repetition, suspension, accelerations and decelerations reveals a shared capacity for dance and the visual arts to explore temporal elasticities and thus create propositions to radically transform our experience of time. As Jasper Johns piece in Cunningham's *Walkaround Time* (1968) (p. 138) clearly demonstrates, time is always produced, distorted, accelerated and compressed by the sheer presence of objects (sculptures, paintings – both secrete a kind of time). This is why the assemblage of objects and bodies secrete temporal durations that confuse the status of both. The Belgian visual artist Jan Fabre used duration's capacity to fuse and confuse bodies and things in his choreographic work *Das Glas in Kopf Wird Vom Glas* (The Glass in the Head Becomes Glass, 1987): a line of ballerinas slowly moving towards the audience for fifty minutes re-aligns dance as a mode for creating time-images. Duration is perhaps most poignantly used in Merce Cunningham's last recorded performance, his dance rendition (or choreographic translation) of John Cage's silent music composition *4'33"*. Documented in a film by Tacita Dean titled *Merce Cunningham performs STILLNESS (in three movements) to John Cage's composition 4'33" with Trevor Carlson, New York City, 28 April 2007* (2008), Cunningham's quiet and deeply moving still dance on a chair secretes and unveils the endless temporality held deep within each passing instant, confirming that the micro-dance of a still body is the first condition for the creation of a distention in time.

Tracing Movement

How do visual arts and dance track the transient *par excellence* – movement? Dance does not produce durable objects, but belabours itself into visibility, sometimes leaving behind evidence of its fleeting acts. Such tracing reveals dance's economy of visibility as one that resists entrapment and arrest – as demonstrated by African-American choreographer Bill T. Jones in *Ghostcatching* (1999) (p. 140). In this collaboration with media artists Paul Kaiser, Shelley Eshkar and Marc Downie, Jones dances before a motion-capture device, which transforms movement into series of digital traces. Despite the apparatus, Jones's motions seem to always confound entrapment, creating virtual images that reveal the trace as fugitive of its own marking. Perhaps this fugitivity of the dancing trace is what attracts visual artists with a political message to movement. If Yves Klein had invested in tracing by problematically dragging women as 'living brushes' or as passive puppets to the sound of music, several women artists took aim at his masculinist gesture and created painterly-choreographic counter-acts that reclaimed the privilege of inscribing, tracing and marking the world's surface while strongly rejecting control and manipulation. Janine Antoni's

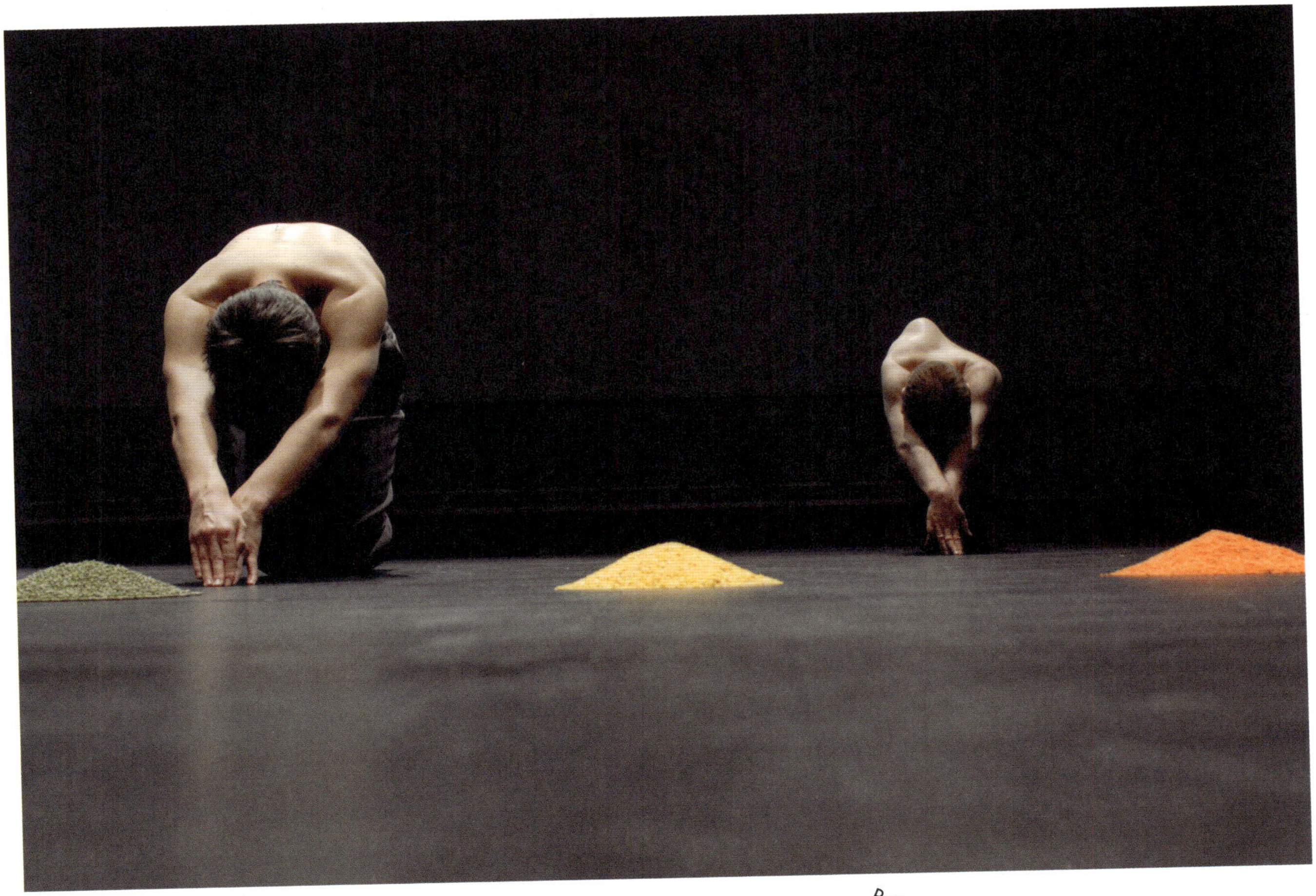

Raimund Hoghe, *Bolero Variations*, 2007

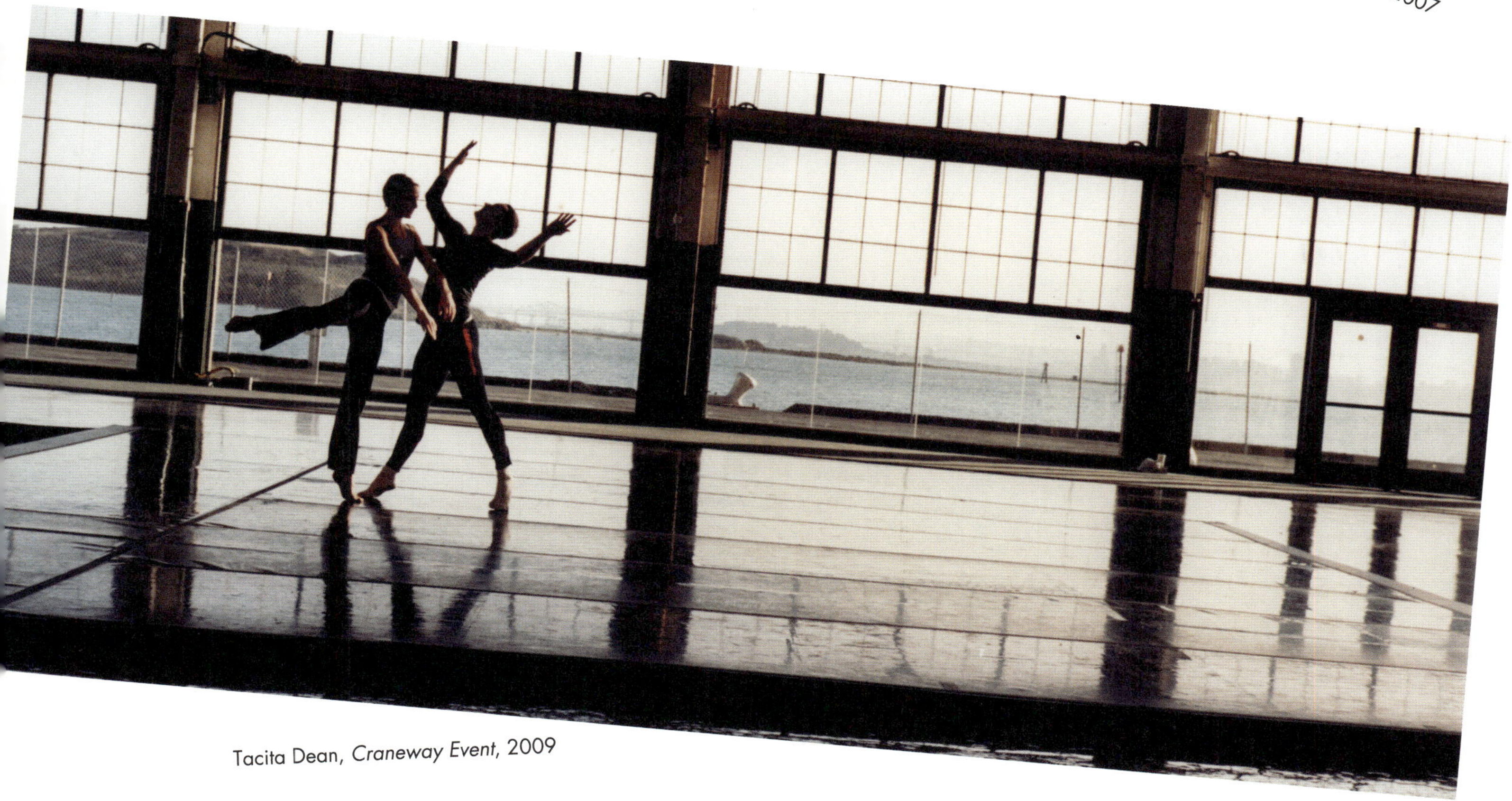

Tacita Dean, *Craneway Event*, 2009

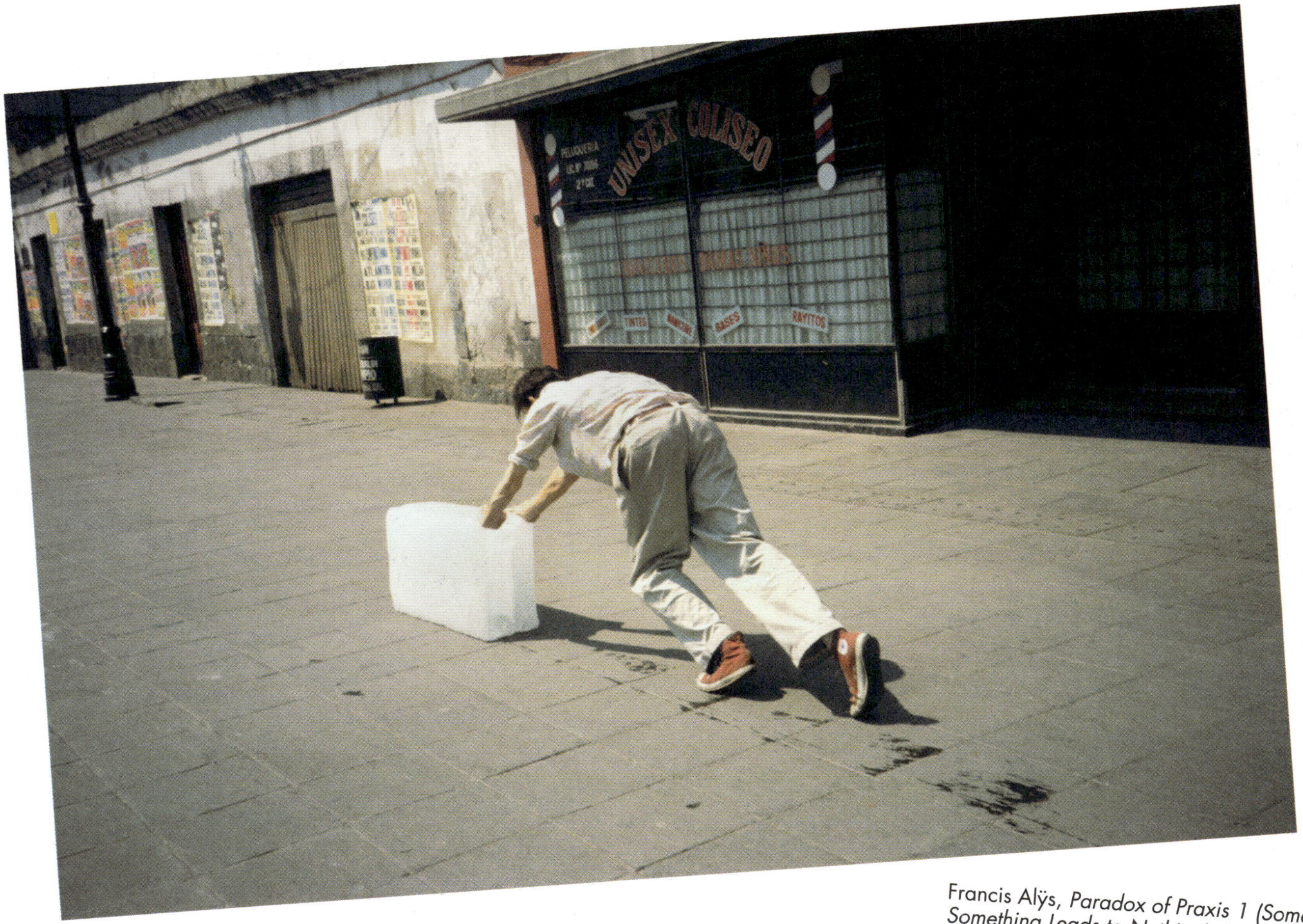

Francis Alÿs, *Paradox of Praxis 1 (Sometimes Making Something Leads to Nothing)*, 1997

Loving Care (1993) (p. 140) 'parodies the male-dominated legacy of Abstract Expressionism',[20] prolonging the gesture initiated by Japanese artist Shigeko Kubota in *Vagina Painting* (1965), where she used a scatological position and a brush attached to her crotch to paint red marks on paper on the floor. In *Loving Care* Antoni, on her hands and knees, dipped her long hair in a bucket filled with black hair dye and painted the whole floor of the Anthony d'Offay Gallery in London. Kubota and Antoni (as well as Ana Mendieta in her *Body Tracks* series (1974), or Carolee Schneeman in *Up To and Including her Limits* (1976), among others) redefined tracing as a necessary dance for a feminist politics of memory and presence. Francis Alÿs, in *Paradox of Praxis* (1997), identified a paradoxical essence in tracing. He pushed a large block of ice through the hot streets of Mexico City until it dissolved into a small puddle. This action reveals that, just like the movement of labour it tries to mark, tracing's ultimate destiny is eventually the production of its own erasure.

Making Space

'Making space' can be seen as the activity that opens up social possibilities for dance and the visual arts as they move away from their expected sites of presentation and make surprising appearances in unexpected places. Ralph Lemon, in a series of works titled *Freedom Bus Rides* (2003), created dances and actions in and for the streets, woods, rivers, half-dismantled buildings and living rooms of strangers in the South of the United States during several trips that followed the freedom rides of the Civil Rights movement of the early 1960s. Lemon's dances are exemplary of a desire to make another social and political space for movement. In a different vein, but with the same political and poetic verve, Mendieta's *Untitled (Burial Pyramid)* (1974) (p. 143), as well as many of the pieces in her *Silueta* series, carves out negative spaces with her body's impression, which then acquire a life of their own – between cenotaph and act. Mendieta referred to these works as 'a dialogue between the landscape and the female body' in order to 'reassert my ties with the earth'.[21] In this series, Mendieta re-asserts how a body is not *in* space, but it is *itself* space. Derrida once remarked that dance not only 'changes place' but 'above all changes *places*'. The collaborative piece by Brazilian choreographer Gustavo Ciríaco and Austrian Andrea Sonnberger *Here Whilst We Walk* (2006), as well as the work of the German collective Ligna, show how simple and unusual reorganisations of bodies and their situation in space activate new possibilities for rethinking the urban. Creating mute assemblages of bodies, and dispersing them in the city, these works literally show dance changing places.

Gravity/Falling

Gravity has been used in painting, dance and sculpture to foreground an aesthetics of forces. In visual arts, Jackson Pollock's drip paintings activated gravity as a force to be used compositionally, allowing painting to remove itself even further from representation. They also made a spectacle out of the physicality of the painter's work. This spectacle is fully revealed as performance in Kazuo Shiraga's sessions of painting with his feet while dangling from a rope over a stretched canvas on the ground (p. 9). Richard Serra, in his film *Hand Catching Lead* (1968) (p. 145) uses gravity as a compositional element in order to probe the physics of an ephemeral act. As several chunks of lead regularly fall across the frame of the film, Serra's hand tries to grasp them, mostly failing to do so. The piece reveals the essential tensions between a physical force (gravity) and a psychological will (an artist's intentionality). Significantly, Serra mentions how he was 'very interested in dance' at the time he made the film.[22] Bruce Nauman also explored tensions at play between the gravitational force and the force of a human will in works such as *Wall/Floor Positions* (1968), *Bouncing in the Corner No. 2 Upside Down* (1969) or *Tony Sinking into the Ground Face Up and Face Down* (1973).

In several of choreographer Trisha Brown's *Equipment Pieces*, the gravitational pull must both be revealed and mastered. In *Man Walking Down the Side of a Building* (1970) (p. 144) or in *Walking on the Wall* (1974), Brown uses harnesses and pulleys to suspend her dancers so that a new space for a body's presence may be carved within the urban and the representational space of the museum, respectively. William Pope.L, in his *Great White Way* (2000-5) (p. 144), crawled from the Statue of Liberty to the Bronx along Broadway in New York City dressed as Superman. Pope.L's project to 'give up verticality' aims at kinetically and politically investigating the grounds upon which our lives are built and demolished.

Gustavo Ciriáco, Andrea Sonnberger, *Here Whilst We Walk*, 2006

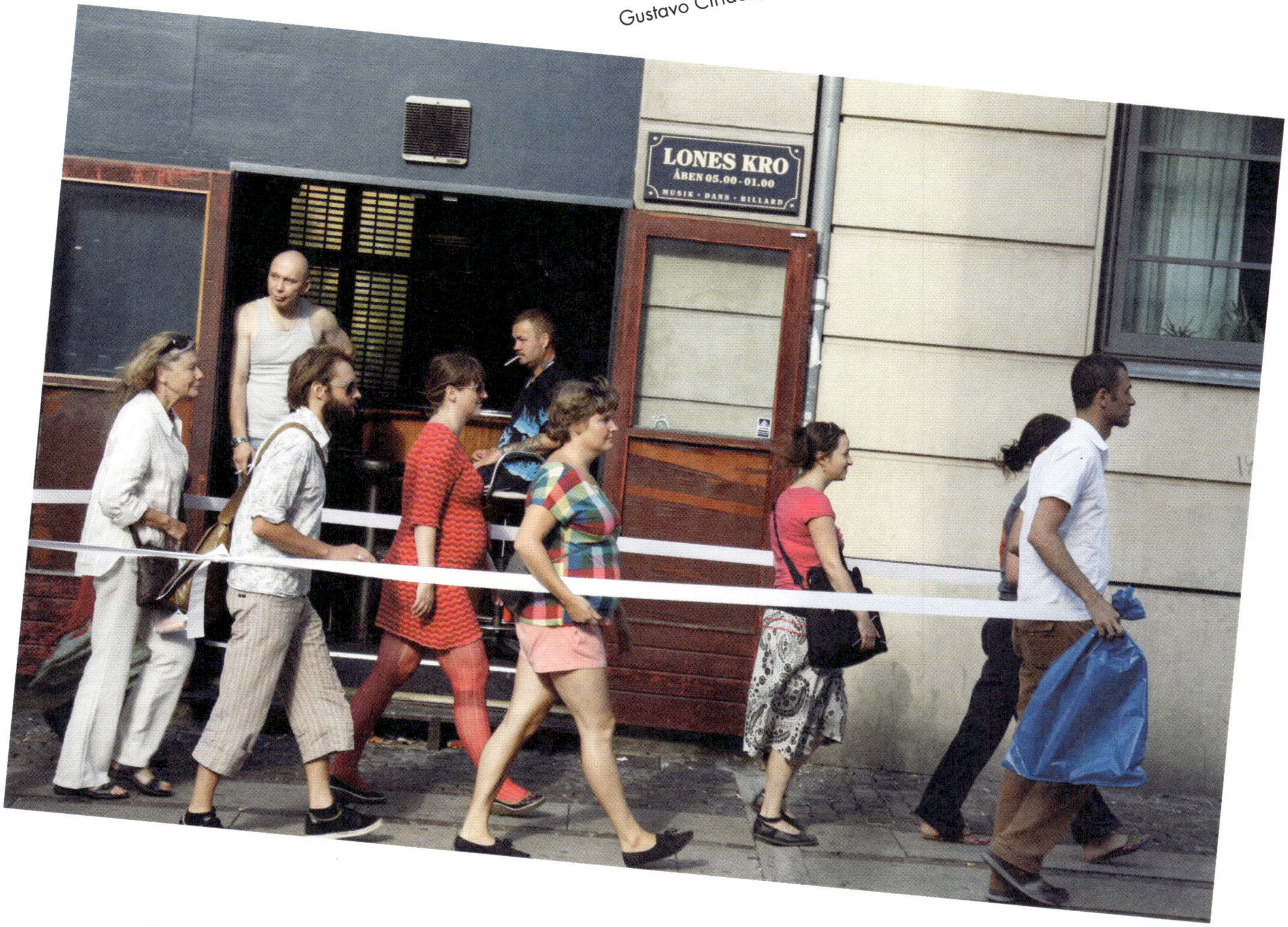

Scoring/Choreographing/Commanding

Since the late 1950s there has been a direct, literal connection between choreography (understood more literally as 'the writing of movement') and the visual arts thanks to the latter's embracing of scores. These allowed to 'dematerialise' the art object, thus becoming an essential tool for Conceptual art in the 1970s. According to Drew Daniel, 'Conceptual art drew its strategic mobility from the example of the music score.'[23] But it may be perhaps more accurate to say that Conceptual art scores drew their intrinsic performativity from the rich history of dance notations. Simone Forti, Yoko Ono, Vito Acconci, Bruce Nauman, Allan Kaprow and George Brecht all produced scores that could be called choreography.

In Adrian Piper's *Making Space* (1970), 155 sheets of paper set out 'choreographed systematic locations for the feet, which create rational stepping patterns that define an area of silent individual movement against a surrounding environment increasingly cramped by crowds of various kinds (shopping, parading, marching, protesting, partying, etc.).' Scores reveal how social behaviour is preconditioned by a series of invisible, reified and naturalised commands to which one yields unawares. The question is how to reveal those hidden choreographic commands structuring the everyday, in order to resist their imposition of behaviours, acts and motions. Cuban artist Tania Bruguera exposed the hidden social forces choreographing our everyday in *Tatlin's Whisper's* # 5 (2008) (p. 147). Two trained anti-riot horses mounted by two trained anti-riot police agents enter the Turbine Hall at Tate Modern and start enacting their tactics of crowd control. The public yields to the choreographed display of authority, and is moved, cornered, immobilised, displaced and funnelled according to the commanding dance of the horses and their riders. In *Laugh* (2006), German performer and choreographer Antonia Baehr, following a line similar to Allan Kaprow's or Steve Paxton's dissections of quotidian behaviours for their happenings and dances, creates a hybrid form of dance and music concert to scored pieces of laughter. Having commissioned several composers to write the scores, Baehr reveals in her highly virtuosic renditions of the most varied forms of laughing the fuzzy line between the utterly spontaneous and the carefully choreographed: a burst of laughter may not be an uninhibited expression of the self, but a social choreography sustaining the illusion of a natural and free subjectivity.

Dancing

Dancing performs an odd function in representation. Apparently a break from language and signification, it usually erupts to express an excess of feeling – revealing in those moments not necessarily 'the body' but the social and affective forces that transverse a body and bind it to a collective. Visual artists have used dance to identify, define and subvert those social forces and limits, creating pieces that are at times embarrassingly private, at times utterly humorous, and most of the time highly political. Nauman remarked about his famous Studio Films of 1967–68 (for instance, *Dance or Exercise Around the Perimeter of a Square*; *Revolving Upside Down*; *Walking in an Exaggerated Manner Around the Perimeter of a Square*) (p. 143): 'I thought of them as dance problems without being a dancer.' Reflecting on these 'dance problems', he commented on how the distance and boundaries between 'body movements' and 'sculptural concerns' had 'gotten a lot smaller' after he created the works.[24]

Oiticica invested in a similar collapse of distance between sculpture and dance, most clearly in his *Parangolés* of the late 1960s (p. 155). Capes made out of 'poor' materials and rich colours, engraved with words and objects, the *Parangolés* fuse objecthood and dancing since they truly *are* only when the person wearing them dances the samba, thus enriching the definition of an object. As Oiticica wrote: 'The experience of dance (of samba) therefore gave me the exact idea of what creation through the corporeal act may be, a continuous transformability. On the other hand however, it revealed what I call the "being" of things, that is, the static expression of objects.'[25]

Probing how performances of racial identity have a direct relationship to dancing informs Adrian Piper's *Funk Lessons* (1983). Leading workshops where she would teach participants how to dance the funk, Piper used dance as a medium through which the performativity of racial identity could be examined. She had already used dance as a medium at the beginning of her career, and more recently she has continued to consider dance as a major motif, as is clear in her film *Shiva Dances with the Art Institute of Chicago* (2004). Since the mid-1990s, works such as Tracey Emin's *Why I Never Became a Dancer* (1995) (p. 150), Mike Kelley's *Pole Dance* (1997) (p. 151), and Nevin Aladag's *Familie Tezcan* (2001), *Raise the Roof* (2007) (p. 151) and her *Dance Invasions* (2007–9) are some of the many examples of the uses of dancing as material in the visual arts. In Daniel Guzmán's *NY Groove* (2004), dance crosses through different types of masculinities, as four men strolling on a busy street pass to each other an infectious, irresistible rhythm. This irruption of dance amidst the quotidian indicates its potentiality for disrupting habits that choreograph us.

4. BEYOND LIMITATIONS

The Minimalist artist Sol LeWitt wrote in 1968: 'When words such as painting and sculpture are used, they connote a whole tradition and imply a consequent acceptance of this tradition, thus placing limitations on the artist who would be reluctant to make art that goes beyond the limitations.'[26] Going beyond limitations, the exchange of creative modes has fuelled the concurrent histories of dance and visual arts in the past five decades. Today, it has become extremely difficult to qualify works by the artists included in this exhibition and archive as belonging exclusively within strict categories of 'sculpture', 'dance', 'installation', 'drawing', 'performance', 'video-art' and 'body art' etc. In this desire for a limitless crossing over, co-formation and co-transformation of dance and visual arts, a dynamics can be identified where imaging as movement and dancing as imaging becomes the driving force – a visuality closer to corporeality, and a dancing closer to things.

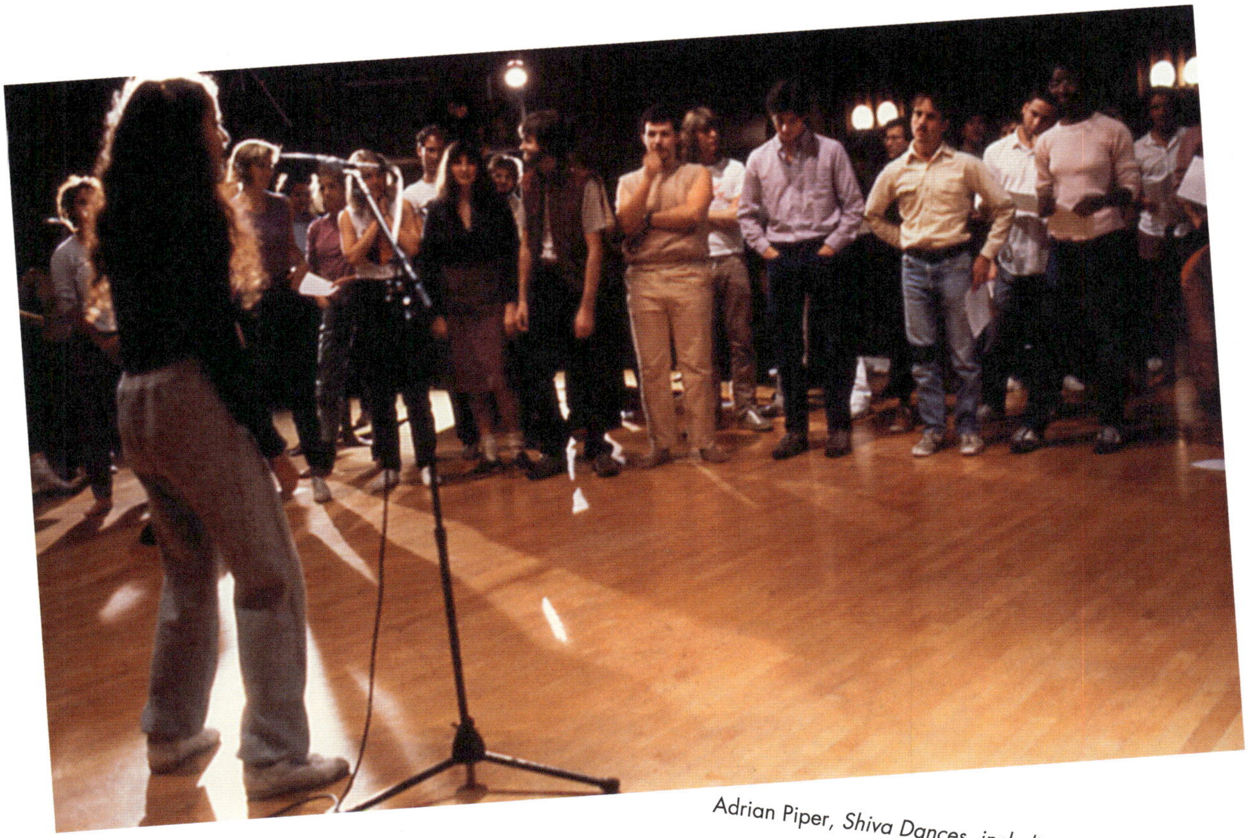

Adrian Piper, Shiva Dances, including Funk Lessons (1983), 2002

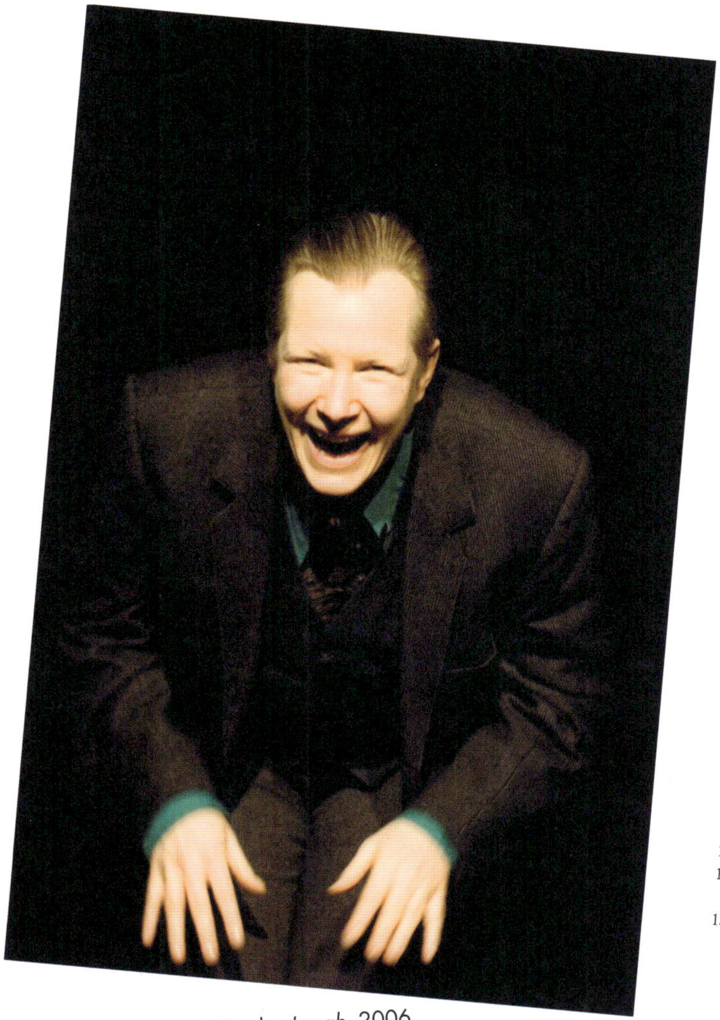

Antonia Baehr, *Laugh*, 2006

1 For a detailed definition of choreography, see Susan Leigh Foster's essay in this catalogue.
2 This piece has had many iterations, and its title has changed throughout. In 1994, for instance, it was performed at Centre Georges Pompidou with the title *Passage: traversant les écrans de papier*.
3 Daisy Peccinini (ed.), *Objeto na Arte Brasileira – Brasil Anos 60*, FAAP, São Paulo, 1978, p.98.
4 Tracey Warr (ed.), *The Artist's Body*, Phaidon, London, 2000, p. 54.
5 Susan L. Foster, *Choreography and Narrative: Ballet's staging of Story and Desire*, Indiana University Press, Bloomington, Ind., 1996, p. 24.
6 Heinrich von Kleist, 'On the Marionette Theatre', first published in four installments in the daily *Berlin Abendblätter* from December 12 to 15, 1810.
7 Robert Morris, 'Notes on Movement', in *Happenings and Other Acts*, Routledge, New York and London, 1995, p. 170.
8 Hélio Oiticica, 'Dance in My Experience. (Diary Entries). 1965/66', in *Participation*, Claire Bishop (ed.), London: Whitechapel, 2006, p. 105, (emphasis added).
9 Merce Cunningham, 'Space, Time, and Dance,' in *Merce Cunningham: Fifty Years*, Melissa Harris (ed.), Aperture, New York, 1997 [1952], p. 66.
10 Yvonne Rainer, 'A Quasi Survey of Some "Minimalist" Tendencies in the Quantitatively Minimal Dance Activity Midst the Plethora, or an Analysis of *Trio A*', in *Minimal Art. A Critical Anthology*, Gregory Battcock (ed.), E.P. Dutton, New York, 1968 [1966], p.269.
11 Yvonne Rainer, op. cit., p. 269.
12 Randy Martin, *Critical Moves*, Duke University Press, Durham, 1998, p. 6.
13 Michael Newman, 'The Material Turn in the Art of Western Europe and North America in the 1960s', in *Beyond Preconceptions: The Sixties Experiment*, ICI, New York, 2000, p. 73.
14 Rosalind Krauss, *Passages in Modern Sculpture*, MIT Press, Cambridge, MA and London, 1981, p.19, (emphasis added).
15 Yvonne Rainer, op. cit., p. 269, (emphasis added).
16 Robert Morris, 'Notes on Dance', in *Happenings and Other Acts*, Mariellen Sandford (ed.), Routledge, New York and London, 1995 [1965], p. 168.
17 Yvonne Rainer, op.cit., p. 266.
18 See particularly Robert Morris, 'Notes on Sculpture', in *Minimal Art. A Critical Anthology*, Gregory Battcock (ed.), E.P. Dutton, New York, 1968 [1966], p.2249.
19 Nancy Spector, 'Introduction', in *Singular Forms (Sometimes Repeated): Art from 1951 to the Present*, Guggenheim Museum, New York, 2004, p. 17.
20 Tracey Warr, *The Artist's Body*, Phaidon, London, 2000, p. 66.
21 Op. cit., p. 168.
22 Annette Michelson, 'The Films of Richard Serra: An Introduction', in *Richard Serra*, Hal Foster and Gordon Hughes (eds.), MIT Press, Cambridge, MA and London, 2000. p. 26.
23 Drew Daniel, 'Next to Nothing', in *Singular Forms (Sometimes Repeated): Art from 1951 to the Present*, Guggenheim Museum, New York, 2004, p. 74.
24 Janet Kraynak, *Please Pay Attention Please. Bruce Nauman's Words*, MIT Press Cambridge, MA and London, 2006, p. 142. For a discussion of Nauman's work as dance, see André Lepecki, *Exhausting Dance: Performance and the Politics of Movement*, Routledge, London and New York, 2006.
25 Hélio Oiticia, op. cit., p106.
26 Sol LeWitt, 'Sentences on Conceptual Art', in *Six Years: The Dematerialization of the Art Object*, Lucy Lippard (ed.), University of California Press, Berkeley. 1997 [1968], p. 75.

WALKAROUND TIME
EXHIBITED WORKS INCORPORATING A TIMELINE OF ART & DANCE

Works marked in bold with * are part of the exhibition *Move: Choreographing You*. See pp. 134–151 for the Archive List of Works

50

Jackson Pollock
Autumn Rhythm: Number 30, 1950
'action painting', oil on canvas
266.7 x 525.8 cm
The Metropolitan Museum of Art, New York

John Cage, Merce Cunningham and Robert Rauschenberg
Theater Piece #1, 1952
Performance at Black Mountain College, Black Mountain, North Carolina, 1952

Saburo Murakami
At One Moment Opening Six Holes, 1955
Performance at '1st Gutai Art Exhibition' held at the Ohara Kaikan Hall, Tokyo, October 1955

Atsuko Tanaka
Electric Dress, 1956
Performance sculpture at '2nd Gutai Art Exhibition' held at Ohara Kaikan Hall, Tokyo, October 1956

Tatsumi Hijikata
Kinjiki, 1959
Performance at a dance festival, Tokyo, 1959

***Allan Kaprow**
***18 Happenings in 6 Parts*, 1959/2010**
Series of Happenings at Reuben Gallery, New York, October 1959
Reinvented in 2010 by Rosemary Butcher for *Move: Choreographing You*
Courtesy Allan Kaprow Estate. This project was made possible by Hauser & Wirth, Zurich, London, New York
With support from the Trinity Laban Conservatoire of Music and Dance
A Southbank Centre Commission
Performed 26–28 November 2010, Royal Festival Hall, London
(See additional credits p. 174; illus. pp. 40–3)

60

Yves Klein
Anthropometries of the Blue Period, 1960
Public performance at the Galerie Internationale d'Art Contemporain, in Paris, March 1960

Simone Forti (with Robert Morris and Yvonne Rainer)
See-saw, 1960
Performance at the Reuben Gallery, New York, December 1960

***Simone Forti**
***Hangers*, 1961**
Performance
Ropes, wood
First performed at the loft studio of Yoko Ono, New York, 1961
Courtesy the artist
(illus. pp. 46–7)

***Simone Forti**
***Huddle*, 1961**
Performance
First performed at the loft studio of Yoko Ono, New York, 1961
(illus. p. 44)

Andy Warhol
Dance Diagram (Tango), 1961
Synthetic polymer paint on canvas
181 x 132 cm
First shown at Stable Gallery, 1962

Robert Morris
Column, 1961
Performance, Living Theatre, New York, 1962

Judith Dunn (with Deborah Hay, Lucinda Childs, Yvonne Rainer, Alex Hay and Robert Rauschenberg)
Acapulco, 1963
A Happening at Judson Memorial Church, New York, 6–7 December 1963

Yvonne Rainer and Charles Ross
Room Service, 1964
Performance, Concert of Dance #13, Judson Memorial Church Sanctuary, New York, 1964

Lygia Clark
Caminhando, 1964
Art experiment, paper and scissors, 1964

Robert Morris and Babette Mangolte with Carolee Schneemann
Site, 1964
Film of performance, b&w, 5 minutes 11 seconds

***Anna Halprin and Anne Collod**
parades & changes, replays
re-interpretation of Anna Halprin's *Parades & Changes* by Anne Collod, 1965/2010
First performed in Stockholm, 5 September 1965
Performed 27 November 2010, Queen Elizabeth Hall, London
This project was made possible with support from Cultures France
(See additional credits p. 174; illus. pp. 48–51)

***Yvonne Rainer**
***Trio A*, 1966**
Performance
First performed at the Judson Memorial Church, New York, 10 January 1966
(illus. p. 52)

Robert Rauschenberg (with John Cage, David Tudor, Yvonne Rainer, Deborah Hay, Robert Whitman, Steve Paxton, Alex Hay, Lucinda Childs and Öyvind Fahlström)
Nine Evenings, 1966
Series of performances at the 69th Regiment Armory, New York, 13–23 October 1966

Samuel Beckett
He, Joe, 1966
Performance for television, first broadcast by Süddeutscher Rundfunk, Stuttgart, 13 April 1966

***Franz Erhard Walther**
***Für Zwei / For Two (Nr. 31, 1. Werksatz / First Work Set)*, 1967**
Light tarpaulin fabric
124 x 46 cm
Courtesy Peter Freeman Inc., New York and Galerie Jocelyn Wolff, Paris
(illus. pp. 56–7)

***Franz Erhard Walther**
***Für Zwei / For Two (Nr. 31, 1. Werksatz / First Work Set)*, 1967**
[exhibition copy]
Light tarpaulin fabric
124 x 46 cm
Courtesy Franz Erhard Walther Foundation

***Franz Erhard Walther**
***Photo relating to Für Zwei / For Two (Nr. 31, 1. Werksatz / First Work Set)*, 1967**
Inkjet print of b&w photograph (exhibition copy)
18 x 24 cm
Photographer Timm Rautert

Courtesy Timm Rautert and Franz Erhard Walther Foundation

***Franz Erhard Walther**
***Work Drawing relating to Für Zwei / For Two (Nr. 31, 1. Werksatz / First Work Set)*, 1967/69**
Pencil, watercolour, casein paint, glue-tape on paper
29.6 x 21 cm (double-sided)
Courtesy Franz Erhard Walther Foundation

Merce Cunningham (with Andy Warhol and David Tudor)
Rainforest, 1968
Performance, Buffalo, New York, 9 March 1968

Merce Cunningham (with Jasper Johns after Marcel Duchamp)
Walkaround Time, 1968
Performance, Buffalo, New York, 10 March 1968

***Simone Forti**
***Sleepwalkers*, 1968/2010**
Performance
First performed at Galleria L'Attico, Rome 1968
Performed 27 November 2010 in the Queen Elizabeth Hall Foyer, London

Bruce Nauman
Slow Angle Walk (Beckett Walk), 1968
Video, b&w, 60 minutes, 1968

***Lygia Clark.**
***Camisa-de-força / Straight Jacket*, 1968**
Mesh object with weights
Dimensions variable
Courtesy 'The World of Lygia Clark' Cultural Association
(illus. p. 60)

***Lygia Clark**
***A casa é o corpo. Penetração, ovulação, germinação, expulsão / The House is the Body. Penetration, ovulation, germination, expulsion*, 1968**
800 x 400 x 335 cm
Courtesy 'The World of Lygia Clark' Cultural Association
(illus. p. 62)

Bruce Nauman
Walking in an Exaggerated Manner around the Perimeter of a Square, 1969
Film, b&w, 10 minutes, 1969

***Franz Erhard Walther**
***Körpergewichte / Body Weights (Nr. 48, 1. Werksatz / First Work Set)*, 1969**
Light tarpaulin fabric
650 x 22 cm
Courtesy Peter Freeman Inc., New York and Galerie Jocelyn Wolff, Paris
(illus. p. 59)

***Franz Erhard Walther**
***Körpergewichte / Body Weights (Nr. 48, 1. Werksatz / First Work Set)*, 1969 [exhibition copy]**
Light tarpaulin fabric
650 x 22 cm
Courtesy Franz Erhard Walther Foundation

***Franz Erhard Walther**
***Photo relating to Nr. 48 First Workset: Körpergewichte / Body Weights*, 1969**
Inkjet print of b&w photograph (exhibition copy)
18 x 24 cm
Photographer: Timm Rautert
Courtesy Timm Rautert and Franz Erhard Walther Foundation

70

Rebecca Horn
Unicorn, 1970
Performance, Hamburg, 1970

Trisha Brown
Walking on the Wall, 1970
Equipment piece, Whitney Museum of American Art, New York, 1970

***Trisha Brown**
***The Stream*, 1970**
Wood, metal pots
Courtesy the artist
(illus. pp. 66–7)

***Trisha Brown**
***Floor of the Forest*, 1970**
Equipment piece
First performed in and around 80 Wooster Street, New York, 18 April 1970
Performed 15–17 October 2010, Queen Elizabeth Hall, London
Part of Dance Umbrella 2010 Celebrating Trisha Brown
(illus. p. 64)

Merce Cunningham (with Bruce Nauman)
Tread, 1970
Performance, Brooklyn, New York, 5 January 1970

***Bruce Nauman**
***Green Light Corridor*, 1970**
Painted wallboard and fluorescent light fixtures with green lamps
Dimensions variable: approx. 300 x 1220 x 305 cm
Courtesy Solomon R. Guggenheim Museum, New York. Panza Collection, Gift, 1992 92.4171
(illus. p. 68)

***Robert Morris**
***bodyspacemotionthings (Log)*, 1971/2010**
Log
Approx. 250 x 30 cm
Courtesy the artist, Sonnabend Gallery, New York and Sprüth Magers Berlin London
(illus. pp. 70–1)

***Robert Morris**
***bodyspacemotionthings (See-saw)*, 1971/2010**
Plywood
244 x 244 cm
Courtesy the artist, Sonnabend Gallery, New York and Sprüth Magers Berlin London
(illus. p. 72)

***Lygia Clark**
***Rede de elástico / Elastic Net*, 1973**
Rubber bands
Dimensions variable
Courtesy 'The World of Lygia Clark' Cultural Association
(illus. p. 63)

***Franz Erhard Walther**
***Zweiteiliges Standstück / Standing Piece in Two Sections*, 1974**
Iron
Each: 206 x 35 x 8 cm
Courtesy Peter Freeman Inc., New York

Ana Mendieta
Body Tracks, 1974
Performance, Franklin Furnace, New York, March 1974

***Trisha Brown**
***Drift*, 1974**
Performance
First performed at Art Now, Kennedy Center, Washington D.C., 2–3 June 1974
Performed 17–19 October 2010 along the Thames between

EXHIBITED WORKS INCORPORATING A TIMELINE OF ART & DANCE (CONTINUED)

Southbank Centre and
Tate Modern, London

***Dan Graham**
***Present Continuous Past(s)*, 1974**
New media, video installation
Courtesy Centre Pompidou,
Paris, France
Musée National d'Art Moderne/
Centre de Création Industrielle
(English venue only)
(illus. p. 74)

***Dan Graham**
***Two Viewing Rooms*, 1975**
New media, video installation
Two-way mirror, fluorescent lights,
video camera and monitor
250 x 250 x 600 cm
Courtesy Collection Marc and
Josée Gensollen, Marseille
(German venues only)
(illus. pp. 76–7)

***Simone Forti**
***Striding Crawling*, 1975/2010**
Performance
First performed at Seibu Theater for
the Art Today Festival, Tokyo, 1975
Performed 27 November in the
Queen Elizabeth Hall Foyer, London

***Simone Forti**
***Angel*, 1976**
Multiplex hologram by Lloyd Cross
53.3 x 41.9 x 30.5 cm
Courtesy The Box, Los Angeles
(illus. p. 46)

Trisha Brown and Babette Mangolte
Watermotor, 1978
16mm film, b&w, 7 mins., 52 secs.

Charles Atlas and Merce
Cunningham
Locale, 1979
'Filmdance', first performed in
New York, January/February 1979

Lucinda Childs (with Sol Lewitt and
Philip Glass)
Dance, 1979
Performance at the Brooklyn
Academy of Music, Brooklyn,
New York, 29 November 1979

Trisha Brown and Robert
Rauschenberg
Glacial Decoy, 1979
Performance, Walker Arts Center,
Minneapolis, 7 May 1979

Jasper Johns
Dancers on a Plane, 1979
Oil on canvas with objects
196 x 162.5 cm
First shown at Kunstmuseum Basel,
1979

80

Eleanor Antin
Recollections of My Life with
Diaghilev, 1980
Performance at Ronald Feldman
Fine Arts, New York, 1980

Rosemary Butcher (with Heinz
Deiter Pietsch)
Spaces 4, 1981
Performance, Riverside studios,
London, 1981

Gilbert & George
Bend It, 1982
Film, 3 mins., 16 secs.

***Franz Erhard Walther**
***Über Haupt / Over Head*, 1984**
Cotton and wood
185 x 65 x 30 cm
Courtesy the artist

Charles Atlas and Michael Clark
Hail the New Puritan,
'mockumentary', 1985–6
Film, 84 mins., 47 secs., colour

Siobhan Davies
Wyoming, 1988
Performance, Riverside studios,
London, 1988

90

Felix Gonzalez-Torres
Untitled (Go-go Dancing Platform),
1991
Performance installation, Andrea
Rosen Gallery, New York, 1991

William Pope.L
Tompkins Square Crawl, 1991
Performance, Tompkins Square Park,
New York, July 1991

La Ribot
13 Piezas distinguidas, 1993
Series of performances, Actividades
Culturales Universidad de
Salamanca, Spain, August 1993

Jérôme Bel
Jérôme Bel, 1995
Performance, Bellones-Brigittines,
Brussels, 1 September 1995

Steve McQueen
Five Easy Pieces, 1995
16mm film/video transfer, 7 mins.

Boris Charmatz
Aatt enen tionon, 1996
Performance at La Halle aux Grains/
Scène Nationale de Blois for the
Festival Dansez Maintenant, 9
February 1996

***João Penalva**
***Widow Simone (Entr'acte, 20 years)*,**
1996
Handwritten and printed paper,
photographs, polystyrene sheets,
felt, pins, ballet bars, lamps, steel
tracking, steel cables, electrical
cables, linoleum dance flooring,
video monitors, digital video discs,
digital video disc players, amplifiers,
loudspeakers
Installation
Dimensions variable
Courtesy Collection of Ministry
of Culture of Portugal

Videos in the installation:
The Clog Dance*, Act II, *La Fille Mal
***Gardée*, 1960**
Film, colour, sound, 2 mins., 20 secs.

***Widow Simone (Entr'acte, 20 years)*,**
1996
Film, b&w, sound, U-Matic
transferred to DVD, 29 mins., 7 secs.

***Unclogged*, 1996,**
Film, b&w, sound, U-Matic
transferred to DVD, 2 mins., 20 secs.
(See additional credits p. 174; illus.
pp. 82–5)

Xavier Le Roy
Self Unfinished, 1998
Performance, Substanz Festival,
Cottbus, Germany, 6 November
1998

***Mike Kelley**
Adaptation: Test Room Containing
Multiple Stimuli Known to Elicit
Curiosity and Manipulatory
Responses/A Dance Incorporating
Movements Derived from
Experiments by Harry F. Harlow and
choreographed in the manner of
***Martha Graham*, 1999/2010**
Choreography by Anita Pace
Metal, plastic, fabric, glass,
aluminum and fibreglass
350 x 1800 x 730 cm
Courtesy the artist and Gagosian
Gallery, London

Films in the installation:
Test Room Containing Multiple
Stimuli Known to Elicit Curiosity and
***Manipulatory Responses*, 1999**
Film, 51 mins., 18 secs., colour, silent

***A Dance Incorporating Movements Derived from Experiments by Harry F. Harlow and choreographed in the manner of Martha Graham*, 1999**
Film, 8 mins. 32 secs., b&w, silent

Both courtesy the artist and Electronic Arts Intermix (EAI), New York
(See additional credits p. 174; illus. pp. 86–9)

00

***William Forsythe**
City of Abstracts
Choreographic object, 2000
Video installation
Video software development: Philip Bußmann; Production Management: Julian Gabriel Richter
Courtesy the Forsythe Company
(See additional credits p. 174; illus. pp. 106–7)

***Tino Sehgal**
***Instead of Allowing Some Thing to Rise up to Your Face, Dancing Bruce and Dan and Other Things*, 2000**
Performance, S.M.A.K. Gent, 2000
(Munich venue only)

Michael Clark and Sarah Lucas
Before and After: The Fall,
Performance, Sadler's Wells, London, 24 October, 2001

***Tino Sehgal**
***This is Good*, 2001**
First shown at the exhibition 'I promise it's political', at the Museum Ludwig, Cologne, 2002
(Düsseldorf venue only)

Trisha Brown
It's a Draw, 2002
Performance, Theatre du Hangar, Montpellier, France, 1 July 2002

***Tania Bruguera**
***Untitled (Kassel)*, 2002**
Dimensions variable
MMK Museum für Moderne Kunst, Frankfurt am Main
Acquired with the generous support of the 3x8 Fonds, an initiative of 12 Frankfurt companies and the City of Frankfurt/Main
(illus. pp. 90–3)

***Boris Charmatz / Musée de la Danse**
***héâtre-élévision*, 2002**
(Pseudo performance)
Conception and choreography : Boris Charmatz
Installation
52 mins.
Courtesy the artist and Musée de la danse / Centre chorégraphique national de Rennes et de Bretagne
(illus. pp. 94–7)

Rui Chafes and Vero Mantero
Eating the Heart Out, 2004
Performance, Portuguese Pavilion, 26th Biennial São Paulo, September 2004

Francis Alÿs
The Green Line, 2004
Performance, Jerusalem, 2004

***Franz West**
***Selbstbeschreibung / Self Description*, 2004**
Epoxy resin, metal, monitor, text, computer and camera
Courtesy of the artist

****EVERYBODYS***
Générique, 2005
Performed on 28 November 2010, Purcell Room, Queen Elizabeth Hall, London

Joan Jonas
The Shape, the Scent, the Feel of Things, 2005
Performance installation, Dia:Beacon, New York, 2005

Akram Khan and Antony Gormley
Zero Degrees, 2005
Performance, Sadler's Wells, London, 8 July 2005

Robin Rhode (with Jean-Baptiste André)
The Storyteller, 2006
Performance, Haus der Kunst, Munich, 2006

***Michael Kliën with Steve Valk**
***Choreography for Blackboards*, 2006/2010**
First performed in Limerick, Ireland, 2006
Music: Volkmar Kliën
Lighting: Dave Guy
Performed 26 & 27 November 2010, Hayward Gallery, London
Supported by Culture Ireland and The Arts Council/ An Chomhairle Elalaíon
(illus. pp. 98–9)

Carlos Amorales (with Galia Eibenschutz, Julien Lede, and Eri Eibenschutz)
Spider Galaxy, 2007
Performance installation, Museo Tamayo Arte Contemporaneo, Reforma y Gandhi, Bosque de Chapultepec, Mexico City, 16–17 October 2007

Russell Maliphant and Isaac Julien
Cast No Shadows, 2007
Film and performance, Sadler's Wells, London, 3–4 October 2007

***Nevin Aladağ**
***Raise the Roof*, 2007**
Original video installation and performance on a rooftop near the Spree River, Berlin, 2007
Performed 27 & 28 November 2010, Purcell Room, Queen Elizabeth Hall, London

Tacita Dean and Merce Cunningham
Merce Cunningham performs STILLNESS (in three movements) to John Cage's composition 4'33" with Trevor Carlson, New York City, 28 April 2007, 2008
Film, 6 x 16mm colour films with optical sound, approximately 5 mins. each

***Christian Jankowski**
***Rooftop Routine*, 2008**
AV installation
Dimensions variable
Courtesy the artist and Klosterfelde Gallery, Berlin
(illus. pp. 100–3)

Akram Khan and Juliette Binoche (with Anish Kapoor)
in-i, 2008
Performance, Lyttleton National Theatre, London, 18 September 2008

Santiago Sierra
The Penetrated, 2008
Performance, El Torax, Terrassa, Spain, 12 October 2008

Boris Charmatz / Musée de la Danse
expo zéro, 2009
An 'exhibition without objects',
Le Garage, Rennes,
19 & 20 September 2009

***Siobhan Davies**
***Minutes*, 2009**
Siobhan Davies Dance
Conceived and directed by Siobhan Davies for *The Collection*
Three parts created and performed by: Catherine Bennett and Matteo Fargion; Henry Montes and Deborah Saxon; Matthias Sperling
First performed at Victoria Miro Gallery, 24 March – 9 April, 2009
Performed 27 & 28 November 2010, Hayward Gallery, London
(See additional credits p. 174)

EXHIBITED WORKS INCORPORATING A TIMELINE OF ART & DANCE (CONTINUED)

Mike Kelley
Day is Done Judson Church Dance, 2009
Performance, Judson Memorial Church, 17–19 November 2009

Ioannis Mandafounis, Fabrice Mazliah, May Zarhy
Zero, 2009
Festival Automne en Normandie, 21–22 November 2009

***La Ribot**
***Llámame Mariachi*, 2009**
First performed at La Comédie de Genève during La Bâtie-Festival de Genève, Geneva, 29–31 August 2009
Performed 26 November 2010, Purcell Room, Queen Elizabeth Hall, London
(See additional credits p. 174; illus. p. 121)

***William Forsythe**
***The Fact of Matter*, 2009**
Choreographic Object
Plastic rings, textile webbing
Dimensions variable
Courtesy the Forsythe Company
The Forsythe Company with the Biennale Art, Venice and the Ursula Blickle Foundation
(See additional credits p. 174; illus. pp. 104–5)

***Janine Antoni**
***Yours truly*, 2010**
Paper from gallery guide, ink
Courtesy the artist and Luhring Augustine, New York
(illus. pp. 108–9)

Rosemary Butcher (with Daria Martin, Cathy Lane, Matthew Butcher & Melissa Appleton)
Lapped Translated Lines, 2010
Performance, Sadler's Wells, London, 1–3 October, 2010

***Pablo Bronstein**
***Magnificent Triumphal Arch in Pompeian Colours*, 2010**
Mixed media
Dimensions variable
Courtesy Herald St., London
(illus. p. 110)

***Isaac Julien**
***TEN THOUSAND WAVES*, 2010**
AV installation
Courtesy of Isaac Julien and Victoria Miro Gallery, London/Galería Helga de Alvear, Madrid/ Metro Pictures, New York
(See additional credits p. 174; illus. pp. 114–17)

***La Ribot**
***Walk the Chair*, 2010**
50 folding chairs
Dimensions variable
Courtesy the artist
***Walk the Chair* has been made possible with the collaboration of the State Corporation for Spanish Cultural Action Abroad (SEACEX)**
(illus. pp. 118–19)

***Thomas Lehmen**
***Schrottplatz*, 2010**
Performed 9 November, Purcell Room, Queen Elizabeth Hall, London
A Southbank Centre Co-production
Supported by Kunststiftung NRW
Thanks to Tanzwerkstatt Berlin, Arizona State University School of Dance
(See additional credits p. 174)

***Xavier Le Roy**
***Low Pieces*, 2010**
Performed 28 November, Queen Elizabeth Hall, London
(See additional credits p. 174)

***Xavier Le Roy and Mårten Spångberg**
***production*, 2010**
Performance
***production* is supported by Portland Green Cultural Projects**
(illus. p. 122)

***The OpenEnded Group with Wayne McGregor**
***Stairwell*, 2010**
Three-screen 3D digital projection
Movement: Wayne McGregor
(illus. pp. 124–7)

Mathilde Monnier and Dominique Figarella
Soaopéra, 2010
Performance, Centre Pompidou, 17–21 November 2010

***Franz West**
***Ion*, 2010**
Two epoxy resin casts, 2 DVS, 2 pedestals
***Adaptive 1*, 1975–76 (cast 2010)**
90 x 57 x 6 cm
Pedestal: 34 x 151 x 150 cm
***Adaptive 2*, 2006 (cast 2010)**
35 x 40 x 11 cm
Pedestal: 83 x 52 x 35 cm
Screen: 210 x 223 x 56 cm
Performer: Ivo Dimchev
Courtesy the artist and Gagosian Gallery, London
(illus. p. 78)

***Franz West**
***Diwan*, 2010**
Steel, foam, linen
100 x 230 x 85 cm
Courtesy the artist

Simone Forti: *Hangers* and *Huddle*; Yvonne Rainer: *Trio A*; Franz Erhard Walther: *Für Zwei* and *Körpergewichte*; Tania Bruguera: *Untitled (Kassel)*, 2002; Pablo Bronstein: *Magnificent Triumphal Arch in Pompeian Colours*; Xavier Le Roy and Mårten Spångberg, *production* are activated with the participation of alumni of Trinity Laban Conservatoire of Music and Dance and have been supported by The Felix Trust for Art. Trisha Brown: *Floor of the Forest* and *Drift* are activated with the participation of students of Trinity Laban Conservatoire of Music and Dance and dancers from Candoco Dance Company.

Compiled by Noémie Solomon and Chelsea Fitzgerald

DANCE BIBLIOGRAPHY

References

Benbow-Pfalzgraf, Taryn and Glynis Benbow-Niemier. *International Dictionary of Modern Dance*. Detroit, Mich.: St. James Press, 1998.

Craine, Debra and Judith Mackrell. *The Oxford Dictionary of Dance*. Oxford: Oxford University Press, 2000.

Le Moal, Philippe. *Dictionnaire De La Danse*. Librairie De La Danse. Paris: Larousse, 1999.

Rousier, Claire. *L'Histoire De La Danse: Repères Dans Le Cadre Du Diplôme d'État*. Paris: Centre national de la danse, 2000.

Historical and Cultural Analysis

Burt, Ramsay. *Alien Bodies: Representations of Modernity, 'Race' and Nation in Early Modern Dance*. London; New York: Routledge, 1998.

Male Dancer: Bodies, Spectacle, Sexualities. London, New York: Routledge, 1995.

Carter, Alexandra, ed. *Rethinking Dance History: A Reader*. London; New York: Routledge, 2004.

The Routledge Dance Studies Reader. London; New York: Routledge, 1998.

Daly, Ann. *Critical Gestures: Writings on Dance and Culture*. Middletown, Conn.: Wesleyan University Press, 2002.

Desmond, Jane. *Meaning in Motion: New Cultural Studies of Dance*. Durham, NC: Duke University Press, 1997.

Dils, Ann and Ann Cooper Albright. *Moving History Dancing Cultures: A Dance History Reader*. Middletown, Conn.: Wesleyan University Press, 2001.

Foster, Susan Leigh. *Corporealities: Dancing, Knowledge, Culture, and Power*. London; New York: Routledge, 1996.

Reading Dancing: Bodies and Subjects in Contemporary American Dance. Berkeley: University of California Press, 1986.

Foster, Susan Leigh, ed. *Choreographing History*. Unnatural Acts. Bloomington: Indiana University Press, 1995.

Franko, Mark. *The Dancing Body in Renaissance Choreography (c. 1416–1589)*. Birmingham, Ala.: Summa Publications, 1986.

Grau, Andrée. *Europe Dancing: Perspective on Theatre Dance and Cultural Identity*. London; New York: Routledge, 2000.

Kelley, Jeff, ed. *Essays on the Blurring of Art and Life*. Berkeley and Los Angeles: University of California Press, 1996.

Lansdale, Janet and June Layson. *Dance History: An Introduction*. London; New York: Routledge, 1994.

Manning, Susan. *Modern Dance, Negro Dance: Race in Motion*. Minneapolis: University of Minnesota Press, 2004.

Ecstasy and the Demon: Feminism and Nationalism in the Dances of Mary Wigman. Berkeley: University of California Press, 1993.

Michel, Marcelle and Isabelle Ginot. *La Danse Au XXe Siècle*. Librairie De La Danse. Paris: Bordas, 1995.

Morris, Gay. *Moving Words: Re-Writing Dance*. London; New York: Routledge, 1996.

Reynolds, Nancy and Malcolm McCormick. *No Fixed Points: Dance in the Twentieth Century*. New Haven: Yale University Press, 2003.

Rousier, Claire. *Être ensemble: Figures de la communauté en danse depuis le XXe siècle*. Paris: Centre national de la danse, 2003.

La Danse en solo: Une figure singulière de la modernité. Paris: Centre national de la danse, 2002.

Thomas, Helen. *Dance, Modernity, and Culture*. London; New York: Routledge, 1995.

Philosophical, Aesthetic and Literary Theories

Arbeau, Thoinot. *Orchesography; a Treatise in the Form of a Dialogue Whereby all Manner of Persons may Easily Acquire and Practise the Honourable Exercise of Dancing* [Orchesographie, 1588]. New York: Dance Horizons, 1966.

Bernard, Michel. *De La Création Chorégraphique*. Paris: Centre national de la danse, 2001.

Copeland, Roger and Marshall Cohen. *What is Dance? Readings in Theory and Criticism*. Oxford; New York: Oxford University Press, 1983.

Feuillet, Raoul-Auger and John Weaver. *Orchesography* [Chorégraphie, ou L'art de décrire la dance par caractères, figures, et signes démonstratifs, 1699]. Farnborough: Gregg, 1971.

Franko, Mark. *The Work of Dance: Labor, Movement, and Identity in the 1930s*. Middletown, Conn.: Wesleyan University Press, 2002.

Dancing Modernism/Performing Politics. Bloomington: Indiana University Press, 1995.

Goellner, Ellen W. and Jacqueline Shea Murphy. *Bodies of the Text: Dance as Theory, Literature as Dance*. New Brunswick, N.J.: Rutgers University Press, 1995.

Hantelmann von, Dorothea. *How to do things with art. Zur Bedeutsamkeit der Performativität von Kunst*. Zurich: Diaphanes, 2007.

Hewitt, Andrew. *Social Choreography: Ideology as Performance in Dance and Everyday Movement*. Post-Contemporary Interventions. Durham: Duke University Press, 2005.

Lepecki, André, ed. *Of the Presence of the Body: Essays on Dance and Performance Theory*. Middletown, Conn.: Wesleyan University Press, 2004.

Louppe, Laurence. *Poétique De La Danse Contemporaine*. Bruxelles: Contredanse, 2004.

Traces of Dance: Drawings and Notations of Choreographers. Paris: Editions Dis Voir, 1994.

Noe, Alva. *Action in Perception*. Cambridge, Mass: MIT Press, 2004.

Noland, Carrie and Sally Ann Ness, eds. *Migrations of Gesture*. Minneapolis: University of Minnesota Press, 2008.

Noverre, Jean Georges. *Letters on Dancing and Ballets* [Lettres sur la danse et sur les ballets, 1760]. New York: Dance Horizons, 1966.

Rameau, Pierre. *The Dancing Master*. [Le Maître à danser, 1725]. New York: Dance Horizons, 1970.

Modern Dance

Albright, Ann Cooper. *Traces of Light: Absence and Presence in the Work of Loie Fuller*. Middletown, Conn.: Wesleyan University Press, 2007.

Anderson, Jack. *Art without Boundaries: The World of Modern Dance*. Iowa City: University of Iowa Press, 1997.

Brandeburg, Hans. *Der Moderne Tanz*. München: Georg Müller, 1917.

Brown, Jean Morrison, Naomi Mindlin, and Charles Humphrey Woodford. *The Vision of Modern Dance: In the Words of its Creators*. 2nd ed. Hightstown, N.J.: Princeton Book Co., 1998.

Duncan, Isadora and Sheldon Cheney. *The Art of the Dance*. New York: Theatre Arts Books, 1970.

Fuller, Loie. *Fifteen Years of a Dancer's Life: With some Account of Her Distinguished Friends* [Quinze ans de ma vie.]. New York: Dance Horizons, 1978.

Garelick, Rhonda K. *Electric Salome: Loie Fuller's Performance of Modernism*. Princeton: Princeton University Press, 2009.

Hawkins, Erick. *The Body is a Clear Place and Other Statements on Dance*. Hightstown, N.J.: Princeton Book Co, 1992.

Hewitt, Andrew. *Social Choreography. Ideology as Performance in Dance and Everyday Movement*. Durham, NC and London: Duke University Press, 2005.

Humphrey, Doris. *The Art of Making Dances*. Hightstown, N.J.: Princeton Book Co, 1991.

Kendall, Elizabeth. *Where She Danced: The Birth of American Art-Dance*. Berkeley: University of California Press, 1984.

Laban, Rudolf von and Lisa Ullmann. *The Mastery of Movement*. Plymouth: Macdonald and Evans, 1980.

Martin, John Joseph. *The Modern Dance*. Brooklyn: Dance Horizons, 1965.

Robinson, Jacqueline. *Modern Dance in France: An Adventure, 1920–1970*. Choreography and Dance Studies. [Aventure de la danse moderne en France.]. Vol. 12. Amsterdam: Harwood Academic Publishers, 1997.

Shawn, Ted. *Every Little Movement*. Brooklyn: Dance Horizons, 1968.

Stebbins, Genevieve. *Delsarte System of Expression*. New York: Dance Horizons, 1977.

Wigman, Mary. *The Mary Wigman Book: Her Writings*. Middletown, Conn.: Wesleyan University Press, 1975.

Cunningham

Cunningham, Merce and Jacqueline Lesschaeve. *The Dancer and the Dance*. New York: M. Boyars: Scribner Book, 1985.

Cunningham, Merce and Frances Starr. *Changes: Notes on Choreography*. New York: Something Else Press, 1969.

Huschka, Sabine. *Merce Cunningham und der Moderne Tanz. Körperkonzepte,*

Choreographie und Tanzästhetik. Würzburg: Königshausen & Neumann, 2000.

Kostelanetz, Richard and Jack Anderson. *Merce Cunningham: Dancing in Space and Time*. Chicago: Chicago Review Press: Distributed by Independent Publishers Group, 1992.

Vaughan, David and Melissa Harris. *Merce Cunningham: Fifty Years*. New York: Aperture, 1997.

Judsonian Minimalism

Aeschlimann, Roland, Hendel Teicher, Maurice Berger, and Addison Gallery of American Art. *Trisha Brown–Dance and Art in Dialogue, 1961–2001*. Andover, Mass.; Cambridge, Mass.: Addison Gallery of American Art, Phillips Academy; Distributed by MIT Press, 2002.

Antin, David; Berger,Maurice; Criqui, Jean-Pierre; Krauss, Rosalind; Michelson, Annette and Mitchell, W.J.T. Robert Morris. *The Mind/Body Problem*. New York: Solomon R. Guggenheim Museum, New York, 1994.

Banes, Sally. *Democracy's Body: Judson Dance Theater, 1962–1964*. Ann Arbor, Mich.: UMI Research Press, 1983.

Terpsichore in Sneakers: Post-Modern Dance. Boston: Houghton Mifflin, 1980.

Brown, Trisha, et al. *Trisha Brown: So That the Audience Does Not Know Whether I Have Stopped Dancing*. Minneapolis: Walker Art Center, 2008.

Burt, Ramsay. *The Judson Church Theater: Performative Traces*. London, New York: Routledge, 2005.

Carrol, Noel. 'Yvonne Rainer and the recuperation of the everyday life'. In *Yvonne Rainer: Radical Juxtaposition 1961–2002*. Philadelphia, Penn.: Rosenwald-Wolf Gallery, The University of the Arts, Philadelphia, 2002.

Forti, Simone. *Handbook in Motion*. The Nova Scotia Series–Source Materials of the Contemporary Arts. Halifax N.S.; New York: Press of the Nova Scotia College of Art and Design; New York University Press, 1974.

Halprin, Anna and Rachel Kaplan. *Moving Toward Life: Five Decades of Transformational Dance*. Hanover: Wesleyan University Press, 1995.

Lambert, Carrie. *Being Watched: Yvonne Rainer and the 1960s*. Cambridge: The MIT Press, 2008.

Novack, Cynthia Jean. *Sharing the Dance: Contact Improvisation and American Culture*. Madison, Wis.: University of Wisconsin Press, 1990.

Morris, Robert. 'Notes on dance' [1965]. In *Happenings and Other Acts*. New York: Routledge, 1995.

Rainer, Yvonne. *Works 1961–73*. New York: New York University Press, 1974.

'No to Spectacle ...' In *Tulane Drama Review* 10, 1965.

'A Quasi Survey of Some 'Minimalist' Tendencies in the Quantitatively Minimal Dance Activity Midst the Plethora, or an Analysis of *Trio A*'. In *Minimal Art: A Critical Anthology*, edited by Gregory Battecock. Berkeley: University of California Press, 1995, pp. 263–273.

Rainer, Yvonne, et al. *Radical Juxtapositions 1961–2002*. Philadelphia: The University of the Arts, 2003.

Ross, Janice. *Anna Halprin: Experience as Dance*. Berkeley: University of California Press, 2007.

Wood, Catherine, ed. *Yvonne Rainer: The Mind is a Muscle*. One Work. London: Afterall, 2007.

Contemporary Conceptualism

Charmtaz, Boris and Isabelle Launay. *Entretenir: À propos d'une danse contemporaine*. Paris: Les Presses du réel, 2003.

Frétard, Dominique. *Danse Contemporaine: Danse Et Non-Danse, Vingt-Cinq Ans d'Histoires*. Le Cercle Chorégraphique Contemporain. Paris: Cercle d'art, 2004.

Hochmuth, Martina, Krassimira Kruschkova et al. *It Takes Place When it Doesn't: On Dance and Performance since 1989*. Frankfurt: Revolver Book, 2006.

Hoffmann, Christine, ed. *Bruce Nauman, Interviews 1967–1988*. Amsterdam: Verlag der Kunst, 1996.

Lemon, Ralph. *Tree: Belief, Culture, Balance*. Middletown, Conn.: Wesleyan University Press, 2004.

Lemon, Ralph and Tracie Morris. *Geography: Art, Race, Exile*. Middletown, Conn.: Wesleyan University Press, 2000.

Jordan, Stephanie. *Striding Out: Aspects of Contemporary and New Dance in Britain*. London: Dance, 1992.

Lepecki, André. *Exhausting Dance: Performance and the Politics of Movement*. New York; London: Routledge, 2006.

Le Roy, Xavier. 'Self-Interview', in *True Truth About the Nearly Real*, Frankfurt: Mouson, 2002, pp. 44–56.

Performance Research, 'Bodiescapes', volume 8, no. 2 (June 2003); 'Moving Bodies', volume 8, no. 4, (December 2003); 'On Choreography', volume 13, no. 2 (June 2008).

Ploebst, Helmut. *No Wind no Word: Neue Choreographie in Der Gesellschaft Des Spektakels = New Choreography in the Society of the Spectacle: 9 Portraits*. München: K. Kieser, 2001.

Rousier, Claire, ed. *La Ribot*. Paris: Centre national de la danse, 2004.

Siegmund, Gerald. *Abwesenheit: Eine performative Ästhetik des Tanzes – William Forsythe, Jérôme Bel, Xavier Le Roy, Meg Stuart*. Bielefeld: Transcript, 2006.

(Post) Expressionism in Germany and Japan

Climenhaga, Royd. *Pina Bausch*. New York; London: Routledge, 2008.

Hogue, Raimund. *Pina Bausch: Tanztheatergeschichten*. Frankfurt: Suhrkamp, 1986.

Horton, Sondra. *Hijikata Tatsumi and Ohno Kazuo*. Routledge, 2006.

Merewether, Charles, ed. *Art Anti-Art Non-Art: Experimentations in the Public Sphere in Postwar Japan 1950–1970*. LA: The Getty Research Institute, 2007. (On Gutai)

Servos, Norbert, Gert Weigelt, and Hedwig Müller. *Pina Bausch–Wuppertal Dance Theater, Or, the Art of Training a Goldfish: Excursions into Dance*. Köln: Ballett-Bühnen-Verlag, 1984.

TDR: The Drama Review: 30.2 (summer 1986) and 44.1 (Spring 2000). Both issues on Butoh.

Viala, Jean and Nourit Masson-Sekine. *Butoh: Shades of Darkness*. Tokyo: Shufunotomo, 1988.

Art and Dance Exhibitions

Francis, Richard, Susan Sontag, David Vaughan et al. *Dancers on a Plane: Cage, Cunningham, Johns*. London: Anthony d'Offay Gallery, 1989.

Art & dance. Boston: Institute of Contemporary Art, 1982.

Dance with Camera. Philadelphia: Institute of Contemporary Art, 2009.

The Dance in Art. introduction by Stephen Longstreet. Alhambra, Ca.: Borden Pub. Co., 1968.

La danse, texte de Roland Schaer. Paris: Editions de la Réunion des musées nationaux, 1986.

Benbow-Pfalzgraf, Taryn and Glynis Benbow-Niemier. *International Dictionary of Modern Dance*. Detroit, Mich.: St. James Press, 1998.

Craine, Debra and Judith Mackrell. *The Oxford Dictionary of Dance*. Oxford: Oxford University Press, 2000.

Le Moal, Philippe. *Dictionnaire De La Danse*. Librairie De La Danse. Paris: Larousse, 1999.

Luckow, Dirk and Traub, Susanne, eds., *Open the Curtain. Kunst und Tanz im Wechselspiel/ Interplay between Art and Dance*. Kunsthalle zu Keil der Christian-Albrechts-Universität, LB Kiel, 2003. Rousier, Claire. *L'Histoire De La Danse: Repères Dans Le Cadre Du Diplôme d'État*. Paris: Centre national de la danse, 2000.

Tanz in der Moderne. Munich: Haus der Kunst, 1996.

Tanz, Sehen. Siegen: Museum für Gegenwartskunst, 2007.

Weisbeck, Markus, ed. Suspense. Kraichtal: Ursula Blickle Stiftung; Zürich: JRP/ Ringier Kunstverlag AG, 2008.

Compiled by Noémie Solomon

COPYRIGHT CREDITS

The publisher has made every effort to contact all copyright holders. If proper acknowledgement has not been made, we ask copyright holders to contact the publisher. All works of art are © the artist unless otherwise stated.

Bas Jan Ader © Bas Jan Ader Estate 2010
George Brecht © DACS 2010
Boris Charmatz © Boris Charmatz/ Musée de la danse 2010
Tracey Emin © Tracey Emin. All rights reserved, DACS 2010.
Valie Export © DACS 2010
William Forsythe © The Forsythe Company 2010
Simone Forti (Hangers, Sleep Walkers) © the artist and The Box, Los Angeles 2010
Bill Jones © 1999 Bill T. Jones, Paul Kaiser, Shelley Eshkar
Allan Kaprow (scores) © J. Paul Getty Trust
Babette Mangolte (Roof Piece) photo © 1973 Babette Mangolte (All rights of reproduction reserved)
Babette Mangolte (Watermotor) photo © 1978 Babette Mangolte (All rights of reproduction reserved)
Ana Mendieta © Estate of Ana Mendieta Collection
Peter Moore photo © Estate of Peter Moore/ VAGA, NYC
Robert Morris © ARS, NY and DACS, London 2010
Hans Namuth photo © 1991 Hans Namuth Estate
Bruce Nauman © ARS, NY and DACS, London 2010
Adrian Piper © APRA Foundation, Berlin
Vaughan Rachel photo © ARS, NY and DACS, London 2010
Robert Rauschenberg © Estate of Robert Rauschenberg. DACS, London/ VAGA, New York 2010
Carolee Schneeman © ARS, NY and DACS, London 2010
Richard Serra © ARS, NY and DACS, London 2010
Fujiko Shiraga © Fujiko Shiraga and the former members of the Gutai Art Association
Meg Stuart © Meg Stuart/ Damaged Goods 1991 (restaged 2002)
Andy Warhol © The Andy Warhol Foundation for the Visual Arts / Artists Rights Society (ARS), New York / DACS, London 2010

PHOTOGRAPHIC CREDITS

The provider of the image is listed first, followed by the name of the photographer in brackets.

Courtesy Center for Creative Photography, University of Arizona (Hans Namuth) p. 9(t)
Courtesy Ashiya City Museum of Art & History pp. 9(b), 132, 134l
Courtesy The Getty Research Institute, Los Angeles (980063) pp. 10, 41, 42b, p. 147r, (Vaughan Rachel) p. 40, (2006. M.24, photo by Peter Moore) p. 11
© Tate, London 2010 pp. 12, 70–1
Distributed by Electronic Arts Intermix. Courtesy Sperone Westwater, New York p. 13
Courtesy Marian Goodman Gallery, New York p. 14
Courtesy Kelley studio (André Morin) p. 16t, (Fredrik Nilsen) p. 86–7
Courtesy Herald St, London and Franco Noero, Turin pp. 19, 113
Courtesy Merce Cunningham Dance Company p. 37, (Richard Rutledge) p. 23t, (James Klosty) p. 27
Courtesy Moderna Museet / Stockholm p. 23b
Courtesy the artists (Jaap de Graaf) pp. 24–5
Courtesy Alexander Gray Associates, New York, NY p. 25
Courtesy the photographer (Peter Moore) p. 28t
Courtesy the Estate of Samuel Beckett and Photo BBC Images & Archives p. 28b
Courtesy The Library of Congress p. 33
Reproduction by permission of the Laban Library and Archive p. 34
Courtesy the artists and Herald St., London p. 43t
© Hugo Glendinning pp. 44–5, 46t, 46b, 52–3, 55, 58b, 59, 60, 66, 78, 90–1, 93, 102–3, 104, 105, 108, 108, 110, 118t, 118b, 119, 122
Courtesy the artist and The Box, Los Angeles p. 134r, (Ann-Marie Rounkle) p. 46t
Courtesy of The Box Gallery p.47
Courtesy the photographer (Jérôme Delatour) pp. 48–9, 50, 51
Courtesy the artist p. 54
Courtesy Peter Freeman Inc (Timm Rautert) pp. 56–7
Courtesy CAC Brétigny (Steve Beckouet) p. 58t
Courtesy of 'The World of Lygia Clark' Cultural Association pp. 62, 63
Courtesy Trisha Brown Company, Inc. p. 67, p. 145b, (Isabel Winarsch/ documenta 12) pp.64–5
Courtesy the photographer and Trisha Brown Company, Inc. (© Adam L. Weintraub, www.adamw.com) p. 64b
© Solomon R. Guggenheim Museum, New York. Panza Collection, Gift, 1992. 92.4171 (Erika Ede) p. 68
© Stephen White pp. 72–3, 74–5, 92, 94–5, 116, 124
Courtesy the Gensollen collection pp. 76t, 76b, 77
Courtesy Archiv Franz West p. 80b, (Friedl Kubelka, Wien) p. 80t, Octavian Trauttmansdorff) p. 81t
Courtesy the artist (Mario Valente) pp. 82, 84bl
Courtesy the artist p. 83
Courtesy the artist (Simon Starling) pp. 84t, 84br
Courtesy the artist (Freddy Dalgetty) p. 85
Courtesy of the photographer (Alastair Muir) pp. 88t, 88b
Courtesy Anna van Kooij – Springdance (© Anna van Kooij) pp. 96–7
Courtesy the artist (Hans-Jürgen Hermann) pp. 98t, 98b
Courtesy Evening Standard (Alex Lentati) p. 102
Courtesy the artist and Lisson Gallery pp. 100–1
Courtesy The Forsythe Company (Julien Gabriel Richter) pp. 106, 107
Courtesy the artist and Victoria Miro Gallery, London pp. 114–5, 117
Courtesy the artist (Gilles Jobin) pp. 120–1
Courtesy the artist (Vincent Cavoroc) p. 125
Courtesy The OpenEnded Group p. 140t, (Marc Downie, Shelley Eshkar, Paul Kaiser) p. 126
Courtesy the artists p. 127
Courtesy the artist (Peter Schmidt) p. 135l
Courtesy of the Peter Moore Estate p. 135r
Courtesy of the artist and 'The World of Lygia Clark' Cultural Association, Rio de Janeiro p. 136l
Courtesy Electronic Arts Intermix (EAI), New York pp. 136r, 137r, p. 143bl, p. 146r, p. 151r
Courtesy the artist and Hauser & Wirth p. 137l
Courtesy BROADWAY 1602, New York (Babette Mangolte) p. 138tl, 138bl, 142
Courtesy Cunningham Dance Foundation (James Klosty) p. 138r
Courtesy the artist (© L. Bernaerts/ I. Müller/ driest ontwerpen) p. 139l
Courtesy Siobhan Davies Dance (Pari Naderi) p. 139r
Courtesy Margarete Roeder gallery p. 140bl
Courtesy the artist and Luhring Augustine, New York (Prudence Cumming Associates) p. 140br
Courtesy the artist and Hauser & Wirth (videography: Mike Cram) p. 141l
Courtesy the Yves Klein Archives p. 141r
Courtesy Galerie Lelong and Alison Jacques Gallery p. 143t
Courtesy the artist (Chris Ha) p. 143br
Courtesy the artist (Pruznik/ Grey) p. 144
Courtesy the Bas Jan Ader Estate and Patrick Painter Editions p. 145tl
Courtesy Gagosian Gallery p. 145tr
Courtesy Arts Council Collection, Southbank Centre, London (Stephen White) p. 146l
Courtesy the artist and Tate Modern (Sheila Burnett) p. 147l
Courtesy of the Estate of Robert Rauschenberg (Wagner International Photography) p. 148l
Courtesy Simon Lee Gallery, London and Patrick Painter Inc., Los Angeles p. 148tr
Courtesy the photographer (Paulo Pimenta) p. 148br
Courtesy Meg Stuart/ Damaged Goods (Chris Van der Burght) p. 149
Courtesy White Cube p. 150l
Courtesy the artist p. 150r
Courtesy the artist p. 151l
Courtesy the artist (Katrin Schoof) pp. 152, 153
Courtesy the artist (Herman Sorgeloos) p. 154
Courtesy Projeto Hélio Oiticica (Andreas Valentin) p. 155l, 155r
Courtesy the artist (Hugo Glendinning) p. 156
Courtesy the artist (©Rosa-Frank.com) p. 159t
Courtesy the artist, Frith Street Gallery, London, and Marian Goodman Gallery, New York (Michael Vahrenwald) p. 159b
Courtesy David Zwirner, New York p. 160
Courtesy the artists (Torben Huss) p. 161
Image courtesy APRA Foundation, Berlin p. 163t
Courtesy of the artist (© Marc Domage) p. 163b

ADDITIONAL CREDITS FOR ARCHIVE FILMS AND ILLUSTRATIONS

Illustrations

pp. 134–5: Simon Forti, *Slant Board*, Performance at Stedelijk Museum, Amsterdam, photographer unknown, 1982. Gutai group, *Gutai members in front of the work by Atsuko Tanaka at the Outdoor Gutai Art Exhibition, Ashiya Park*, 1956.Susanne Linke, *Im Bade Wannen*, photo of performance by Peter Schmidt, 1980. Yvonne Rainer, *Continuous Project – Altered Daily*, photo of performance © Peter Moore, 1970.

pp. 136–7: Eleanor Antin, *Caught In The Act*, film still, 1973. Lygia Clark, *Memoria do Corpo*, film still, 1984. Paul McCarthy, *Experimental Dancer (short), Edit 1*, 1975. Carolee Schneeman, *Meat Joy*, film still, 1964.

pp. 138–9: Trisha Brown, Babette Mangolte, *Watermotor*, film still, 1978. Merce Cunningham, Charles Atlas, after Marcel Duchamp's Large Glass in the Philadelphia Museum of Art, supervised by Jasper Johns, *Walkaround Time*, photo of performance by James Klosty, 1968. Siobhan Davies Dance, *Minutes*, photo of performance at Victoria Miro Gallery, London, by Pari Naderi, 2009. Ivana Müller, While We Were Holding It Together, photo of performance by L.Bernaerts, I.Müller and driest ontwerpen, 2006.

pp. 140–1: Janine Antoni, *Loving Care*, photo of performance with Loving Care hair dye 'Natural Black' at Anthony d'Offay Gallery, London, by Prudence Cumming Associates, 1993. Bill Jones, *Ghostcatching*, film still, 1999. Yves Klein, *Fire Paintings and Anthropometries*, performance at Gaz de France, Saint-Denis, Paris, 1961. *Tom Marioni drawing* Out of Body, Free Hand Circle *in the Guggenheim Museum*, photographer unknown, 2009. Paul McCarthy, *Face Painting – Floor, White line*, film still, 1972.

pp. 142–3: Trisha Brown, Babette Mangolte, *Roof Piece*, photo of performance by Babette Mangolte, 1973. Rosemary Butcher, *5-Sided Figure*, photo of dance performance at Riverside Studios, London, by Chris Ha, 1979. Ana Mendieta, *Burial Pyramid, Yagul, Mexico*, film still, 1974. Bruce Nauman, *Walking in an Exaggerated Manner Around the Perimeter of a Square*, film still, 1967–8.

pp. 144–5: Bas Jan Ader, *Fall 1, Los Angeles*, film still, 1970. Trisha Brown, *Man Walking Down the Side of a Building*, film still, 1974. William, Pope.L, *Great White Way*, photo of performance by Pruznik/ Grey, 2005. Richard Serra, *Hand Catching Lead*, film stills, 1968.

pp. 146–7: Tania Bruguera, *Tatlin's Whispers #5*, decontextualisation of an action, photo of performance view at UBS Openings: Live The Living Currency, Tate Modern, by Sheila Burnett, 2008. Valie Export, *Body Tape*, film still, 1970. Allan Kaprow, *Routine: score*, 1973.

pp. 148–9: Pina Bausch, *Café Müller*, photo of performance by Paulo Pimenta, 1978. Robert Rauschenberg, *Linoleum*, photo of performance by Wagner International Photography, 1966. Jim Shaw, *The Whole: A Study in Oist Integrated Movement*, installation view at Simon Lee Gallery, London, photographer unknown, 2009. Meg Stuart / Damaged Goods, Disfigure Study, photo of performance by Chris Van der Burght, 1991 (restaged with new cast and score, 2002).

pp. 150–1: Helio Oiticica and Ivan Cardoso, *H.O.*, film still, 1979. Nevin Aladağ, *Raise the Roof*, film still, 2007. Tracey Emin, Why I Never Became a Dancer, film still, 1995. Mike Kelley, Pole Dance, film still, 1997

Films

pp. 134–5: Anna Halprin , *Parades and Changes*, 1965. Choreography by Anna Halprin. Music by Folke Rabe and Morton Subotnick. Sculpture by Charles Ross. Performed by members of the Dancer's Workshop Company of San Francisco.

Yvonne Rainer , *Continuous Project - Altered Daily*, 1969–1970. Filmed by Michael Fajans. Choreography by Yvonne Rainer. Performed by the members of the Grand Union.

pp. 136–7: Michael Clark, *Heterospective*, 1989. Recorded at the Anthony d'Offay Gallery in London 1989. Fragment selected: 'Heroin'. Choreography: Michael Clark. Music: The Velvet Underground.

Michael Clark, *Ludd Gang*, 1988. Fragment from 'Hail the New Puritan'. Choreography: Michael Clark. Music: The Fall.Costumes: Leigh Bowery. Set design: Trojan. Dancers: Michael Clark, Julie Hood, Matthew Hawkins and Ellen van Schuylenburch.

Michael Clark, *Venus in Furs*, 1988. Fragment from 'Because We Must' Choreography: Michael Clark. Music: The Velvet Underground. Costumes: Leigh Bowery. Dancers: Leigh Bowery, Leslie Bryant, Joachim Chandler, Michael Clark, Dawn Hartley, Matthew Hawkins, David Holah, Amanda King, Rachel Lynch-John, Russell Maliphant, Gisela Mariani, Leesa Philips.

pp. 138–9: Siobhan Davies, *Different Trains*, 1990/1993. Venue: Opera de Lille, France.Choreographer: Siobhan Davies. Music: Steve Reich. Design: David Buckland. Garments: David Buckland. Lighting: Peter Mumford. Dance Artists: Gill Clarke, Paul Douglas, Sean Feldman, Jeremy James, Elizabeth Old, Deborah Saxon. Musicians: Sophie Harris (cello), Steven Smith (violin) , Clive Hughes (violin), Nic Pendlebury (viola).

Siobhan Davies, *Minutes*, 2009 Conceived and directed by Siobhan Davies for The Collection. Three parts created and performed by: Catherine Bennett and Matteo Fargion, Henry Montes and Deborah Saxon, Matthias Sperling.

pp. 142–3: Boris Charmatz / Musée de la Danse, *Horace-Benedict*, 2001. Direction: Dimitri Chamblas and Aldo Lee. Filmed at the Col du Semnoz (FR) during Ouvrée, artistes en alpage, a project by Boris Charmatz/association edna (2000). Siobhan Davies, *This Side to Body*, 2002. Venue: Millennium Bridge, London. Choreographer: Siobhan Davies. Film Director: David Buckland. Dance Artists: Gill Clarke.

Meg Stuart, *Revisited*, 2007. 27–28 April 2007, Time Festival, Ghent. Anna Viebrock's set design for visitors. Installed in the open air in a square in Ghent to host two afternoons of improvisation by Meg Stuart and Damaged Goods. Filmed and edited by Britt Mesdagh. Production: Damaged Goods, Time Festival (Ghent), Kunstencentrum Vooruit (Ghent).

pp. 146–7: Steve Paxton, *Satisfyin' Lover*, 2001. Choreography by Steve Paxton. Presented by Brooklyn Academy of. Music in association with Baryshnkiov. Productions; White Oak Dance Project. Artistic Direction by Mikhail Baryshnikov. Videotaped in performance at the BAM Howard Gilman Opera House, Brooklyn, NY one June 7, 2001

pp. 148–9: Jae Eun Choi, *Anger, Pleasure, Sorrow, Comfort*, 2007. Performer: Ushio Amagatsu. Camera work: Eugenio Polgovsky. Editing : Jae eun Choi, Hiroyuki Tanimoto. Composing: Cristian Manzutto.

Michael Clark, *BBC Old Grey Whistle Test*, 1984. Danced to The Fall track 'Lay of the Land'. Choreography: Michael Clark. Costumes: Leigh Bowery. Dancers: Michael Clark, Julie Hood, Matthew Hawkins and Ellen van Schuylenburch.

DD Dorvillier, *Nottthing is importanttt*, 2007. Choregraphed and Directed by DD Dorvillier. Music and sound installation by Zeena Parkins. Lighitng Design by Thomas Dunn. Sound installation Design: Doug Henderson. The Cast: Danielle Goldman, Martin Lanz Landazuri, Alejandra Martorell, Andrea Maurer, Paul Neuninger, Mina Nishimura, Peter Sciscioli, Otto Ramstad, and Elizabeth Ward.

William Forsythe, *The Loss of Small Detail*, 1991. Music: Thom Willems. Stage/ lighting: William Forsythe. Costumes: Issey Miyake. Film: 'Hund im Schnee', Helga Fanderl. Color film: 'Between Mediums', Fiona Léus. Text: William Forsythe, Yukio Mishima, Jerome Rothenberg (selections from 'Technicians of the Sacred'). Premiere: 11 May 1991, Opernhaus, Frankfurt am Main.

Meg Stuart, *Disfigure Study*, 1991/2002. Filmed and edited by Phillipp Hochleichter. Copyright 2007. (Filmed on December 16th 2006 at Volksbuhne am Rosa-Luzemburg-Platz, Berlin). Production: Klapstuk (Leuven), The Kitchen (New York), Streaks of Crimson (Brussels) (1991); Damaged Goods (1996, 2002). Co-production remake 2002: STUK (Leuven).

Meg Stuart and Philipp Gehmacher with Niko Hafkenscheid, *Maybe Forever*, 2006. Filmed and edited by Philipp Hochleichter/Smith&Kurtz. Copyright 2008. Production: Damaged Goods, Mumbling Fish (Vienna). Co-production: Kaaitheater (Brussels), Wexner Center for the Arts (Columbus, OH), Theatre de la Ville (Paris), Volksbuhne am Rosa-Luxemburg-Platz.

ADDITIONAL CREDITS FOR EXHIBITED WORKS

João Penalva
The Clog Dance, Act II, *La Fille Mal Gardée*, 1960
Choreography: Frederick Ashton; Music: Ferdinand Hérold /John Lanchbery; Performers: Brian Shaw as Widow Simone and members of The Royal Ballet Covent Garden; Video Director: John Vernon
© 1981 National Video Corporation Ltd. – Royal Opera House Covent Garden, Courtesy NVC Arts

Widow Simone (Entr'acte, 20 years), 1996
Text: João Penalva; Voice: Leslie E. Spatt (Recorded at 17:10h, 17.08.1996); Performer: João Penalva (Filmed at 18:20h, 19.08.1996); Camera: Simon Withers

Unclogged, 1996,
Choreography: João Penalva; Music: Laurence Crane/ Andrew Renton; Performer: João Penalva; Camera: Simon Withers. Filmed at The Hackney Empire Variety Theatre, London, 05.08.1996

Allan Kaprow
18 Happenings in 6 Parts, 1959/ 2010
Reinvented in 2010 by Rosemary Butcher for *Move: Choreographing You*
Installation artists: Matthew Butcher and Pablo Bronstein; Performers: Elena Giannotti, Dennis Greenwood, Ben Ash, Lauren Potter; Visual Artist and Sound Co-ordination: Edwin Burdis; Writing and text co-ordination: Professor Susan Melrose; Technical and; Project Managements: Karsten Tinapp; Researcher: Stefanie Sachsenmaier

Mike Kelley
Test Room Containing Multiple Stimuli Known to Elicit Curiosity and Manipulatory Responses, 1999
And *A Dance Incorporating Movements Derived from Experiments by Harry F. Harlow and Choreographed in the Manner of Martha Graham*, 1999
With: Sonia Kazorov, Kristen Hernstein, Dion Derizzo, David Bicha, Anita Pace, Carl Burkley. Choreography: Anita Pace. Production Supervisor: Patti Podesta. Camera: Robert Elhardt, Greg Kucera (Dance), Lighting Assistant: Derth Adams. Editor: Greg Kucera. Crew: Catherine Sullivan, Cameron Jamie, Abram Boosinger, Joycelyn Shipley (Dance). Courtesy the artist and Electronic Arts Intermix (EAI), New York

William Forsythe
City of Abstracts, 2000
The Forsythe Company is supported by the city of Dresden and the state of Saxony as well as the city of Frankfurt am Main and the state of Hesse. The Forsythe Company is Company-in-Residence of both the Festspielhaus Hellerau in Dresden and the Bockenheimer Depot in Frankfurt am Main. With special thanks to Ms. Susanne Klatten for supporting The Forsythe Company

William Forsythe
The Fact of Matter, 2009
Producer: Julian Gabriel Richter
The Forsythe Company is supported by the city of Dresden and the state of Saxony as well as the city of Frankfurt am Main and the state of Hesse. The Forsythe Company is Company-in-Residence of both the Festspielhaus Hellerau in Dresden and the Bockenheimer Depot in Frankfurt am Main. With special thanks to Ms. Susanne Klatten for supporting The Forsythe Company

Anna Halprin and Anne Collod
parades & changes, replays re-interpretation of Anna Halprin's *Parades & Changes* (1965) by Anne Collod, 1965/2010
Conception, artistic direction: Anne Collod in dialogue with Anna Halprin and Morton Subotnick
Re-interpretation and performance: Boaz K Barkan, Nuno Bizarro, Alain Buffard, Anne Collod, DD Dorvillier, Vera Mantero
Music: Morton Subotnick
Assisted by Sébastien Roux
Artistic collaboration: Cécile Proust
Costumes: Misa Ishibashi
Stenography: Anne Collod, Mikko Hynninen
Stenographic elements: Misa Ishibashi, Alain Gallissian
Graphic elaboration of the scores: Mathias Poisson
Technical direction: Nicolas Barrot
Light technician: Philippe Bouttier
Thanks Yves Godin
Management Henri Jules Julien
This project was made possible with support from Cultures France production ...& alters coproduction Festival d'Automne à Paris / Les Spectacles vivants – Centre Pompidou Paris / Biennale de la Danse de Lyon / Centre National de Danse Contemporaine d'Angers / Le Manège de Reims – Scène Nationale / Centre Chorégraphique National de Montpellier Languedoc Roussillon with the help of New England Foundation for the Arts / FUSED (French US Exchange in Dance) / French American Cultural Society / ADAMI / DRAC Île de France / SPEDIDAM / Fondation Beaumarchais / CulturesFrance / Services culturels, Consulat Général de France à San Francisco / Services culturels, Ambassade de France aux USA. and Culturgest Lisbonne / Le Vivat Scène Conventionnée d'Armentières / Micadanses Paris / Les Laboratoires d'Aubervilliers, Parc et Grande Halle de La Villette Paris.

Isaac Julien
TEN THOUSAND WAVES, 2010
With: Mazu: Maggie Cheung. Blue Goddess: Zhao Tao. Lover: Yang Fudong. Calligrapher: Gong Fagen. Narrators: Benedict Wong; Jennifer Lim. Poems: Wang Ping.
Director of Photography: Zhao Xiaoshi. Editor: Adam Finch. Music: Maria de Alvear; Jah Wobble and the Chinese Dub Orchestra. Producer: Maggie Still. Executive Producer: Virginia Ibbott. Associate Producer: Huang Fan. Produced by the LUMA Foundation.
Courtesy of Isaac Julien and Victoria Miro Gallery, London/Galería Helga de Alvear, Madrid/Metro Pictures, New York. Made with the kind support of the Udo and Anette Brandhorst Foundation; Colección Helga de Alvear; and the Linda Pace Foundation. Supported by the National Lottery through Arts Council England and Le Centre national des arts plastiques (Image/Mouvement), Ministère de la culture et de la communication. The artist would also like to thank Toby Devan Lewis and those who wish to remain anonymous for their kind support.
Isaac Julien is represented by Galería Helga de Alvear, Madrid; Metro Pictures, New York; Victoria Miro Gallery, London; Roslyn Oxley9 Gallery, Sydney; Almine Rech Gallery, Brussels and ShanghART Gallery, Shanghai.

Thomas Lehmen
Schrottplatz, 2010
Choreography, concept, text: Thomas Lehmen
Dramaturgical collaboration: Victoria Perez Royo
Artistic collaboration: Lucy Cash
Production: Thomas Lehmen, Christine Peterges
Co-produced by: PACT Zollverein, South Bank Centre London

La Ribot
Llámame Mariachi, 2009
Direction: La Ribot
Interpretation: Marie-Caroline Hominal, La Ribot, Delphine Rosay
Light creation: Daniel Demont
Light and video technician: Sandrine Faure
Sound technician: David Scrufari

Xavier Le Roy
Low Pieces, 2010
Concept and choreography: Xavier Le Roy
Performers: Sasa Asentic, Jefta Van Dinther, Mette Ingvarsten, Anne Juren, Krõõt Juurak, Neto Machado, Luis Felix Miguel, Jan Ritsema & Xavier Le Roy
Production: Le Kwatt – Montpellier, France. Coproduction: TanzquartierWien – Vienna, DRAC Languedoc-Roussillon, France.

ACKNOWLEDGEMENTS

First and foremost we would like to thank the artists for their generosity and enthusiasm.

The following individuals and institutions kindly lent to the exhibition:

Bas Jan Ader Estate; Anthology Film Archives; ARTPIX; Arts Council Collection, Southbank Centre; Ashiya City Museum of Art & History; Luhring Augustine; Axiom Films; The Box; Żak Branicka; Broadway 1602; Trisha Brown Company; Centre Pompidou; Lucinda Childs Dance; Michael Clark Company; Merce Cunningham Foundation; Siobhan Davies Dance; Deutsches Tanzfilminstitut Bremen; Electronic Arts Intermix (EAI); The Forsythe Company and the Ursula Blickle Foundation; Peter Freeman Inc.; Gagosian Gallery; The Getty Research Institute; Vilma Gold; Alexander Gray Associates LLC; Solomon R. Guggenheim Museum; Haunch of Venison; Hauser & Wirth; Herald St; Hijikata Archives; Holzwarth Publications GmbH ICKamsterdam – Emio Greco | PC; Alison Jacques Gallery; Klosterfelde Gallery; Allan Kaprow Estate; Akram Khan Company; L'Arche Editeur; l'association fragile / christian rizzo; Harris Lieberman Gallery; Lisson Gallery; Sprüth Magers; Victoria Miro Gallery; Meredith Monk/The House Foundation for the Arts; MMK Museum für Moderne Kunst; Musee de la Danse; Museu Colecção Berardo; Museum of Modern Art New York; The New York Public Library for the Performing Arts; O Rumo do Fumo-Edificio, Lisbon; Patrick Painter Editions; Maureen Paley; Adrian Piper Research Archive Foundation; Primary Information; Estate of Robert Rauschenberg; RE.AL; Margarete Roeder Gallery; Rosas; Perry Rubenstein Gallery; Sonnabend Gallery; SWR Media Services GmbH; Tate; Troubleyn/Jan Fabre; VAGA –Visual Artists and Galleries Association Inc.; Videoda; Video Data Bank; Shoshana Wayne Gallery; Atelier Franz West; 'The World of Lygia Clark' Cultural Association; Yves Klein Archives; Galerie Jocelyn Wolff; Franz Erhard Walther Foundation; David Zwirner.

We would like to thank the following individuals, galleries and studios of the participating artists:

Gabriela Corchado, Bas Jan Ader Estate; Adam Harris and Jenni Biggs, Advanced Digital Ltd.; Tamara Bloomberg, Allan Kaprow Estate; Robert Haller, Anthology Film Archives; Arnaud Antolinos; Fredericka Hunter, ARTPIX; Mizuho Kato, Ashiya City Museum of Art & History; Natalia Sacasa, Luhring Augustine; Richard Donnelly, British Broadcasting Corporation (BBC) Active; Lydia Bell; Angela Bernstein; Aniko Erdosi and Anke Kempes, Broadway 1602; Rebecca Davies and Tricia Pierson, Trisha Brown Company; Pat Catterson; Jacqueline Caux; Pedro Machado and Stine Nilsen, Candoco Dance Company; Vincent Cavaroc; Christine van Assche, Emilie Choffel, and Valerie Degrelle, Centre Pompidou; Miryam Charim Galerie; Amanda Shank, Lucinda Childs Dance Company; Tazuko Horigome , Jae-eun Choi Studio; Ellen van Schuylenburch, Michael Clark Company; Kevin Carr, Kevin Taylor and David Vaughan, Merce Cunningham Foundation; Bettsy Gregory, Dance Umbrella; Siobhan Davies, Franck Bordese, Alison Proctor, Siobhan Davies Dance; Heide-Marie Hartel, Deutsches Tanzfilminstitut Bremen; Ivo Dimchev; Rebecca Cleman, Electronic Arts Intermix; Carol Emshwiller; Tom Cullen and Nick Joyce, Enigma FX; Dr. Vera Battis-Reese, Dorsey Bushnell, Philip Bußmann, Julian Richter and Max Schubert, The Forsythe Company; Peter Freeman, Peter Freeman Inc.; Chloe Barter and Serena Cattañeo, Gagosian Gallery; Marc and Josée Gensollen; Emma Gladstone; Jeannie Freilich, Gladstone Gallery; Michelle Reyes, Felix Gonzales-Torres Estate; Karina Daskolov, Marian Goodman Gallery; Kristin Kolich, Alexander Gray Associates, LLC; Francien Eppens, ICKamsterdam - Emio Greco | PC; Lydia Grey; Portland Green, Portland Green Cultural Projects; Lori Mahaney, Guggenheim, New York; Sian Ede, Gulbenkian Foundation; Guy Gypens; Claudia Stockhausen, Haunch of Venison; Tina Köhler and Julienne Lorz, Ulrich Wilmes, Haus der Kunst, Munich; Adrian Heathfield; Hans Werner Holzwarth, Holzwarth Publications GmbH; Rosalind Horne; Philippe Siauve, Yves Klein Archives; Jessica Vaughan and Philip Abraham, Tessa Jackson; Alison Jacques Gallery; Molly Taylor and Tamsin Wright, Isaac Julien Studio; Doris Krystof, Kunstsammlung Nordrhein-Westfalen; Mary-Clare Stevens, Mike Kelley Studio; Marek Pomocki, Akram Khan Company; Matt Corrall and Kite Design Ltd.; Martin Klosterfelde, Sil Egger, Klosterfelde Gallery; Anneke Koblik, Kramlich Collection; Sabine Lacaze, L'Arche Editeur; Catherine Meneret, l'association fragile / christian rizzo; Amanda Levete, Alvin Huang, Gemma Douglas and Tanya Rainsley, Amanda Levete Architects; Kris Latocha and Jessie Washburne-Harris, Harris Lieberman; Greg Hilty and Silvia Sgualdini, Lisson Gallery; Yuki Miyake; Charlie Morrissey; Nicky Molloy; Olivia Georgia, Meredith Monk/The House Foundation for the Arts, Inc; Martina Hochmuth, Jean-Michel Hugo, and Frédéric Vannieuwenhuyse, Musée de la danse; Ulrich Lang, MMK Museum für Moderne Kunst; Kitty Cleary, Museum of Modern Art New York; Mark Nash; Tanisha Jones, The New York Public Library for the Performing Arts; Miriam North; Oliver Evans, Maureen Paley; Dominique Palfreymen, The Felix Trust; Jenelle Porter, Philadelphia Institute of Contemporary Art; James Price; Ben Pugh; Folk Rabe; Hazel Singleton, Random Dance; Matt Magee, Robert Rauschenberg Studio; Sofia Campos, RE.AL; Susanna Recchia; Rares Donca, La Ribot Studio; Anne Van Aerschot, Rosas; Molly Klais Springer, Perry Rubenstein Gallery; Patricia Romão, O Rumo do Fumo-Edifício; Keisuke Sakurai; Jochen Sandig; Kerstin Schroth; Noémie Solomon; Xan Price and Jason Ysenburg, Sonnabend Gallery; Marcelo Spinelli; Andreas Gegner, Sprüth Magers Berlin London; Morton Subotnick; Markus Jochem, SWR Media Services GmbH; Ursula Popp, Tanztheater Wuppertal Pina Bausch GmbH; Kathy Noble, Tate; Alexey Moskvin and Sofie Roberts, Tate New Media; Mamie Tinkler; Mirella Bartrip, Gill Clarke, Melanie Clark, Susan Sentler, and Lizzie Kew-Ross, Trinity Laban Conservatoire of Music and Dance; Mark Guerden, Troubleyn/ Jan Fabre; Luciano Foglia, David Hoe, Kishi Takayoshi, and Waiming Wee, Unit9.; Lisa Nelson, Videoda; Laura Lord, and David Thain, Vilma Gold; Pamela Caserta, Walker Art Center; Suzanne Walther, Franz Erhardt Walther Foundation,; Alexandra Wellensiek; Ines Turian, Atelier Franz West; Sandrine Djerouet-Stenstad, Galerie Jocelyn Wolff; Alessandra Clark, 'The World of Lygia Clark Cultural Association'; Asia Żak, Żak Branicka; John Zwaenepoel; Ben Berlow and Stephanie Stockbridge, David Zwirner.

We would like to thank the participants who performed throughout the exhibition, organised by Trinity Laban Conservatoire of Music and Dance:

Vanessa Abreu, Irina Baldini, Gemma Bass-Williams, Hrafnhildur Benedikstdottir, Luke Birch, Irene Cena,James D'Arcy, Paola Di Bella, Nathalia Mello, Mara Domenici, Ina Dokmo, Hannah Erlman, Martina Francone, Andrew Graham, Andrej Gubanov, Alexandrina Hemsley, Pauline Huguet, Ruska Tuuli Hynynen, Helka Kaski, Elizabeth Denise Litchfield Sells, Martina Malvasi, Christopher Matthews, Fernanda Munoz-Newsome, Katy Pearce, Amanda Marie Prince-Lubawy, Andrea Samain, Megan Saunders, Saffy Setohy, Alice Tatge, Lucille Teppa, Daisy Thompson, Else Karen Kerstin Tunemyr, Rosalie Wahlfrid, Emelie Wangstedt, Helena Webb, Cat Westwood.

At Southbank Centre, we would like to thank:

Tamsin Ace, Kath Boddy, Amy Botfield, Ali Brikci-Nigassa, Gemma Broughton, Mark Butler, Sarah Cashman, Becca Connock, Kate Cunningham, Janet DeLuca, Thomas Edge, Helen Faulkner, Chelsea Fitzgerald, Mark Foster, Pamela Griffin, Anna Gritz, Rahila Haque, Rachel Harris, Jessica Hemming, Lucy Jefferies, Helen Luckett, Curtis Mackie, Eva Martinez, Alison Maun, Siobhan McCracken Nixon, Athena Morse, Rafal Niemojewski, Sarah O'Reilly, Sarah Ragsdale, Mary Richards, Faye Robson, Julia Sawyer, Nicky Shaill, Vicky Skelding, Helen Slater, Jon Smalldon, Rebecca Smith, Claire Louise Staunton, Luisa Summers, Heather Walker, Helena Zedig. The Hayward technical team lead by Matt Nightingale and Dave Wood supported by Ciaran Begley, Jeremy Clapham, Jon Glazier, Nicky Goodge, Mark King, Jeremy Leahy, Roberto Marsura, Declan McMullan, Pat O'Connor, Amy Simpson, Jonny Winter and Jim Woodall. We wish to thank them as well as the many others who helped install the exhibition for their excellent work.

Finally, we would like to acknowledge:

Sam Forster Ltd (build, consultation and fabrication); Amanda Levete Architects (exhibition design); Melanie Mues, Mues Design (graphic design); Philip Miles (graphics production and installation); Aideen Malone (lighting); Unit9 (archive design).

NOTES ON AUTHORS

Eleonora Fabião is a performer, performance theorist and Associate Professor at the Federal University of Rio de Janeiro, School of Communication.

Susan Leigh Foster, choreographer and scholar, is author of *Reading Dancing* (1986) and *Choreographing Empathy* (2010).

Isabelle Graw is Professor of Art Theory and Art History at the Städelschule in Frankfurt and co-founder of *Texte zur Kunst*.

Anna Gritz is Assistant Curator at the Hayward Gallery, London.

Martin Hargreaves is the editor of *Dance Theatre Journal* and Programme Leader of the MA 'Dance Theatre' at Trinity Laban Conservatoire of Music and Dance, London.

Paul Kaiser is a digital artist and writer and member of The OpenEnded Group.

André Lepecki is Associate Professor in Performance Studies at New York University.

Julienne Lorz is Curator at Haus der Kunst, Munich.

Helen Luckett is Interpretation Manager at the Hayward Gallery, London.

Siobhan McCracken Nixon is Assistant Curator at the Hayward Gallery, London.

Eva Martinez is Dance and Performance Programmer at Southbank Centre, London.

Nicky Molloy is currently a freelance curator, previously Head of Dance and Performance at Southbank Centre, London.

Peggy Phelan holds the Ann O'Day Maples Chair in the Arts at Stanford University.

Stephanie Rosenthal is Chief Curator of the Hayward Gallery, London.

Noémie Solomon is a dancer, choreographer and writer, and teaches at Tisch, New York University and Marymount Manhattan College.

Åsmund Thorkildsen is Director of the Drammen Museum, Norway.